# Ethics in the AI, Technology, and Information Age

EDITED BY

MICHAEL BOYLAN
*MARYMOUNT UNIVERSITY*

WANDA TEAYS
*MOUNT SAINT MARY'S UNIVERSITY*

ROWMAN & LITTLEFIELD
*Lanham • Boulder • New York • London*

Acquisitions Editor: Natalie Mandziuk
Acquisitions Assistant: Sylvia Landis
Sales and Marketing Inquiries: textbooks@rowman.com

Credits and acknowledgments for material borrowed from other sources, and reproduced
with permission, appear on the appropriate pages within the text.

Published by Rowman & Littlefield
An imprint of The Rowman & Littlefield Publishing Group, Inc.
4501 Forbes Boulevard, Suite 200, Lanham, Maryland 20706
www.rowman.com

86-90 Paul Street, London EC2A 4NE, United Kingdom

British Library Cataloguing in Publication Information Available

**Library of Congress Cataloging-in-Publication Data**

Names: Boylan, Michael, editor. | Teays, Wanda, editor.
Title: Ethics in the AI, technology, and information age / edited by
  Michael Boylan, Wanda Teays.
Description: Lanham : Rowman & Littlefield, [2022] | Includes
  bibliographical references and index.
Identifiers: LCCN 2021052276 (print) | LCCN 2021052277 (ebook) | ISBN
  9781538160749 (cloth) | ISBN 9781538160756 (paperback) | ISBN
  9781538160763 (ebook)
Subjects: LCSH: Technology—Moral and ethical aspects. | Artificial
  intelligence—Moral and ethical aspects. | Internet—Moral and ethical
  aspects.
Classification: LCC BJ59 .E865 2022 (print) | LCC BJ59 (ebook) | DDC
  174/.96—dc23/eng/20211222
LC record available at https://lccn.loc.gov/2021052276
LC ebook record available at https://lccn.loc.gov/2021052277

♾™ The paper used in this publication meets the minimum requirements of American
National Standard for Information Sciences—Permanence of Paper for Printed Library
Materials, ANSI/NISO Z39.48-1992.

Michael:
*To Andrew (my father) who thought there
were no "downsides" to technology—especially
after network radio and the refrigerator*

Wanda:
*To Silvio, whose interest in technology is only
bounded by the constraints of time*

# Contents

# Acknowledgments

We are grateful to our editor, Natalie Mandziuk, and the team at Rowman & Littlefield. Thank you so much for all your encouragement and support.

Thanks also to the contributors to this timely anthology. We are grateful to you for the ideas and insights expressed in your chapters. And thanks to you, our readers, for sharing an interest in this growing field of technology ethics.

# Preface

Some have claimed that the making of tools is what (in a primitive way) has separated us from other animals and has allowed the development of language—and reason itself.[1] Thus, the relationship between technology and what it means to be human goes back to the very beginning.

A more recent starting point might be the Industrial Revolution that continued for a hundred and fifty years and then gave way to the Information Age—including social communications, artificial intelligence, and an interface with robots and technology that influences almost everything from health to warfare. Thus, the way humans interface with technology creates a panoply of new possibilities of action—many of which bring with them ethical problems. We cannot be so overwhelmed with the efficiency of production provided by machines that we ignore moral problems that may be important.

This conflict between prudential advantage and ethical norms is at the heart of applied ethics. It is our hope that this collection of essays helps readers think about some of these issues within domains in the world we live in. We seek to promote discussion on how we might take the best from technology while avoiding possible ethical pitfalls.

This area of discourse will, we believe, continue to grow as one of the primary areas of interest in applied ethics in the years to come.

This is just the beginning!

—Michael Boylan and Wanda Teays

# THEORETICAL BACKGROUND

# Ethical Theory, Applied Ethics, and Professional Ethics

# CHAPTER 1

# Ethical Reasoning

*Michael Boylan*

## Abstract

This essay introduces the reader to an outline of some of the principles involved in ethical reasoning, including the contrast between prudential decision-making and using one of the established ethical theories to drive outcomes.

### KEYWORDS

prudential decision-making, ethical decision-making, utilitarianism, deontology, ethical intuitionism, virtue ethics, ethical non-cognitivism, ethical contractarianism, ethical non-cognitivism, personal worldview imperative

## Introduction

What is the point of studying ethics? This is the critical question that will drive this chapter. Many people do not think about ethics as they make decisions in their day-to-day lives. They see problems and make decisions based upon practical criteria. Many see ethics as rather an affectation of personal taste. It is useful only when it can get you somewhere. Is this correct? Do we act ethically only when there is a "win-win" situation in which we can get what we want, and also appear to be an honorable, feeling, and caring person?

# A Prudential Model of Decision-Making

In order to begin answering this question we must start by examining the way most of us make decisions. Everyone initiates the decision-making process with an established worldview. A worldview is a current personal consciousness that consists in one's understanding of the facts and values that reside in the world. It is the most primitive term to describe our factual and normative conceptions. This worldview may be one that we have chosen, or it may be one that we passively accepted as we grew up in a particular culture. Sometimes, this worldview is wildly inconsistent. Sometimes, this worldview has gaping holes so that no answer can be generated when confronted by a tricky situation. Sometimes it is geared only to perceived self-interest. And sometimes, it is fanciful and can never be put into practice. Failures in one's personal worldview model will lead to failures in decision-making.

One common worldview model in the Western world is that of celebrity fantasy. Under this worldview, being a celebrity is everything. Andy Warhol famously claimed that what Americans sought after most was "fifteen minutes of fame."[1] Under this worldview model we should strive to become a celebrity, if only for a fleeting moment. What does it mean to be a celebrity? A celebrity is someone who is seen and recognized by a large number of people. Notice that this definition does not stipulate that once recognized, the object is given positive assent. That would be to take an additional step. To be seen and recognized is enough. One can be a sinner or a saint—it is all the same. To be recognized is to be recognized. If this is the end, then it is probably easier to take the sinner route. In this way, the passion for celebrity is at heart contrary to ethics.

Another popular worldview model is practical competence. Under this model the practitioner strives to consider what is in his or her best interest and applies a practical cost-benefit analysis to various situations in order to ascertain whether action x or action y will maximize the greatest amount of pleasure for the agent (often described in terms of money). Thus, if you are Bernie Madoff (a well-known financial swindler), you might think about the risks and rewards of creating an illegal Ponzi scheme as opposed to creating a legitimate investment house that operates as other investment houses do. The risks of setting off in your own direction are that you might get caught and go to prison. The rewards are that you might make much more money than you would have done under the conventional investment house model. Since you think you are smarter than everyone else and will not get caught, the prudential model would say, "Go for it!" Madoff did get caught, but who knows how many others do not? We cannot know because they *have not been caught*. But even if you are not caught, is that the best worldview approach? The prudential worldview model says *yes*.

# Another Worldview Approach

What if we felt that the prudential worldview approach was lacking? Might there be another way to structure the worldview that controls how we act? If it's contrary to pure prudentialism, then it must be structured upon a different set of principles.

I have used the principles of axiomatics (logical, systemic presentations) to formulate an alternative to the prudential approach. It begins with a set of principles we can use to structure our personal worldview.

# The Personal Worldview Imperative

The personal worldview imperative is that "All people must develop a single comprehensive and internally coherent worldview that is good and that we strive to act out in our daily lives."[2] There are four parts to the personal worldview imperative: completeness, coherence, connection to a theory of the good, and practicality. Let's briefly say something about each.

First is *completeness*. Completeness refers to the ability of a theory or ethical system to handle all cases put before it and to determine an answer based upon the system's recommendations. This is functionally achieved via the good will. The good will is a mechanism by which we decide how to act in the world. The good will provides completeness to everyone who develops one. There are two senses of the good will. The first is the *rational good will*, which means that each agent will develop an understanding about what reason requires of us as we go about our business in the world. Completeness means that reason (governed by the personal worldview and its operational ethical standpoint) should always be able to come up with an answer to a difficult life decision. In the case of ethics, the rational good will requires engaging in a rationally based philosophical ethics and abiding by what reason demands. Often this plays out practically in examining and justifying various moral maxims—such as maxim alpha: "One has a moral responsibility to follow-through on one's commitments, *ceteris paribus*."

This maxim is about promise-making—call it maxim alpha. For example, one could imagine that an employer named Fred hired Olga on the basis of her résumé and a Skype interview, which did not reveal her mobility challenges (she needs a walker to get from points A to B for perambulation). Fred promises Olga the job, but when she shows up to work Fred determines that Olga does not fit the *image* of the company that he wishes to exude: *vibrant*, *athletic*, and *potent*. A person in a walker is discordant to this image. Even though the job is a desk job (sitting in a cubicle), Fred wants to fire Olga. What should Fred do? The rational good will (as Fred himself has developed it via maxim alpha) says that Fred should carry through with his promise to Olga since there is no conflicting moral issue that would invoke the ceteris paribus clause in the maxim. For Fred to act otherwise would be an instance of denying completeness based upon the rational good will. Fred should keep his promise to Olga and let her work for him.

Another sort of good will is the *affective* or *emotional good will*. We are more than just rational machines. We have an affective nature, too. Our feelings are important, but just as was the case with reason, some guidelines are in order. For the emotional good will we begin with sympathy. Sympathy will be taken to be the emotional connection that one forms with other humans. This emotional connection must be one in which the parties are considered to be on a level basis. The sort of emotional connection I am talking about is open and between equals. It is not that of a superior "feeling sorry" for an inferior. Those who engage in interactive human sympathy that is open and level will respond to another with care. Care is an action-guiding response that gives moral motivation to assisting another in need. Together sympathy, openness, and care constitute love.

In the above case on promise-making Fred wouldn't be making and justifying moral maxims such as maxim alpha. Instead, Fred would be developing his capacity to sympathetically connect with other people—call this maxim beta. If Fred sympathetically connected with Olga and her disability that has nothing to do with her ability to carry out the job as advertised, his caring response would guide him toward maintaining his promise to Olga because to do otherwise would sever the sympathetic connection. Fred would not be acting like a loving person if he did otherwise. The shared community worldview of *vibrant, athletic,* and *potent* need not be compromised because these are basically characteristics of the human spirit and not of the physical body. Olga can do her desk job with *joie de vivre* that reflects the company's shared community worldview. Thus, Fred, acting on maxim beta, should refrain from firing Olga.

Thus, the two sorts of good will (affective and rational—set out via maxims alpha and beta) work together to promote keeping Olga on the job so long as she can do the work—disability should not be a factor here.[3]

When confronted with any novel situation, one should utilize the two dimensions of the good will to generate a response. Because these two orientations act differently it is possible that they may contradict each other. When this is the case, I would allot the tiebreaker to reason. Others demur.[4] Each reader should consider her own response to such an occurrence.

A second part of the personal worldview imperative is *coherence*. People should have coherent worldviews. This also has two varieties: deductive and inductive. Deductive coherence speaks to our not having overt contradictions in our worldview. An example of an overt contradiction in one's worldview would be for Sasha to tell her friend Sharad that she has no prejudice against disabled individuals and yet in another context tell jokes about disabled persons. The coherence provision of the personal worldview imperative says that you shouldn't change who you are and what you stand for depending upon the context in which you happen to be: you should either support people with disabilities or excoriate them; waffling between the two is incoherent.

Inductive coherence is different. It is about adopting different life strategies that work against each other. In inductive logic a conflicting strategy is called a sure-loss contract.[5] For example, if a person wanted to be a devoted family man and husband and yet also engaged in extramarital affairs, he would involve himself in inductive incoherence. The very traits that make him a good family man—loyalty, keeping one's word, sincere interest in the well-being of others—would hurt him because he is a philanderer, which requires selfish manipulation of others for one's own pleasure.

The good family man will be a bad philanderer and vice versa. To try to do both well involves a sure-loss contract. Such an individual will fail at both. This is what inductive incoherence means. From the point of view of a disabled person this second form of coherence involves a self-assessment of what can and cannot be done: to seek for both will lead to a sure-loss contract. This creates a reality of the possible in which the disabled person can try to find self-fulfillment.

Third is *connection to a theory of the good—the most prominent theory being ethics.*[6] The personal worldview imperative enjoins that we consider and adopt an ethical theory.[7] It does not give us direction, as such, to which theory to choose except that the chosen theory must not violate any of the other three conditions (completeness, coherence, and practicability). What is demanded is that we connect to a theory of ethics and use it to guide our actions.

Now, the personal worldview imperative does not dictate *which* ethical theory the agent should adopt to meet this third requirement. The most common candidates are discussed below.

# Theories of Ethics

There are various ways to parse theories of ethics. I will parse theories of ethics according to what they see as the ontological status of their objects. There are two principal categories: (1) the realist theories that assert that theories of ethics speak to actual realties that exist, and (2) the anti-realist theories that assert that theories of ethics are merely conventional and do not speak about ontological objects.

## REALIST THEORIES

### *Utilitarianism*

Utilitarianism is a theory that suggests that an action is morally right when that action produces more total utility for the group than any other alternative. Sometimes this has been shortened to the slogan: "The greatest good for the greatest number." This emphasis upon calculating quantitatively the general population's projected consequential utility among competing alternatives appeals to the same principles that underlie democracy and capitalism (which is why this theory has always been very popular in the United States and other Western capitalistic democracies). Because the measurement device is natural (people's expected pleasure as an outcome of some decision or policy), it is a realistic theory. The normative connection with aggregate happiness and the good is a factual claim. Advocates of utilitarianism point to the definite outcomes that it can produce by an external and transparent mechanism. Critics cite the fact that the interests of minorities can be overridden.

### *Deontology*

Deontology is a moral theory that emphasizes one's duty to complete a particular action because the action itself is inherently right and not through any other sort of calculations, such as the consequences of the action. Because of this non-consequentialist bent, deontology is often contrasted with utilitarianism, which defines the right action in terms of its ability to bring about the greatest aggregate utility. In contradistinction to utilitarianism, deontology will recommend an action upon principle. "Principle" is justified through an understanding of the structure of action, the nature of reason, and the operation of the human will. Because its measures deal with the nature of human reason or the externalist measures of the possibility of human agency, the theory is realist. The result is a moral command to act that does not justify itself by calculating consequences. Advocates of deontology like its emphasis on acting upon principle or duty alone. One's duty is usually discovered via careful rational analysis of the nature of reason or of human action. Critics cite the fact that there is too much emphasis upon reason and not enough on emotion and our social selves in the world.

## SWING THEORIES (WHICH MAY BE REALIST OR ANTI-REALIST)

### *Ethical Intuitionism*

Ethical intuitionism can be described as a theory of justification about the immediate grasping of self-evident ethical truths. Ethical intuitionism can operate on
the level of general principles or on the level of daily decision-making. In this
latter mode many of us have experienced a form of ethical intuitionism through
the teaching of timeless adages, such as "Look before you leap," and "Faint heart
never won fair maiden." The truth of these sayings is justified through intuition.
Many adages or maxims contradict each other (such as the two above), so that
the ability to properly apply these maxims is also understood through intuition.
When the source of the intuition is either God or Truth as they independently
exist, then the theory is realist. The idea here is that everyone who has a *proper*
understanding of God or of Truth will have the same revelation. When the
source of the intuition is the person herself, living as a biological being in a social
environment, then the theory is anti-realist, because many different people will
have various intuitions and none can take precedent over another.

### *Virtue Ethics*

Virtue ethics is also sometimes called agent-based or character ethics. It takes
the viewpoint that in living your life you should try to cultivate excellence in all
that you do and all that others do. These excellences or virtues are both moral
and non-moral. Through conscious training, for example, an athlete can achieve
excellence in a sport (a non-moral example). In the same way, a person can
achieve moral excellence as well. The way these habits are developed and the
sort of community that nurtures them all come under the umbrella of virtue
ethics. When the source of these community values is Truth or God, then the
theory is realist. When the source is the random creation of a culture based upon
geography or other accidental features, then the theory is anti-realist. Proponents
of the theory cite the real effect that cultures have in influencing our behavior.
We are social animals, and this theory often ties itself to communitarianism,
which affirms the positive interactive role that society plays in our lives. Detractors often point to the fact that virtue ethics does not give specific directives on
particular actions. For example, a good action is said to be one that a person
of character would make. To detractors, this sounds like begging the question.

## ANTI-REALISTIC THEORIES

### Ethical Non-Cognitivism

Ethical non-cognitivism is a theory that suggests that the descriptive analysis of language and culture tells us all we need to know about developing an appropriate attitude in ethical situations. Ethical propositions are neither true nor false, but can be analyzed via linguistic devices to tell us what action-guiding meanings are hidden there. We all live in particular and diverse societies. Discerning what each society commands and admonishes is a task for any person living in a society. We should all fit in and follow the social program as described via our language and society. Because these imperatives are relative to the values of the society or social group being queried, the maxims generated hold no natural truth value and, as such, are anti-realist. Advocates of this theory point to its methodological similarity to deeply felt worldview inclinations of linguistics, sociology, and anthropology. If one is an admirer of these disciplines as fundamental, then ethical non-cognitivism looks pretty good. Detractors point to corrupt societies and state that ethical non-cognitivism cannot criticize these from within (because the social milieu is accepted at face value).

### Ethical Contractarianism

Ethical contractarians assert that freely made personal assent gives credence to ethical and social philosophical principles. These advocates point to the advantage of the participants being happy or contented with a given outcome. The assumption is that within a context of competing personal interests in a free and fair interchange of values, those principles that are intersubjectively agreed upon are sufficient for creating a moral "ought." The "ought" comes from the contract and extends from two people to a social group. Others universalize this, by thought experiments, to anyone entering such contracts. Because the theory does not assert that the basis of the contract is a proposition that has natural existence as such, the theory is anti-realist. Proponents of the theory tout its connection to notions of personal autonomy that most people support. Detractors cite the fact that the theory rests upon the supposition that the keeping of contracts is a good thing; but why is this so? Does the theory presuppose a meta-moral theory validating the primacy of contracts? If not, then the question remains: What about making a contract with another creates normative value?

For the purposes of this text, we will assume these six theories to be exhaustive of philosophically based theories of ethics or morality. In the subsequent chapters of this book, the reader should try to access which ethical point of view is being assumed by the author—with the advantages and shortcomings that such a theory possesses.

The final criterion in the personal worldview imperative is *practicability*. It is important that the demands of ethics and social/political philosophy (including human rights) be doable and its goals be attainable. This is especially important to consider when one is disabled. One must accept the body one is in at the moment and consider what is possible. This does not mean to "settle" for something less. But it also does not mean that one should hang upon scientifically unwarranted dreams of having one's disability reversed.

A *utopian* command may have logically valid arguments behind it but also be existentially unsound—meaning that some of the premises in the action-guiding argument are untrue by virtue of their being unrealizable in practical terms. If, in a theory of global ethics, for example, we required that everyone in a rich country gave up three-quarters of their income so that they might support the legitimate plight of the poor, then this would be a utopian vision. Philosophers are all too often attracted to tidy, if perhaps radical, utopian visions. However, unless philosophers want to be marginalized, we must situate our prescriptions in terms that can actually be used by policymakers.

Philosophers involved in human rights discourse must remember that these theories are to apply to real people living in the world. In taxation policy, for example, at some point—let's say at the point of a 50% income-tax rate—even the very wealthy among us will feel unjustly burdened and will rebel and refuse to comply with the policy. Thus, it is utopian to base a policy upon the expectation that the rich will submit to giving up 75% of their income. An *aspirational* goal (by contrast) is one that may be hard to reach but is at least possible to achieve (it does not violate principles of human nature or structural facts about the communities that inhabit the world). For the purposes of this essay, the aspirational perspective will be chosen over the utopian.

The purview of the personal worldview imperative is the individual as she interacts with other individuals in the world. Each of us has to do as much as possible to take stock of who we are and what we realistically think we can and should be. Our personal consciousness is in our power to change what is within our power. Though factors of environment and genetics are not to be dismissed, in the end it is the free operation of our will that allows us to confront the personal worldview imperative as a challenge for personal renewal. The acceptance of the personal worldview account means that it is in our power to create our ethical selves. The personal worldview imperative thus grounds a theory of personhood that is part of the foundation of natural human rights.

CHAPTER 2

# "Nature" as a Background Condition

*Michael Boylan*

## Abstract

This essay suggests that "nature" is a background condition that is fundamental to evaluating changes to nature—such as various technologies. It is the contention of this essay that we should be careful about intentionally going *against nature*. This calls for the application of the principle of precautionary reason to ascertain possible negative consequences. This does not disallow fundamental change, but merely advocates a "go slow" approach.

KEYWORDS

nature, Aristotle, shared community worldview imperative, the common body of knowledge, protecting nature

## Part I: What Is Nature?

Aristotle introduces our discussion in *Posterior Analytics* II.1: "There are four questions we can ask about the [natural] objects we know (*epistametha*): the fact (*hoti*); the reasoned fact or cause (*dioti*); the question about the modal existence of the entity (*ei esti*); and the question of definition or essence (*ti esti*)."[1] In the context of this essay I'd contextualize this as ultimately searching for a definition of nature that can be the basis of our discussion. But "definition" is last on Aristotle's list.

Why is that? It is because the definition must be the result of experience (*empeiria*) that itself allows one to have confidence in her beliefs about what the fact *actually is* (*hoti*) and its structure and modalities within various contexts (*ei esti*) in order to speculate on the causal structure that underlies its operation (*dioti*). As has been the case in the past, this author is greatly influenced by Aristotle's approach to understanding nature.[2] However, this essay will use this general structure and move beyond the Stagirite's exposition (though using this structure in part one).

## PRIMITIVE POSITS

*Nature* is a term full of meanings.[3] For our purposes, let us begin with an understanding of nature in its contextual sense (the brute facts observed, *hoti*): we view nature as being *outside* us. But this does not mean that we, also, are not a part of nature (though some make this mistake in issues concerning the environment).[4] There is an historical/religious tradition that views nature as outside of us just like children are outside of the parents but a part of the family. This is the tradition that talks about being "stewards of nature." It goes back to the *scala naturae*.[5] This model owes much to Aristotle's notion of the three sorts of living entities (souls, *psuche*, including plants, animals, and humans).[6]

In addition, we have two understandings of denotation: the individual and the group. It has been this author's practice in the past to stipulate this distinction by the use of a lowercase n and capital N.[7] Thus "nature" will refer to individuals and their capacities/executions while "Nature" will refer to larger groups—such as species, genera, et al., including integrated systems such as ecosystems, and more general systems such as biomes, biota, and the earth's biosphere. By using language this way, we can be more exact in our denotative referents (*ei esti*, above).

This sort of distinction helps a little in making clear the "inclusion problem" cited above: whether the individual looking around sees Nature as the *other* that does not include herself since she is an individual human and humans are exceptional in this scheme, residing at the top of the *scale naturae*. Though said human, let's call her "Sue," resides in Nature, her nature is as a power figure: on the Board of Directors for the corporation, Nature. Though she is nominally a part of the larger scheme, it is only as one of the ruling executives, trumped solely by God (if she is a theist) or by nothing else save the physical laws governing the interaction of states of matter (if she is an agnostic or atheist).

If this analysis is correct, then *why* is this so (*dioti*)? I have argued in a recent book that the European and Chinese traditions used the concept of Nature as the source of limitation on human excesses up until the seventeenth century in

Europe and until the nineteenth century in China.[8] Under this earlier account Nature was recognized as more powerful than humans—especially regarding natural disasters such as hurricanes, tornadoes, floods, tsunamis, earthquakes, and volcanic eruptions. In this way, an abstract Nature is seen as a force apart from living organisms (plants, animals, and humans) and nonliving entities (earth, air, and water). This force was viewed by some as Divine.[9]

What occurred (once a general reverence for Nature was withdrawn, around the seventeenth century for Europeans) was that this particular collection of human civilizations replaced Nature with some other reverential object based upon human technological power—weapons using gunpowder and lead bullets along with improved naval vessels that could travel with large cargos for long distances. The new reverential object became colonial conquest ("discovering" and "civilizing" the "primitive world") and then European powers expropriated riches from their aggressive land thievery. This made these empire builders believe that *they were* Masters of the Universe, and thus masters over Nature.[10] They came, they saw, and they conquered. Then they destroyed the land configurations and substituted their own visions of majesty in their stead, constructing cities with brick buildings, roads, and monumental cathedrals that redefined the landscapes. This is what a master of the universe believes is in his job description.

Though for hundreds of years the magisterial attitude among Europeans and their thralls was supreme, there were a few architectural renegades such as Frank Lloyd Wright (1867–1959) who thought that organic approaches of *fitting into* the existing physical space rather than *conquering it* was a better goal.[11] This was also the goal of many conquered indigenous peoples who also often set out the organic in their architectural vision, fitting into the landscape rather than refashioning it in their own image. The standard European approach marks a transition by embracing a community worldview of dominion.[12]

In the worldview of dominion, the powerful individual (and by extension his cadre of helpers) rejects the perspective of the Natural community for that of a personal scope of control: *This plot of land belongs to me. I own it. I may do whatever I want with it!* This is the mantra. Such individuals think that they are entitled to shave down mountains, change the course of rivers, eliminate wetlands, pollute air and water, create new mountains (landfills with piled toxic waste)—all because they view nature as *the other*, which they can own and do with it what they will. The *dioti* here is constructed around power to execute a personal, natural vision of *what is*.

Part of what is behind this worldview is what I've called the "egg carton" community worldview.[13] Under this view people wish to fulfill their nature by doing as they wish without any interference from others (just like eggs in an egg carton are protected from touching any other egg in the carton). Such an aspirational vision is also thought to be possible as if we all were detachable units that can operate on our own apart from any interaction with other people or with Nature.

It is the contention of this author that such visions of personal human independence/autonomy are factually inaccurate concerning our existence on Earth and are normatively false depictions of what we should aspire to individually as our nature. This is because we are intertwined with Nature—including the human community along with terrain, climate, plants, and animals. Our fates are *not* separate. The *scala naturae* model is the wrong way to think about our existence. In its stead we should consider a model of various community memberships in which we participate.

## LIVING IN COMMUNITY

One important piece of the (*hoti* and *ei esti*) is to describe the manner of how it is we situate ourselves into communities. It has been this author's contention that a better *dioti* than the exclusive, individualistic perspective of who we are and how we *ought* to understand the way forward is to jettison extreme individualism in favor of a worldview that accepts the concept of community.

Under this account *individuals* live within a community. There are constraints upon individuals regarding how we should act (since purposive action defines the *mode* of our human nature, *ei esti*),[14] but our focus here is on the manner that individuals live in various communities: human communities (close at hand and extended throughout the world) and within Natural communities (close at hand and extended throughout the world). Like the individual perspective, the community perspective is normative and governed by imperatives for action.

A brief review of these various perspectives that set out their normative structure are as follows. First, the shared community worldview imperative tells us that human communities are close at hand, and that *"Each agent must contribute to a common body of knowledge that supports the creation of a shared community worldview (that is itself complete, coherent, and good) through which social institutions and their resulting policies might flourish within the constraints of the essential core commonly held values (ethics, aesthetics, and religion)."* There are five important parts of this imperative that deserve attention.

The first criterion is *agent contribution*. This means that members of a community are responsible for being active members. Ethically, one cannot completely shift this responsibility to others. Even in communities in which there are elected officials, this does not absolve each person in the community from periodically checking to see whether she thinks the community is doing what it says it's doing and whether what it says it's doing is proper policy. When it isn't the case that what it says it's doing is proper policy, then that member of the community has an obligation to engage whatever institutional mechanisms of protest and change are open to her.

The second criterion is the reference to the *common body of knowledge*. The common body of knowledge represents what is culturally accepted to be good, true, and beautiful about the world. Most of these understandings are non-moral in character. For example, music scales in the Middle East (which are based upon the tar and sitar) have tonal combinations that are different than those admired in Europe (which are based upon different source instruments). Each audience has been accustomed to their own musical sounds so that they appreciate the familiar combinations as beautiful. The reason that this concept is relevant here is that many communities (especially most macro communities) are diverse. To create acceptance within some communities, it is necessary that, at a minimum, one recognizes the non-moral character of these differences. I call these non-moral differences *legitimate cultural relativism*.[15] People should be as tolerant as possible about accepting these alternate forms of non-moral behavior (the dynamics of *dioti*).

The case with moral relativism is more difficult. Moral relativism is a logical consequence of the moral anti-realists. These individuals contend that there is no science of the right and wrong in human action because there are no real moral objects at all.[16] For the moral relativist all prescriptions about normative right or wrong are merely social constructions that have arbitrarily occurred via accidents in human history. Thus, when we say that "Action x is right in society y," we are only giving a factual, anthropological report. We are *not* saying anything universal about the human condition. This is because universal generalizations are the outputs of science only and describe things that really *are* (ontological objects). Since the moral anti-realists deny the efficacy of the moral realist scenario, it would be possible to give an anthropological report of murder and the shrinking of heads in some society and stop right there. No one in another anthropological tradition could call it wrong except as an expression of cultural imperialism. From this vantage point, global ethics would translate into merely an inevitable power play to impose the values of one culture over another. This results in ethical relativism.

The moral realists, on the other hand, point to natural criteria that can prove the existence of moral rules that govern humans—such as the prohibition against murder. These criteria can be based in group happiness (in the case of utilitarianism) or in absolute duty that is grounded in reason or the nature of human action (in the case of deontology). The swing theories (virtue ethics and ethical intuitionism) require a direct connection to a source of *what is* (such as God or Truth) to validate the virtue or the intuition. Without this connection to such a source, virtue ethics and ethical intuitionism revert to anti-realism.[17]

Sometimes the moral and the non-moral become confused. In these situations, one must refer back to the personal worldview imperative[18] and the relevant theory of ethics that has been embraced in order to separate an ethical from a non-ethical practice.[19] It is easy to be prejudicial against what is new or unfamiliar. When the unfamiliar is merely different and nonethical, then the common body of knowledge must expand to accommodate it (*legitimate cultural relativism*). When the unfamiliar is immoral, then the common body of knowledge should give direction for the proper way to exclude such an input to the community (for example, Charles Manson's killing cult).

The third criterion describes common traits shared by the personal worldview imperative: *complete, coherent, and connected to a theory of good* (social/political philosophy). As per our embrace of the common body of knowledge, these pivotal criteria allow the members of the community to evaluate new members to the community so that they might be accepted or not. New doesn't necessarily mean bad.

The fourth criterion enjoins that the *creation of social institutions* occurs within the guidelines set out by the imperative. The way communities act is via the creation of institutions that represent the worldview of the micro or macro group. It is important that the institutions that are so created actually represent the sense of the shared worldviews of the group's members. It is certainly possible for an institution to be created that loses its original mission and strays in the way that it operates. When this occurs, it is the community's responsibility to put the institution back on course (by either revising or eliminating it).

Finally, the last part of the imperative is an acceptance of the *diversity of the community in terms of core values: ethics, aesthetics, and religion*. The acceptance of diversity is very important. This is because autonomy will necessitate that there will be no "standard" or "normal" citizen. There is not an essentialist template by which we can measure. On the contrary, people are different. Embracing these differences and allowing institutional space for them is morally and practically important. There is a limit to this acceptance—not all core values will be consistent with the personal worldview imperative (as per criteria two and three above). The default position in the shared community worldview imperative is that diversity is *prima facie* good and a healthy state of affairs for the micro or macro community. The burden of proof to the contrary is upon those who believe that such behavior is unethical.

It is the position of this author that these five aspects of the shared community worldview imperative lay the groundwork for ethical human communities that operate effectively for all their members (*hoti, dioti,* and *ei esti*).

Secondly, the complementary theoretical construct is an imaginative construction that extends community membership to those beyond the conventional boundaries of our micro and macro groups.[20] To intellectually grasp this aspect of community membership we need to import a new concept: the extended community. The extended community is one in which the agent is remotely connected. For example, I live in suburban Maryland just outside Washington, DC. I am a member of various micro communities (such as my college and various groups associated with my wife and children) and macro communities (such as my city, county, state, and nation).

In each of these I have some direct or indirect contact that is proximate and tangible. I can go into the District of Columbia. I can write my congressperson or senator. I can get into my car or travel via public transit directly to the physical domains of the state or national capital. Each of these is connected proximately to me through a tangible, operational, institutional structure that operates (in theory) under the principle of sovereignty set out above.

Now, the extended community is a little different (*hoti*, *dioti*, and *ei esti*). Even though I travel there by rail, sea, or air, I do not have immediate access. I must present a passport. I can be denied entrance. I have many fewer tangible institutional rights in a foreign country than I do at home. The foreign culture is different than my national culture. In some cases, I may be completely ignorant about its customs, government, and social circumstances. The media often makes it more difficult for me to find out facts on many foreign nations—particularly those that are poor and don't seem to fit our perceived national interest. Because of these aspects of remoteness there may be a famine occurring in Mali or severe storm damage on one of the islands of Indonesia that many in the United States (for example) don't even know about.

International ignorance is a large cause of international apathy. To address a background condition necessary for morality and global justice we must embrace a third sort of worldview imperative: the extended community worldview imperative, which states that *"Each agent must educate himself and others as much as he is able about the peoples of the world—their access to the basic goods of agency, their essential commonly held cultural values, and their governmental and institutional structures—in order that he might create a worldview that includes those of other nations so that individually and collectively the agent might accept the duties that ensue from those peoples' legitimate rights claims, and to act accordingly within what is aspirationally possible."*

The extended community worldview imperative (seeing one's community as extended throughout the world) has three principal parts. The first has to do with self and micro community education[21] about the peoples of the world (*hoti*). This educational exercise should include important facts like geographical situation, political and institutional structures, culture, and how the people fare with respect to the basic goods of agency (see chapter 3). This education process should be ongoing. The point is to allocate space in one's consciousness and in the consciousness of those in your micro community to the existence and lives of others remote from you. Because this is an ethical imperative, obedience is not optional.

The second feature has to do with the way you incorporate others into your worldview (*ei esti*). Fulfilling this has to do with the operation of one's imagination. The imagination is the power of the mind that makes real and integrates what is abstract into lived experience, and vice versa. When one educates oneself about the lives of others, the imagination steps in and makes possible rational and emotional applications of the good will. Thus, one might possess enough (particularity via education and the imagination) that one could be able rationally to assess one's duties in response to others' valid rights claims. Also, one will be able to create fictive reconstructions of the people in these countries based upon intersubjective facts so that one can create an extended style of sympathy. Normally sympathy requires two people to be in direct contact. In the extended variety of sympathy, all that is needed is enough facts to generate an image of some typical person living in the country such that the vividness of their particularity will generate a constructed variety of the actual person-to-person contact of proximate sympathy. In this way, the rational and affective good will act together to exhort one to action on behalf of another.

The third feature refers to an action response (*dioti*). Those in other countries who have legitimate rights claims are entitled to our responding via our correlative duties. Ignorance of their plight does not absolve us of our responsibility. What often gets in the way is that we view those in the extended community as having their own society (which is viewed as the proximate provider of goods and services). Because our world is set up on the model of individual sovereign states, it seems to many that each country should take care of its own. The community model offers some support to this analysis.

However, in the end this sort of parochialism fails because the boundaries of states are not Natural facts but socially constructed conventions. Where one country ends and another begins is an artifact of history and military conquest. Since few of us (except the *kraterists*)[22] believe that might confers normative goodness, this position should be rejected. The boundaries of states are artificial and do not indicate Natural divisions (even when the boundary between states is a mountain range or a river).

Thinking in this way is important because it shows that the way we parse ourselves (via geography, language, or culture) is rather arbitrary. There is a much stronger sense (based upon human biology) that our existence as *homo sapiens* is the only real robust boundary that counts among our species.[23] However, there is much truth in the old adage "Out of sight, out of mind." When we are ignorant of the plight of others and when we haven't undergone the imaginative connection of the other to ourselves, then it is certainly the case that we will be less likely to be moved to action.

The extended community worldview imperative exhorts us all to educate ourselves about the plight of others in the world and then to respond with individual and corporate action according to our abilities to act effectively. It must become a top priority issue to us all.

Thirdly, when we add the other components of the Natural community, we come up with two more community worldview imperatives: the eco-community worldview imperative and the extended eco-community worldview imperative. Let us begin with the eco-community worldview imperative (the eco-community close at hand, *hoti*): *"Each agent must educate herself about the proximate Natural world in which she lives relating to her agency within this eco-system: (a) what her natural place in this order is vis-à-vis her personal agency; (b) how her natural place (vis-à-vis her personal agency) may have changed in recent history; (c) how her social community's activities have altered the constitution of the Natural order and how this has effected community agency; (d) the short-term and long-term effects of those changes vis-à-vis agency, and (e) what needs to be done to maintain the natural order in the short and long term so that the ecosystem might remain vibrant."*[24]

First there is the requirement that people educate themselves as much as is practically possible about the proximate environment in which they live. This will require particular attention to the land, water, air, animal life, plant life, and meteorological events. In the age of the Internet, it should be possible for a large number of people on earth to obtain easy access to these facts.[25] What is important, of course, is that they connect to reputable scientific sources.

Second is the personal recognition that individual humans live in interaction with their Natural surroundings and that they should contextualize such interactions personally.

Third requires a sense of recent history of the local environment. This creates a personal baseline by which one might assess how one has been affected by climate change.

Fourth and last is for the agent who has just assessed how she has been affected to examine various sustainability policy proposals and gather enough information that she can decide which course she will endorse and then work vigorously for enactment of those policy proposals.

Just as when we focused upon the human community it was necessary to go beyond to the extended human community, so also it is the case with the eco-community. The extended eco-community worldview imperative is, *"Each agent must educate herself about the world's biomes: freshwater, saltwater, arid regions, forests, prairies and grasslands, tundra, and arctic regions. This education should be ongoing and should include how the relative stability and Natural sustainability is faring at various points in time. This knowledge will entail a factual valuing that also leads to an aesthetic valuing. Since all people seek to protect what they value,*[26] *this extended community membership will ground a duty to protect the global biomes according to what is aspirationally possible.*

This imperative prescribes first educating oneself about the scientific *facts* of the world. This doxastic responsibility is primary. Far too often people create beliefs that are unsupported by hard data.[27] This is irresponsible and immoral.[28] As the late New York senator Daniel Patrick Moynihan is reputed to have said, "We are all entitled to our own opinions, but not to our own facts."[29] What this means is that people must do the best to seek out reputable sources of scientific information on key extended environmental questions, such as the $CO_2$ in the troposphere, over discrete meteorological air spaces and the trends that follow from this.

Now it is probably the case that large numbers of individuals are deficient in science education so that they would not be able to engage at this level except for broad generalizations that might be skewed by news outlets (on traditional media or on social media). I would suggest that these individuals go to local libraries (in countries that have these public resources) and engage with the librarians on how they can educate themselves objectively on issues facing the scientific community's assessment of how various perturbations are altering Nature.[30]

A second normative duty is to transition from factual understanding to aesthetic valuing. It is my contention that this is a seamless process and the foundational grounding for an anthropocentric approach to environmental ethics.[31] Understanding the operation of a complex biological system will result in an intellectual valuing of that system. To value a system is to undertake a duty to protect said system. Thus, the second part of the extended eco-community worldview imperative is to undergo this process. It all begins with education, and it ends with an intellectual-cum-aesthetic appreciation that translates into a duty to protect.

In the end, the extended eco-community worldview imperative entails a duty to protect all of the world's Natural biological and nonbiological material systems (such as earth, air, and water) according to our resources. Since this duty extends only to humans, this account is anthropocentric. And though the shared community worldview imperatives (in their various forms) emphasize the communal duties incurred, because human communities are comprised of many individual humans, these duties apply to each individual within the community via my personhood account, the personal worldview imperative.

This constitutes the definition of Nature within the context of community dynamics (*ti esti*).

# Part II: Why Should We Care?

## THE ETHICAL CONSTRAINTS ON INTERFERING WITH NATURE

If we accept the depiction in part I of this essay, then we already have an argument outline on why we should care:

1. There are two sorts of understandings of N/nature: (a) nature that refers to individuals (tokens), and (b) Nature that refers to larger, general groups (types)[32]—A(ssertion)
2. The systemic, operational mechanisms of both nature and Nature are intricate, complex, and difficult fully to understand—F(act)
3. Whenever one comes to a correct, partial understanding of intricate and complex systemic mechanisms there follows a reaction that is akin to aesthetic appreciation—A
4. Aesthetic value appreciation incurs a duty to protect that which has been valued—F[33]
5. When one engages with nature/Nature and comes to an understanding (on some level) of the causal operation of these systemic mechanisms one will value nature/Nature, and as a result, be obliged to protect nature/Nature—1–4
6. Coming to terms with understanding nature/Nature involves a model that situates individuals within communities (both proximate and remote)—A
7. There are (at least) two large understanding of communities that all humans must recognize: human communities and N/natural communities—A
8. Properly understanding the human communities and the N/natural communities requires an accommodation and engagement in both proximate and remote versions of the same—6, 7
9. Duties follow from recognizing obligations that people have toward others—such as human and Natural communities both proximate and remote—F[34]

10. All humans have a duty to engage in and protect their human and their natural/Natural communities—5–9

### Argument One: The Recognition, Valuing, and Protection of Nature

Once we accept Argument One, it is incumbent upon us to ascertain what are the constraints upon our activities that do not arise from n/Nature. This area of development might be termed *artificial*. All technology is artificial. One popular definition of humans is as toolmaking animals.[35] The *making* (ποεῖν + τεχνή/ *poein + techne*) is at the etymological center of the realm of the technological, which is a novel creation that will augment the realm of Nature by *homo sapiens*. One way to think about these additions is by using the language of the ancient Greek physical philosophers. The given order, Nature (φύσις/*phusis*) exists. The *making* can either accord with Nature (κατα φύσιν/*kata phusin*) or it can go against the Natural grain and thus interrupt, change, or go against Nature (παρα φύσιν/*para phusin*).[36] Thus, one distinction of importance is between *kata phusin* and *para phusin*.[37]

If, from part I, there is a general duty to protect Nature (*phusis*), then *ceteris paribus* one should only *make things* that are in accord with nature (*kata phusin*). But what would this mean? How much elasticity does Nature possess? At what point are we really *harming* Nature? And to what extent are we harming it?

This is an issue in much dispute.[38] In the nineteenth century in Britain, during the rise of the first Industrial Revolution, the climate was heavily affected.[39] The conceptual dissonance on this is noted in a painting of J. M. W. Turner, *Rain, Steam, and Speed: The Great Western Railway*. In the painting we are presented with three facts: (1) There is a train (a new *making*) coming right at us over the Waterloo Bridge in London (metaphorically a symbol of *augmented* Nature going into the future); (2) There is a rowboat (the old *kata phusin*) going in the opposite direction (a vision of the past); and (3) In the midst of it all is an

Illustration: J. M. W. Turner, *Rain, Steam, and Speed: The Great Western Railway*, National Gallery of Art, London.

atmosphere of pollution (the present *para phusin* caused by the new technology). Turner makes his visual case that this is the direction of *human makings* in the nineteenth century in Britain. Depending upon whether one identifies with the locomotive or the rowboat, one judges positively or negatively on this.[40]

This artistic rendering illustrates a critical possible conflict between Humans (considering themselves atop the *scala naturae*) and Nature (the broader class that includes humans as members). The fact that humans often get this logical relation confused is the source of much confusion. The human making, *poein* + *techne* (now to be referred to in shorthand as *technology*) is the output of human activity. It is executed *within* a Natural construct. But because it originates from its own designs narrowly understood, it can create *community* (human and/or Natural) disruption.

*Community disruption* is an important concept. It occurs when one member of a community acts as if they live in a "community of one." Everyday examples of this are within the shared community worldview of a micro community.[41]

This debate in the nineteenth-century context of Britain is complicated by another variable: a static versus a dynamic view of Nature, viewed as a system with various perturbations that affect the output. Often Nature was thought of as some sort of enclosed garden upon which humans (both separated and apart as per part I) enter and gaze at this exotic *other* to ascertain whether they are satisfied or not.

There are echoes here of the Garden of Eden. In this theologically based model there is a sub-portion of Nature that is especially set out as being perfect from the anthropocentric viewpoint so long as one obeys certain rules—the principal one being not eating the fruit of the Tree of the Knowledge of Good and Evil.[42] In the narrative as depicted by John Milton, what was really behind God's prohibition to Adam and Eve was an attempt to frame the story in terms of the seventeenth-century scientific revolution—putting these dynamic ideas of a changing view of Nature (cutting-edge but controversial science) into the mouth of Eve.[43]

The unchanging view of Nature took another hit in the nineteenth century with Darwin and other advocates of *evolutionary theory*.[44] The dogma in this essay is that the static view is the wrong way to view Nature. Nature is in constant flux[45] so that in species$_1$ the environment$_1$ might prosper in time$_1$, but when we approach time$_2$ the environment may change to environment$_2$ such that some existing and nascent species will prosper and some others will go extinct—such as species$_1$. This is just a factual discussion of change, but many of the evolutionary folk (harkening back to the *scale naturae*) thought that this was a modern way to provide an explanation for the *superiority* of humans in Nature (however they are situated: outside-looking-inside or *partially* inside).[46]

The social *evolutionary* attitude is also often countered by an antithetical *devolutionary* attitude. In the former account, people expect that human life in Nature will always *improve*.[47] There is much incentive among most politicians around the world to trumpet this possibility. That's how they stay in power (so long as they are a part of the traditional ruling party).

The *devolutionary* attitude is rather different. These folks contend that things were better in the past and are now deteriorating. Vastly different social/political groups can take this position. For example, in Hesiod's *Theogony* it is asserted that in the past, there was an age of gold. It was a far better time to be alive on earth; things were much better as opposed to the present, lower age of iron.[48] Some politicians around the world cynically set out a similar account of the status quo to support either their election or a revolution to change things in order to return to a previous age that was better.[49]

## Caring for and Protecting Nature

Another aspect of "caring" about Nature concerns whether Nature, as such, possesses positive normative value. In Argument One it was argued that humans who view nature/Nature carefully will find it to be a web of complicated systems and that when people come to understand some of the mechanism of a complicated system something akin to an aesthetic reaction occurs and this, in turn, fosters a caring attitude of protection for the system(s) so assessed. This mechanism must be linked to outcomes that are positive in their own terms (such as ongoing sustainable biocentric diversity that is beneficial to promoting and maintaining life).[50]

But more is needed and the only way to get there, in this author's opinion, is to refer to the anthropocentric attitude that a well-operating Nature helps human nature(s) to thrive. This must undergird the value/duty relation because without it, we are faced with mere factual posits. This is not an ethical egoistic position because it is made on behalf of all humanity. If anything, it approaches either a utilitarian justification (not this author's preferred stance) or a contextual condition that allows human action to continue (the author's preferred position). An example of this position would be the following argument.[51]

1. The Nature of humans, as a species, is to seek to execute purposive action according to (at least) a rudimentary understanding of deductive, inductive, and abductive logic—A[52]
2. To execute purposive action, Humans require various goods of agency set out hierarchically in the Table of Embeddedness—A[53]
3. All humans will value as "prudentially good" that which allows them personally to act—F

4. All humans, personally, will value as "prudentially good" the acquisition of as many goods from the Table of Embeddedness as possible (in hierarchical order)—1–3
5. Respecting the general grounds of action, all humans are alike—F
6. Respecting the general grounds of human action, logically there can be no idiosyncratic preference—5
7. Whatever attaches as an essential Natural condition of a species viewed contextually from the various community worldview imperatives (shared human, extended human, eco, and extended eco) is proper to that Natural species' condition—F
8. To be "mutually life-affirming in an environmental perspective" is a fundamental positive normative environmental value—A[54]
9. Whatever is proper to a Natural species' condition is morally good if the summation of all and every Natural species' conditions (i.e., general, generic conditions) are mutually life-affirming in an environmental perspective—5–8
10. The prudential values set out in premise 4 (for individuals) can be generally life-affirming in an environmental perspective—9
11. Prudential values for particular individuals in an environmental context become general moral values when they attach to generic Natural species' conditions—9, 10

---

12. The prudential values set out in premise 4 are morally good and incur positive moral duties on all (capable of voluntary action) to facilitate outcomes that are life-affirming in an environmental perspective—4, 9, 11

### Argument Two: The Moral Perspective of Human Nature within the Environmental Perspective

Argument Two, though it begins with prudential values (seen from the perspective of individual natures), *transcends to the ethical* when the understanding of the relationship between humans and their fundamental definition is generalized within the environmental context. This is because there is no longer an agent acting for herself only. Rather, the logical substitution instance is a generically described individual and, as such, could be understood as applicable to any substitution instance for the variable that has undergone universal generalization.

Along with some undergirding mechanism such outcomes can be projected into a law-like structure.[55] This depiction of humans as situated within their environmental communities (severally understood) constitutes a fundamental structure of ethical duty.[56]

## *The* Making *and the* Things Made

Earlier in this chapter, Nature, as an existent ontological entity, was contrasted with things created by humans, "the making." The making was connected to a process described as an art or *techne*. Nature was set out as primary to human making because humans do not make themselves. This assessment relies upon a principle about *making*: "There is a priority in *making* that gives priority to the maker over the artifact created (that which is made)."[57]

This relationship does not depend upon *knowing* the identity of the maker. For example, Nature (as an all-encompassing material system affecting all living things and that which supports them) exists, and within this systemic structure, brings about the conditions whereby life and its supporting components (air, land, and water) came to be and are sustained. Humans are a part of this grand system. But Humans did not create it. It was created by some systemic material agency since by the Principle of Sufficient Reason, everything that *is* must owe its existence to some material, causal explanation.[58] Under this account the material system, Nature, is understood to be the named entity that is responsible for our very human existence.

As such, under the hierarchy of the making and the output of the making (things made), we owe a level of respect and precaution when dealing with the operation of Nature's systems when we go about *our* making of artificial devices (*teche* => technology). In a situation in which there was a conflict between human making and the material system, Nature, the status of the latter should trump the former.[59] This can be seen in Argument Three.

1. There is a priority in the process of making that puts the *maker* above the output of the *maker (things made)*—A
2. The status of priority in the process of making means that the operation of and the interests in *the maker* always trump the operation of and the interests in *the things made*—A
3. Nature's relation to Humans is as *maker* to the output *made*—F
4. The operation of and the interests in Nature's systemic operation always trump the operation of and the interests in Human's own *making*—1–3
5. The operation of and the interests in Human artifacts (technology) are always subservient to the ultimate interests of Humans—1, 4

---

6. The operation of and interests in Human artifacts (technology) are always subservient to the operation of and interests in Nature's systemic operation—4, 5

*Argument Three: The Priority of the Maker over the Maker's Output*

Argument Three has some interesting corollaries. Among these are that if we rank the priority normatively, from the vantage point of the thing made, the maker is (in an important sense) normatively good. This would make Nature (from the point of view of Humans and all other living things) *good*. In turn, if Nature is good and if technology created by Humans harms the operation of Nature, then that human technology is *bad* and ought not to be adopted. This gradation of the evil is a function of how much harm Nature incurs.

Since the level of harm and the elasticity of Nature to rebound from temporary or ongoing harm is speculative at best, the principle of precautionary reason[60] dictates that we should refrain from harming Nature whenever it is in our power to do so. It is one thing to see how such a corollary would apply in prohibiting air, water, and land pollution. This seems very straightforward. However, more difficult cases (beyond the scope of this essay) are when one proffers technology that seeks to *improve* Nature. A pivotal example of this is in genetic engineering.[61]

If we try to *improve* the genome by the use of "knock out" gene strategies (which will affect future generations) for fatal genetic diseases or genetically based handicaps, are we "helping" or "hurting" Nature? In the earlier terminology, is it *kata phusin* or *para phusin*? This is a difficult question and may turn on other criteria such as the difference in somatic treatment versus germ line alterations. There are arguments that can be made on each side of this and related controversies. It is not the purpose of this essay to solve these and other such important practical issues, but rather to offer a theoretical framework by which the discussion should proceed.

What we are left with in this second section of the essay is a moral commitment to care for Nature. This moral commitment is based upon what Nature *is* (a series of concentric and overlapping human and Natural communities that are symbiotic). The study of Nature creates the value/duty relationship that outlines the ground of general moral duty from the human side. This general ground becomes more practical when it is specified that there is a moral prohibition not to interfere in a harmful way with our human makings because Nature stands in relation to all of us as "maker." As such, Nature's makings (which includes us) require the respect owed to a maker not to have its own artifacts come back to harm it. This second principal grounds our practical duties to Nature and acts as a firm moral limitation on human technology.

Section 2

# Humans and Machines: A New Ethical Paradigm?

# CHAPTER 3

# Transformative Technologies, the Status Quo, and (Religious) Institutions

*Morgan Luck and Stephen Clarke*

## Abstract

In this chapter we consider, and criticize, a range of definitions of transformative technology, before offering our own definition. According to our definition, transformative technology significantly transforms existing states of affairs; that is, it transforms the status quo. We anticipate, and head off, two possible objections to our definition before ending with a brief discussion of a well-known form of cognitive bias, status quo bias, which can be used to explain much of the opposition to the introduction of transformative technologies, much of which emanates from existing institutions, including religious institutions.

KEYWORDS

cognitive bias, institutions, irreversible change, religion, status quo bias, transformative technology

## Introduction

Transformative technology is widely discussed but there is a noticeable lack of agreement about what constitutes transformative technology. In this chapter we consider, and criticize, a range of definitions of transformative technology, before offering our own definition. According to our definition, transformative technology significantly transforms existing states of affairs; that is, it transforms the status quo.

We anticipate, and head off, two possible objections to our definition before ending with a brief discussion of a well-known form of cognitive bias, status quo bias, which can be used to explain much of the opposition to the introduction of transformative technologies, much of which emanates from existing institutions, including religious institutions.

# 1.0 What Are Transformative Technologies?

What are transformative technologies? It's not entirely clear. People "are often ambiguous in what they consider transformative" (Gruetzemacher & Whittlestone 2019, 2). As such, the term

> remains somewhat fuzzy. Many of the discussions focus on the marvels of the technology itself, others focus on its pathway of development, adaptation and adoption, and still others address the impacts of the technology on the economy and society. (Phillips 2007, 13)

We aim to reduce this fuzziness. We begin by introducing common examples of transformative technologies. We then use these examples to evaluate current accounts of transformative technology and to provide a new account of it.

# 1.1 Some Common Examples of Transformative Technologies

The oral contraceptive pill is a clear example of transformative technology (Pridmore-Brown 2006, 790). From the time "the pill" was first approved for use in the United States in 1960 it has played a key role in enabling women to control their own fertility. This, in turn, has enabled them to invest more in education and in their careers, transforming the workforce.

The Organisation for Economic Cooperation and Development (OECD) provides further examples of transformative technologies.

> The list of transformative and potentially transformative technologies is long, from quantum computing and advanced energy storage, to new forms of 3D printing, big data analytics and neurotechnologies. Three technologies are outlined here whose impacts have the potential to be particularly far-reaching: AI, the IoT and blockchain. (2018, 13)

Also, Clarke and Roache (2012) provide the following examples of transformative technologies:

> Some novel technologies offer potentially great opportunities to transform our lives, making us faster, stronger, more resistant to disease and so on. These include human enhancement technologies, cloning, stem cell research and the use of pre-implantation genetic diagnosis to select embryos for non-disease traits. (27)

With these examples in place we can build a general picture of what is meant by transformative technologies. To help provide some focus, we will consider the following questions:

- Could any type of technology be a transformative technology?
- Must transformative technologies be multipurpose?
- Must transformative technologies be general purpose?
- Do transformative technologies merely have the potential to transform?
- Must transformative technologies bring about positive changes?
- Must transformative technologies bring about irreversible changes?

To help answer these questions, we shall now consider some current accounts of transformative technology.

# 1.2 Could Any Type of Technology Be a Transformative Technology?

Let us begin with a narrow account of transformative technologies. Riva et al. (2015) state that "'Transformative Technology' is a technologically mediated experience that supports positive, enduring transformation of the self-world" (308).

This account limits transformative technologies in various respects. We focus here on the claim that transformative technologies must mediate experiences.

In psychology a technology that mediates experience is one that gives you information about an experience that the experience itself doesn't provide immediately. For example, a birdwatching smartphone app might tell you the name of the bird you are taking a picture of. The bird's name is not relayed by looking directly at the bird; that is, this information is not immediate. So, seeing the bird's name pop up on your phone is an example of a mediated experience. The problem with this limitation is that not all examples of transformative technologies mediate experience.

Many technologies commonly taken to be transformative would be excluded under this account. These include 3D-printed on-demand houses, cloning, stem cell therapies, the contraceptive pill, and electricity. These technologies do not obviously mediate experiences. Riva et al. (2015) might argue that these are not examples of transformative technologies, since they don't fit their account. However, when giving an account (as opposed to a definition) one should aim to capture the key ways in which the term is used, and this involves accounting for common examples.

# 1.3 Must Transformative Technologies be Multipurpose?

Consider next an account given by Woodly (2002).

> Transformative technologies can be broadly defined as technologies with
>
> 1. many varied purposes;
> 2. applications or impacts on large parts of society and the economy;
> 3. much scope for improvement initially;
> 4. strong complementarities with other technologies; and
> 5. long term effects on values, power structures and ideas. (2)

Woodly doesn't limit transformative technology to a particular type. However, this account also fails to capture some common examples of transformative technologies. To see why we can focus on point 1: the claim that transformative technologies have many varied purposes.

The contraceptive pill seems like a clear case of a transformative technology. However, arguably it only serves a single purpose: to stop ovulation. Teleportation seems like a potential future transformative technology. Yet, arguably, it too only serves a single purpose: to move matter instantly from one location to another. Of course, it might be argued that such technologies do have multiple purposes. The pill can prevent pregnancy and help regulate the menstrual cycle. Teleportation could be used to reduce traffic and pollution, and open up new holiday destinations. There are two points to consider in response to this line of reasoning.

First, the purpose of every technology can be broken into smaller parts in similar ways. Take the humble rolling pin. Its purpose is to roll malleable items into sheets. However, we could break this purpose up: to help make bread, to help make cookies, to help make pastries, and so on. If such an argumentative move were acceptable, then Woodly's first criterion would seem redundant, as nearly every technology's purpose could be given the same treatment.

Second, even if we assume that all past examples of transformative technology are multipurpose, this doesn't rule out future transformative technologies that are single-purpose. For example, let us imagine that an immortality pill was developed that had a single purpose—to stop people from aging. This technology would surely have a huge impact on people's lives. And to suggest it wasn't transformative merely because it didn't have other purposes seems wrongheaded.

# 1.4 Must Transformative Technologies Be General Purpose?

LaFleur et al. assert that "Technologies become transformative when they evolve into general purpose technologies (GPTs) that enable productivity gains across many sectors of the economy" (2017, 5).

Although many transformative technologies are also clearly general-purpose technologies (such as the stream engine, electricity, and computers), and perhaps all general-purpose technologies are transformative technologies, it is not clear that all transformative technologies are general-purpose technologies.

The contraceptive pill is a good counterexample to this account, as the pill was clearly transformative, but not general purpose. That is, it does not perform a generic function; it has instead a narrow (although massively important) range of uses (e.g., to prevent pregnancy). And again, future technologies, such as the immortality pill, look like they might also fail to qualify as general purpose.

This restriction should also be dropped to allow for the possibility that a technology might have a huge impact upon our lives, but do so in a very focused way.

# 1.5 Do Transformative Technologies Merely Have the Potential to Transform?

Miller and Keoleian tell us that "A transformative technology is a product or process that has the potential to fundamentally change existing markets, develop new markets, lead to changes in consumer behavior, or significantly alter major supply chains" (2015, 3067).

It seems clear that if technologies such as mind-uploading, the immortality pill, and teleportation were developed, future generations would most certainly look back upon them as transformative of society. But should we currently consider them to be transformative technologies merely because they *might* bring about significant social change? Miller and Keoleian think "yes." We think otherwise.

To make our point, consider an invention from 1922: Fiske's reading machine. At the time it was made publicly available, this machine was lauded as a game-changer; a machine that "the present art of printing may be revolutionized by" (Winters 1922). Fiske's reading machine consisted

> of a tiny lens and a small roller for operating this eyepiece up and down a vertical column of reading-matter, is a means by which ordinary typewritten copy, when photographically reduced to one-hundredth of the space originally occupied, can be read with quite the facility that the impression of conventional printing type is now revealed to the unaided eye. (407)

By drastically reducing the size of text, while maintaining its readability, Fiske's reading machine promised to reduce the cost of printing, reduce the space required to store texts, increase the mobility of texts, and increase the accessibility of texts. The reading machine had the potential to make these transformative changes; however, they were never made because the new and potentially transformative device proved unpopular and was never widely used anywhere. So, is Fiske's reading machine a transformative technology?

Assuming, as we are, that the machine did have the potential to bring about the required changes, Miller and Keoleian would deem the technology to be transformative. This is despite the fact it failed to bring about such changes. The notion of a transformative technology that failed to transform anything seems very odd to us.

We propose that only technologies that have brought about the required changes are transformative technologies. Those technologies that have the *potential* to bring about the required changes, but have yet to do so, are *potential transformative technologies*. It might also be useful to employ a subcategory. Potential transformative technologies that we expect *will* (as opposed to merely might) bring about the required changes, but have yet to do so, are *future transformative technologies*.

Fiske's reading machine was a potential transformative technology, but it never became an actual transformative technology. The contraceptive pill is a transformative technology. Nanotechnology, which "is expected to become a key transformative technology of the twenty-first century" (Michelson et al. 2008), is a future transformative technology.

# 2.0 A New Account of Transformative Technology

So far we have considered some common examples of transformative technologies and used them to help evaluate current accounts of the term. We now change tack. In this section we present a new account of transformative technology. Let us begin by considering what transformative technologies are actually changing.

Shah & Shay (2019) state that, simply defined, a transformative technology is any technology that inspires a substantive change.

But a change to what? To help us figure this out, it is interesting to note that some technologies resist change. Refrigerators keep our food from spoiling. The Thames Barrier keeps London from flooding. The pill keeps women from conceiving. Each of these technologies is intended to stop change from occurring. Yet these technologies also managed to change norms. It was normal for foods to spoil earlier, for London to occasionally flood, and for women to conceive more often. In each case the status quo—the existing state of affairs—was changed. Our view is that when a technology *significantly* alters the status quo, especially with regard to social and political matters, it constitutes a transformative technology.

The status quo is changing all the time in various ways. And sometimes in just small, subtle, and incremental ways. Not all these changes are significant. For example, the introduction of the VCR changed the status quo in minor ways. People no longer had to miss their favorite television shows if they were unable to watch television at a particular time. But this change probably doesn't qualify as significant. So, the VCR would fail to be a transformative technology in our account. With this significant qualification in place, our account can be presented as follows,

> X is a transformative technology for Y if and only if X is a technology that significantly transforms the status quo of Y.

Transformative technologies are explicitly relative on this account. Their relative nature allows for the possibility that a technology might radically transform the lives of some people, but not of others. For example, although the steam train changed the status quo of the British people in the early 1800s, this technology did not have the same impact on all non-British people at the time. Our account allows for the possibility that the steam engine was a transformative technology relative to the British in the 1800s. But it was not a transformative technology relative to humanity as a whole at this time.

Although this account is simple, versatile, and avoids the problems raised in the previous sections, it doesn't eliminate "fuzziness" completely. The idea that transformative technology brings about *significant* transformations naturally raises the question, "What is a significant transformation?" It is tempting to explicitly define the term "significant" to address this question. However, this would be a mistake. Given the multitude of ways different things can be important to different groups, the term is likely to resist such an analysis.

Let us now consider some possible objections to our account.

## 2.1 Must Transformative Technologies Bring About Positive Changes?

Some may object to our account as it doesn't limit transformative technology to technology that has positive effects. For example, Riva et al. stipulate that "'Transformative Technology' are technologically-mediated experiences that support positive, enduring transformation of the self-world" (2015, 308).

This stipulation is problematic. The effects of technology can change over time. The rise of AI might initially yield very positive effects for humans, unless and until AIs themselves rise up and enslave humans, as some fear. Also, synthetic neurotransmitters may be able to help usher in a new era of mental health, but could be used by repressive governments to surveil and control thought. Are such technologies transformative whilst bringing about positive changes, but then cease to be once they bring about negative changes? Or were they never really transformative technologies in the first place, as the negative consequences ultimately outweighed the positive?

Both of the aforementioned options seem problematic. To suggest a technology that has brought about drastic and profound effects is not transformative, because it later brings about even more drastic and profound effects, skews our common understanding of the term "transformative." These issues are avoided if we allow transformative technologies to have neutral, positive, and/or negative effects.

## 2.2 Must Transformative Technologies Bring About Irreversible Changes?

Some may object to our account for not limiting transformative technologies to those that bring about irreversible effects. This limitation is suggested by Gruetzemacher & Whittlestone's (2019) account of transformative technologies:

> We suggest that what should be considered core to the notion of a transformative technology is that it contributes to irreversible changes across some domain or aspect of society. Although we agree that transformative technologies need only change "some domain or aspect of society," we disagree that these changes must be irreversible. (4)

There is general agreement that transformative technologies bring about lasting, significant changes. They are not faddish, like tamagotchis, the Nintendo Power Glove, or the Zip drive. With a fad technology, after the initial stir, people largely move on. The changes they bring about are in effect reversed; the previous status quo returns. However, the changes brought about by transformative technologies are not significant *because* they are irreversible. Why? Because few technologies bring about irreversible changes. To understand why, let us again consider an apocalyptic event.

Imagine that after some cataclysm (a nuclear winter, asteroid impact, or virus) humanity is reduced to a handful of survivors. One can easily envision life returning to something more akin to prehistoric subsistence living, where the effects of blockchain, stem cell research, and AI are no longer felt. This possibility demonstrates that the effects of most technologies can be reversed. It is entirely possible for us to revert to a prior way of living.

A less dramatic example would be political changes that effectively reverse the social changes brought about by technology. For example, currently in the United States, "29 states out of 50 have a majority of anti-abortion lawmakers in their legislatures and are actively enforcing ways to limit access to the procedure" (BBC, 2021). Were such efforts successful, many of the effects of abortion technology would be reversed—that would be the point of the legislation. It takes little imagination to see how other political changes might reverse the social changes caused by the introduction of the morning after-pill, stem-cell research, cloning, etc.

So, given that it is possible to reverse the changes of most technologies "across some domain or aspect of society" (Gruetzemacher & Whittlestone 2019, 4), it follows that either no technology is transformative, or the irreversibility limitation is wrong. We opt for the latter.

# 3.0 Opposition to Transformative Technologies and Status Quo Bias

Many transformative technologies that are now generally regarded as positive were regarded by a significant portion of the population as negative at the time that they were introduced. A striking example is in vitro fertilization (or IVF). IVF has transformed the lives of many women, enabling them to delay pregnancy and have children at a later age than they would be able to otherwise. It has also transformed the lives of other women who would never have been able to have children at all were it not for IVF. These days IVF has obtained widespread acceptance across the globe. Over eight million IVF-assisted births have occurred worldwide since the first IVF birth in 1978.[1] About 5% of births in Australia in 2020 occurred with the assistance of IVF (UNSW Media 2020).

When IVF was first used in 1978 it aroused widespread opposition, particularly from religious authorities. It was alleged by several of these authorities that the use of IVF amounted to "playing God." It was also feared that its use would set humanity down a "slippery slope," leading to the use of other forms of fertility treatments that were more clearly immoral. The stakes were reckoned to be very high indeed. According to the editors of *Nova Magazine*, test-tube babies were "the biggest threat since the atom bomb" (Henig 2003, 64).

According to Leon Kass, the head of George W. Bush's President's Council on Bioethics, "the idea of the humanness of our human life and the meaning of our embodiment, our sexual being and our relations to our ancestors and descendants" were all placed in jeopardy by the introduction of IVF (Henig 2003, 64). Some of the opposition to IVF from the late 1970s and early 1980s had a circular quality to it, with opponents highlighting fears that children who were conceived with the assistance of IVF might be bullied by other children on the grounds that they were "test-tube babies," even if there were no substantive reasons to object to IVF and even if children born with the assistance of IVF were no different in appearance from other children.

The fears associated with allowing the introduction of IVF have dissipated. This may be because, among other things, they were not based on considered reasoning but were, for the most part, the result of *post hoc* reactions. Many of the people who experienced unease about the possibility of allowing IVF were motivated to find or invent reasons to oppose it that would not have been reasons for them had they not had an initial sense of unease about the introduction of IVF. They may have felt such a sense of unease as a consequence of the activation of a cognitive bias that appears to be widespread—a bias in favor of the status quo, coupled with a sense that the status quo was coming under threat.

The status quo in 1978 was that IVF was not used, and indeed was not possible. Someone who was opposed to IVF in 1978, as a result of status quo bias, would not, all things being equal, oppose IVF in 2021. Indeed, they would now oppose the introduction of restrictions on the use of IVF as the new status quo in 2021 is that IVF is widely used.

Not all preferences for the status quo are the result of cognitive bias. Sometimes it is rational to prefer the status quo to change. However, there is strong evidence that status quo bias is widespread and that many preferences for the status quo are a consequence of cognitive bias rather than a consequence of well-considered reasoning.[2] Status quo bias appears to be the result of a number of underlying cognitive biases, the two most important being the "endowment effect" and "loss aversion" (Kahneman et al., 1991).

The endowment effect leads people to ascribe greater value to what they currently possess over that which they might potentially possess in the future. For example, if given the choice between keeping a dollar we already have, or swapping it for a dollar and one cent, a surprising number of us would stick with the dollar. This effect inhibits change, at least in respect of changes that have an impact on items that can be owned. Loss aversion is the result of a tendency we have to feel more harmed by losses than we feel benefitted by gains. For example, losing a dollar feels bad far more than finding a dollar feels good.[3]

Because children are not usually regarded as being owned, the endowment effect is probably not relevant to the example of status quo bias against IVF. However, loss aversion is highly relevant here. The introduction of IVF in 1978 offered the prospect of both potential gains and potential losses. IVF appeared to lead to potential gains for the women who stand to benefit from its use and appeared to offer potential losses to the society that it threatened to disrupt. We can see with the benefit of hindsight that such fears of losses were ill-founded. But this would not have been apparent to many at the time. Because such potential losses tend to loom larger in ordinary human cognition than do potential gains, as a result of loss aversion, opposition to IVF was widespread.

The endowment effect is relevant to status quo bias against the introduction of forms of transformative technologies that are owned. A good example is the automobile, which was the subject of extraordinary skepticism when it was first introduced (Winton 1911/2017). Large numbers of people were utterly convinced, without being able to explain why, that a "horseless carriage" would never be successful. A good explanation for their evidence-free skepticism about horseless carriages was that many of them owned horses and carriages and placed a high value on them, as a result of the endowment effect. When they compared their highly valued horses and carriages to the possibility of horseless carriages, which they did not own, the potential horseless carriages they imagined were invariably disvalued when compared to their actual horses and carriages, and so the endowment effect fueled their skeptical attitudes about the possibility of successfully functioning automobiles.

The widespread nature of status quo bias contributes to the appeal of political conservatism. Political conservatives are people who either prefer the status quo with respect to social and political arrangements over other possible arrangements, or hold that it is not feasible to change society so as to enable a more preferable set of arrangements to be instituted. Some conservatives may have good reasons to prefer the status quo to alternatives or may have good reasons to suppose that it is not feasible to change society in such a way as to implement available alternatives. But other conservatives do not articulate good reasons and the *post hoc* reasons that appear to motivate them are driven by feelings of discomfort in relation to the prospect of altering the status quo. A key cause of such discomfort is status quo bias.[4]

Because political conservatives place a high value on current social and political arrangements, it is understandable that they would both oppose the introduction of IVF in the late 1970s and also support the retention of IVF programs in 2021.[5] In the late 1970s the introduction of IVF threatened to alter existing social and political arrangements. However, in 2021 IVF has been offered to women for over forty years and IVF programs are now part of the social and political status quo. To conservatives it will appear that IVF programs have proved their worth by surviving the "test of time."[6]

# References

Bostrom, N., and Ord, T. (2006). The reversal test: Eliminating status quo bias in applied ethics. *Ethics, 116*: 656–679.

Clarke, S. (2016). The reversal test, status quo bias and opposition to human cognitive enhancement. *Canadian Journal of Philosophy, 46*(3): 369–386.

Clarke, S. (2017). A prospect theory approach to understanding conservatism. *Philosophia, 45*(2): 551–568.

Clarke, S., & Roache, R. (2012). Introducing transformative technologies into democratic societies. *Philosophy and Technology, 25*(1): 27–45.

Franklin, U. (1990). *The real world of technology.* Annasi.

Ghildial, P. (2021, May 28). *The looming battle over abortion in the US.* BBC News. https://www.bbc.com/news/world-us-canada-57208053.

Gruetzemacher, R., & Whittlestone, J. (2019). *Defining and unpacking transformative AI.* Effective Altruism Global. arXiv. https://www.arxiv-vanity.com/papers/2001.04335/.

Henig, R. M. (2003). Pandora's baby. *Scientific American, 288*(6): 62–67.

Jovanovic, B., & Rousseau, P. (2005). General purpose technologies. In P. Aghion and S. Durlauf (Eds.), *Handbook of Economic Growth* (pp. 1181–1224). Elsevier.

Kahneman, D. (2011). *Thinking, fast and slow.* Farrar, Straus, and Giroux.

Kahneman, D., Knetsch, J. L., & Thaler, R. H. (1991). Anomalies: The endowment effect, loss aversion and status quo bias. *Journal of Economic Perspectives, 5*(1): 193–206.

LaFleur, M., Bruckner, M., & Pitterle, I. (2017). *Frontier issues: The impact of the technological revolution on labour markets and income distribution.* United Nations Department of Economic and Social Affairs.

Michelson, E., Sandler, R., & Resnik, D. (2008). Nanotechnology. In Mary Crowley (Ed.), *From birth to death and bench to clinic: The Hastings Center bioethics briefing book for journalists, policymakers, and campaigns* (pp. 111–116). The Hastings Center.

Miller, S. A., and Keoleian, G. A. (2015). Framework for analyzing transformative technologies in life cycle assessment. *Environmental Science & Technology, 49*(5): 3067–3075.

Organisation for Economic Cooperation and Development. (2018). *Transformative technologies and jobs of the future.*

Phillips, P. W. B. (2007). *Governing transformative technological innovation: Who's in charge?* Edward Elgar.

Pridmore-Brown, M. (2006). Gender and technology. *The European Legacy, 11*(7): 789–793.

Riva, G., Villani, D., Cipresso, P., Repetto, C., Triberti, S., Di Lernia, D., Chirico, A., Serino, S., & Gaggioli, A. (2016, April 7–9). *Positive and transformative technologies for active ageing* [Paper presentation]. *Medicine Meets Virtual Reality* (22), NextMed/MMVR. Los Angeles, CA.

Scruton, R. (2014). *How to be a conservative.* Bloomsbury Continuum.

Shah, D., & Shay, E. (2019). How and why artificial intelligence, mixed reality and blockchain technologies will change marketing we know today. In A. Parvatiyar & R. Sisodia (Eds.), *Handbook of advances in marketing in an era of disruptions* (pp. 377–390). SAGE.

Taipale, S. (2009). *Transformative technologies, spatial changes: Essays on mobile phones and the Internet.* University of Jyvaskyla.

UNSW Media. (2020, September 6). *Almost one in 20 babies in Australia born through IVF.* https://newsroom.unsw.edu.au/news/health/almost-one-20-babies-australia-born-through-ivf.

Winston, B. (2008). Hula hoop or contraceptive pill? Misunderstanding the nature of the social impact of technology. *Navigationen-Zeitschrift für Medien-und Kulturwissenschaften, 8*(2): 139–150.

Winters, S. R. (1922). An invention that may reduce the size of our books to a fraction of their present bulk. *Scientific American, 126*: 407.

Winton, A. (2017, January). Get a horse! America's skepticism toward the first automobiles. *Saturday Evening Post.* https://www.saturdayeveningpost.com/2017/01/get-horse-americas-skepticism-toward-first-automobiles/. (Original work published 1911.)

Woodley, B. (2002). *The impact of transformative technologies on governance: Some lessons from history.* Institute on Governance.

CHAPTER 4

# Transhumanism
## IS THIS A STEP FORWARD?

*Felicia Nimue Ackerman*

## Abstract

Transhumanism promotes technology to radically enhance human intelligence, health, happiness, and longevity. Objections have been raised to transhumanism both in principle (that it would go against nature) and in practice (that it would be unfeasible or that the benefits would not be worth the costs). This essay argues against both sorts of objections, concluding that there is nothing wrong with transhumanism in principle and that it offers hope of a better future in practice.

**KEYWORDS**

enhancement, longevity, nature, transhuman, unnatural, John Stuart Mill

## Introduction

We mustn't improve our biology,
Despite all its limits and pains.
If God had approved of technology,
He would have endowed us with brains.[1]

Is transhumanism a step forward? What is transhumanism, anyway? My discussion will rely on the following characterization:

> Transhumanism [is a] social and philosophical movement devoted to promoting the research and development of robust human-enhancement technologies. Such technologies would augment or increase human sensory reception, emotive ability, or cognitive capacity as well as radically improve human health and extend human life spans. Such modifications resulting from the addition of biological or physical technologies would be more or less permanent and integrated into the human body. [This] will herald the increase in human consciousness, physical strength, emotional well-being, and overall health and greatly extend the length of human lifetimes.[2]

How could this fail to be a step forward? What could be wrong with a longer, happier, healthier, and smarter life? For example, as John Harris points out, "most people fear death, and the prospect of personal extended life-span is likely to be welcomed."[3] His claim is supported by a 2003 CNN survey that asks, "If it were possible, would you like to live 500 years?" Warning that the survey "is not scientific and reflects only the opinions of those Internet users who have chosen to participate," CNN reports that of the 31,905 responses received, 45% said yes, 39% said no, and 16% said they were not sure.[4]

Since the advantages of transhumanism are obvious, I will focus on objections that have been made to it. These objections can be divided into three categories.

The first category is empirical, involving claims that the objectives of transhumanism are unfeasible. The second category is philosophical, involving claims that transhumanism is undesirable in principle. The third is a hybrid category, involving claims that transhumanism would be harmful in practice, or at least that its benefits would not be worth the costs. Being a philosopher and bioethicist, I will focus on the second and third categories. Objections in the first category are best assessed by scientists.[5]

# Objections to Transhumanism in Principle

Why would anyone consider transhumanism undesirable in principle? A common objection is that transhumanism is in some sense unnatural or goes against nature. But what is wrong with going against nature? Religious believers may have reason to believe that nature is good if they believe that God created the laws of nature. Unbelievers, however, have excellent reason to deny that nature is uniformly good. As John Stuart Mill points out,

> in sober truth, nearly all the things which men are hanged or imprisoned for doing to one another, are nature's everyday performances.

> Killing, the most criminal act recognized by human laws, nature does once to every being that lives; and in a large proportion of cases, after protracted tortures such as only the greatest monsters whom we read of ever purposely inflicted on their living fellow-creatures.[6]

Note also the characterization, commonly attributed to Alfred, Lord Tennyson, but in fact in use earlier, of nature as "red in tooth and claw."[7]

What does it even mean to say that something is unnatural or goes against nature? Mill says,

> the word "nature" has two principal meanings: it either denotes the entire system of things . . . or it denotes things as they would be, apart from human intervention. In the first of these senses, the doctrine that man ought to follow nature is unmeaning; since man has no power to do anything else than follow nature. In the other sense of the term, the doctrine that man ought to follow nature, or in other words, ought to make the spontaneous course of things the model of his voluntary actions, is equally irrational and immoral.[8]

In Mill's second sense of the word "natural," what is natural is contrasted with what is done with the aid of technology, as in what we now call natural death or natural childbirth. But only the most extreme Luddite would hold that the introduction of technology is inherently and invariably bad. Advocates for natural death or natural childbirth generally exclude only certain sorts of technologies, rather than advocating that hospice patients or women in labor forgo central heating, air conditioning, and electricity. While Mill's claim that "Everything that is usual appears natural,"[9] is an obvious overgeneralization, familiarity (as well as bias) surely plays a role in judgments of naturalness.[10] Heart transplants, for example, once struck many people as unnatural but are often taken for granted today.

A third sense of the word "natural" has to do with natural law in the religious sense. Religion lies outside the secular scope of this essay, although it is worth noting that the secular glorification of what is "natural" may involve the export of traditional values into a milieu lacking the religion that grounded them. As the Catholic writer G. K. Chesterton says in a different context: "The modern world is full of the old Christian virtues gone mad."[11] With respect to the possibility of a greatly extended human lifespan, Sherwin B. Nuland expresses this sort of secular glorification as follows:

> The first of the early exponents of the experimental method, and therefore of science, often spoke of what they called the animal economy, and of the economy of nature in general. If I understand them correctly, they were speaking of that kind of natural law which

exists to preserve the earth's environment and its living forms. That natural law . . . evolved by straightforward Darwinian principles of planetary survival, very much as did every species of plant or beast. For this to continue, mankind cannot afford to destroy the balance . . . by tinkering with one of its most essential elements, which is the constant renewal within individual species and the invigoration that accompanies it. For plants and animals, renewal requires that death precede it so that the weary may be replaced by the vigorous. This is what is meant by the cycles of nature.[12]

Mankind, for all its unique gifts, is just as much a part of the ecosystem as any other zoologic or botanic form, and nature does not distinguish. We die so that the world may continue to live. . . . The tragedy of a single individual becomes, in the balance of natural things, the triumph of ongoing life.[13]

Nuland also says,

among living creatures, to die and leave the stage is the way of nature—old age is the preparation for departure, the gradual easing out of life that makes its ending more palatable not only for the elderly but for those to whom they leave the world in trust.[14]

These passages offer rhetoric but no reason to believe that future increases in human longevity would destroy the world (any more than past increases did). And the final sentence is cruel in its implication that old people's natural deterioration is good because it makes them more willing to die and makes their children and grandchildren more willing to see them go.

Thomas Nagel points out that

observed from without, human beings have a natural lifespan and cannot live much longer than a hundred years. A man's sense of his own experience, on the other hand, does not embody this idea of a natural limit. His existence defines for him an essentially open-ended possible future, containing the usual mixture of goods and evils that he has found so tolerable in the past.[15]

Note also that Andrew Stark considers a drug "artificial enhancement," and hence taboo, if it brings its users to a level no one had reached by nonmedical means such as diet.[16] He introduces this stipulation in response to Joseph Rosen's remark that "were he given permission by a medical ethics board, he would try to engineer a person to have wings."[17] But why would it be so terrible (rather than so wonderful) if technology enabled people to reach levels of power, intelligence, and longevity previously absent among humans? For that matter, why would it be so terrible if Joseph Rosen engineered wings for informed and consenting adults in a world where neither money nor biological side effects were a problem?

The conservative approach of the President George W. Bush's Council on Bioethics stresses "the danger of degradation in the designed, considering how any proposed improvements might impinge upon the nature of the one being improved"[18] and maintains that "to have an identity is to have limits."[19] But Ray Kurzweil points out that the essence of being human lies not in our limits but "in our ability to supersede our limitations."[20] What, after all, could be more distinctively human than our human intelligence and rationality, which is precisely what enables us to supersede what would otherwise be our limitations?

# Objections to Transhumanism in Practice: Harms to Transhuman Individuals Themselves

I now turn to arguments that transhumanism would be harmful in practice. I will distinguish two types of harm: harm to the transhuman individuals themselves and harms to society. The first is predicted by Bush's Council on Bioethics, which holds that a greatly extended lifespan would deprive these long-lived people of such virtues as interest and engagement, seriousness and aspiration, beauty and love, and virtue and moral excellence.[21] I have argued elsewhere against these claims.[22] Here I will simply mention that it is cruel to deny people a benefit because of an unsubstantiated fear (or, except in the case of one's minor children, a substantiated one) that it might damage their characters.

Consider also Erik Erikson's view that old people who approach death without fear manifest wisdom, because "healthy children will not fear life if their elders have integrity enough not to fear death."[23] Erikson's empirical claim is unsubstantiated, and his philosophical claim offers no reason to suppose that old people lack integrity or wisdom if they value life enough to fear its end.

Thomas Lynch takes this one step further, suggesting that we do not deserve a greatly increased lifespan because we would not make good use of the extra time. Lynch even begrudges us the extra three decades that the twentieth century brought to the average human lifespan in America. Claiming that "the returns . . . are mixed" on the extra time we have had so far, Lynch laments that with our extra time, "we neither cured the common cold nor secured peace in the Balkans, but we did invent the Wonderbra and no-load mutual funds. . . . We also golfed more and watched more sitcoms."[24] Lynch seems to think an extended lifespan is like an education at a very selective school. You have to qualify for it by showing you are likely to put it to good use. But why should an extended lifespan be something you have to deserve?

A more humane objection to a greatly extended lifespan involves the possibility that a very long life might be boring. But, as David Gems points out, "Some people seem especially able to enjoy endless repetition of the same experience."[25] Furthermore, there are some experiences whose repetition few people find boring. As Richard Momeyer recognizes, "so long as appetite remains strong, food and sexual union remain satisfying."[26]

If boredom is taken to be a reason against a greatly extended lifespan, the bar for acceptable quality of life has been raised remarkably high. "Bored to death" is a figure of speech.[27] How many people deem boredom a fate literally worse than death? Christine Overall considers the possibility that the boredom would be so extreme as to be "analogous to the experience of severe insomnia, in which, having been awake for seemingly endless hours without respite, one feels tired of being awake and exhausted by being oneself and wants only the nothingness of unconsciousness that is afforded, temporarily, by deep sleep."[28] This is hardly true of my own experience of severe insomnia, which has led me to long for sleep not as a respite from consciousness but as a means to an improved state of consciousness upon awakening. Moreover, insomnia frequently includes the unpleasant state of physical exhaustion, which is not necessarily part of boredom.

But sensual satisfactions are far from all that can keep long-lived people from boredom. Transhumans, with their greatly expanded mental capacities, could also be continually learning new things. Furthermore, transhumanism would hardly have to be compulsory, so people could choose to forgo it, just as some people nowadays choose to forgo higher education and life-extending medical care and technology.[29] Of course, people who opt out of transhumanism would still find their world changed by it. Like those in our society who opt out of cyberspace, they might feel unhappy and displaced. But their loss seems small when measured against the gains for those enjoyed by transhumans.

# Objections to Transhumanism in Practice: Harms to Society

How else might transhumanism harm society? One possibility is that young people will resent it if the old stick around too long, especially if these old people are robust enough to compete with the young for resources and professional advancement. Daniel Callahan has argued that "older people who stay longer in the work force . . . will close out opportunities for younger workers coming in."[30] But technological advances can create new resources and opportunities. As S. Jay Olshansky points out in criticizing Callahan, "we saw warnings of this kind before when women began to join the work force. A result was that women added nearly $3 trillion to the economy, and businesses owned by women employ nearly 16 percent of the work force."[31]

Callahan, however, doubts that there are "potential social benefits" to an increased human lifespan. He asks, "Is there any evidence that more old people will make special contributions now lacking with an average life expectancy close to 80?"[32] Callahan assumes that old people's continued existence needs to be justified in terms of their making "special contributions." But what about the social benefit inherent in prolonging the lives of old people who want to stay alive? In failing to recognize that this huge benefit to old people is a social benefit, Callahan is writing old people out of society.

This dismissive attitude also underlies Callahan's statement that "an important and liberating part of modern life" has been that "the old retire from work and their place is taken by the young. A society where the aged stay in place for many more years would surely throw that fruitful passing of the generations into chaos."[33] He overlooks the possibility that this passing is neither fruitful nor liberating to the old. Moreover, it is meanspirited and ageist to hold that the old should die in order to avoid giving the young grounds for resentment.

It is even more meanspirited to expect old people to die to liberate their adult children from the pressure of parental expectations. According to Ezekiel Emanuel,

> parents also cast a big shadow for most children. Whether estranged, disengaged, or deeply loving, they set expectations, render judgments, impose their opinions, interfere, and are generally a looming presence for even adult children. This . . . is inescapable as long as the parent is alive. . . . And while children can never fully escape this weight even after a parent dies, there is much less pressure to conform to parental expectations and demands after they are dead.[34]

But, although feelings may be mixed, an adult either would on balance welcome her parents' deaths or she would not. If she would not, transhumanist life extension would accord with her preferences for her parents (and, of course, quite likely eventually for herself). If she would, why should such a selfish preference be honored?[35]

Another potential harm to society involves the possibility that transhumanism would increase social inequality because only the rich would be able to afford it. But the remedy is to make transhumanism available to all rather than to none. This may well happen in the long run. Medical technology is an area where the "trickle down" effect actually occurs—nowhere near enough, in my view, but somewhat.

Heart transplants, for example, although initially available in America only to the wealthy, are now covered by Medicare. Old Americans who need new hearts are much better off now than they would have been had egalitarian concerns prevented the development of heart-transplant technology. And if transhumanism doesn't trickle down fast enough, we can subsidize it by increasing taxes on the rich, avoiding war unless America is invaded or at least endangered, and giving people higher priority than piping plovers and their ilk.[36]

Two further points are worth noting here. First, many technologies that are now widely available were initially available only to the rich, and rejecting technology for reason of temporary inequities would stymie progress. Second, preindustrial societies were hardly models of egalitarianism.

An additional possible harm to society is that transhumanism could increase the life and power of some pernicious people. Concerned about the "chilling . . . prospect of power concentrated relentlessly into the hands of a few undying individuals—and particularly into the hands of tyrants,"[37] Gems argues that a greatly extended lifespan represents "a very serious threat to humanity in the long term."[38] A parallel objection, however, could have been made to any life-extending medical advance, such as chemotherapy and antibiotics. A tyrant who dies of an infection at thirty will do less harm than one who lives vigorously into his seventies. But it is cruel to object to medical advances for fear that such advances might prolong the active lives of some dreadful people.

Moreover, a short lifespan is hardly an effective deterrent against tyranny, for one tyrant can replace another, as often already happens. Particularly inappropriate for his argument is Gems's admonition, "Remember the words of O'Brien to Winston Smith in Orwell's *1984:* 'If you want a picture of the future, imagine a boot stamping on a human face—forever.'"[39] No increased longevity was envisioned in *1984. Tyranny arose from a totalitarian system*—and is best prevented by a democratic one.[40]

How else might transhumanism damage society? According to Charles C. Mann, it is "fundamental to human existence" that "every quarter century or so children take over from their parents."[41] But this claim should be seen in light of other things that have been deemed fundamental to human existence, such as slavery and the subjugation of women.[42] A conservative worldview rejects change because of the possibility of unspecified, unanticipated harm. Social conservatives offered similar objections against the emancipation of women and against same-sex marriage.

# Conclusion

Consider again Mill's maxim that what is usual appears natural. People found the possible damages resulting from the emancipation of women, gays, and lesbians so distressing because they did not find the longstanding injustices visited against these groups distressing enough. The same may be true of transhumanism. Do we find the possibility of harm resulting from transhumanism so upsetting because we do not find illness, pain, suffering, and avoidable early death distressing enough? The theory of adaptive preferences holds that we adapt our preferences in response to available options.[43] Transhumanism offers the hope of new and better options. Imagine the following message from our transhuman future.

"Children of the present age,
Reading this indignant page,
Know that in a former time,
Longer life was thought a crime.

"Elders needing doctors' care
Cost us more than we can spare.
Elders who retain their health
Rob the young of jobs and wealth.
Fourscore years are all you need.
Seeking more reveals your greed.
Live your numbered years with zest.
Then go sweetly to your rest.

So the pundits used to say
Till we reached a better day.
Children, how our lifespans grew:
I'm 300—you'll be too."[44]

# Bibliography

"180 Years Old? Experts Debate Limit of Aging." *CNN*. July 19, 2003. http://www.cnn.com/2003/HEALTH/07/19/aging/index.html.

Ackerman, Felicia Nimue. "Assisted Suicide, Terminal Illness, Severe Disability, and the Double Standard." In *Physician-Assisted Suicide: Expanding the Debate*, edited by Margaret P. Battin, Rosamond Rhodes, and Anita Silvers, 149–61. New York: Routledge, 1998. Reprinted in Jennifer A. Parks and Victoria S. Wike. *Bioethics in a Changing World*. Upper Saddle River, NJ: Prentice Hall, 2009.

Ackerman, Felicia Nimue. "Death Is a Punch in the Jaw: Life-Extension and Its Discontents." In *The Oxford Handbook of Bioethics*, edited by Bonnie Steinbock, 324–48. Oxford: Oxford University Press, 2009.

Ackerman, Felicia Nimue. Letter to the Editor. *The Atlantic*. October 2005.

Ackerman, Felicia Nimue. "More about More Life." *The Hastings Center Report* 33, no. 6 (November–December 2003): 5.

Ackerman, Felicia Nimue. "Song of a Better Day." *Providence Journal*. January 31, 2014. https://www.providencejournal.com/article/20140131/OPINION/301319880?temp late=ampart.

Boeree, C. George. "Erik Erikson." General Psychology. Shippensburg University. Accessed August 17, 2021. http://webspace.ship.edu/cgboer/genpsyerikson.html.

Callahan, David. "On Dying after Your Time." *New York Times*. November 30, 2013. https://www.nytimes.com/2013/12/01/opinion/sunday/on-dying-after-your-time .html.

Chesterton, Gilbert K. "Orthodoxy: The Suicide of Thought." Page by Page Books. Accessed August 17, 2021. https://www.pagebypagebooks.com/Gilbert_K_Chesterton/ Orthodoxy/The_Suicide_of_Thought_p1.html.

Colburn, Ben. "Autonomy and Adaptive Preferences." *Utilitas* 23, no. 1 (March 2011): 52–71. https://doi.org/10.1017/S0953820810000440.

Emanuel, Ezekiel J. "Why I Hope to Die at 75." *The Atlantic*. October 2014. https:// www.theatlantic.com/magazine/archive/2014/10/why-i-hope-to-die-at-75/379329/.

Gems, David. "Is More Life Always Better? The New Biology of Aging and the Meaning of Life." *Hastings Center Report* 33, no. 4 (August 2003): 31–39.

Hamilton, Craig. "Chasing Immortality: The Technology of Eternal Life; An Interview with Ray Kurzweil." *What Is Enlightenment?* (September–November 2005).

Harris, John. "Intimations of Immortality." *Science* 288, no. 5463 (April 7, 2000): 59. https://doi.org/10.1126/science.288.5463.59.

Huston, Tom. "We Will Be the Lords of Creation: Envisioning Our Immortal Future with Science Fiction Writer Robert J. Sawyer." *What Is Enlightenment?* (September–November 2005).

Lynch, Thomas. "Why Buy More Time?" *New York Times*. March 14, 1999. https:// www.nytimes.com/1999/03/14/opinion/why-buy-more-time.html.

Mann, Charles C. "The Coming Death Shortage." *The Atlantic*. May 2005. https://www .theatlantic.com/magazine/archive/2005/05/the-coming-death-shortage/304105/.

Mill, John Stuart. "John Stuart Mill on the 'Subjection of Women.'" *Making of America*. University of Michigan. Accessed August 17, 2021. https://quod.lib.umich.edu/m/ moajrnl/acw8433.1-01.012/381:9?page=root;size=100;view=text.

Mill, John Stuart. "Nature." In *Three Essays on Religion: Nature, the Utility of Religion, and Theism*, 3–65. London: Longmans, Green, Reader, and Dyer, 1874.

Momeyer, Richard W. *Confronting Death*. Bloomington: Indiana University Press, 1988.

Naam, Ramez. *More Than Human: Embracing the Promise of Biological Enhancement*. New York: Broadway, 2005.

Nagel, Thomas. "Death." University of Colorado Boulder. Accessed August 17, 2021. https://rintintin.colorado.edu/~vancecd/phil150/Nagel.pdf.

Nuland, Sherwin B. *How We Die: Reflections of Life's Final Chapter*. New York: Vintage, 1995.

Olshansky, S. Jay. Letter to the Editor. *New York Times*. December 1, 2013. https://www .nytimes.com/2013/12/05/opinion/when-life-goes-on-and-on.html.

Orwell, George. *1984*. Project Gutenberg Australia. 2008. http://gutenberg.net.au/ ebooks01/0100021.txt.

Overall, Christine. *Aging, Death, and Human Longevity: A Philosophical Inquiry.* Berkeley: University of California Press, 2003.

The President's Council on Bioethics. *Beyond Therapy: Biotechnology and the Pursuit of Happiness.* New York: ReganBooks, 2003.

Stark, Andrew. *The Limits of Medicine.* Cambridge: Cambridge University Press, 2006.

# CHAPTER 5

# AI and Human Rights

## PRESENT AND FUTURE MORAL CHALLENGES

*Mark Vopat*

## Abstract

It is often the case with many technologies that once we recognize that we can do something, we rarely ask whether we ought to do it. Historically, technological innovation has in many cases leapt before it looked. Our current development and implementation of artificial intelligence (AI) has outpaced our consideration of the implications that technology has on human well-being and human rights. In this chapter I examine the moral challenges AI poses to human rights, both from the perspective of currents rights holders, as well as from the perspective of potential rights holders.

**KEYWORDS**

artificial intelligence, moral community personhood, rights, well-being

## 1. Introduction

A few years ago I was invited to sit on a panel discussion on the topic of artificial intelligence. The other panelists included a logistics specialist at a trucking company, the director of technology for a "smart city," a professor of robotics engineering, and a computer scientist. At one point the panel discussion turned to a new machine named Flippy that was being tested by the fast food restaurant chain Caliburgers. Flippy is a robot that can cook burgers and clean the grill with little human assistance. When it was noted that such a machine, if widely used, would displace a large number of fast-food workers, one panelist responded: "Well, who really wants to work at a fast-food restaurant anyway?" Another panelist noted that these were jobs normally held by high school kids, so we shouldn't be concerned with their part-time employment options.[1]

The panelists were nearly unanimous in their admiration of the progress made by artificial intelligence. One was enthralled by the increased efficiency and savings logistical artificial intelligence had garnered with their company. Another was excited about the prospect of fully automated public transportation that would more efficiently transport people around the city. And what about the bus and truck drivers who would be replaced because of this technology? The general consensus was that they would retrain, or that their displacement would open up new opportunities in other areas of the economy. What wasn't considered was the possibility that those other areas would also one day no longer need living, breathing, human beings.

It is often the case with many technologies that once we recognize that we can do something, we rarely ask whether we ought to do it. Historically, technological innovation has in many cases leapt before it looked. Our current development and implementation of artificial intelligence has outpaced our consideration of the implications that technology has on human well-being and human rights. In this chapter I examine the moral challenges AI poses to human rights, both from the perspective of currents rights holders, as well as from the perspective of potential rights holders.

# 2. Laying the Groundwork

## 2.1 ARTIFICIAL INTELLIGENCE

One of the difficulties in talking about AI is that there is not a single definition, but a number of proposed definitions of what it is. These definitions are often couched in the desired goal of an AI system. In general we can define AI systems as those that are *behavior based* or those that are *reasoning based*.[2]

Behavior-based AIs are those that are designed to act like humans, or ideally to act rationally. Systems that act human might, for example, be able to pass a Turing test.[3] Although the machine may be able to fool the human participant into believing that they are dealing with another human being, the machine itself need not be conscious. Behavior-based AI is focused on the outcomes of the system.[4] This type of AI does not think the way human beings think, but it is able to process large amounts of information and act upon that information. This type of AI is often referred to as artificial narrow intelligence (ANI). One example of ANI is the AI that tracks your credit card use and sends you a text message when it detects suspicious or unexpected activity on your account. The system is able to use your home address and pair that information with where you may have just purchased breakfast, and then filled up the tank in your car. It then compares that information with the fact that you just bought lunch 1,000 miles away from those other locations.

What the AI can't understand is that you did all those things on the way to the airport with a ticket purchased on another credit card that offers better air miles rewards. The system in this case is drawing a rational or logical conclusion based on a series of algorithms and then acting accordingly. As this example demonstrates, ANI's impact can be measured by the way this technology affects the rights of human beings.

On the other hand, reasoning-based AI are those artificial intelligences that are designed to think like human beings or ideally to think rationally. This is the AI that we see in works of science fiction: Commander Data of *Star Trek: The Next Generation*, HAL of *2001: A Space Odyssey*, and WOPPR (Joshua) of *War Games*. This type of AI does not simply *behave* as if it were human, it is actually engaging in human-like thought processes. This type of AI is often referred to as artificial general intelligence (AGI).[5]

Both ANI and AGI pose moral challenges for human rights, but they do so in different ways. In the case of the former, the challenges are primarily those of how human moral agents construct and use ANI, and how it affects the rights of living, breathing human beings. In the case of AGI, while there are issues regarding how it may affect the rights of human beings, the effect is on our conceptions of personhood and who is a rights bearer.

## 2.2 HUMAN RIGHTS

Any discussion of the impact artificial intelligence has on human rights should begin with at least a general idea of what is meant by "human rights." Although there are several traditions in the philosophic literature, human rights are generally defined as those owed to individuals independently of any state recognition. The individuals who are owed rights are those who are part of the *moral community*. Once a person is determined to have moral standing within the moral community, they are by that membership entitled to certain rights. Although the specifics of any particular theory of rights may differ, I will assume for our purposes here a standard liberal conception of rights.

There are a number of different liberal theories, and they all share certain general features. In "The Common Faith of Liberalism,"[6] Jean Hampton argues that there are five major commitments common to all liberal traditions:

1. A commitment to the idea that people in political society must be free.
2. A commitment to equality of the people in political society.
3. A commitment to the idea that the state's role must be defined such that it enhances the freedom and equality of the people.
3a. The state has the best chance of securing the freedom and equality of its citizens when it is organized as a democracy.
3b. The state can only ensure freedom by pursuing policies that implement toleration and freedom of conscience for all citizens.
3c. The state must stay out of the individual's construction of his own life plans—his own "conception of the good."[7]

The first three of Hampton's commitments provide an umbrella for all the different types of rights people often cite. If people are to realize their own individual conception of the good life, they will need a robust set of rights. These rights include the right of conscience to explore different worldviews free from the scrutiny of others, and the freedom to associate with others who share similar views. People need to be free from oppression so that they may worship, work, and live in a manner compatible with the good life they have chosen. And this freedom from oppression may also entail that as moral agents they require certain goods necessary for their survival. It also seems necessary that they have a say in the way their society is structured and that they should be free to express those views. As we will see in the next section, many of these rights and freedoms are threatened by our use of various forms of ANI.

# 3. Moral Challenges of ANI

Artificial narrow intelligence permeates nearly every aspect of our digital life. It tracks our credit card usage, remembers our route to work, offers to pull up the map on our phone, offers movie recommendations based on what we have previously viewed, and it may even inform us of discounts on products that we were previously viewing on Amazon. While many may find this type of ANI helpful, there is also a more troubling side.

Take, for example, the AI used in facial recognition software. In January of 2020, Robert Julian-Borchak Williams was arrested by Detroit police for allegedly shoplifting $3,800 worth of jewelry. The arrest was based primarily on the identification of Mr. Williams by facial recognition software. The software matched Mr. Williams's driver's license photo to a grainy still photo capture from surveillance footage from the scene of the crime. He was arrested and held for thirty hours before being released on bail. Two weeks later—after contacting a lawyer who quoted him a price of $7,000—Mr. Williams appeared in court, only to have the prosecution ask to have the case dismissed with prejudice.[8]

A number of factors went into Mr. Williams's wrongful arrest, but the most central element was the AI that misidentified Mr. Williams as the perpetrator. It has been known for some time that facial recognition software is both inaccurate and biased. In a 2019 study completed by the US Department of Commerce's National Institute of Standards and Technology, researchers found that facial recognition software tended to be racially biased depending on where the software was developed. As the report noted,

> false positive rates are highest in West and East African and East Asian people, and lowest in Eastern European individuals. This effect is generally large, with a factor of 100 more false positives between countries. However, with a number of algorithms developed in China this effect is reversed, with low false positive rates on East Asian faces. With domestic law enforcement images, the highest false positives are in American Indians, with elevated rates in African American and Asian populations; the relative ordering depends on sex and varies with algorithm.[9]

For many, facial recognition AI promises to help protect citizens against potential terrorist attacks or aid in the apprehension of criminals. In practice, AI software—developed by private companies—is often inherently biased. Depending on which datasets are used, who is doing the programming, and who is training the software, this type of AI can pose a direct threat to individual liberty and due process.

## ATLAS OF AI

In her book *Atlas of AI: Power, Politics, and the Planetary Costs of Artificial Intelligence+*,[10] Kate Crawford documents the myriad ways that ANI threatens the well-being and rights of human beings. These threats come in the form of questionably collected personal data, racially biased data, and the abrogation of human decision-making in favor of machines. Crawford's examination of AI is unique in that it looks at both the resources necessary for the construction of this technology and the impact this technology has once deployed.

One way this technology impacts human beings is illustrated by the energy needed to perform natural language processing (NLP). For example, many of us are unaware of what is involved behind the scenes when we ask our Echo Dot to turn on a light. We don't consider the energy, raw materials, and human labor necessary to construct the large server farms that store and process this information. ANI systems that run the NLP models used by companies such as Apple, Amazon, Google, and Microsoft use massive amounts of energy to perform this relatively simple task. As Crawford notes, a study completed by researchers at the University of Massachusetts Amherst in 2019 stated that the carbon footprint of just one of the various NLP systems consumed an enormous amount of energy. As Crawford writes,

> The initial numbers were striking. Strubell's team found that running only a single NLP model produced more than 660,000 pounds of carbon dioxide emissions, the equivalent of five gas-powered cars over their total lifetime (including their manufacturing) or 125 round-trip flights from New York to Beijing.[11]

Of course, this is just an example of one NLP model being used by one company. There are multiple companies using multiple models, all consuming massive amounts of energy and pushing that environmental cost onto society.

A similar issue arises when we examine the raw materials necessary for the manufacturing of the components necessary to create the machines running the AI. Many of these nonrenewable precious metals are found in places that are not politically stable. As Crawford writes,

> There are seventeen rare earth elements: lanthanum, cerium, praseodymium, neodymium, promethium, samarium, europium, gadolinium, terbium, dysprosium, holmium, erbium, thulium, ytterbium, lutetium, scandium, and yttrium. They are processed and embedded in laptops and smartphones, making those devices smaller and lighter. . . . But extracting these minerals from the ground often comes with local and geopolitical violence.[12]

Even if these elements could be extracted without geopolitical violence, there still remains the environmental cost of mining operations in these countries. So aside from the problem of rights violations due to worker exploitation, there is the added violation of the fundamental human right to access clean air and water.

Finally, another example of how ANI directly impacts human rights is its use in data mining. Data mining is the process of finding patterns or useful information through the analysis of large amounts of information known as datasets.[13] While the acquisition of the datasets themselves raises moral questions, it is the application of ANI to these sets that is concerning.[14] For example, Crawford notes how even anonymized data, once mined, can reveal very personal information:

Even when datasets are scrubbed of personal information and released with great caution, people have been reidentified or highly sensitive details about them have been revealed. In 2013, for example, the New York City Taxi and Limousine Commission released a dataset of 173 million individual cab rides, and it included pickup and drop-off times, locations, fares, and tip amounts. The taxi drivers' medallion numbers were anonymized, but this was quickly undone, enabling researchers to infer sensitive information like annual incomes and home addresses. . . . But beyond individual harms, such datasets also generate "predictive privacy harms" for whole groups or communities. For instance, the same New York City taxi dataset was used to suggest which taxi drivers were devout Muslims by observing when they stopped at prayer times.[15]

Access to large datasets that can be analyzed by highly complex machine algorithms poses a substantial threat to a person's right to privacy.

The focus here has been on how artificial narrow intelligence continues to pose a threat to individual rights.[16] The examples given have noted that the improper application of ANI can have an impact on justice by threatening one's due process rights, one's right to not be harmed by AI's negative environmental impacts, and one's right to privacy.

# 4. Moral Challenges of AGI

Unlike artificial narrow intelligence, artificial general intelligence presents a different set of challenges for human rights. There are two fundamental moral challenges raised by AGI. First there is the issue of whether a machine that has attained AGI has rights. The second issue is whether or not we should bring such beings into existence.

Before delving into this issue a few preliminary remarks are in order. It is important to note that there are no known instances of AGI. We may examine the potential impact of AGI in an exercise in anticipatory ethics—ethics that attempts to anticipate the problems that may be caused by emerging technologies.[17] I will proceed under the hypothetical assumption that we have overcome the technological hurdles and have achieved reason-based AI.[18] Let us assume that AI now has all the abilities of flesh-and-blood human beings. It is sentient, conscious, can have desires, can have desires about its desires, and can communicate with others. It is—aside from its physical constitution—a thinking, feeling being.[19]

## 4.1 AGIS, RIGHTS, AND PERSONHOOD

One standard answer to the question of who is a rights bearer is that a rights bearer is one who is a member of the moral community. But this then raises the question of how one becomes a member of the moral community. One common answer to this question is that one is a member of the moral community if one meets certain criteria of personhood. In this section I argue that AGI (should they come into existence) ought to be treated as members of the moral community and thus rights bearers.

### *Personhood*

The nature of personhood is not without controversy, and thus the question of AI having personhood raises many of the same philosophical problems with defining persons in general. To begin, I shall assume the fairly widespread acceptance of the distinction between human beings and persons. *Human being* is a biological classification. Beings that have certain physical and genetic characteristics are biologically human. On the other hand, *person* is a moral category, in which being biologically human is not a necessary condition. Assuming it is true that being biologically human is not a necessary or sufficient condition for personhood, then it follows that some biological humans are not persons, and some persons are not biologically human beings.

### *Mary Anne Warren*

There are several different views on what constitutes a person. Not surprisingly, the issue of whether AGIs ought to be considered persons overlaps significantly with the personhood issues in the debate on the morality of abortion. In "On the Moral and Legal Status of Abortion,"[20] Mary Anne Warren argues that rights require membership in the moral community. But to be considered part of the moral community requires one to be a person.

According to Warren, there are a number of criteria we appeal to when determining whether something is a person. These criteria include the following:

1. consciousness (of objects and events external and/or internal to the being), and in particular the capacity to feel pain;
2. reasoning (the developed capacity to solve new and relatively complex problems);
3. self-motivated activity (the activity which is relatively independent of either genetic or direct external control);
4. capacity to communicate—by whatever means, messages of an indefinite variety of types, that is, not just with an

indefinite number of possible contents, but on indefinitely
many possible topics;

5. presence of self-concepts and self-awareness either individual
or racial, or both.[21]

Although Warren readily admits that there may be problems creating precise definitions of the criteria, they do capture the features we generally look for
when determining personhood. Furthermore, it seems clear that if something
were to meet *all* of the criteria, we would be hard pressed morally to deny that it
was a person. Similarly, if something met *none* of these criteria, we could be reasonably certain that something was not a person. By noting that at the extremes
the determination of personhood is relatively straightforward, Warren is able to
avoid any debate over necessary and sufficient conditions.[22]

Given that the description of AGI as a sentient, conscious being that can
communicate with others, have desires, etc., meets all five of Warren's criteria,
there is little rationale for claiming that it is not a person.[23] As such, we would
be morally obligated to admit that artificial being into the moral community.

In fact, Warren holds that such beings should be considered persons and
thus members of the moral community. As she writes,

> Citizens of the next century should be prepared to recognize highly
> advanced, self-aware robots or computers, should such be developed,
> and intelligent inhabitants of other worlds, should such be found, as
> people in the fullest sense, and to respect their moral rights.[24]

### Shelly Kagan

Warren's view of personhood is not the only one that supports the idea that
AGI are persons in all the important senses. Shelly Kagan also has a theory of
personhood that supports the notion of rights-bearing AI. In his article "What's
Wrong with Speciesism?"[25] he argues that there are good intuitive grounds for
accepting the view that "other things being equal, human interests count *more*
than corresponding animal interests."[26] That being said, Kagan goes on to say
that while we normally assign greater weight to the interests of human beings,
it is not really the fact that they are human that justifies this greater emphasis.
According to Kagan, it is really the case that most of us endorse *personism*, being
part of what he terms a *person species*.

According to Kagan, to be a personist is just to hold that if a being is rational, self-conscious, aware of itself as one among others, and these factors are
extended over time, the being qualifies for personhood and thus membership in
the person species.[27] By adopting these ideas, Kagan believes he can account for
our intuitions about the moral status of other types of beings.[28] Imagine we were

asked the moral status of an alien like E.T. Most of us would not say that E.T. (if he existed) was not entitled to "human" rights. Beings like E.T.—though not biologically human—would in Kagan's view be part of the person species. This inclusion is justified on the grounds that E.T.'s interests are similar enough to our own in all the morally relevant ways.

Kagan's person species view, applied to AGI, would also entitle it to human rights. Failure to recognize this would be to engage in a form of prejudice, which he defines as holding "a view on the basis of evidence that you wouldn't otherwise consider adequate."[29] If one accepts that beings that meet criteria such as those spelled out by Warren and Kagan are persons, and if AGI by definition has all of those characteristics, then the reason for denying it personhood is mere prejudice.

### Objections to AGI as Persons

Although there are compelling arguments for ascribing personhood to AGIs based on their similarities to human rights bearers, not all philosophers agree that meeting certain criteria is what grounds rights. In "Granting Automata Human Rights: Challenge to a Basis of Full-Rights Privilege,"[30] Lantz Miller argues that even if AGI were achieved, such beings would still not be entitled to human rights. Miller's argument is powerful in the sense that he does not attempt to deny the characteristics of AGI that were assumed above. Rather, he argues that it is the ontological status of machines that counts against granting them rights.

There is for Miller a fundamental ontological difference between human beings and machines. This difference lies in the way in which each comes into existence. Human beings are purposeless beings—they are not the product of some normative choice and are thus outside the scope of morality. On the other hand, automata come into existence through an act of human choice, and thus fall within the scope of morality.[31] It is the "existential normative neutrality" of human beings that distinguishes them from sentient machines.

According to Miller, natural rights theory does not make any assumptions about how human beings came into existence, or what their purpose is, or what individuals must do. Rights exist because we have no comprehensive doctrine that provides human beings with a purpose. Absent a known purpose, we should publicly recognize every person's right to realize their own conception of the good. Since automatons have a known or knowable purpose, we need not grant them rights. As Miller writes,

> Those X's need not come into existence because their constructors
> need not build them. Humans, by contrast, may well have simply

come into existence without having to have had any constructors build them or without any given purpose. Their rights rest upon their given existence and their freedom from anyone's purpose. An automaton must have a purpose—its constructor's purpose in constructing it, even if that purpose be merely to construct such an entity.[32]

Although Miller's focus on the ontological status of AI is unique, Gorden and Pasvenskiene have rightly pointed out that it appears fundamentally flawed. This flaw lies primarily in Miller's reliance on the fact–value distinction. The fact that AIs come into existence with a purpose, whereas human beings apparently do not, says nothing about the moral status of either being. As they write,

> The bare fact that human beings do not have a particular *existential purpose* does not convey anything by itself. This fact is relevant only if one adds the premise that human beings who have been born without a purpose are morally superior to other entities, have a full moral status, and therefore should enjoy human rights. Miller does not provide a justification for this additional premise.[33]

Unless one accepts the intuition that human beings are morally special, Miller's argument fails. Moreover, it seems that Miller is engaging in a kind of prejudice that Kagan would also find objectionable. An AGI that could go beyond its initial purpose or redefine that purpose on its own would surely no longer be subject to another being. Similarly, if we encountered an AGI from another world, would our inability to determine its purpose entail that those nonbiological entities are somehow now ontologically persons, while those on earth are not? It seems far more reasonable to simply ask whether some AGI exhibits certain characteristics that we recognize as constituting moral persons.

## 4.2 AGI AND ITS IMPACT ON HUMAN RIGHTS

If AGIs are moral persons, then the issues we have with them are similar to those we have with genetically human persons. Questions about justice, fairness, welfare, and rights that we have regarding biological persons would need to be extended to include artificial persons. While the specific needs of such beings would be different than biological beings, the conceptual issues would be the same.

On the other hand, since we are engaging in a form of anticipatory ethics it is appropriate to ask whether we should create or bring into existence such beings. It is clear that creating AGIs would impact the well-being of current rights holders. For example, AGIs would not suffer the same limitations as biological beings. They would not require sleep, or become sick or fatigued. Such beings would likely be better at doing many of the jobs that human agents rely upon. The potential physical and mental superiority of such beings would ultimately threaten the well-being of others. In this sense, AGIs pose similar concerns and challenges to those that were discussed with ANIs. The difference lies in our ability to question whether, morally speaking, we ought to bring such beings into existence *before* such beings have been admitted into the moral community.

# 5. Conclusion

The reality of ANI and the possible realization of AGI offers fertile ground for future moral inquiry. Both bring with them challenges and indeed threats to human well-being and human rights. The threat to human rights is currently seen in the various ways ANI has become part of our everyday lives.

Although ANI has been shown to have a negative impact on human rights, there is nothing inherently bad about this technology. The technology itself is morally neutral; it is the implementation of the technology that is at times morally questionable. As such, a moral evaluation of AI is really an evaluation of the way in which *human* moral agents use the technology. If ANI poses a threat to the environment, it is only because we have chosen to use nonrenewable forms of energy to power it.

If certain minerals are acquired by exploiting people and countries, it is only because we have chosen to ignore these injustices. If data has been gathered and used indiscriminately, it is because we have failed to respect the right of people to determine who has access to their information. These issues are ultimately social, political, moral, and economic issues that deserve greater examination in the philosophic literature. In many instances the question that needs to be asked is not can we use AI in a particular way, but whether we ought to do so.

These questions only become more pressing as AI develops. The presentation here has assumed one of two options: AI as a non-sentient tool, or AI as a self-aware being. It is likely that as the technology evolves, there will be machines that fall somewhere in the middle. These machines may have some rudimentary awareness, without that awareness constituting personhood. It is here that a whole new area of moral inquiry will be necessary. In many ways these middle-ground forms of AI raise issues that are not dissimilar to those raised with regard to the ethical treatment of animals.

The creation of semiautonomous or semiconscious beings would create questions not only about rights, but also about how such beings should be integrated into our current socioeconomic systems. If tedious and dangerous physical labor could be replaced by complex, semiconscious machines, a radical reorganization of economic systems might be required. If machines are doing the work, how are human beings going to sustain themselves? For example, Elon Musk of Tesla recently announced his company's plan to create a humanoid robot that would perform many of the mundane, physically demanding tasks currently done by humans. When asked about the economic impact of such machines, he stated:

> "Essentially, in the future, physical work will be a choice," Musk said during the presentation. "This is why I think long term there will need to be a universal basic income," he added.[34]

Whether or not one agrees with the idea of a universal basic income, there is no doubt that AI poses questions that will require a radical rethinking of this technology's relationship to human rights, human well-being, and human institutions.

PART TWO

# APPLICATIONS

Section 1

# The Practical Scope of Technology Ethics

CHAPTER 6

# Is There a Need for a New, a Technology, Ethic?

*David E. McClean*

## Abstract

A technology should continually acquit itself, as it is applied to its primary purposes. That is, it should serve to help improve or at least to not negatively disrupt the integrity of natural systems and human culture, or lead to psychological maladies in the form of substantive levels of mental illness and spiritual malaise when its primary function is carried out as intended. It must be a continual acquittal because its impacts may not be known for years, perhaps even decades.

KEYWORDS

technology ethics, technoethics, AI, environmental ethics

## Introduction

To say that we human beings are living in "the age of technology" seems correct. On the other hand, it is also incorrect. For human beings have made use of technology for millennia (as have quite a few other species). To clear up that point, I will define (somewhat unoriginally) what I mean by "technology." By "technology" I mean the process and end result of forging (construed broadly) tools (including devices, methods, and plans), the purpose of which is to help achieve some goal. It is correct to say that we are living in "the age of technology" if what is meant is that we have become preoccupied with it (i.e., with the process and end result of forging tools to achieve goals), and most of our goals

79

have to do with solving mundane problems, some serious (e.g., fighting patho-
gens and removing microplastics from the oceans) and some not so serious (e.g.,
improving the realism of computer games and extending the useful life of tennis
balls; the not-so-serious varieties I will refer to hereafter as "problems").

It may be fair to say, and I would argue, that we have become so enthralled
with the application of technology to our problems and "problems" that the
tail of technology is now wagging the dog of human agency. The energies and
time invested in toolmaking and mundane problem-/"problem"-solving have
become manic. Indeed, the age of technology may be construed, as well, as the
age of *technomania*, and technologists—those who spend most of their time on
toolmaking (and this includes, fitting with my definition, coders and software
developers)—may be thought of as *technomaniacal*.

But it is not just the technologists who are technomaniacal; it is also the case
that we users of technology are as well, at least in the sense that many of us are
no longer even capable of leaping out of the technology ruts in our minds and
back onto a plane of thought on which *ars gratia artis* and the liberal arts abide.
Not only has our technomania given us a means-ends (that is, instrumental and
transactional) approach to living that consumes much if not most of our time
but also our enthrallment has blinded us to the conundrums and dilemmas
that so much of it has presented—from problems associated with the disposal
of nuclear waste to those associated with habitat loss for many species. Beyond
these conundrums and dilemmas, the creation of the Internet—which may soon
approximate what Teilhard de Chardin (as well as Vladimir Vernadsky) called
the "noosphere"—has enabled all sorts of communication, much of it instant,
unheard of, and even unimagined by many who comprised the generations just
preceding our own.[1] The speed and volume of this communication has created
rafts of legal and ethical questions, many of which still have no satisfactory
answers. For example, when so many can publish their ideas with no editorial
review, who really is a *journalist*? How do you police social media and when do
you censor content? Who decides? Etc.

So pervasive a phenomenon screams for a robust and evolving *ethic* of
technology, just as was needed for environmental ethics, as captured in philosopher Richard Routley's landmark essay, "Is There a Need for a New, an
Environmental, Ethic?"[2] But in a time of technomania, in which few stop to ask
fundamental questions concerning the development and deployment of technology, we have also lost a good deal of our agency, a sense that we can ablate or
mitigate the conundrums and dilemmas by deciding to do less problem-solving
and "problem"-solving. This loss of agency is profound, for our humanity cannot be construed without reference to it. Beyond this, many new technological
innovations, such as cryptocurrencies and high frequency trading, come with
their own hazards.

Beyond these examples, we can consider what we are doing with genes. For example, genetic manipulation and the pursuit of human enhancements carry with them possibilities that worry many ethicists and other informed observers. It is one thing to treat diseases or to correct a body that has been badly damaged in an accident (i.e., problem-solving), and quite another to use the technologies that empower human beings to do these things to be pressed into service for the purpose of forging cosmetic changes (such as making one's body more muscular or changing the color of one's eyes) or to enhance one's social standing by, for example, making one a better conversationalist or more empathetic (i.e., "problem"-solving), as explored in some depth by philosopher Michael J. Sandel in his book, *The Case Against Perfection* (2007).

It is even questionable whether all "diseases" should be treated or eradicated, since enduring certain negative somatic challenges (say, the common cold or headaches) or mental challenges (say, mild depression or anxiety) would not seem to warrant the manipulation of our genes, especially since we cannot be sure that we have grasped all of the unintended consequences of such manipulation (mild depression and anxiety can spur creativity and increase our capacity to handle negative emotions, and learning to control them by learning to reroute bad thought patterns such as catastrophizing can be character-building).[3]

And who decides (always a question that sharpens attention)? We are the products of billions of years of evolution. It is true that evolution forged a biome in which we find many unpleasant biological challenges—one need only consider COVID-19. But there are hundreds of others challenges, from malaria to leprosy to schizophrenia. Yet, while some (depending on the species, of course) succumb to these challenges, most members of most species have flourished as the temporary end result of processes of natural selection (though all members of all species eventually die).

We have only known about DNA for a relative blink of an eye when compared to the eons of time that elapsed as our present biota evolved to take its current shape. Do we know enough about our genes (or, for that matter, the genes of other species) to alter them and with any certainty that we have not set into motion something that produces unpleasant or even horrific consequences? Should we be in pursuit of "perfect bodies" using genetic or cybernetic enhancements, and what would happen if everyone had one? To reiterate and expand upon some key questions, should parents be allowed to select the color of their children's eyes, and assure that they would be super-intelligent or super-compassionate, all via genetic manipulation? What would be lost were such "perfections" simply handed to us through a process of gene manipulation rather than through *striving*? What would happen to human *character*?

What would happen to human goals? Who would get to benefit from enhancement technologies? The very wealthy only? Could genetic and cybernetic manipulation lead to two or more classes of human beings—those who are enhanced and so "better" and those who are not? And what would be the latter's fate? And to reiterate and expand on another point, our literature is filled with struggles of people who worked to overcome, through *choice, diligence,* and *prolonged commitment,* bodily, mental, and emotional limitations, and those struggles shaped some of them into people we have come to admire. What happens when striving ends because outcomes can be almost guaranteed in a laboratory? What would happen, to paraphrase William James from his essay "What Makes a Life Significant?" were the "fruit" to merely be eaten, with no effort devoted to planting or harvesting?[4]

Beyond these questions looms a larger one, once relegated to science fiction: At what point do human beings cease being human beings and become, through "enhancements," *a new species*? Then come the questions that follow that one: Is such transhumanism akin to *genocide*? If not, why not? What kind of world would such a new species forge? At what point do "enhancements" cease, or do they go on indefinitely?

What about artificial intelligence (AI) and its potential to solve many human problems and "problems" and achieve many human goals? AI is already assisting in the diagnosis and treatment of diseases, creating efficiencies in transportation, assisting in the management of risks of all types, and helping organizations like FedEx and important and active maritime ports solve logistical and loading problems in a small fraction of the time it would take humans to do so. Indeed, AI is being deployed in *many* industries, from health care to gaming. But what is AI? AI refers to the capacity of a computer to autonomously engage with its environment to solve problems and "problems" relevant to that for which it was tasked, without additional human intervention (programming). But the incredible speed at which computers do these things has caused us to think about the potential dangers of computers that can, effectively, "think for themselves" (I use scare quotes here because whether or not what AI machines do is actual "thinking" is still a subject of debate; it depends on what one means by "thinking," and whether the capacity to do millions of calculations using massive datasets is nothing more than, well, just lots of and more intricate calculations).[5]

The ethical concerns and control worries associated with AI are wide-ranging. For example, there is the problem of what has been called "the singularity," that point at which computers will be able to perfect and change their own programming with *no* involvement of human beings, become self-aware, and do so at speeds far beyond the capacity of human beings to grasp or control (and supplant human beings as the dominant intelligence on Earth, assuming that is what we are presently).[6] At what point might a computer simply "decide" to launch a series of events in the real world in order to accomplish its own aims (this is the "Skynet" scenario, as played out in the movie *Terminator*)? Then there is the problem of *superintelligence*, which concerns a computer/machine far surpassing the intelligence of any single or even a thousand highly educated and highly intelligent human beings.[7]

Are we ready to live in a world of such super-intelligent and perhaps self-aware machines? Would human beings come to be the servants or slaves of such super-intelligent machines, rather than the other way around? Also, there are questions that concern *transhumanism*, the notion that human consciousness might one day be uploaded into a machine (or, in a less fantastic conjecture, humans and machines might otherwise "merge," creating millions or billions of beings that are *largely* part human and *largely* part machine [i.e., true *cyborgs*]), after which (and on the assumption that) the human body, as born via the natural biological process, is shed as superfluous and as a hindrance because "too primitive" and prone to injury and disease, or is otherwise too "limited" in its function. One may think of Agent Smith's tirade to Morpheus in the first *Matrix* movie (1999), referencing the real world of human beings, the world outside of the multisystem software realm that is Smith's realm, the world of blood and sweat, of sights and sounds and smells:

> I hate this place. This zoo. This prison. This reality, whatever you want to call it, I can't stand it any longer. It's the smell, if there is such a thing. I feel saturated by it. I can taste your stink and every time I do, I fear that I've somehow been infected by it.
>
> *He wipes sweat from Morpheus' forehead, coating the tips of his fingers, holding them to Morpheus' nose.*
>
> Repulsive, isn't it?
>
> *He lifts Morpheus' head, holding it tightly with both hands.*
>
> I *must* get out of here, I *must* get free. In this [Morpheus's] mind is [the] key.
>
> My key.
>
> *Morpheus sneers through his pain.* [Emphases added.][8]

There are questions, too, about how super-intelligent machines are to be treated by human beings. Would they have rights, and if so, how would those rights be determined and enforced? Such questions have been treated in science fiction, such as in the television series *Star Trek* (Lt. Commander Data's moral and political status was more than once the subject of an episode) and in the movies *Bicentennial Man* (1999) and *Blade Runner* (1982).

There are those who believe that AI poses serious threats to humanity as well as nonhuman forms of life—indeed, *existential* threats. These include technologists and scientists themselves—Bill Gates (of Microsoft), Elon Musk (of Tesla), and the late Stephen Hawking (a theoretical physicist at Cambridge University) are just a few of the informed technologists and scientists who have sounded the alarm about the potential for machines imbued with AI to do significant harm to humanity. Stephen Hawking has gone so far as to suggest that AI could lead to the end of the human species.[9] Philosopher Nick Bostrom has sounded similar alarms. But is the horse out of the barn, so to speak? Is it too late to reconsider the creation of super-intelligent machines, to ask some basic questions that perhaps were sidelined or simply not considered as computer science blossomed since the 1950s? Are the ends that AI is intended to serve worthy ends, or is AI merely a super-improved means to unimproved ends?

While AI is intended to solve problems (and "problems"), considering that many of these are of our own making (we only have thorny logistical challenges because we have decided that we needed to travel almost at will and to send goods all around the globe in response to market demands), what changes in human *culture and values* could obviate the need for the sorts of problem-/"problem"-solving that AI does and will do more efficiently than human beings using "ordinary" computing power? What about the new problems and "problems" that AI will *create* as it solves old ones, and won't those be far more complex and thornier than can even be imagined presently? What capabilities will AI give human beings that it might be best human beings *did not have* (e.g., to clone an army of soldiers from somatic cells, or to create super-viruses that can be weaponized by a military and used to kill millions in but a few days). Here, AI meets genetic engineering and such new techniques as derived from "CRISPR" (clustered regularly interspaced short palindromic repeats), whereby genes can be altered with precision to, at least so far, assist in providing therapies or cures for genetic diseases, such as sickle cell anemia, *but without any assurances that the technology will be limited to therapeutic uses.*[10]

What of an assumption that AI will be used only for salutary purposes? Is such an assumption wise or is it rather unwise in the extreme, given that so many technological advancements to date have been used for ignoble or destructive ends? Are we soon to enter a period in which, for example, super-intelligent machines learn to hack into government databases and "the internet of things" with blazing speeds and quickly erase their tracks, which will require that other super-intelligent machines be marshalled to check their malicious efforts, also with blazingly fast countermoves, in a frenzy of super-fast thrusts and parries that go on as part of endless cyber warfare—while all we humans will be able to do is stand back and watch in, perhaps, horror? This is not a future scenario, but rather one that is developing now, as documented in Nicole Perlroth's book *This Is How They Tell Me the World Ends: The Cyberweapons Arms Race* (2019).

# An Ethic for Technology

As our technological capacities were refined and made more complex (in many cases) over the centuries (especially the last two centuries), to reach a fever pitch in the last one hundred years or so, our capacity to *predict* their impacts has not kept up, although it has improved. That improvement has involved laws that require such undertakings such as environmental impact studies and product safety testing. Yet because of the complexities involved in the creation of each new tool (plastic buttons and other small plastic devices or parts thereof, for example, which were not *foreseen* to be a cause of death in sea birds, but are), it is not always possible to predict what those impacts will be.[11]

The Earth is tiny when compared to the size of its celestial home, but it is, nevertheless, an extremely complex and dynamic system (at least as humans perceive dynamism and complexity), and so it is very difficult to model the effects of our toolmaking either spatially (i.e., around the planet and across natural systems) or temporally (i.e., through time). Because of this, the philosopher Hans Jonas argued that a new approach to ethics is required. Jonas warned, in *The Imperative of Responsibility: In Search of an Ethics for the Technological Age*, that

> with certain developments of our powers the nature of human action has changed, and, since ethics is concerned with action, it should follow that the changed nature of human action calls for a change in ethics as well: this not merely in the sense that new objects of action have added to the case material on which received rules of conduct are to be applied, but in the more radical sense that the qualitatively novel nature of certain of our actions has opened up a whole new dimension of ethical relevance for which there is no precedent in the standards and canons of traditional ethics.[12]

Ethical questions about technology are not new. They have led to a whole field of study referred to as "technoethics." According to Rocci Luppicinni, a scholar of communication as well as a philosopher:

> Juxtaposed with the coming of powerful new scientific and technological advances, is a major push to rediscover the ethical dimension of technology across the [natural] sciences, social sciences, and humanities. Literature on ethics and technology are in abundance which focus on key areas of technology dedicated to the diverse areas of research and theory in use today.
>
> Surmounting debates and scholarly inquiry across multiple disciplines and applied fields of study connected to technology form the basis of an emerging field known as Technoethics (TE). Technoethics . . . is concerned with all social and ethical aspects of the design,

development, utilization, management, and evaluation of sciences and technology in society. As an interdisciplinary field, it utilizes theories and methods from multiple knowledge domains to provide insights on ethical dimensions of technological systems and practices for advancing a technological society. Technoethics provides a systems theory and methodology to guide a variety of separate areas of inquiry into technology and ethics.[13]

As one might glean from the above description of technoethics, it is an area of broad inquiry that runs the gamut of the sciences and technologies. While the work done in technoethics is very useful, there appears to be no metaethics that guides it. It draws from a range of "traditional" ethical theories, from deontology to virtue ethics. What might be useful as a metaethics is, perhaps, not an *ethics* at all, but rather an *ethic*. What work would such an ethic do? To answer that question, we might look to Aldo Leopold, who broke new ground in his areas of work and inquiry, conservation and environmental philosophy ("philosophy" in the broader rather than the truncated academic sense of the word). Leopold gave us not an ethics but an *ethic*, his famous "land ethic," which states:

> The "key-log" which must be moved to release the evolutionary process for an ethic is simply this: quit thinking about decent land-use as solely an economic problem. Examine each question in terms of what is ethically and esthetically right, as well as what is economically expedient. A thing is right when it tends to preserve the integrity, stability, and beauty of the biotic community. It is wrong when it tends otherwise.[14]

Given the blizzard of ethical considerations that emerge from disparate areas of technological research and production, what might serve as a technology ethic, an ethic that guides our thinking in the midst of this blizzard, as Leopold's has served to guide the thinking of designers, planners, agronomists, and conservationists as regards the uses of and incursions into the natural world? I would now like to suggest such an ethic, using the "land ethic" as a model. My technology ethics is as follows:

> *The "key-log" which must be moved to release the evolutionary process for a technology ethic is this: cease thinking about technology solely in terms of solving immediate human problems and the immediate commercial benefits of those solutions. Consider each proposed and extant technology in terms of its impacts across natural systems, human culture, and human psychology. A technology should continually acquit itself, as it is applied to its primary purposes. That is, it should serve to help improve or at least to not negatively disrupt the integrity of natural systems and human culture,*

*and it should not lead to psychological maladies in the form of substantive
levels of mental illness and spiritual malaise when that primary function
is carried out as intended. It must be a continual acquittal because its
impacts may not be known for years, perhaps even decades.*

There are some apparent and significant problems with this technology
ethic. But you will note that I adopted the language from Leopold's "land
ethic," which stipulates that an ethic such as the proposed will only release
an "evolutionary process." Thus, neither the "land ethic" nor my "technology
ethic" is the final word, but rather it is a place to commence serious deliberation and reflection. Both Leopold's land ethic and my technology ethic can be
criticized as being too vague, but an ethic *must* be somewhat vague. Indeed, a
common feature of an ethic is its vagueness. It is intended to begin the process
of focusing the mind at a higher level of abstraction, after which one can tackle
more granular matters. An ethic serves as a cognitive funnel to guide thinking
and affect in a certain direction, in this case away from the idea that one need
only be concerned with the successful direct application of a new technology in
a *narrow context*.

Another problem is that this ethic may seem to impose an impossible
requirement on technologists and other innovators—that of precision prognos-
tication concerning the disparate consequences across systems and over time.
But there are answers to these criticisms of vagueness and impossible prognosti-
cation, answers that derive, in part, from a now clear history that demonstrates
the dangers of truncated and monomaniacal thought as regards technological
innovations. We are now much more aware of at least the *kinds* of questions
that we should ask as new technologies are deployed and brought to market. We
are no longer naïve, no longer children playing in the dark. What John Dewey
called "the method of intelligence" has us asking questions concerning just about
all new technological innovations. If it's a device, how might it be used, and if
used in the ways that we *can* anticipate, what might be the harms? If it's a new
*service*, how will it be deployed and made available, and what will be the effects
on those who use it? If it's a chemical, how might it spread into habitats and
ecosystems, and with what results?

If it's a new innovation in the *mode* of doing some task, what might be the
impacts on tasks related to the pre-innovation mode, and who might be the winners
and losers be? The technology ethic I am proposing is, essentially, a requirement
to constrain the "release" of a new technology into the "environment" by engaging in serious systems-thinking before, during, and after deployment. In the
1980s, for example, as the personal computer became increasingly affordable and
popular, there were questions raised about the future of work, some of which
were quite prescient, and some not (for example, while calculations of various

kinds become easier because of spreadsheet software, the predictions about the end of paper usage lagged far behind what many thought would be the case).

We can now see more clearly, as well, that technological innovations can have significant social, emotional, and mental health costs. The Internet gave humanity the power to stay in constant communication with other people, some on the other side of the planet, almost instantly. The potential to forge new relationships, learn different cultures and languages, and expand one's knowledge became enormous. However, with this came the end of boundaries that separated work time from family and leisure time, the vectors for engaging in organized crime and moral depravity of various types, and a growing incapacity to engage in (or desire to engage in) direct face-to-face communication and socializing, as discussed in Robert D. Putnam's insightful though controversial book, *Bowling Alone: The Collapse and Revival of American Community* (2000). Social media, which is used daily for salutary undertakings, has also given us the phenomena of trolling, cyberbullying, cyberstalking, and deep fakery, and has been implicated, quite convincingly, in the mental health problems of tens of thousands, if not millions, of Americans, in some cases even in their suicides.[15]

The sort of stock-taking that my technology ethics proposes is not mere run-of-the-mill cost-benefit analysis, though clearly it does call for a form of such analysis. The stock-taking goes well beyond typical environmental impact studies and commercial cost-benefit calculations. It takes us, ultimately, into the complicated considerations that technoethics calls for, but it first provides a cognitive lens that reminds us why moving into those complicated considerations is critical.

CHAPTER 7

# The Social Worlds of Technology

*Marvin T. Brown*

## Abstract

How we see the role of technology in addressing our environmental crisis depends a lot on the story we tell. One story tells how changes in technology parallel changes in human communication and consciousness. It makes the mistake of taking social evolution for human evolution. Another story tells a social story (of American Prosperity) in which technology belongs to its trends, and is a current threat to our planet. To change the trends of American Prosperity that endanger our habitat, one must return to its origin in the Atlantic commerce of people and land, acknowledge its legacy, and correct the injustices it caused.

KEYWORDS

human evolution, empathy, social evolution, American prosperity, social justice, double consciousness

## Introduction

Although we see a growing consensus that we face an environmental crisis, and that technology will have an important role in addressing it, we remain cautious in our efforts to adequately change current social and economic trends. Our degree of hesitancy depends a lot on the social story or narrative in which we live. These stories create the context or what we can call a "social world" in which we interpret current possibilities. Of the multiple stories told in different circles, I want to tell and reflect on two: the story of how technological innovation has affected human consciousness and the story of the tragedy of American Prosperity.

We don't think a lot about social worlds. We usually take ours for granted and view them as natural, rather than composed of stories and patterns of behavior—as social. One of the best ways to learn about a social world is through comparison and contrast, which is the strategy employed here. I will compare a story of the coevolution of technology and empathy taken from Jeremy Rifkin's book, *The Empathic Civilization* (2012), and a story of American Prosperity taken from my book, *A Climate of Justice* (2021).[1] The task here is not only to tell the stories, but also to evaluate them. I just don't believe an evil empire, or even a simply bad one, will have the gumption or fortitude or whatever it takes to transform our current socioeconomic systems to be sustainable. So, we need to understand the social worlds in which we live, to evaluate them, and to find some source for turning their current trends toward a more sustainable direction.

In his book *Communication and the Human Condition*, W. Barnett Pearce sorts out four different forms of communication or social worlds: monocultural, ethnocentric, modern, and cosmopolitan.[2] In monocultural social worlds, everyone believes the same story, and their story serves as a way to coordinate their activities. People in ethnocentric social worlds also share the same story but see their story as superior to others' stories and organize their world in terms of "us and them." Moderns, on the other hand, easily dismiss historical stories and focus on what's new. "Whatever is newer is better." Cosmopolitan social worlds take a more balanced approach, listening to the stories of other communities and sharing their own. Instead of creating unity by believing in the same stories, and focusing on whatever is new, cosmopolitan social worlds find unity through the very process of inquiry, sharing, and learning.

In a sense, the environmental crisis seems to push us to a modernistic social world that puts aside historical narratives and focuses on what's new, but the modernistic social world has trouble distinguishing between good and bad. Just because it's new doesn't make it right. So, we are left with trying to practice cosmopolitan communication during which we listen to different stories, with one ear open to ethical standards that help us to tell a good story from a bad one, or, we could also say, a good social world from a bad one.

So, how do we tell a good social world from a bad one? First, we look at what social worlds do. Pearce says that social worlds—forms of communication—do three things: provide coherence, coordination, and mystery.

> The way communication works is grounded in three universal aspects of the human condition: persons interpret their environment and their experience; they interact with their fellows, and they remind themselves that there is more to life than the immediate moment.[3]

So, what would be some ethical criteria we could use to evaluate how well a social world performs these three functions? In general, the task of ethics is to help us to do good and to avoid evil. In this case, since there are any number of "good" stories, we will focus on the ethical task of developing standards for avoiding evil, or for not making mistakes, by applying an ethics of coherence, coordination, and mystery.

A story has coherence when the parts fit together. The question, of course, is which parts. What goes with what? Let's say that a story only has coherence when it has not omitted events and episodes that are necessary for understanding the history that the story tells. The ethical standard for coordination is that it must not create and maintain out-of-balance and unstable social relations. And a good mystery? Let's say that it reminds us that there is more to life than the mere facts of daily existence. The meanings of these three ethical standards should become clearer when we apply them to our two stories.

# The Story of the Coevolution of Technology and Empathy

The story that technological transformations create social transformations has been told numerous times, and in some sense, it seems true. I have chosen Jeremy Rifkin's telling because he focuses on how changes in technology have transformed human consciousness in terms of our capacity for empathy. Empathy refers to the phenomenon of understanding what another person is feeling, such as when someone's sadness makes us sad as well. At the same time, the evolution of technology has also increased planetary entropy—the transformation of assets from useful energy to wasted energy—that now threatens the survivability of the planet. His picture of our global crisis, in other words, is a contest between empathy that connects us all and entropy that threatens our planet. Rifkin's hope is that what he calls "the third industrial revolution" could escape the rule of entropy by fundamentally reorganizing production and distribution through the use of renewable and sustainable technologies plus an empathic consciousness.

The main theme of Rifkin's story is that as humans have gone through major changes in energy production and consumption, and changes in communication technology, they have also experienced new forms of consciousness and an expanded range of empathy. In the historical section of Rifkin's book, he deftly sorts out the relationships among all these parallel transformations. I created the following chart that reflects my reading of his story of major shifts.

| | Energy production | Communication | Consciousness | Empathy impulse |
|---|---|---|---|---|
| Hunter/forger Urban Christianity | Body Hydraulic/ agriculture | Oral Script/ writing | Mythological Theological | Blood ties/tribe Religious affiliation |
| First Industrial Revolution | Steam/coal | Print | Ideological | National boundaries |
| Second Industrial Revolution | Electric | Telephone/other technologies | Psychological | Global empathy |
| Third Industrial Revolution | Sun, wind, and water renewables | Internet/social networks | Dramaturgical | Age of empathy |

Although this chart leaves out the details of Rifkin's story, it's not that difficult to understand the overall plot. You can see that the development of human communities from hunter/forgers to what Rifkin calls the Third Industrial Revolution parallel changes in energy production, communication technology, and human consciousness, which then also cause changes in empathy. This coevolution of technology and human consciousness has now brought us to an "Age of Empathy" like we have never experienced before. As he says, "A distributed, collaborative, non-hierarchical society can't help but be a more empathic one."[4] Increased empathy gives rise to a "biosphere consciousness" that could lay the foundation for saving the planet.[5]

If this were the only story we knew, we might be quite optimistic, because it appears that evolution is on our side. The question is whether we can keep up with it. Remember the saying that if there is a will, there is a way. In this story, the way—technology—seems to inspire the will. The second story doesn't disagree so much about the way—technology—but does have a different approach to understanding the will.

# The Tragedy of American Prosperity

All other things being equal, prosperity, of course, is a good thing. Prosperity indicates well-being and happiness, security, and, well, prosperity. American Prosperity promises to provide all these things. However, if everyone enjoyed prosperity even close to the amount that those who enjoy American Prosperity do, we would need four to five earths. We only have one. The tragedy is that our social systems plow ahead as though everything was possible: a classic case of hubris with the added characteristic, in this case, of white supremacy.

American Prosperity has its origin in the Atlantic commerce of people and land beginning in the sixteenth century. Taking the land on the Atlantic Coast and using enslaved labor allowed the colonists to export products such as tobacco and later cotton to European nations. Technological developments in shipping, agriculture, and finance facilitated wealth creation for both Europeans and the colonists. The American Revolution ensured that the colonies continued to have access to cheap land and cheap labor, which increased the wealth of white Americans. Northern and Southern politicians then agreed to allow the practice of slavery until 1865. After the short period of Reconstruction, the establishment of Jim Crow in the Southern states, discrimination in the North, and the banishing of Indians to reservations ensured the continuance of cheap labor and cheap land for American Prosperity.

Following Reconstruction, a peculiar story emerged that acknowledged the North's victory in the Civil War but claimed that the Southern cause was more noble and honorable. This story of the "lost cause" prevented the nation from moving toward a more inclusive society and instead made heroes of Confederate generals and then reestablished a racial hierarchy that held sway until the middle of the twentieth century. The civil rights movements of the 1960s disrupted the existing social patterns, and the environmental movement exposed the destructive effects of American Prosperity on the natural environment.

These challenges to continued economic growth, consumption, and wasteful spending were largely silenced with the election of Ronald Reagan, and our nation has become more and more divided as the pressures from social injustices and the climate continue to erode the people's trust in our civic institutions. We did get rid of segregated water fountains, but as Michelle Alexander pointed out in her book *The New Jim Crow*, we have filled our prisons with Black citizens through discriminatory drug policies and sentencing guidelines.[6] Although some would say we are not a racist society, it really depends on where one looks. The political scientist Charles Mills gives us one perspective:

> In a phrase, I would say it's [racism] the political economy of racialized capitalism: the legacy of these systems (chattel slavery, colonialism) both globally (as North-South domination) and in particular nations (the former colonizing powers, the former colonies, the former white settler states). . . . So this inherited system of structural advantage and disadvantage, which was heavily racialized, continues to affect life chances today, thereby reproducing "race" and racial identities as crucial social categories. . . . So racism is most illuminatingly seen in this social and historical context—as an ever-evolving ideology linked with group domination and illicit advantage—rather

than in the framework of individual "prejudice" favored by main-stream social theory.[7]

We need to understand that what Mills calls "this social and historical context" defines the social climate of American Prosperity. This is also the context for making the changes necessary for a sustainable future. This story of American Prosperity does not disagree with our earlier story on technology as the way to a sustainable future, but it does have different assumptions about the will: the process of choosing a path forward.

In the story of the coevolution of technology and empathy, the basic dynamic is between evolutions in technology and human consciousness and the "will" that resides in human consciousness. The second story on American Prosperity is about "social evolution" rather than "human evolution," which means that the "will" has a social rather a human location. So, before we complete an ethical analysis, we need to know whether this distinction between human and social locations makes a difference.

# Human and Social Evolution

In his book on cosmopolitism, Kwame Appiah gives us this hypothetical: "If a normal baby girl born forty thousand years ago were kidnapped by a time machine and raised in a normal family in New York, she would be ready for college in eighteen years."[8] Our basic human capacity, in other words, has not changed. By most accounts, human evolution ended about 315,000 years ago. Since then, we have had a long history of "social evolution" as human communities spread out of Africa to other continents. These migrations did change some characteristics of these communities, such as skin color and facial features, which demonstrate that social changes can alter ever so slightly our genetic makeup. In a sense such epigenetic changes are markers of our ancestors' social history. According to Ancestry.com, I am 53% Scottish, which does not mean that I am a different human being than someone who is 53% Nigerian. It just means that our ancestors lived in different geographic locations.

Technology, of course, also belongs to some social world. One could imagine a "natural" rather than "social" story of technological developments, but such a story is told in a social language, in a social community, and for social reasons. Once we see the coevolution of technology and empathy as a social story, then we can set it alongside our second story and evaluate both stories, beginning to form an ethics of coherence.

# The Ethics of Coherence

If we all lived in the same social world, we would not be talking about coherence. It would be taken for granted. Living in a pluralistic society makes a difference. Once we know of multiple social worlds and stories, we can examine how they are related to one another by applying the following ethical principle of coherence:

> If you cannot understand A without understanding B,
> then you cannot understand B without understanding A.

If we applied the principle to the relationship between white and Black America, it would look like this:

> If you cannot understand Black America without understanding white America,
> you cannot understand white America without understanding Black America.

Or, what about this version:

> Just as you cannot understand Africa without understanding Europe,
> you cannot understand Europe without understanding Africa.

Once you start applying the principle, it becomes clear that the social worlds in which we live today correspond much more to a cosmopolitan perspective than either a monocultural or even modernistic one. Our true social identity emerges from the interdependent relationships of the different groups that belong to the same history. Furthermore, including the disparate experiences of white and non-white Americans in an expanded social story creates an innovative context for responding to our environmental challenges.

When we turn our attention to our other story, the coevolution of technology and empathy, we see a European/American story written as though it had its own coherence. If you recognize modern European history belonging to the larger story of the Atlantic triangular trade involving Europe, Africa, and the Americas, then a story limited to technology and empathy is incoherent.

One could also call the American Prosperity story incoherent because there is more to American Prosperity than the people and the land. There is also, of course, technology. "If you cannot understand American Prosperity without understanding technology, then you cannot understand technology without understanding American Prosperity." Coherence also means that technology cannot be understood by itself, but rather must be coupled with our understanding of American Prosperity. They exist together. So, let's see what that entails.

# American Prosperity and Technology

Technological advances in ship building and navigation were necessary for the development of the Atlantic triangular trade, as were the refitting of ships for the Middle Passage. Should one accuse technology of crimes against humanity? I don't think so. We don't accuse IBM of crimes against humanity for their invention of punch cards that the Nazis used to keep track of prisoners in their concentration camps. Technology may have made these crimes against humanity possible, but they were not inevitable.

Technological innovations have also advanced the prosperity of many Americans, in such areas as health care, agriculture, transportation, communication, banking, and so on. Many of us, myself included, have greatly benefited from these innovations. Technology has also been used to protect American Prosperity with a long history of innovations in military technology.

From the use of the Remington rifle in the Indian Wars, to the nuclear bombs dropped on Hiroshima and Nagasaki, to Agent Orange in Vietnam, to the use of drones in Iraq, military technology has been a promoter and protector of American Prosperity. It would be incoherent to exclude it from the story of American Prosperity. As Daniel Sarewitz points out:

> The science and technology agenda of the United States government, for example, is dominated by the development of military technologies that are, for the most part, of no conceivable benefit in the developing world. Indeed, the widespread proliferation of modern weaponry peddled by the United States and other industrial nations continues to add to the woes of the South. The US space program, though more benign than weapons programs, similarly, has little connection to the development needs of the South. Yet defense and space together constitute almost 70% of the federal R&D budget.[9]

It's true, you cannot understand American Prosperity without understanding the military, and it may be that you cannot understand technology without understanding the military. Any coherent story would include all three. It's a mistake, in other words, to think of technology as existing by itself. Like money, in spite of appearances to the contrary, technology always exists in social worlds and within social relations.

Let's conclude our application of the principle of coherence by saying that a good story needs to include a big enough social world in which the relevant groups are recognized and their relationships, even when broken and in need of repair, are acknowledged. Once we recognize the parts that belong to a good story, then we can review how they are related to each other, how they are coordinated.

# The Ethics of Coordination

If everyone shares the same beliefs, then coordination is not an issue. People just fit in with the role they have been given. It becomes an issue with pluralism, with differences. If the differences are seen as "human" differences, then some people usually end up "coordinating" their relationships with others by setting up some form of hierarchy. In the case of the coevolution of technology and empathy, it doesn't appear that the issue of coordination is a problem because the story focuses on human empathy, not different social groups.

As Rifkin says, "Empathy is a communion of kindred spirits, and it's elicited in a temporal and special zone that transcends distinctions based on social status."[10] In this zone, we experience "the awareness of the vulnerability we all share, and when expressed it becomes a celebration of our common yearning to live."[11]

While the experience of vulnerability may be universal, we are not all vulnerable for the same reasons. Some groups are vulnerable—such as civilians in war zones or refugee camps—because of their social circumstances. Others may "feel" vulnerable while reading their morning newspaper about civilians pleading for food. Empathy may help privileged people understand the plight of others but does little to help them understand the relationship between their circumstances and the circumstances of others. For that to happen, we need to not only have a human conscience but also a social conscience.

# Social Consciousness

Some of us have benefited from the social world of American Prosperity as owners and investors. This does not prevent us from also recognizing the urgent need to change the direction of American Prosperity to save our planet. Instead of a single consciousness, we need to remain conscious of both the dynamics of the social world in which we exist and of ourselves as critics and agents for change. This experience may remind you of W. E. B. Du Bois's famous notion of double consciousness. His description does not match my experience, but it does inform it:

> It is a peculiar sensation, this double-consciousness, this sense of always looking at one's self through the eyes of others, of measuring one's soul by the tape of a world that looks on in amused contempt and pity. One ever feels this twoness—an American, a Negro; two souls, two thoughts, two unreconciled strivings; two warring ideals in one dark body, whose dogged strength alone keeps it from being torn asunder.[12]

White people, of course, cannot replicate this experience of double consciousness. We can, however, learn from Du Bois's description how to interpret our own experiences. If we want to achieve coherence as white Americans, then we must develop some sort of dual or multiple consciousness. We can recognize, for example, that we live in a social world made to benefit people like us and made to the detriment of others, and we can also recognize our responsibility for repairing its injustices. We have not only a social identity, in other words, but also a personal identity.

If we are socially conscious of our different experiences, then we can figure out how to coordinate living together in a habitat for all of us. Figuring this out invites us to reflect on the meaning of mystery in and between our social worlds.

# The Ethics of Mystery

Barnett Pearce defines mystery as "the remembering that there is more to life than the immediate moment."[13] What can we remember that serves this function? Does the story of the coevolution of technology and human consciousness give us something to remember? The story does travel from hunter-gather communities to the current Third Industrial Revolution, but this story is one of development, so why would one remember earlier stages? Like the modernistic kind of communication, the journey's importance resides in its destination. Achieving "biospheric consciousness," for Rifkin, is not about "remembering" something, but rather about participating in the future that evolution has brought to us.

The different stages, in other words, do not impinge on the present. The present, for Rifkin, arrives without impairments or distresses. The evolutionary process may have gone through social turmoil, but it now arrives unscathed and full of promise. The stages through different Industrial Revolutions, in other words, were without lasting damage. Ta-Nehisi Coates offers another view of the Second Industrial Revolution in his book, *Between the World and Me*:

> Once, the Dream's parameters were caged by technology and by the limits of horsepower and wind. But the Dreamers have improved

themselves, and the damming of seas for voltage, the extraction of coal, the transmitting of oil into food, have enabled an expansion in plunder with no known precedent. And this revolution has freed the Dreamers to plunder not just the bodies of humans but the body of the Earth itself. The Earth is not our creation. It has no respect for us. It has no use for us. And its vengeance is not the fire in the cities but the fire in the sky. Something more fierce than Marcus Garvey is riding on the whirlwind. Something more awful than all our African ancestors is rising with the seas. The two phenomena are known to each other. It was the cotton that passed through our chained hands that inaugurated this age. It is the flight from us that sent them sprawling into the subdivided woods. And the methods of transport through these new subdivisions, across the sprawl, is the automobile, the noose around the neck of the earth, and ultimately, the Dreamers themselves.[14]

The dream of the automobile—the noose around the neck of the Earth—represents the refusal to see the Earth's limits, which is the basic hubris of American Prosperity, the hubris that prevents us from seeing that our possibilities are becoming more and more limited as we try to make things better rather than try to change them.

If we follow the ethics of coherence, the story of American Prosperity is a story of remembering. Its coherence involves bringing historical events together that have been separated. This remembering does entail the experience of empathy as Rifkin describes. As we remember the suffering of those who were vulnerable to the forces of American Prosperity, we can feel our own vulnerability. We should not pretend, however, that our experiences of vulnerability are similar.

If those of us who have enjoyed the privileges of American Prosperity experience the human vulnerability of those who have suffered from it, and if we then look at our social world from their social experience of it, we can see our hubris. Having a dual consciousness of the social vulnerability of others and our social privilege, in other words, could create an awareness that "there is more to life than the immediate moment."

The "mystery" is that experiencing our broken relationships with others can invoke in us a response—a response to repair not only our relations with others but also with the Earth. After all, the extraction of value from other persons occurred with the same mentality as the extraction of value from the Earth. Repairing one will enable us to repair the other.

If we can remember this, we may be able to receive an invitation to take up a dualistic perspective of American Prosperity, accept the harm it has done and is doing to people and the planet, and then change its course, thereby preserving our planet.

As was said earlier, "If there is a will, there is a way." Well, technology is part of the way, but it does not create the will. Just because something is possible—even sustainability—does not mean it will happen. It depends on our will. What kind of will? The heroic will? The tragic will? Or the will of the steward, of the caretaker? It's the people who have taken care of us—provided us food, built and cleaned our houses, babysat our kids, held the dying, and dug the graves for the dead—who know how to approach a fragile and sick planet. Instead of following the technocrats or the heroes of American Prosperity to learn what we need to know, we need to listen to the voices of the caretakers and join them in transforming our social world into a world of caretakers. Theirs is the will that will find a way.

# The Ownership of Technology and Technology Transfer

# CHAPTER 8

# Ownership of Information Technology

*David Koepsell*

## Abstract

Modern information technologies rely on electronic and optical signals transmitting data, expressions, and other signals around the world. Digital networks account for trillions of dollars' worth of worldwide commerce, but the nature of their objects is complicated and has proven to be a challenge for customary and legal modes of ownership of expressions. Intellectual property law governed expressions and inventions for the past couple of hundred years, but software and other digital objects, due to their ephemeral and nonphysical natures, pose some ontological, ethical, and regulatory challenges discussed in this chapter.

KEYWORDS

digital commons, intellectual property, cyberspace, ontology, ethics of information

## Introduction

Perhaps one of the most complicated markets in the world at the start of the twenty-first century is that which consists of digital objects. Software, networks, and the transaction of data in worldwide information systems working at the speed of light now account for about eight trillion USD, and this market continues to grow.[1] Information technologies are thousands of years old but have recently begun to evolve rapidly, consistent with the evolution of silicon and other digital storage and transmission technologies at the rate described by Gordon Moore in 1965. "Moore's Law" posits that the computational ability of integrated circuits (silicon chips, CPUs, GPUs, and other technologies involved in IT) doubles every year.[2]

This hypothesis became law over time as his predictions came true. The burgeoning rate of increasing computational capacity has coincided with a growth in the market for integrated circuits, which have become more affordable, ubiquitous, and endemic to our societies. It is barely conceivable to live without the ability to immediately communicate with anyone in the world through robust, decentralized networks, using high bandwidth video and audio. Our networks are now awash in data and communication, hosting innumerable forms of creativity, and overflowing with raw and curated data of all sorts. Much of the value of that multi-trillion-dollar market described above derives from intellectual property (IP) protection. Copyrights, patents, and trademarks are considered a necessary part of the digital milieu. Here, we will discuss what IP is, how IP fits into our information technology (IT) use and its institutions, and consider some questions and problems of IP in IT and potential alternatives.

# Owning Expressions

For most of human history, the idea that one could "own" something that couldn't be enclosed or held somehow (like land enclosed with fences, or hammers in toolboxes, etc.) was nonexistent. A book or parchment might be possessed, but the stories, pictures, or recipes in them were not "owned" by anyone, even the author. When Shakespeare was making himself famous as England's greatest playwright, there were no copyrights.[3] This had been the case for thousands of years. The plays of Aristophanes and Sophocles, and the dramatic epics of Homer, were freely performed, memorized, passed down from generation to generation, written into physical storage devices like books and scrolls, and the authors of these plays and texts could claim no revenue from all those subsequent performances, recitations, or physical copies.

Philosophically, we can distinguish two types of entities involved in each of these creations: types and tokens. A copy of a book with the story *The Iliad* in its pages is a token.[4] It takes up space, it is a unitary object, its possession excludes all other possessions, the space it takes up excludes all other objects, etc. The story *The Iliad* is a type, it can be retained in memory, spoken from one person to any number of people, shared without limit, and distributed without limit, without excluding other things any particular point in space, and without being diminished in its entirety when copied, published, disseminated, or otherwise instantiated in any number of tokens.[5]

Over time, creators who were rewarded through only some portion of the distribution of the types they created sought the help of the state to protect their creations. Shakespeare made his money through the patronage of the crown, which supported his plays monetarily. But he also used an ancient form of protection typically reserved for trespasses upon physical property: force, of a sort. First, only plays that had been authorized by the crown could be performed in England, and the company's copy of the script needed to be stamped by the sovereign's appointed Master of Revels. No copies were generally made of the official script, and no performance of the play could occur without the company's physical possession of the stamped official script. While nothing would prevent others from memorizing the play, as indeed for centuries the Homerian epics had been memorized and recited without physical copies, the state enforced the sole right for the performance of Shakespeare's (and others') plays through this bureaucracy, backed by the threat of state force.

About three hundred years ago, states began creating new sorts of rights for authors, formalizing monopolies over the distribution of copies of tokens and types with patents and copyrights. Copyrights and patents have evolved and spread throughout the world, protecting generally the original expression of some *type* by limiting who may reproduce and sell copies, essentially.[6] Nothing protects ideas themselves. Ideas still cannot be "owned" in any legal sense. As types, they are not prone to exclusivity of possession, and there is no diminution of an idea when held by more than one mind at once. Rather, the laws of intellectual property use the state to provide monopolies to creators over the physical instantiation of ideas in tokens and their "first sales" for some period of years. The first patents and copyrights expired after some short period of time, often around ten or fourteen years.[7] Now, the patent term worldwide is about twenty years on average and the copyright term varies based upon numerous extensions of the protected period, which in the United States, for example, is the lifetime of the author plus seventy-five years.

All of this remained relatively easy to understand and enforce until the advent of modern information technologies. Previously, copying ideas into physical tokens and disseminating them was difficult enough that IP "piracy" was relatively expensive and possible to detect when done at some moderate scale. That's not to say there wasn't significant IP piracy compounded by the fact that nations had their own IP laws and regimes and they typically didn't reach beyond their borders, so enforcement was almost impossible internationally. Modern information technology changed all that. When creative works could be copied in unlimited numbers and distributed instantly worldwide, the regimes created to enforce individual ownership of original expressions through regulating the dissemination of tokens became not only very difficult, but virtually meaningless. Let's look at the complications, legal history, and current state of

IP in IT and then consider why our classical conceptions of owning expressions may be mistaken.

# IP and IT: A Brief History

For quite some time, no one assumed that one of the primary objects of information technology, namely software, was capable of being copyrighted. At best, some had tried to patent software with little resistance, but both the culture and nature of software writing in the early days of computers inspired a sort of wide-open network of sharing algorithms and code across and between university departments and eventually hobbyists using software and networks as the new realm of cyberspace began to blossom.

Complicating the application of copyright to software was something that had been the case in US law for some time: a sort of direct-perception test as to whether an expression was a reproduction under copyright law. The 1908 White-Smith case dealt with player piano rolls. In sum, player piano rolls were not considered "direct reproductions" of protected expressions because humans alone could not perceive the expressions. When a piano roll (which is like an old computer punch card) was put in a player piano, the court held that the roll became part of a machine, and machines can't be copyrighted. The case prompted an amendment to US copyright law in 1909 that introduced a compulsory license for manufacturers of machines that reproduced copyrighted works, and then in 1976, another amendment made clear that a reproduction of a work of authorship includes any "material object . . . in which a work is fixed . . . and from which the work can be perceived, reproduced, or otherwise communicated, either directly or with the aid of a machine or device," thus eliminating any "direct perception test." It wouldn't be until the 1980s that several cases eventually clarified that copyright encompassed computer code.[8]

Software exists in numerous forms, often simultaneously, and in ways that confound most of our ordinary understandings of the definitions of a machine, a book, a performance, or an idea. The complicated nature of software, I have argued, has actually revealed a deficiency in the law of intellectual property in general where types of expressions in similar media are distinguished radically and without logical consistency. Cyberspace, software, and information technology in general have revealed that the world of artifacts is both simpler than we thought it was or treated it for several hundred years, and is in need of reconsideration if the promise of new technologies is to be achieved.

The dichotomy between books and machines, between aesthetic and utilitarian expression embodied in the laws of copyright and patent, are now suspect as the backbone of the new worldwide IT economy blurs the lines between all of those suspect classifications. While it is now clearly the legal case that software is copyrightable *and* sometimes patentable, there are a number of reasons to revisit the general question of why and whether property and ownership frameworks are rationally applied to the underlying objects, and if some other way to conceive of these objects makes sense and is more ethical.

# Problems of IP in IT

Software complicated the legal landscape historically and even long after courts and states expanded IP to clearly include software objects. While copyright has protected written works for hundreds of years, and patents have protected machines and other inventions, software is a bit like both. Code is written by humans using languages that are decipherable by humans, and then used in a computer, which causes the computer to act in certain ways. The source and object codes are different qualitatively. Computers only act upon "binary" code, the ones and zeros that force logic gates to open and close, and such code is not like any written work that could be protected under traditional copyright principles.

Moreover, source code consists of algorithms, and for centuries algorithms were not protectable by copyright.[9] A recipe for a cake is not the sort of original expression that one could copyright, which is why food blogs have so much extra verbiage besides the recipe itself. That excess verbiage, original expressive elements other than the simple algorithms involved in the actual mixing and baking of a cake, is protected by copyright as long as it is original.

Software, at its core, is like a recipe. It consists of instructions that take inputs and produce outputs deterministically. The results may be the display or performance of some original expression, but as the court reasoned in the player piano case, the software acting within a computer is like the deterministic physics of parts in a machine. Machines and other compositions of matter are patented under the theory that monopolies over the production of inventions encourage the risk and investment in the trial and error needed to create new, useful things. Like copyrights, intended to encourage creators to develop new original expressions, patents are artificial monopolies that make up for the fact that no natural enclosure or act can prevent the reuse or expression of things already created and circulated to the public.[10]

In the early days of software, "hacking" primitive code on primitive machines was pursued largely for the challenge, not necessarily to develop IP that could make companies wealthy. Early code was often released to public listservs and published widely for people to play with using their new home PCs, or for students at universities to run on their school's servers.[11] But with the commercialization of computer technology, and the mass production and dissemination of personal computers, came the ability of companies like Microsoft, for instance, to corner the market on operating systems and software for use by a wide audience. With that came IP protection to prevent loss of profits by those who could easily copy software using the very tools that enable it.

Unlike most machines, software can be reproduced infinitely and quickly. Unlike most written works or other original expressions, artists or creator's guilds, or other institutional and customary modes of protection of creators' rights, software is vulnerable to widespread copying. Xeroxing a whole book is more expensive and awkward than its worth, whereas quickly copying a floppy disk with *Sim City* on it costs only the price of a blank disk. Because of the ease with which software objects and digital beings can be reproduced, the emerging software industry began in earnest in the 1980s to apply and enforce copyright to software and to enlist the force of states and their laws to prevent lost profits due to copying of purchased software. Thus began a war over intellectual property rights in information technology that continues to this day. It also marked a philosophical debate about the role of IP in general, the nature of IT specifically, and economic theories regarding profit and property that challenge many of our basic assumptions about creation and money.

# Is IT Property, Really?

Copyrights and patents have now been applied to much of the digital world. Information technologies are now accepted to be well-encompassed by the laws of intellectual property. Even while the nature of the underlying objects remains problematic, the courts are now largely unperturbed by the vague nature of the distinctions between the subjects of patent and copyright, and the logically dual nature of software and other digital beings as hybrid objects that exist simultaneously as algorithms, machines, and expressions. While software should challenge our assumptions about the distinctions in types of objects made for hundreds of years under the law of IP, we have settled into a steady state of accepting that these categories are real, meaningful, and mostly useful.

Intellectual property regimes were created a few hundred years ago to create a new form of monopoly not afforded by nature. While possession, control, exclusivity, and rivalry associated with "real" property (land) and "moveables" (other physical objects) precede the laws that recognize the formality of ownership of these things, no similar facts obtain for expressions, ideas, or inventions. Ideas cannot be fenced in except, perhaps, by the act of keeping a secret. Ideas once expressed can be disseminated infinitely among minds, and expressed again anywhere without diminution of the original idea or expression. The relatively recent invention of intellectual property worked rather smoothly for a while in the sense that its objects seemed to be clear, and clearly distinguishable. A light bulb is not a novel, and a movie is not a steam engine.

Physical and expressive reality was still the substrate for protectable objects such that expressions that were not "fixed" in some tangible form were not copyrightable. But what distinguished a physical book from a printing press, really? The development of IT revealed that these distinctions were themselves loosely construed, even while custom and ordinary perceptions seemed to show them to be qualitatively different. IT showed us that the book and the printing press, and the manners in which ideas are instantiated in each, are fundamentally similar if not exactly the same. All are expressions of ideas; some ideas are "aesthetic" in nature and others are "utilitarian." But even those distinctions are suspect.

Modern information technologies use digital transmission of electronic impulses across transistors and networks to enable video, audio, interactive virtual realms, computation, connections to sensors, data distribution and analysis, artificial agents, and other nearly instantaneous, worldwide communication and phenomena. The operations of electric and optical impulses to trigger logical gates are quite unlike the very first forms of computation, which were more obviously mechanical. The seemingly ephemeral and even apparently ethereal nature of "cyberspace" confounds most of our notions of ordinary property.

Your relation to data on your hard drive, or in a cloud server, is unlike your relation to the hard drive or the server themselves. Your relationship to the books on your bookshelves is similarly unlike the relation between you and the stories in the books on your bookshelves. The property relations among all of these sorts of objects are complex and prone to misunderstandings, and the emerging and changing nature of information technologies leaves many people confused about the extent of their property claims or rights.

There are parts of modern IT networks that are clearly property in the traditional sense. The physical infrastructure upon which all IT depends is real property, unenclosable, exclusive, and rivalrous. The possession and ownership of these sorts of objects is not in doubt and is backed up by thousands of years of custom and law. The information flowing and residing in these networks is also prone to a type of property claim now that there are intellectual property regimes, but for the most part, the IT that is part of and flowing through your corner of cyberspace is not your property. Property claims and rights for digital reality in modern IT are complicated nests of licenses, patents, and copyrights among numerous parties who create the digital (rather than physical) infrastructure of modern cyberspace.

The "Internet" is the physical and digital backbone of a growing amount of worldwide communication in every medium. It consists of decentralized hosts, routers, and switches that move digital signals around a robust, redundant network first designed to withstand nuclear war. Its fundamental digital technol-ogies are generally unowned, nonproprietary, and open source. That is, the code that runs on the switches and moves all of our Internet communications is not patented; the code is published and well-known; and anyone is able to explore, build upon, modify, and even improve the code without paying any royalties to any "owner" of the IP. On the other hand, most people using the Internet do so on PCs and other machines whose code is largely locked up by complex webs of property rights, including patents and copyrights over the operating systems for those machines and the software running on them.

That code is not published; is obscure to the user; cannot generally be modi-fied, used, or improved upon; and cannot be copied or disseminated without paying a royalty to the IP owners. While this state of affairs is now common and expected, it isn't necessary, and some of the philosophical underpinnings of the modern communication and computer age have impelled some to develop alternate schemes, more akin to the state of affairs that obtains for the digital infrastructure of the Internet, for the user end of the network. Freeware, open-source, and other schemes for developing and disseminating software outside of traditional IP frameworks continue to vie for market share in the brave new world of modern IT. Below, we will explore how they work, the motivation for non-IP alternatives for IT, and the degree to which they may be succeeding.

# The Ephemera of Cyberspace

Most of us consider the online realm, and much that is computer-mediated, to be largely ephemeral. We can see and interact with computers, and they mediate communications and other experiences, but the workings of modern informa-tion technologies remain in large part obscure, difficult to grasp, and sequestered from us. The "virtual" realm isn't really "real" the same way IRL (in real life) is, and the things that occur among and within computers and other appliances of modern information technologies are ephemeral, effervescent, fleeting, and disembodied.[12]

Ideas are ephemeral. Among human creations, ideas are perhaps the most difficult things to pin down, to draw borders around, to weigh or measure, and certainly to contain. Even after the advent of intellectual property law, ideas remained unprotectable, uncontainable, and not prone to any claims of owner-ship. They are specifically excluded from IP and have long been. Often, people confuse the nature of IP as some form of protecting ideas, but this is a miscon-ception. IP protects only for a limited time the expression of original ideas. Ideas alone cannot be contained under any legal or practical scheme. It is the nature of ideas that they spread easily, readily, and far. The impossibility of ideas to be containable or monopolized without infringing individual liberty harshly or violently is reason enough for their exclusion from IP law. But another reason is that ideas are a lot like the wind. You may feel them, sense their movements, even witness them being expressed in some form, but you cannot defy their tendency to remain ephemeral. Unlike expressions of ideas that become fixed in some medium, ideas themselves cannot be contained at all.

Many expressions, too, are ephemeral. Live performances, speeches, improvised songs and poems, raps, or other fleeting temporal expressions that do not become fixed in any medium are also not amenable to IP protection. The world of ephemera has long been excluded from any property protection. For a long time too, information technologies were seen as hosting ephemera. Math, laws of nature, languages, and digital communications pulsing through electronic or optical networks at the speed of light, binding together communications and computations across borders instantaneously, all seemed too far afield from the realm of ordinary experience to be subject to property claims. In fact, early networks and time-shared computers developed around them cultures of sharing and openness. The spirit that Levy captures in his history of the early Internet, *Hackers*,[13] is one of communalism, play, and open exploration of a new technology that many thought would lead to a sort of virtual utopia, where everyone would finally be able to express themselves fully and freely far beyond the constraints of the physical world.

Cyberspatial objects, digital beings, and much of the software infrastructure of modern information technologies are largely free both metaphysically and legally.[14] Only those elements that are new, original, creative, inventive, or otherwise prescribed by IP laws must be paid for through licenses or other schemes like royalties. Nonetheless, much of the architecture of the Internet was created without regard to IP. Where a worldwide network crosses hundreds of national boundaries, must remain adaptive to new technologies and creative trends, and should be as frictionless as possible, property regimes pose more of a risk of hindrance than accommodation. In the early days of the auto industry, the potential risk to commerce due to patents helped convince the various auto manufacturers to create patent pools and agreements not to pursue claims against each other for using patented technologies that were best left as accessible standards. Interoperability was deemed so important that it overcame the profit potential of monopolies over certain technologies necessary for a national automobile infrastructure to work. The same was true for the early development of the Internet and its various related technologies, now all part of our modern information infrastructure.[15]

One way to think about property rights in general is in contrast to other sorts of domains and the nature or absence of property claims over them. Besides land and ideas, two opposite poles of property rights and claims, both practically and legally, there are other sorts of things that are potentially amenable to property claims, though regimes that could or sometimes do recognize them do so to only a limited extent, and with difficulty. For ages, certain parts of the world have been recognized as belonging to something called "the commons." There is a long history of information technology infrastructures being treated similarly, with swaths devoted to the public at large.

# The Digital Commons

The development of the earliest legal "commons" in the West can be traced back to the beneficence of sovereigns. "Commoners" were unlanded poor who often had no property of their own, save some grazing animals at best. The crown set aside rights for commoners to use otherwise underdeveloped parts of the crown's land (which often ranged over the whole state) for grazing, and even settling in the case of England, providing one could build a habitable shack within the period between sunrise and sunset. The notion of the commons has since been extended to general human rights to various unenclosable natural resources as well, including sunlight, air, water, and other difficult to enclose and absolutely necessary goods. Besides what we might call "commons by choice" (extensions of the sovereign's beneficence in setting aside public goods, now in the form of national parks, etc.) the air, sunshine, water, and other similar phenomena might be called "commons by material necessity."

The commons by necessity are those parts of the universe that can be used with exclusivity, but that cannot be fully monopolized practically. To the degree that much of cyberspace is similarly difficult to contain, to fully monopolize, or to dominate without competition, so too might a fair amount of modern information infrastructures be commons by material necessity. Even if they are not, there are strong ethical claims about why they should be treated as commons, and there is a rich history of the hacker community doing so that evolved around the Internet in its earliest incarnations, and pervades its use and culture even now.

While the modern phenomenon of IP protection affords a pseudo-property right over expressions that have been argued by many proponents to have enabled and encouraged creativity and inventiveness that would not have occurred without such rights, many of those involved in the earliest forms of modern IT have eschewed property rights altogether, opting for treating the digital realm as a commons, and all of its inventiveness as part of a broader, social goal. The central theme of the ethic that promotes digital beings as necessarily a commons is that "information wants to be free." This is a restatement of sorts of the truism that information is free in the form of ideas. As discussed above, nothing can contain ideas, not even IP laws. Rather, expressions have been granted certain state-sanctioned monopolies for limited periods of time. But those who have sought to preserve freedom and fluidity of information in cyberspace embrace the notion that an unhindered and unbounded virtual domain is best for all of us, and that monopolization of information is unproductive and even morally wrong.[16]

There is a burgeoning part of digital being that is free by design, and where creators are defying the short history of IP to create without property claims at all. Open-source licenses, GNU-based software, freeware, and other forms of production and creation without recourse to state monopoly rights have flourished and are valued significantly, both emotionally and monetarily. One prime example is Linux, a free operating system that accounts for more than 2% of market share for operating systems (OSes), and which has been estimated to be worth over $1.4 billion USD. It was created and is maintained by a community of worldwide volunteers who continue to work democratically to improve its code, and to donate their time and labor to its existence. Because it is open source, others can repackage and sell it, and companies like Red Hat, which built its fortune on maintaining and packaging the Linux OS without IP protection, do just that. In 2018, Red Hat was acquired by IBM for $34 billion USD.

There is ethical and monetary value in doing good things, creating without the necessity of property claims, and in providing valuable and useful services to users. This insight has driven billions of dollars' worth of creation in modern IT, and has made fortunes and spread good will. It is at the core of the philosophy that early cyberspace pioneers embraced, and it remains an active part of the community of users and developers of IT even now.

# CHAPTER 9

# The Fight for Digital Sovereignty

*Luciano Floridi*

## Abstract

Digital sovereignty, including the question of who ultimately controls AI, seems, at first glance, to be an issue that concerns only specialists, politicians, and corporate entities. And yet the fight for who will win digital sovereignty has far-reaching societal implications. Drawing on five case studies, this chapter argues that digital sovereignty affects everyone, whether digital users or not, and makes the case for a hybrid system of control that has the potential to offer full democratic legitimacy as well as innovative flexibility.

KEYWORDS

AI, digital technology, European Union, legitimacy, sovereignty

## Introduction

*Digital sovereignty* seems to be very important, given the popularity of the topic these days. True. But it also sounds like a technical issue, which concerns only specialists. False. Digital sovereignty, and the fight for it, touches everyone, even those who do not have a mobile phone or have never used an online service. To understand why, let me start with four episodes. I shall add a fifth shortly.

**June 18, 2020:** The British government, after having failed to develop a centralized coronavirus app not based on the application programming interface (API)

provided by Google and Apple,[1] gave up, ditched the whole project (Burgess 2020), and decided to start developing a new app in the future that would be fully compatible with the decentralized solution supported by the two American companies.

This U-turn was not the first: Italy (Longo 2020) and Germany (Busvine and Rinke 2020; Lomas 2020) had done the same, only much earlier. Note that, in the context of an online webinar on COVID-19 contact-tracing applications, organized by Renew Europe (a liberal, pro-European political group of the European Parliament), Gary Davis, global director of Privacy & Law Enforcement Requests at Apple (and previously deputy commissioner at the Irish Data Protection Commissioner's Office), stated that, "Google/Apple can disable the system [i.e., the contact-tracing app] on a regional basis when no longer needed."[2] This is *power as control*, as I shall explain presently, and it is clear who has it and can exercise it, as far as the coronavirus apps and the API are concerned.[3]

**July 7, 2020:** Mike Pompeo, the US secretary of state, announced the intention of his government to ban TikTok (Clayton 2020). India had already banned it (Singh 2020) together with many other Chinese apps, including WeChat, following clashes at the India–China border in the Himalayas. TikTok is an app used to create and share short amateur music videos. Translated into forty languages, it has over eight hundred million active users every month. Something used to enjoy singing, dancing, comedy, and lip-syncing short videos would seem harmless.

However, the videos can contain social or political messages, for example. And the fear is that the app can collect personal data, including sensitive metadata such as user geolocation, and may be used to support China's espionage and infiltration, hence the possible ban. However, things may soon change. At the time of this writing, Microsoft announced the following:

> Following a conversation between Microsoft CEO Satya Nadella and President Donald J. Trump, Microsoft is prepared to continue discussions to explore a purchase of TikTok in the United States. Microsoft will move quickly to pursue discussions with TikTok's parent company, ByteDance, in a matter of weeks, and in any event completing these discussions no later than September 15, 2020. During this process, Microsoft looks forward to continuing dialogue with the United States Government, including with the President. The discussions with ByteDance will build upon a notification made by Microsoft and ByteDance to the Committee on Foreign Investment in the United States (CFIUS). The two companies have provided notice of their intent to explore a preliminary proposal that would involve a purchase of the TikTok service in the United States, Canada, Australia, and New Zealand and would result in Microsoft

owning and operating TikTok in these markets. Microsoft may invite other American investors to participate on a minority basis in this purchase.[4]

**July 16, 2020:** The Court of Justice of the European Union (EU) concluded that the United States did not offer sufficient guarantees about the surveillance and the security of personal data, and therefore invalidated the EU-US Privacy Shield, the agreement that regulates the transfer of the data of European users to processors in the United States for commercial purposes.[5]

**July 20, 2020:** Huawei is a leading Chinese company in the production of 5G networks and systems. If the EU decided to ban the use of its technology for security reasons, following in this the United States and Great Britain, then China threatened that it might retaliate against two European companies, Nokia and Ericsson (Mukherjee 2020).

These are just a handful of examples, during some ordinary weeks in the life of the digital revolution. They could be multiplied, the reader may have others in mind, and I shall refer to one more in a moment. But the common thread that unites them is getting clear: these are all episodes in the fight for *digital sovereignty*, that is, for the *control* of *data*, *software* (e.g., AI), *standards* and *protocols* (e.g., 5G, domain names), *processes* (e.g., cloud computing), *hardware* (e.g., mobile phones), *services* (e.g., social media, e-commerce), and *infrastructures* (e.g., cables, satellites, smart cities)—in short, for the *control of the digital*.

Let me clarify that by "control" I mean here the ability to influence something (e.g., its occurrence, creation, or destruction) and its dynamics (e.g., its behavior, development, operations, and interactions), including the ability to check and correct for any deviation from such influence. In this sense, control comes in degrees and above all can be both pooled and transferred. This is crucial since we shall see that the ultimate form of control is individual sovereignty, understood as self-ownership, especially over one's own body, choices, and data.

The fight for digital sovereignty is an epochal struggle not only of all against all but also of anyone allied with anyone, with variable alliances changing according to interests and opportunities. The most visible clash is between companies and states, and it is asymmetric. On the one hand, companies *design*, *produce*, *sell*, and *maintain* the digital. This *poietic* (that is, creative) power over the digital means that states depend on companies for almost anything that is digital, to the extent that, for example, companies have in some contexts become the first line of defense when it comes to cyberattacks.

On the other hand, states have the power to *regulate* the digital, and this is a powerful form of *cybernetic* (in the original, Greek sense of piloting or steering[6]) control, exercised by determining what is legal or not, incentives and disincentives, kinds and levels of taxation, policies for public procurement, as well as modalities and costs of compliance.

The usual narrative that regulations could stifle or even kill innovation and destroy whole industrial sectors is also an acknowledgement of the power of the cybernetic state. It is a significant counterbalance to the other narrative, about the impossibility of regulating the digital because states and regulations arrive always too late with respect to fast-moving companies and their nimble operations. The real point is that, between companies and states, the former can determine the nature and speed of change, but the latter can control the direction of change.

In this asymmetric dialectic, sometimes states use domestic companies for political ends, to fight other states. Companies may try to trick or bypass states and their legislation, but they also rely on "home" states to defend them against foreign states that oppose them. And sometimes companies fight with their own "home" states, as was the case with the Twitter–Trump clash (Posner 2020). Finally, companies may fight against each other.

For example, Microsoft lost against Google in the competition for hegemony over the *search business* (Microsoft had 2.44% vs. Google's 91.54% of market share in 2020[7]), but won an important victory against Amazon, IBM, and Oracle for the hegemony over cloud computing by securing the US Department of Defense cloud computing contract (Joint Enterprise Defense Infrastructure or JEDI), worth up to $10 billion over a period of ten years (Lardinois 2019; Tsidulko 2020), while Google lost against Facebook repeatedly in the competition for hegemony over the *social* business, by shutting down first Orkut, then Google Buzz, and finally Google Plus (Vítečková 2020).

It would be interesting to write a history of when multinational giants have failed to beat other multinational giants at their own game, or have learned to avoid competing among each other, because it would be a history of *de facto* monopolies and how a *pax digitalis* of non-belligerence emerged among such actors. While waiting for such a history, let us return to the topic of digital sovereignty. We have seen that it is generating some confusion. To orient ourselves, let us take a step back.

*Sovereignty* is a form of legitimate, controlling power. It is the power of the captain of the ship, to adopt and adapt Plato's cybernetic analogy. The debate about who can exercise it, how, on what, and for what purposes has contributed to shaping the modern age. This is the period that begins, unanimously and conventionally, in 1492, with the discovery (in the sense of Europeans realizing the existence) of America, but that generates controversies about its exact end. Modernity of size $S$ ends with the French Revolution (1789). Size $M$ goes all the way to the Congress of Vienna (1814–1815). Size $L$ lasts until the outbreak of the First World War (1914). I prefer the *XL*, which runs until the end of the Second World War (1945).

I shall return to the justification of this preference presently. Before, we can now qualify as *national sovereignty* the controlling power exercised by the state on its territory, on the resources that are found in it, and on the people who live there. It is a phenomenon and a concept entirely modern (in the sense of the term just seen) and totally analog, in terms of time, space, and the physicality of things. But the modern age is over, even in its XL version. And our contemporary age is not just *postmodern*.

This is a characterization that indicates only what our age is no more, but says nothing about what it actually is (note that XL is the only "size" of modernity that can accommodate *postmodernity* as a chronologically meaningful category). More informatively, our age is above all the *digital age* (nobody should be surprised by this taxonomy: technology has always helped us to date periods of human evolution, from the Stone Age to the Iron Age).

And in the digital age, the infosphere is not a territory; data are not a finite, scarce, rivalrous, natural, nonrenewable resource like oil (so much the worse for the poor analogy); digital assets are largely private and subject to market forces; and our profiles are created, owned, and exploited not just by states but also by multinationals, which, as the word indicates, are globalized. For all these reasons (and several others, see Floridi 2014, 2020), the digital age is forcing us to rethink the nature of sovereignty. Modern analog sovereignty is still necessary but increasingly insufficient, exactly like the state. Contemporary digital sovereignty is needed as well, in order to provide effective, democratic forms of control through appropriate regulation. But who should exercise it *de facto* and *de jure*?

The first two decades of the century saw the emergence of a sort of *de facto digital corporate sovereignty*. It is that form of controlling power that is supported by those who argue that corporate self-regulation is sufficient, that legislative intervention is unwelcome and unnecessary, and that any required checks and balances of corporate digital power will come from a competitive, laissez-faire approach and market-based equilibria. We saw that this digital corporate sovereignty is built on hegemonic positions or *de facto* monopolies, which enjoy both poietic and cybernetic power over the digital, and on the shift from the individual as a voter-consumer to the individual as a follower-user. Let me comment on both points.

About the first point, I already mentioned how multinationals fail to compete with each other. The logic of winner takes all, the Matthew effect, dominates contemporary capitalism, especially in the digital industry and network economies. Once cumulative advantages create a monopolistic regime, there is no real competition, no real consumer's choice, and therefore no real accountability of the companies that dominate specific markets. Time has come to introduce the fifth example to exemplify what I mean.

**July 29, 2020:** Jeff Bezos (Amazon), Tim Cook (Apple), Sundar Pichai (Google), and Mark Zuckerberg (Facebook), were questioned during a hearing of the House Judiciary Subcommittee on Antitrust, Commercial, and Administrative Law on "Online Platforms and Market Power, Part 6: Examining the Dominance of Amazon, Apple, Facebook, and Google." Chairman David N. Cicilline gave the following opening statement, worth quoting at length:

> Open markets are predicated on the idea that if a company harms people, consumers, workers, and business partners will choose another option. We are here today because that choice is no longer possible. . . . Because concentrated economic power also leads to concentrated political power, this investigation also goes to the heart of whether *we, as a people, govern ourselves, or whether we let ourselves be governed by private monopolies.* American democracy has always been at war against monopoly power. Throughout our history, we have recognized that concentrated markets and concentrated political control are incompatible with democratic ideals. When the American people confronted monopolists in the past—be it the railroads and oil tycoons or AT&T and Microsoft—we took action to ensure no private corporation controls our economy or our democracy. We face similar challenges today. . . . Their ability to dictate terms, call the shots, upend entire sectors, and inspire fear represent *the powers of a private government.* Our founders would not bow before a king. Nor should we bow before the emperors of the online economy.[8]

Corporate digital sovereignty is not just a philosopher's idea, but a political reality. This leads me to the second point about the shift from voters-consumers to followers-users.

In the second half of the twentieth century, democracy and capitalism were seen as two sides of the same coin because both were assumed to be accountable to people, through competition, which was based on political (voting) and purchasing (buying) choices, respectively. We just saw that Cicilline's statement assumes this premise. It is also implicit in classics such as von Mises (2005), for example. So, it was coherently (if mistakenly) thought that exporting capitalism would have meant exporting democracy. In particular, it was thought that China would have become a democracy through the Trojan horse of capitalism. It did not work.

The two phenomena were merely traveling in parallel for a while, in some Western countries. Whether the misleading narrative was a naive mistake or an evil plan depends on whom you ask and about whom they are talking. The fact remains that popular sovereignty, as the source of legitimization of political power, including national sovereignty, was seen as the sovereignty of the voter *and* of the consumer, as if these two roles were intrinsically part of the essence of a citizen, as an indissoluble unity, empowered by competition for people's vote and money.

However, since the end of modernity (using the XL concept I introduced before), the progressive fulfillment (or at least the hope thereof) of the consumer's desires first stretched and then snapped away from the voter's needs, like two pieces of blu tack. Marx failed to see (or indeed could not have seen what is now easy to see) that capitalism flourishes by transforming the working class into the shopping class through consumerism, and that to promote consumerism capitalism needs to guarantee a minimum amount of redistribution (or at least creditworthiness) to create an increasing number of customers who can (at least believe they are able to) afford an increasing number of good and services, while fueling in those customers the hope that the future will always be better than the past (tomorrow is not just another day, it is a better day), when they may join (or defend their newly acquired status as members of) the bourgeoisie, to use Marx's vocabulary.

Likewise, liberalism did not see (or again, could not have seen) that the progressive increase in relative prosperity and the hope of future gain deprioritize political participation, hence the demand for change. In both cases, one may quip that the worst enemy of democracy is a credit card. For democracy is more likely to be the demand of the poor than of the rich, or of those who hope to become rich. However, note that this cuts both ways, because democracy and capitalism are not two sides of the same coin: an economic future worse than the present simply motivates people to ask for political change, and when this happens in a democracy this means that sometimes populism arises and democracy is challenged. Our time provides plenty of examples, from Italy to the United Kingdom, from the United States to Brazil.

In the past few decades, increasing prosperity made consumers feel democracy was decreasingly essential, as long as the future was economically better than the present. This was also the time of the great decoupling of social sciences from ethics: after the end of modernity (the XL size) in liberal democracies economy focuses on profit, jurisprudence on compliance, and politics on consensus, while right and wrong are more likely to be treated as a matter of individual choices and preferences.

Today, we know that it takes a lot of pressure to rebel against a repressive regime, and that such pressure is relieved by economic growth. Thus, with an oversimplification (because there are many and complex factors at stake, see for example Roberts et al. [2021]) one may jest that in China the cost of democracy is a yearly growth of the GDP of at least 7% or so: if it is lower than that, then people may start complaining, politically and en masse, because they may want an economically better society through better politics.

When GDP growth is higher than that, students, idealists, activists, and a few other politically minded people may be ready to run serious risks for their freedom and life, and protest for a socially better society, but they remain a minority. More generally, autocratic powers will not be overturned by masses that every year can look forward to a better year. This long premise should help us to understand a fundamental shift in the role of the individual, who, in this century, has moved from being a voter-consumer, empowered by competition, to being a follower-user, disempowered by political and business hegemonies.

In an age when analog reality is increasingly managed and controlled by digital reality, the sociopolitical sovereignty of both appears to be essential for a better democracy and coordinated cooperation to tackle global problems, to make society fairer, and to make development at least sustainable. In Europe, this means asking who should exercise digital sovereignty, whether it be each member state or the European Union.

The distinction is important. When Macron and Merkel speak of digital sovereignty, do they mean the *national* one (France's, Germany's, etc.), or the *supranational* one (the EU's), as when von der Leyen refers to it? The risk, when supporting *national* digital sovereignty, is that states end up supporting *digital sovereignism* or *digital statism*. These are culturally and economically anachronistic positions, which defend an autarchic and mercantilist version of the digital. They range from the rhetoric of national champions, existing or to be created, to the wishful thinking about cloning foreign successes at home. They should both be resisted. Yet the line that separates them from digital sovereignty can be easily blurred, as it sometimes is in the EU.

In the EU, analog sovereignty is articulated on two levels. For example, *tax sovereignty* remains national, to the extent that multinational companies exploit it to game the EU system and play national sovereignties against each other (think of the Apple–Ireland case).[9] But, continuing with the example, *monetary sovereignty* in some cases has become supranational, whenever member states have adopted the euro. Likewise, digital sovereignty should probably be equally articulated, with both national and supranational levels of implementation.

In some fundamental cases, also in view of avoiding digital sovereignism and statism, digital sovereignty could be exercised more easily by the EU, both in terms of feasibility and in terms of added value, resembling the case of monetary sovereignty and what has happened with the Eurozone. We know, for example, that *digital data sovereignty* is more feasible and effective at the EU level, through the General Data Protection Regulation. It may be reasonable to move in the same direction for *AI sovereignty* and *5G sovereignty*, to mention two other key digital areas. The best answer to the multinationals' control of the digital is probably the establishment of a (*de jure* and not only a possibly *de facto*) supra-national digital sovereignty, at the EU level.

The debate on digital sovereignty is not about replacing national modern analog sovereignty, which is necessary but increasingly insufficient. It is about complementing it with a supranational, contemporary digital one—which is often its condition of possibility—to provide to all actors and stakeholders wider benefits of harmonization (e.g., of standards and requirements) and a level play-ing field, as well as to enhance opportunities of coordination. But if this is the case, as I would argue, then at least one more significant problem still remains to be solved: *legitimacy* (Schmitter 2001).

Recall that, if (not yet qualified) sovereignty is the controlling power that legitimizes (transforms power into recognized authority) other forms of power but requires no previous controlling power to be legitimized in its turn, then *national* sovereignty is usually based on *popular* sovereignty, which is taken to be a sort of Aristotelian unmoved mover. The *regressus ad infinitum* is avoided by having individuals pool their self-sovereignties (sovereignty over themselves) through deliberation, negotiation, and voting, to create popular sovereignty, which then legitimizes national sovereignty, which then controls individuals' legal exercise of their self-sovereignties.

The answer to "Quis custodiet ipsos custodes?" is the "custodiendi" them-selves. (Who controls the controllers? The controlled themselves.) This is not a vicious circle but a virtuous spiral, given the shift from individual sovereignty (self-sovereignty) to societal sovereignty (popular sovereignty). Through their lives, individuals join a polity, which is more stable than their existence, and as they come and go, like many short fibers of a rope, they make the rope (popular sovereignty) long and strong.

The question is what happens when digital or analog sovereignty are no longer national but supranational: How can the support of popular sovereignty be expanded to also cover supranational sovereignty? And indeed, can it be? There seem to be several alternatives, sometimes defended and criticized in the EU under the general topic of "democratic deficit." In each alternative, popular sovereignty remains the ultimate source of legitimization of all other forms of sovereignty, including national and supranational sovereignty. What is contro-versial is how exactly this may work.

One way forward is to recall that sovereignty is not like a rivalrous resource that, when given to someone else is no longer in one's possession, and can only be reacquired by taking it back from that someone. It is more like a relation (control), in which one may engage more or less intensely and successfully, but precisely because it is a matter of engagement is never "lost" when exercised or delegated, and is not finite or rivalrous: giving it to someone does not mean being unable to give it also to someone else at the same time.

Such a relational concept of sovereignty enables one to see that the legitimization of sovereignty can be modeled in terms of the topology of the network that seems to be the most appropriate for its structuring. Many network topologies are possible in theory, but three are of political and historical interest here.

In a *fully connected* network topology, each node enjoys popular and national sovereignty, and the nodes are all linked together for some common purposes. Each node is legitimized by its own popular sovereignty, each node can leave the network at any time (secession), and the network itself lacks its own legitimacy over and above the legitimized nodes. This more *distributed legitimacy* is what some supporters of a European confederation of national states (the nodes), for example, seem to have in mind. It can be a strong version of intergovernmentalism, which can deal with fundamental issues such as currency, trade, or defense.

In terms of political design, this network requires no innovation: it is simply a more or less strong network of Westphalian states. As a modern concept, it is well established in terms of common action among sovereign states that pursue shared goals and wish to further shared aims. Since it requires no changes in popular or national sovereignty, it also requires no storytelling to be made popular among voters.

In a *star* network topology (think of spoke–hub distribution), popular sovereignty is placed at the center and directly legitimizes every other peripheral node, represented by other kinds of sovereignty, national and supranational included. The network has its own supranational sovereignty. This more *centralized legitimacy* is what some supporters of a European federation, for example, seem to have in mind. It is simple and classic in terms of political design, representing an updating of the Westphalian state to a federated version, and perhaps for this reason it is also easier to understand, but it may not be popular among voters attached to nationalistic values and policies.

Finally, in a *hybrid* topology, in a partially connected mesh there can be nodes, popular sovereignties that legitimize other nodes, and national sovereignties, which then legitimize some other nodes (e.g., supranational sovereignties), possibly in a mutually legitimizing relation. This more *hierarchical* legitimacy is what some supporters of a multi-speed Europe, for example, seem to have in mind. Its variable geometry is less intuitive and more innovative in terms of political design.

It is also more complex and difficult to implement properly, and because it is largely unprecedented, it requires more and better storytelling to be explained and made popular. But it is not hard to conceptualize, because states can be fruitfully understood today as individual multiagent systems (Floridi 2015, 2016) that pool and transfer their national sovereignties to create supranational sovereignty in some areas.

We saw that the Eurozone provides an excellent example. So, one may argue that popular sovereignty (understood as the pooling of individuals' self-sovereignties) legitimizes national sovereignty as national sovereignty (now understood as the pooling of national multiagent systems of self-sovereignties) legitimizes supranational sovereignty. This is how the "combined sovereignty" of the EU may be understood and promoted. Through the mechanism of "enhanced cooperation,"[10] a hybrid network could support a core of a more federal Europe within a larger, more confederated EU, and one could call the whole the United States of Europe.[11]

Perhaps an EU that currently has different solutions for different kinds of analog sovereignty and only the beginning of some kinds of digital sovereignty may one day opt, as plan A, for a centralized, single form of both analog and digital sovereignty. However, this seems to be unlikely and at best very distant in the future, even assuming it is a preferable strategy. The good news is that this is also not incompatible with an EU that continues to opt, for the foreseeable time, for variable geometries of both analog and digital sovereignty. For some people, this hybrid topology will remain plan B, with the advantage of feasibility and the shortcomings of a compromise, but I would like to argue that it should rather be the focus of some truly innovative design, to transform it into a successful plan A.

A partially connected mesh of individual, popular, national, supranational, and subnational (see, for example, the case in support of indigenous data sovereignty, Taylor and Kukutai [2016]) sovereignties, both analog and digital, could deliver full democratic legitimacy and greater innovative flexibility, if designed successfully. This is not an easy thing to do, but, if I am correct, one day the United States of Europe will not be an intergovernmental or supranational chapter in the history of the Westphalian state and its analog/digital sovereignties, but a new book altogether, neither a confederation nor a federation, but a *differentiated integration* with its own design.

But enough about a possible future. Let me close with a look at the past, and a historical comparison almost entirely incorrect. The fight for digital sovereignty may remind one of the Investiture Controversy, the medieval conflict between the Church/Pope and the State/Emperor in Europe over the ability to choose and install bishops and more generally over secular and spiritual power. Of course, that controversy is very different from anything we are seeing in the fight for digital sovereignty. But I believe that the comparison is not entirely incorrect.

That controversy was a significant stage in the development of the concept of sovereignty, as the etymology of the word makes obvious. Today, the fight is not over secular and spiritual power but over corporate and political power over the digital, yet the roots of this clash are very old. But most importantly that medieval debate reminds us that whoever will win the fight for digital sovereignty will determine the lives of all people on both sides of the digital divide, exactly like the Investiture Controversy affected all people, no matter if they were religious or not. This is why I began this article by saying that digital sovereignty is not just a matter of interest for some specialists. It is already affecting everybody. And this is why it is essential to design it as well as possible, together.

# Acknowledgments

I benefited enormously from several conversations with many members of the Digital Ethics Lab, and above all with Josh Cowls, Hugh Roberts, and Mariarosaria Taddeo, who read a penultimate version of this article and provided some truly excellent suggestions on how to improve it substantially. They are of course not responsible for any remaining mistakes.

# References

Burgess, Matt. "Why the NHS Covid-19 Contact Tracing App Failed." *Wired*, June 19, 2020. https://www.wired.co.uk/article/nhs-tracing-app-scrapped-apple-google-uk.

Busvine, Douglas, and Andreas Rinke. "Germany Flips to Apple-Google Approach on Smartphone Contact Tracing." *Reuters*, April 26, 2020. https://www.reuters.com/article/us-health-coronavirus-europe-tech/germany-flips-to-apple-google-approach-on-smartphone-contact-tracing-idUSKCN22807J.

Clayton, James. "TikTok: Chinese App May Be Banned in US, Says Pompeo." *BBC News*, July 7, 2020. https://www.bbc.com/news/technology-53319955.

Floridi, Luciano. *The Fourth Revolution: How the Infosphere Is Reshaping Human Reality.* Oxford: Oxford University Press, 2014.

Floridi, Luciano. "Hyperhistory and the Philosophy of Information Policies." In *The Onlife Manifesto: Being Human in a Hyperconnected Era,* edited by Luciano Floridi, 51–63. Cham: Springer International Publishing, 2015.

Floridi, Luciano. "Hyperhistory, the Emergence of the MASs, and the Design of Infraethics." In *Information, Freedom and Property: The Philosophy of Law Meets the Philosophy of Technology,* edited by Mireille Hildebrandt and Bibi van den Berg, Chapter 7. London: Routledge, 2016.

Floridi, Luciano. *Il Verde e Il Blu: Idee ingenue per migliorare la politica.* Milan: Raffaello Cortina, 2020.

Lardinois, Frederic. "In a Victory over Amazon, Microsoft Wins $10B Pentagon JEDI Cloud Contract." *Tech Crunch*, October 25, 2019. https://techcrunch.com/2019/10/25/in-a-victory-over-amazon-microsoft-wins-10b-pentagon-jedi-cloud-contract/.

Lomas, Natasha. "Germany Ditches Centralized Approach to App for COVID-19 Contacts Tracing." *Tech Crunch*, April 27, 2020. https://techcrunch.com/2020/04/27/germany-ditches-centralized-approach-to-app-for-covid-19-contacts-tracing/.

Longo, Alessandro. "L'app Immuni cambia. Seguirà il modello decentralizzato di Apple e Google." *Il Sole24Ore,* April 22, 2020. https://www.ilsole24ore.com/art/l-app-immuni-cambia-seguira-modello-decentralizzato-apple-e-google-ADcBF4L?refresh_ce=1.

Morley, Jessica, Josh Cowls, Mariarosaria Taddeo, and Luciano Floridi. "Ethical Guidelines for COVID-19 Tracing Apps." *Nature* 582 (2020): 29–31.

Mukherjee, Supantha. "China May Retaliate against Nokia, Ericsson if EU Bans Huawei: WSJ." *Reuters*, July 20, 2020. https://www.reuters.com/article/us-china-huawei-europe/china-may-retaliate-against-nokia-ericsson-if-eu-bans-huawei-wsj-idUSKCN24L1NW.

Posner, Michael. "What's behind the Trump-Twitter Clash?" *Forbes*, May 29, 2020. https://www.forbes.com/sites/michaelposner/2020/05/29/whats-behind-the-trump-twitter-clash/?sh=56be06ab54f5.

Roberts, Huw, Josh Cowls, Jessica Morley, Mariarosaria Taddeo, Vincent Wang, and Luciano Floridi. "The Chinese Approach to Artificial Intelligence: An Analysis of Policy and Regulation." *AI & Society* 36 (2021): 59–77.

Schmitter, Philippe C. "What Is There to Legitimize in the European Union . . . and How Might This Be Accomplished?" Working Paper, Vienna, Institute for Advanced Studies, 2001. https://jeanmonnetprogram.org/archive/papers/01/011401-01.html.

Singh, Manish. "India Bans TikTok, Dozens of Other Chinese Apps." *Tech Crunch*, June 29, 2020. https://techcrunch.com/2020/06/29/india-bans-tiktok-dozens-of-other-chinese-apps/.

Taylor, John, and Tahu Kukutai. "Indigenous Data Sovereignty: Toward an Agenda." Acton, Australia: Australian National University Press, 2016.

Tsidulko, Joseph. "Pentagon CIO: JEDI Cloud 'Re-Announcement' Should Come by End of August." *CRN*, July 30, 2020. https://www.crn.com/news/cloud/pentagon-cio-jedi-cloud-re-announcement-should-come-by-end-of-august.

Verhofstadt, Guy. *The United States of Europe: Manifesto for a New Europe.* London: Federal Trust for Education and Research, 2006.

Vítečková, Karolína. "The Story behind Google Plus Shutting Down." *Wiredelta*, updated June 22, 2020. https://wiredelta.com/behind-google-plus-shutting-down/#:~:text=The%20main%20reason%20for%20the,are%20less%20than%205%20seconds.&text=As%20it%20turns%20out%2C%20Google,APIs%2C%20connected%20to%20security%20flaws.

von Mises, Ludwig. *Liberalism: The Classical Tradition.* Liberty Fund Library of the Works of Ludwig von Mises. Indianapolis: Liberty Fund, 2005.

# Information Technology and Social Media

# CHAPTER 10

# The Moral Fog of Social Media

*Dean Cocking and Jeroen van den Hoven*

## Abstract

The information and social media revolutions promised great leaps forward for moral agency and the shared life. Instead, there has been widespread depreciation of value and social connections. Pseudoscience and conspiracy theories fueled online, for example, have undermined the authority of science and democracy, and an increase in loneliness has become a major health issue. We focus here on the problem that considered moral realities, otherwise loud and clear, have become obscure to us as we live online. We point the finger at the design and milieu of virtual life at once compounding our preoccupation with self and providing a bonanza of access for big business to manipulate that self.

### KEYWORDS

social media, moral fog, virtual worlds, manipulation, the "self," Edward Bernays, the Metaverse, dream incubation

## Introduction

> "I like the plastic look" —Reality TV Star

The online social revolution has normalized the artificial, the abnormal, the extreme, and the immoral. Fashion-driven plastic surgery, for instance, has exploded along with communities that normalize it, indeed, communities where

131

it is almost required and people compete over it, such as across TikTok, Snapchat, Instagram, Reality TV, and our social worlds more generally.[1] Illnesses such as anorexia get celebrated and health problems like COVID-19 get denied. People are driven to extremes to get attention in saturated waters, or by polarizing echo chambers or filter bubbles. Violence and pornography are instantly accessible to anyone with a smartphone and have spawned huge industries.

The information and social media revolutions promised great leaps forward for self-expression and communication by giving us unprecedented access to a world of information, ideas, and understanding, and to one another. As such, they promised a monumental growth spurt for moral (and more broadly rational) agency and the shared life. What was not (so) foreseen, however, was just how remarkably we would quickly lose sight of valuable understandings and practices, such as ones we have long developed in our traditional worlds concerning our appreciation of value and worthwhile connections to one another.

Polite kids have become bullies online, including toward their offline friends, and an increase in loneliness has been widely associated with smartphone use and become regarded as a major health issue.[2] Pseudoscience and conspiracy theories fueled by the design and milieu of life online have caused the widespread demise of the authority of science and democracy. The promise of fundamental moral (and rational) progress has given way to worries about the social fabric and cultural regress.

# "Just Me and the Internet"

How have we "flipped" to such failures of understanding about value and reality? How have we lost sight of what we otherwise knew well? In *Evil Online* we suggest some answers. In particular, we describe how our social worlds online create "moral fog" that obscures our understanding of value and reality. The problem of moral fog has various forms and has always been a foundational problem for our pursuit of personhood and a worthwhile life. Limits and distortions of understanding come with our nature, for instance, with the subjectivity and contingency of our experience of self, others, and the world around us. The design and milieu of social media platforms, however, has presented something of a perfect storm for exacerbating our problems of limited and distorted understanding.

The design of online communication presents a coalescence of such features as (actual and seeming) social isolation from one another, anonymity, unreality, and a relative absence of a broad suite of social practices and effective laws supporting an individual's appreciation of value and reality. In addition, the milieu of our social media platforms is notably shaped by the business model of its owners, associated businesses, and advertisers. Big data about our attitudes and desires as revealed by our conduct online has been a bonanza for manipulating us to commercial and political ends, and, accordingly, the business of "big data" has exploded.

Such features of the design and milieu of social media platforms now increasingly mediate an individual's engagement with the world. Instead of being directly connected to others and the social practices and laws around me, my understandings of self, others, and my surroundings is now largely the product of engagement between "just me, and the Internet."[3] Our direct connection is to the design and milieu of my social media platform, at once compounding our preoccupation with self and providing a bonanza of access for big business to manipulate that self.[4] As a result, the design and milieu of social media has created online life-worlds that are moral fog machines. These are worlds where moral realities are unclear, not only because we are encountering possibilities and problems we have not yet considered, but where well-considered moral realities that were otherwise very clear to us have become obscure.[5]

This variety of the problem of moral fog has even derailed discussion, understanding, and instruction about problems of evil online. Many are now aware of various problems of life online, including those with which we opened our discussion, and some efforts at better value-sensitive design have appeared.[6] It is a mistake, however, to think that having some awareness of cases and ways in which life online has normalized the artificial, the extreme, and the immoral thereby clears up our problems of moral fog that brought us to these worlds. It is a mistake to think that because we have some awareness of such problems and see some efforts in the right direction that we now understand things clearly, can expect appropriate progress to follow, and can therefore move on and focus our attention elsewhere.[7]

Our knowledge about greenhouse gas emissions presents a devastating illustration of how our awareness, even of the most serious of problems, along with some efforts to redress them, need not amount to anything like appropriate progress. The solid scientific base about the danger of global warming is widely recognized to have been around for about fifty years.[8] In 1985, for example, the Australian government under Prime Minister Hawke established a climate change committee that reported "dire and 100% accurate warnings" thirty-five years ago.[9] In the online case, there is also good evidence of how we can be aware of problems without this providing appropriate guidance of our conduct. Commonly users can be instructed about problems with communication online but lose sight of their awareness when they are online. Many, for example, who can demonstrate they are well aware of privacy risks online, nevertheless conduct themselves online as if they are relatively clueless.[10] Many bullies online could also give you an informed account of online bullying, they just don't see their own conduct online as bullying.[11]

Moral psychology has long focused on describing our capacities[12] to appreciate, even create, value, and understand reality, sometimes even against the odds, such as presented by the "battle-citation" model of moral worth in which duty overcomes conflicting inclination, with which Kant is often associated.[13] We are creators of value, or at least appreciators of value, including sometimes against the most horrendousness of odds.[14] As well, however, our susceptibilities to moral fog and capacities to ignore, fail to appreciate, and to destroy value that we otherwise know well are astonishing.

# The "Century of Self"[15]

## "TORCHES OF FREEDOM"

Edward Bernays, nephew of Sigmund Freud, is widely regarded as the "great-grandparent" of "PR"—public relations. In fact, he coined the term "public relations." He did so to provide a more palatable description for the business of manipulating people than "propaganda." He recognized that the term "propaganda" had the self-defeating impact of alerting people to the attempt to manipulate them. In this "original spin" Bernays set the defining standard for the industry. The manipulation of the masses would need to disguise its intent (on his account, to save democracy):

> The conscious and intelligent manipulation of the organized habits and opinions of the masses is an important element in democratic society. Those who manipulate this unseen mechanism of society constitute an invisible government that is the true ruling power of our country. We are governed, our minds are moulded, our tastes formed, and our ideas suggested, largely by men we have never heard of. . . . It is they who pull the wires that control the public mind.[16]

His infamous early campaign to raise demand for smoking cigarettes among women in 1929 presented a spectacular example of how to disguise intent. He had fashionable women "puff away" at an Easter parade and promoted their look as fashionable more generally (and later as "slimming" and "soothing"). However, his use of the description of cigarettes as "torches of freedom" tapped into the developing recognition of women's oppression and rights of the period, and took the manipulation to a new level. Bernays's campaign to drive people to addiction to cigarettes in the name of their freedom was a phenomenal success. More than this, his cover for intent and gas-lighting of the masses has been one of the most influential and oft-repeated approaches for public relations.

Manipulation disguised as emancipation has become a template for economic and political spin.

There is a very simple and fundamental reason for the effectiveness of the "big lie": the pitch appeals to our pursuit of personhood and a valuable life its foundations. Our development as persons, as valuing beings, and our pursuit of a worthwhile life heavily involves our carving some identity and worthwhile life ourselves, and this involves our developing capacities to make choices to do so. "Torches of freedom" describes (quite well) our development of capacities for choice, our times of evaluative decision-making about how to be and act that "light our path" and illustrate our maturing as moral agents.[17] Moreover, contemporary revolutionary communication technologies, unlike smoking cigarettes, can lay plausible claims to providing "torches of freedom."

Revolutionary communication technology promises radical new ways to enable our becoming valuing beings. Information and social connections are (often) central to our moral development, and the information and social revolutions promised unprecedented "torches of freedom" across both fronts. They provide ways to transcend various and notable limitations and distortions of knowledge, understanding, and connection characteristic of our traditional worlds.

We are presented with very powerful reasons to embrace these revolutions in information and communication technology. Otherwise, we refuse these opportunities to transcend the limits and distortions of experience and understanding of our traditional worlds. We will be choosing to undermine our own pursuit of virtue and value, to be left behind in ways crucial to our pursuit of moral agency and a worthwhile life. Bernays's template for manipulation gets a perfect home in the promotion of revolutionary communication technology, a home that provides very compelling "plausible deniability" for any unwanted results that ensue.

## GROUNDHOG DAY IN THE FOG

The successors of Bernays are now employed by Big Tech and are deeply involved in behavioral advertising, choice modeling, framing, and nudging. Big Tech companies divert attention away from what is actually going on under the cover, claiming that they are just providing mere tools, which are value-neutral and carefree. They are in the business of connecting people, augmenting people's range of options and choice. It is nothing short of amazing just how widespread acceptance of this "pitch" has been.[18]

Media barons have long run a "protection racket" against politicians and competitors to advance their economic interests. Political candidates who come on board get good publicity and protection from bad publicity. Those who refuse and pose an obstacle become the subjects of smear campaigns, along with getting nil or little good publicity where it is due. Media organizations have long run "fake news" campaigns to destroy political (and economic) opponents (and/ or to advance their own interests) and these have invariably been very effective. In short, mass media owners, organizations, and associated businesses have long manipulated the masses to favor their own economic and political interests, used fake news to do so, and thereby hijacked democracy by significantly undermining (and often making a nonsense of) the prospects of a reasonably informed citizenry.

In the world of modern media new plans are now made to influence people even more effectively. We describe the project of "targeted dream incubation" ahead, which aims to influence the dreams of users by means of smart devices such as Siri, Alexa, or smartphones. Serious investments are being made in brain–computer interfaces, such as Musk's NeuroLink.[19] No one knows which urgent global problems on the stock list of UN Sustainable Development Goals we are solving by these "innovations." There is also no sign that Big Tech companies are reflecting on the long-term moral consequences of the way they are digitally reweaving the fabric of society.

Reflection should not so much be concerned with preventing this or that mishap, unfortunate accident, episode of catfishing, identity theft, pranking, and so on. Neither should it be primarily about establishing ethical guidelines, editorial content policies, or corporate ethics boards. Reflection should be concerned with the development of moral sensibilities and the ability to experience instances of moral worth and merit. Instead, our attention spans, attitudes, desires, and rewards are increasingly of the short-term and self-obsessed varieties, cultivated by the communication platforms and possibilities designed by Big Tech.

We live, for example, in worlds where our experiences of self and others are mediated by the images we can present and the virtual worlds we can inhabit, rather than by direct engagement with others. Self/other understanding is no longer (so much) the product (nor is it able to be) of immersion in morally educative activities and experiences regarding self-expression and engagement with others. Actors often report how their celebrity image gets in the way, both of their seeing and engaging with others, and of their ability to see and be "themselves." Their identity and social connection get reduced to the images they and everyone else have of them. Similarly, for all of us living in virtual worlds, our possibilities for reflection and our understanding of self and others are reduced to images.[20]

# Back to the Future

## THE "METAVERSE"

Very recently, founder of Facebook Mark Zuckerberg announced a great leap forward that promises to bring together our traditional and online worlds—the "Metaverse." The term was coined in *Snow Crash*, Neal Stephenson's 1992 sci-fi novel. The term refers to a convergence of physical, augmented, and virtual reality in a shared online space. The idea is that three billion Facebook users have access to Zuckerberg's extended hybrid world that combines our physical world and a virtual-reality-augmented online world. Its basic ontology, physics, categories (time, space, and causality), the social structures of affordances and constraints, and incentive mechanisms, would all be designed and preprogramed. Everything that goes on in such a digital universe is captured.

Users will be able to take their avatars and goods all over the Metaverse. It will be an embodied Internet operated by many different players in a decentralized way, says Zuckerberg.[21] The Metaverse, he says, will bring unprecedented opportunities to individual's creative capacities, to artists, to people who want to work from home and work far from urban centers, and to people whose traditional environments offer inadequate educational and recreational opportunities. The "pitch" continues—this revolutionary communication technology will provide us with "torches of freedom" that supercharge our pursuit of self-governance and a worthwhile life.

Immersion in the Metaverse, however, would guarantee, for example, that digital twins—extensive data doubles—can be built of individuals who spend considerable time there. This would amount to a digital totalitarian environment where autonomy and agency would be a farce, since all renderings of self and other would be Facebook mediated and transformed into software items by unknown and black-box proprietary compilers. If we are worried by the power of Facebook and the fact that it lacks all democratic legitimacy to build and govern human lives by design, we should be freaking out about plans to even try to build a Metaverse.

## IN YOUR DREAMS

In a recent article on the ethical implications of dream incubation technologies, Robert Stickgold et al. describe how a beer company, Molson Coors, has designed a "new kind of advertising campaign" to infiltrate our dreams.[22] The company planned to use targeted dream incubation on approximately one hundred million people a couple of days prior to the Super Bowl. In return for a discount on packs of Coors beer, participants would have their dreams infiltrated with advertising about drinking Coors beer in a "clean, refreshing mountain environment."[23] (During their waking hours they would be exposed to images of this environment along with Coors Beer.) This was an enormous "experiment" to observe the efficacy of dream incubation advertising.

Incredibly, as the authors explain, with current advances in brain imaging that captures the "contents" of the brain and real-time communication between researchers and dreamers, this future is no science fiction fantasy. Business is already using dream incubation technology to insert their products into our dreams. The authors describe, for example, how video game and burger companies are selling their products using dream incubation technology, and describe a burgeoning research industry looking into how to "alter and motivate purchasing behaviour through dream and sleep hacking."[24]

Recent research into our dreams and sleep has shown their importance for shaping our memories, our emotional health, our understanding of the events of our day, and our crafting of our future choices and decision-making. Dream incubation technology has already been sufficiently developed to be effective in a range of ways beneficial to us, such as alleviating depression, trauma, and addiction, and by enabling creativity. As well, as Stickgold et al. suggest, it is not hard to see what a bonanza of new territory dream incubation technology presents for businesses to get access to us, and also just how ubiquitous the technology could so easily become.

We could, for example, passively consume the manipulation through the headphones on our smartphone, or, as the authors suggest, through the smart speakers forty million Americans already have in their bedrooms. As Stickgold et al. say, the potential for science fiction–like misuse is "as obvious as it is ominous."[25] Brain science, as they point out, has already been used to develop "addictive" design across social media and our smartphones, and so our waking lives. The coverage of business across the individual would be complete with effective access to our sleep and dreams.

Elisabeth Anscombe argued in 1958 that the notion of moral obligation didn't make sense in a secular society. According to Anscombe, the notion of moral obligation was associated with a divine authority, and that had disappeared.[26] We think something similar about the dependence of our valuing capacities upon certain social practices and conditions. Thus, as these continue to change so dramatically, ethics as we know it (and have known it for many thousands of years) may well disappear. The felicitous conditions for moral experiences of empathy, worth, merit and excellence, and ethical thinking and discourse may no longer be sustainable by online forms of life.

# Conclusion

The World Wide Web, according to its inventor Tim Berners Lee, spectacularly failed to live up to its initial promise of furthering autonomy, equality, justice, solidarity, and freedom.[27] Instead of leading to more inclusion, sharing, participation, and distribution of power, it has greatly contributed to the centralization of power and accumulation of wealth among a very small group of people who have exploited the dynamics and properties of networks and the network economy optimally.

Our democracies have been massively undermined and compromised by computational propaganda, micro-targeting, and AI-powered nudging and framing techniques. The online world has become the arena of silent but large-scale power grabs and data-driven profit-making.[28] Notwithstanding that there is an outpouring of devastatingly critical analyses of the ugly faces and perverse business models of Big Tech as well as their surreptitious use of sophisticated manipulations via a panoply of dark patterns, A/B testing, and behavioral advertising, their profits and market capitalisation have seen staggering growth.

The fate of moral agency of the past "century of self" may largely now be focused on the manipulation of this self that has become possible with revolutionary mass communication technologies. The connection between individuals and their promotion as consumers (and indeed as objects of consumption themselves) is now far more direct and complete than ever before, and is largely replacing the direct connections of our traditional worlds, both to each other and to our social practices, laws, and institutions.

As social worlds presenting a "metaverse" and colonizing our dreams develop, we will be sold their benefits along the lines of the template for mass manipulation Bernays created with his "torches of freedom" campaign. The information and social revolutions have been remarkably valuable revolutions in information access and connection to others. For many, however, like Bernays's cigarettes, life online has become an unhealthy addiction. More generally, life online has resulted in various, including some extreme and widespread, losses in our ability to appreciate value and reality.

The rise of Big Tech for three consecutive decades has been facilitated by governments and politicians across the world in the grip of neoliberal politics. All have had trouble getting their heads around the impact of computers and telecommunications. The digital tragedy that is now unfolding has many faces, and has a deplorable parallel in the climate tragedy that is unfolding. As we increasingly live online and the fog that prevents valuing thickens, we urgently need to expand our focus beyond the transcendental possibilities and toward understanding and addressing our remarkable capacities to ignore and destroy what we otherwise know and value. As Philip Kitcher asks, "What does it profit a species to gain the entire wisdom of Wikipedia, and lose both the best (or least bad?) form of government and its planet as well?"[29]

# Bibliography

Anscombe, G. E. M. "Modern Moral Philosophy." *Philosophy* 33, no. 124 (January 1958): 1–19.

Aristotle. *Nichomachean Ethics*. Translated by W. D. Ross. Oxford: Oxford University Press, 1980.

Ball, Edward. "The Mind of Dylann Roof." *New York Review of Books* 64, no. 5 (March 23, 2017): 12–16.

Bernays, Edward. *Propaganda*. New York: Horace Liveright, 1928.

Bernays, Edward. *The Engineering of Consent*. Norman: University of Oklahoma Press, 1955.

Cocking, Dean, and Jeroen van den Hoven. *Evil Online*. Oxford: Wiley-Blackwell, Oxford, 2018.

Cocking, Dean, and Jeroen van den Hoven. "Moral Fog and the Appreciation of Value." *Evil Online, Journal of Practical Ethics* (special issue). Oxford: Oxford University Press, 2021.

Cocking, Dean. "Friendship Online." In *Oxford Handbook of Digital Ethics*, edited by Carissa Veliz, 1–22. Oxford: Oxford University Press, 2021.

Frankl, Viktor E. *Man's Search for Meaning*. Boston, MA: Beacon Press, 2006. Originally published 1946.

Henson, Richard, G. "What Kant Might Have Said: Moral Worth and the Overdetermination of Dutiful Action." *The Philosophical Review* 88, no. 1 (January 1979): 39–54.

Kitcher, Philip. "Losing Your Way in the Fog: Reflections on Evil Online." *Evil Online, Journal of Practical Ethics* (special issue). Oxford: Oxford University Press, 2021.

Oreskes, Naomi, and Erik M. Conwa. *The Merchants of Doubt: How a Handful of Scientists Obscured the Truth from Tobacco Smoke to Climate Change*. New York: Bloomsbury Press, 2010.

Stickgold, Robert, Antonio Zadra, and AJH Haar. "Advertising in Dreams Is Coming: What Now?" June 7, 2021. https://dxe.pubpub.org/pub/dreamadvertising/release/1.

Zuboff, Soshanna. *The Age of Surveillance Capitalism: The Fight for a Human Future at the New Frontier of Power*. London: Profile Books, 2019.

# CHAPTER 11

# Becoming Good and Growing Up Online

*Dean Cocking and Brigid Evans*

## Abstract

Growing up online presents unprecedented obstacles to moral development, such as overexposure to bullying and pornography and a culture of pursuing attention, self-obsession, and short-term rewards. Are such problems a reflection of our infancy online? Even if we transcend such extremes, will problems for becoming good online remain? To answer these questions, we need to answer the question of how human beings become good. Moral education has been neglected by modern moral philosophy. Now, in the digital age, we lack contemporary guidance. In this chapter, we fill this gap by applying Aristotle's account of moral education to growing up online and assessing the challenges for becoming good.

### KEYWORDS

moral education, value appreciation, Aristotle, social media, young people, social practices, moral habits, experiments in living

## Introduction

Many are worried nowadays about children and young people growing up online. There are many specific worries about content and threats young people become exposed to, such as pornography and bullying. There are broad worries about how social media platforms are shaping people's lives generally, such as worries about addiction to the short-term rewards designed into these plat-forms—the instant and relentless likes, clicks, and attention.

For some, these problems reflect our infancy online. We are barely a couple of decades into the information and social revolutions. We can imagine a future where life online has matured. A future where we have weeded out the trolls, bullying, relentless self-obsession and pursuit of attention, the dominance of short-term rewards, the objectification, polarization, competitive-comparative understandings of one another . . . and so on. While we can imagine such a future, the way things are does not inspire great confidence that we are heading in the right direction. Second, even if we do transcend such negative extremes, will problems for our becoming good online remain?

To answer these questions, we first need to know what is involved and what is at stake in our moral education. How do human beings become persons? What do they (most) need to become good? These questions have been somewhat neglected by modern philosophy. Now in the digital age, we lack a contemporary guide concerning the impact of growing up online on our moral education. We fill this gap by developing and applying Aristotle's account of moral education to the digital age. Aristotle offers the most influential account of moral education, and in this chapter, we develop his account and use it to illustrate various challenges, some more and some less surmountable, that grow-ing up online presents for becoming good.

# Becoming Good: The Appreciation of Value

The information and social media revolutions have created unprecedented opportunities for moral education in terms of knowledge acquisition and con-nection to a diversity of people, lifestyles, and ideas. We might have reasonably expected that this would have brought with it a commensurate move forward in our moral understanding. After all, exposure and connection to a range of beliefs and lifestyles is commonly thought crucial to moral education. Thus, for instance, it is widely believed that integrated schooling fosters the developing autonomy of children by exposure to attitudes and lives other than those of their parents (or, say, their particular ethnic or sociopolitical group).

Now, children and young people grow up on the World Wide Web, an online life-world where, on a smartphone they rarely put down, they are exposed and connected to cultures and moralities from across the world (present and past). In some ways, this is the most integrated "school" there has ever been. Yet, we have not seen anything like a commensurate move forward in moral understanding, much less in the moral education of children and young people. In fact, the online information and social revolutions have enabled widespread denial of science, disregard for democracy, and social disconnection. Instead of supercharging our moral (and rational) progress, the digital age has presented worries (of notable kind and degree) that we are devolving.[1]

In addition to the above particular and general contemporary worries about online worlds, there is a raft of other important and well-known features of life online implicated in our apparent devolution. For example, social media's business model has an enormous, broad influence on providing online worlds with a dominance of short-term rewards, driving us to seek attention for its own sake and to live in filter bubbles and echo chambers. All such manipulations are designed to maximize our engagement on the platforms, which, in turn, maximizes the commercial interests of its owners, associated businesses, and advertisers. As a result, users have also been increasingly driven to commodify and sell themselves.[2]

To better understand these and other worries about growing up online, we need to look more directly at the nature of moral education. For it is our moral education that ought to guide us in our encounters with these moral missteps and seductions. The prospects for moral education (including maintenance) depend primarily upon the development of our capacities to *appreciate* value. Questions about the foundational nature of our values have long occupied moral philosophy. However, the question of how we appreciate value has not been so widely discussed. In *The Practice of Value*, Joseph Raz makes a spectacular contribution across both fronts, arguing that there is a very tight dependence of values upon social practice: values only come into existence by being presented to us in social practices.[3]

In reply, Christine Korsgaard argues that it is not our shared practices that create values and give us moral reasons; it is *us,* our shared "humanity" as beings capable of evaluative judgment about how to be and what to do. It is our very nature that enables the creating and conferring of value. As evidence, she describes how the appreciation of natural beauty, for instance, need not depend upon social practices supporting such appreciation: "I think you could be dazzled by a spectacular sunset even if it is the only one you ever saw, or if no one in your culture talked about such things."[4]

However, even if we agree with Korsgaard that it is capacities within us, rather than external forces like social practices, that are the ultimate source of value, these capacities within us are very limited and vulnerable. As a result, we commonly fail to appreciate value. Indeed, as Aristotle highlighted, even if values are presented to us through social practices, even if they are made "loud and clear" to us through explicit instruction, we nevertheless routinely fail to appreciate them. While argument, or appeals to moral reasoning, he says, might: "have power to encourage and stimulate the generous-minded among our youth, and to make a character which is gently born, and a true lover of what is noble, ready to be possessed by virtue, they are not able to encourage the *many* to nobility and goodness."[5]

For Aristotle, argument, or the force of moral reason alone, will not suffice to make us (or most of us) good. Whatever force reason might have requires the *prior* support of our having cooperative inclinations to act in right and good ways. However, most of us, he says, are not (overly or unambiguously) blessed by nature to be so inclined. So how do we develop the (generally) required prior support of inclination to behave well to get the enterprise of our becoming good off the ground?

Aristotle's well-known answer is that good habit formation is required and foundational to teaching us to become good. Good habit formation plays this foundational role by supplying the required inclinations to enable the rational understanding and persuasion of argument:

> the soul of the student must first have been cultivated by means of habits for noble joy and noble hatred, like earth which is to nourish the seed. For he who lives as passion directs will not hear argument that dissuades him, nor understand it if he does; and how can we persuade one in such a state to change his ways? And in general passion seems to yield not to argument but to force. The character, then, must somehow be there already with a kinship to virtue, loving what is noble and hating what is base.[6]

While Aristotle thought formal moral lessons and instruction were radically insufficient to motivate us morally, absent of inculcating good habits, he emphasizes the role of reason in directing and regulating the inculcation of good habits. Thus, we come to find pleasure and pains in the right places (i.e., where these places are truly pleasurable and painful). He did not think of (desirable) habit formation as developing instincts that bypass reason. On the contrary, he highlighted how, without reason forming our habits, our habits would become indifferent and resistant to reason.[7] Nevertheless, for reason to play this regulative role, our inclinations will already, or, at once, also need to be amenable to reason. Otherwise, our inclinations will seem unconnected or hostile to appeals to reason.

While the education of our capacities for value appreciation importantly requires habit formation regulated by reason, this will still not be sufficient for maintaining our goodness. As Aristotle also famously argues, we will need the force of the law to support our governance by reasoned habits:

> it is difficult to get from youth up a right training for virtue if one has not been brought up under right laws; for to live temperately and hardily is not pleasant to most people, especially when they are

young. For this reason their nurture and occupations should be fixed by law; for they will not be painful when they have become customary . . . it is surely not enough that when they are young they should get the right nurture and attention: since they must, even when they are grown up, practice and be habituated to them, we shall need laws for this as well, and generally speaking to cover the whole of life . . .[8]

Moral education, then, requires the "right nurture and attention" and the support of laws to enable us to "practice and be habituated" to the right and the good, and so guide our inclinations to track and be regulated by reason.[9] Moreover, to be effective, the nurture, attention, and appropriate censure mechanisms that habituate us to the regulation of reason must operate comprehensively across our lives (i.e., both within the private household and across the broader sociopolitical scene of laws, social practices, conventions, and formal and informal rewards and penalties).

## Obstacles to Becoming Good

A central obstacle to becoming good is human selfishness. Kant championed our capacities of reason to appreciate value irrespective of our inclinations (whether cooperative or not) and irrespective of direction from others, social practices, and the world around us. In a well-known description, he describes how such appreciation (the good will) would "shine like a jewel for itself, as something having its full worth in itself."[10] As well, however, Kant thought it possible that the world had never seen a human being with such purity of focus on the north star of morality, and that our selfishness, what he called our self-conceit (our giving primacy to our "inclinations" over the moral law) was ubiquitous and significant across human nature.[11]

Thus, while Kant and his followers locate the creation of values within individuals rather than social practices, given they also think our self-conceit an enormous obstacle to our capacities to create value, they should concede we nevertheless remain in dire need of social practices to curb our self-conceit and help enable our individual valuing capacities. Irrespective of the dispute between Kantians (like Korsgaard) and others (like Raz) concerning the genesis of our values, we can all recognize the need for social practices to enable our capacities to appreciate values, whether these are values we have created ourselves or they are ones that social practices have presented to us.

As well as self-conceit, there are many other widely shared vices, such as envy, greed, and self-righteousness, presenting notable obstacles to our becoming good. Iris Murdoch highlighted another widely shared obstacle—our anxieties. She describes how our self-conscious condition sources not only our selfishness but also fundamental anxieties.[12] Murdoch tends to run these together, but while our selfishness has long been regarded as the chief obstacle to our becoming good, our anxieties and insecurities of self-consciousness present fundamental obstacles of their own. As well, they require very different kinds of responses.

For example, while punishments may well often be appropriate responses to curb our self-conceit, they do not seem (generally) to be an appropriate way to address our anxieties and insecurities. Instead, our anxieties of self-consciousness need settings and social practices to help lighten their burden and minimize their damaging effects upon our understanding and agency.

Accordingly, we have developed psychosocial practices to help us put them aside, such as by creating safe, protected spaces for play and experimentation. These are settings that allow us to make mistakes, and parents, teachers, mentors, and so on to provide guidance and support (often indirectly) in recognition of how the anxieties and insecurities of self-consciousness undermine us. Thus, the development of our capacities to learn and to appreciate value are significantly and unavoidably socially dependent (i.e., on settings and guidance providing the right kind of attention and nurture to help us, for instance, to set aside and better deal with our widely shared obstacles to learning and valuing).

There is a lot to learn as individuals; we take decades to mature, and there are many obstacles, both internal and external, to block the way. Furthermore, we are never altogether morally mature, at least in the sense of our being able to govern ourselves absent of the support (including censure) of others and the sociopolitical institutions and social practices of the world within which we live. We never become "self-sufficient" in virtue. Our understanding and maintaining of our capacities for valuing remain socially dependent; moral education and maintenance are relational, not just from the beginning, but to the end (but obviously not in the same ways and degrees).

# Growing Up Online

The "nurture and attention" we need from parents, teachers, institutions, social practices, and so forth to guide us toward governance by reason, toward becoming good, must obviously be centrally concerned with addressing the chief obstacles that would undermine our being governed by reason and becoming good. There are many social practices and settings that we have developed over millennia to address and provide the space to help us navigate our way through such obstacles. Mill described how our moral education and the development of our valuing capacities require that we engage in "experiments in living" (i.e., that we practice various lifestyles and ways of being to empower our choices and develop autonomy).[13]

As noted previously, however, the digital age has not delivered the explosion in exposure and connection to varied attitudes and lifestyles one might have imagined. On the contrary, there are significant worries about increasing isolation, polarization, and disconnection from one another. So too for the fate of "experiments in living." Instead of expanding our exposure and our experiments in living to build our moral education, we have seen a great loss, distortion, and hijacking of the practicing and experimenting in living upon which our moral education is built.

The social dependence of our understanding and capacities for valuing is, of course, a double-edged sword. As well as being foundational to our becoming good, this social dependence makes us very vulnerable to settings and guidance that demolish our capacities to become good rather than provide them with the right kinds of nurture and attention. (This is commonly the fate of those who have suffered extreme forms of trauma when they are young.) The failures of the settings and guidance of our online life-worlds provide many varied and extreme illustrations of the social dependence of our understanding and valuing and of just how vulnerable this makes us. The social dependence of valuing, then, is also (all too often) a central obstacle to our becoming good.

There are countless cases of the digital age crushing children and young people's capacities to "practice" and engage in their "experiments in living." The early landmark case of the so-called *Star Wars* Kid highlighted how the massive exposure of innocent play could cause monumental shaming, ridicule, and bullying.[14] In our traditional worlds, we have long engaged in various practices to provide "protective" psychosocial spaces to support the early practicing of young people regarding self-expression, connecting with others, engaging in activities, finding their "scene," and so forth. We very much need to do so as, even without an especially hostile environment (say, of trolls and bullies), our self-consciousness and self-doubts can be utterly crippling to self-expression, communication, and connection with others. It does not take much to set us back, and it takes a lot of help and support to navigate our way forward.

Increasingly, we may address or redress the orgies of shame, trolling, and bullying that have overly characterized the digital age. As suggested earlier, we might imagine a future where we have moved beyond shaming, trolling, bullying, and so forth. Relatedly, many are worried about the problem of not being able to forget, put aside, or move on from things we have done, such as embarrassing or significant mistakes.[15] If our "practicing" risks such mistakes, since they will be around forever to haunt us, the practicing and experiments in living we need for our moral education may face extinction online. Perhaps, however, we can design and regulate life online so that unwanted content can (rightly, appropriately) be removed, and we are not forever haunted by our past and can forget, learn, move on, and so forth.

Even if we can do so, the main worries about the digital age extinguishing various forms of practicing and experiments in living needed for our moral education remain. Lost or distorted online is much of the territory and milieu that provided the psychosocial spaces in our traditional worlds for the practice needed in our moral education. The complex and nuanced plural worlds of our public, private, and intimate lives are largely flatlined as we live on screens. As a result, much of the complex territory enabling significant forms of valuing have been undermined, such as forms of polite disregard and respect for one another's privacy in public, or of quiet communion with one another, for instance, when tragedy or some great difficulty strikes.[16]

Various measures are being undertaken across social media platforms to provide improved moral instruction and regulation, such as algorithms to identify apparent bullying or harassment or prompt reflection with something like: "Is that what you really want to say?" Many online environments require you to agree to rules of conduct before entering the space. Some have introduced "welcome courses" where you go through the values of the space when you first join. Other groups have strike systems of engaging first (for example, they discuss the concerning behavior or belief and attempt to correct or educate), remove second (if the person does not engage in the first step, or repeats their behavior, then they are removed).

The surveillance aspect helps in one important direction—namely, redressing the seeming moral isolation of users by inserting notice that the community, socially and legally, will hold you to (some) account for your conduct, just as we have long done in our traditional worlds—not just to address extremes, but to regulate for pro-social conduct broadly across our ordinary, everyday lives, such as with "Don't walk on the grass" signs.[17]

As described above, however, Aristotle provides a compelling account of the limitations of moral instruction and messaging in moving us to become good. Without inclinations to be moral that have been well trained to be regulated by reason and without the backing of formal and informal laws and social practices, we might as well be delivering our message with the microphone turned off, or by social media posts when the website is down. Insofar as moral education online is restricted to providing reliable information, moral instruction, messaging, appeals to reason, and our "better selves," it will not be very effective.

Similarly, as we have seen, it is also crucial to moral education that a suite of laws and other censure mechanisms, such as negative reactive attitudes from others, apply to us and hold us to account. To be educative, of course, such consequences need to be appropriate to our conduct and explained to help us see the light. As with moral instruction, however, we cannot expect even righteous application of censure to be very effective absent of the support of the right kind of nurture and attention from others and our settings—in particular, accepted and effective authoritative guidance of practice that habituates our inclinations to be regulated by reason. Otherwise, as with the impotence of instruction alone, forms of censure plus such instruction will still miss this central plank of our becoming good.

Authoritative guidance from others is essential for habituating our inclinations to be regulated by reason. This guidance includes modeling good habits and reasoning practices and providing exposure to value, positive and negative reinforcement of habits, and accountability, among a wealth of other supports. Recognizing moral guides as authoritative, however, is vital for taking their messages, their censure and praise, seriously. So too, for understanding and internalizing the reasons and habits we might forge with them.

While it is nothing new to see our guides (parents, teachers) as "out of touch," this sense of disconnect has been exacerbated by the rate at which technology is changing. Traditional moral guides have not necessarily "grown up online"; as a result, the experience and guidance they bring to forging good moral habits online may be lacking. So too, even where good guidance is not lacking, the *authority* of their guidance online may go unrecognized.

The risk is that young people grow up in the new world of social media, where value attribution and norms of conduct are mostly set by their peers. These are worlds where the influence of parents, teachers, and other traditional moral guides has largely been removed, and where, in any case, they may have little generational experience and knowledge to provide much guidance. This digital co-opting of traditional moral education distorts and impedes good habit formation, leading to moral immaturity and poor or immoral habits and character formation.

The limitation of traditional moral guides in influencing online behavior can result in a non-transference of "offline" moral guidance into online interactions. That is, while moral guides may help produce typically pro-social children, those same children may behave immorally online. In reverse, failed moral guidance (either through the limitation of traditional moral guides to extend their moral teaching into online spaces, or where moral guidance is co-opted by online peers ill-suited to develop the moral character of others) can hijack moral character formation. This can lead individuals to take their ill-formed online habits and apply them to the real world.

How do we protect and replicate the moral guidance we need from various key players, institutions, social practices, and settings across our personal and public lives (families, teachers/schools, social practices for recreation)? This relational development in our understanding and practices is critical to our moral education. The engagement and influence of all these players across our personal and public lives, along with the social practices and settings within which they have been developed, primarily provides the dialogue and moral spaces (informal and formal) that support reason regulating our inclinations and habit formation.

For example, our parents effectively monitor the worlds in which we live, such as at home and school, and our teachers have an authoritative place in our education. Online, however, not only has the effective moral guidance of parents taken a huge hit, so too has the rational authority of science and democracy. Likewise, the authority of teachers in physical and political sciences has taken an enormous hit at the hands of the pseudosciences and conspiracy theories gaining widespread traction online.

# Conclusion

The primary issue for moral education and our becoming good is developing our capacities to appreciate value. Developing our valuing capacities is unavoidably and heavily reliant upon the help of others and the sociopolitical worlds within which we find ourselves. However, as we increasingly live online, many of the social practices enabling the dialogue and psychic space to develop this understanding and to receive this guidance have been lost.

The authoritative guidance of our parents, mentors, and teachers has taken a severe hit, swamped and undermined by a sea of misinformation and nonsense online. In any case, however, the right kind of "nurture and attention" for forming habits regulated by reason and the promotion of value appreciation often cannot be replicated online. The territory for expression, communication, and connection with one another is too blunt, riding roughshod over much of the plurality of our traditional worlds upon which many social practices supporting valuing have been developed.

One overused educative response to individuals facing morally challenging environments is that they need to become more resilient (and so we need to teach more resilience). Resilience, of course, is important, especially to help people's moral governance to survive challenging environments. Perhaps, then, given that young people are often at the front line of social media use and cannot rely too much on the guidance of parents, educators, and others who usually lag way behind, resilience does have an important place in moral education as we live online.

The far more fundamental reality and problem, however, is that while we may have special reasons to develop such resilience further, it is folly (indeed, offensive folly) to dump the problem on individuals or to suppose we should expect any such thing without a suite of external world supports. Across the personal and public domains, we need a suite of educative supports, such as role models, reactive attitudes and forms of censure to enable and maintain young people's moral understanding and character, including their resilience. More emphasis needs to be put on identifying and building the capacities of those around the individual so that unreasonable expectations of individual moral resilience are not asked, and where asked, are supported.

There is little chance of returning to our traditional offline worlds without social media platforms. Therefore, the future of moral education will primarily be written in better, more value-sensitive algorithms for these platforms, and many are already working in these design areas. There are some good examples of better value-sensitive designed platforms that support our moral education. Reddit, for instance, aims to restore some authoritative guidance across various issues and so help us sort out misinformation, true from false. So too, false and misleading tweets are being flagged as suspect, with links provided to accurate and trustworthy informants—the flagging of President Trump's tweets being a particularly public example. Similarly, recent posts on Facebook, Twitter, Instagram, and so on that mention COVID-19 or its vaccination are all linked to trusted, accurate information.

Online platforms that give us more reliable information and restore some authority in such ways are, of course, a good thing. Again, however, Aristotle makes a compelling case about the limits of this approach—the limits of providing correct information, even correct explicit instruction about the good, for our becoming good. Accordingly, many of our social practices aiming to enable our capacities for value appreciation are not so much (or even at all) about giving us more, rather than less, accurate information. Many social practices are about providing appropriate mechanisms of censure to curb our selfishness and the morally bad conduct it generates. Here their role is not just to punish and manipulate our self-interest but also to educate our understanding of ourselves and our conduct.

The appropriateness of the measures is especially crucial, since otherwise, where the penalties are too harsh, we create righteous resentment and almost certainly cause any morally educative lessons to be lost. As noted above, life online has delivered something of an orgy of inappropriate punishments—a culture of free-wheeling shame and blame. Perhaps, though, we can turn this around.

In any case, many morally educative social practices are also not just about manipulating self-interest or educating us through censure. Many are about helping us set aside or navigate other common obstacles to our becoming good, such as our significant learning limits and the anxieties of our self-consciousness. Thus, for instance, we have developed social practices and settings to provide safe, protective psychosocial spaces to help us set aside and navigate the crushing effects of self-consciousness and to help us engage in the practicing and experimentation in living that our learning limitations need for us to appreciate value better.

It is hard to see how we can engage in much of this "practicing in public" as we live on screens. The future for becoming good in an online world, therefore, also requires us to better identify the obstacles to becoming good that we can only really address in our traditional worlds, and to focus on how we might improve life offline to deliver the right kind of "nurture and attention" we need to do so.

# References

Aristotle. *The Nicomachean Ethics.* Translated by W. D. Ross. Oxford: Oxford University Press, 1980.

Cocking, Dean, and Jeroen van den Hoven. "Moral Fog and the Appreciation of Value." *Evil Online, Journal of Practical Ethics* (special issue). Oxford: Oxford University Press, 2021.

Kant, Immanuel. *The Groundwork of the Metaphysic of Morals*, Ak 4:394. Translated and analyzed by H. J. Paton. New York: HarperCollins, 1964.

Kant, Immanuel. "Religion within the Boundaries of Mere Reason." In *Immanuel Kant: Religion and Rational Authority*, 39–216. Translated and edited by A. W. Wood and G. di Giovanni. Cambridge: Cambridge University Press, 1996.

Mill, John Stuart. *On Liberty* (vol. 18). In *The Collected Works of J. S. Mill*, 260–67. Edited by J. M. Robson. Toronto: University of Toronto Press, 1977.

Murdoch, Iris. "The Sovereignty of Good over Other Concepts." In *The Virtues: Contemporary Essays on Moral Character*, 84–98. Edited by Robert B. Kruschwitz and Robert C. Roberts. Belmont, CA: Wadsworth Publishing, 1987.

Ronson, Jon. *So You've Been Publicly Shamed?* London: Picador, 2015.

Stuart, Forrest. *Ballad of the Bullet: Gangs, Drill Music and the Power of Online Infamy.* Princeton, NJ: Princeton University Press, 2020.

Wallace, R. Jay, ed. *Joseph Raz: The Practice of Value (The Berkeley Tanner Lectures).* Oxford: Oxford University Press, 2003.

CHAPTER 12

# The Privacy Paradox

*Edward H. Spence*

## Abstract

This chapter will examine and evaluate the reasons for the "privacy paradox" and through a normative analysis of the concept of privacy in the digital age assess its normative implications for individuals and collectively for society. The chapter will first examine and evaluate the normative issues and requirements concerning the privacy of our information as individual agents, as well as our collective responsibility for safeguarding the privacy of our digital information against the normative, manipulative, and invasive normative violations of the Big Tech companies for their gain at the expense of the common good of society and the global community.

**KEY WORDS**

privacy, autonomy, Big Tech, freedom, dual obligation information theory (DOIT)

## Introduction

> Privacy and autonomy are related because losses of privacy make it easier for others to interfere with your life.
> —Véliz 2020, 72

This chapter will examine and evaluate the reasons for the "privacy paradox"[1] and through a normative analysis of the concept of privacy as manifested in the digital age assess its normative implications for individuals and collectively for society. To begin, let me first say that strictly speaking the "privacy paradox" is not a logical paradox as such, but a cognitive inconsistency in how one thinks and how one acts, by commission or omission, which involves a conflict of interest between the epistemic concepts of justification, motivation, and compliance concerning one's beliefs and actions. The chapter will first examine and evaluate the normative issues and requirements concerning the privacy of our information as individual agents, as well as our collective responsibility for safeguarding the privacy of our digital information against the normative, manipulative, and invasive violations of the Big Tech companies for their gain at the expense of the common good of society and the global community.

# A Universal Model for Evaluating the Normative Quality of Digital Information

This section will examine privacy in relation to the normative structure of information, and digital information specifically, to demonstrate that the violation of privacy is ethically wrong and unacceptable. The object is to describe and demonstrate a meta-theoretical framework for the normative evaluation of digital information in terms of its inherent epistemological, ethical, and eudaimonic categories. The aim is to demonstrate the conceptual relationship between information, knowledge, and well-being and the normative commitments to which information, understood as a type of knowledge, gives rise.

My argument for the inherent normative structure of information as a process of communicative action has been examined and demonstrated at length in previous publications (Spence 2021, 2009).[2] In this chapter the primary aim is to provide a summary of that argument sufficient for establishing an initial theoretical standpoint from which to further motivate and develop the normative relationship between information, knowledge, and well-being that would allow us to show how the privacy of one's digital information is an ethical right and its abuse therefore a violation of that right. The demonstration of that normative relationship, at once *epistemic, ethical,* and *eudemonic*,[3] will demonstrate a direct normative link between information and well-being. Its purpose is to provide a methodological approach in terms of a wisdom-theoretic model (Spence 2011) for the normative evaluation of that relationship and its implications and impact for individuals and societies generally, and especially, for the purpose of this chapter, with regard to privacy.

## THE INHERENT NORMATIVE STRUCTURE OF INFORMATION AND KNOWLEDGE

In describing the *dual obligation information theory (DOIT)* (Spence 2009, 2021) this chapter will employ an epistemological account of *semantic information* based on a minimal *nuclear* definition of information (Dretske 1999, 44–45 and 86). Following Luciano Floridi (Floridi 2005), information is defined as "well-formed meaningful data that is truthful" and following Dretske information is defined as "an objective commodity capable of yielding knowledge" and knowledge, in turn, is defined as "information caused belief."

The reference to both Floridi's and Dretske's notions of *information* in this chapter is not intended to make any critical theoretical comparisons between those two accounts of information, which lies beyond the scope of this chapter. It is rather intended to highlight the one essential element that those accounts have in common, namely, that what is necessary for both information and knowledge is truth.

Using the aforementioned minimal account of information, we can now develop an *inherent normative account of information*, which demonstrates and describes the generic epistemological and ethical commitments that necessarily arise in the dissemination of semantic information, specifically as a process of *communication*.[4]

Briefly, the argument is as follows (Spence 2009): insofar as information is a type of knowledge (it must be capable of yielding knowledge, and one must be able to learn from it) it must comply with the epistemological conditions of knowledge, specifically, that of truth. And insofar as the dissemination of information is based on the justified and rightful expectation among its disseminators and especially its users that such information should meet the minimal condition of truth, then the disseminators of information are committed to certain widely recognized and accepted epistemological criteria. Those epistemic criteria will in the main comprise the objectivity as well as the independence, reliability, accuracy, and trustworthiness of the *sources* that generate the information. The epistemology of information, in turn, commits its disseminators to certain ethical principles and values, such as honesty, sincerity, truthfulness, trustworthiness, and reliability (also epistemological values), and fairness, including justice, which requires the equal distribution of informational goods to all citizens. Thus, in terms of its dissemination, as a process of communication, information has an intrinsic normative structure that commits everyone involved in its creation, production, search, communication, consumption, and multiple other uses, to epistemological and ethical norms. These norms being intrinsic to the normative structure of information with regard to all its disseminating modes are rationally unavoidable and thus not merely optional.

## INFORMATION AND UNIVERSAL RIGHTS

The following associated argument is to show that in addition to committing its disseminators to unavoidable epistemological and ethical standards by virtue of its own inherent normative structure in terms of truth, information as a process of *communication* commits its disseminators to respect for peoples' rights to freedom and well-being. This is by virtue of the inherent normative structure of *action* and specifically *informational action*, due to its essential features of freedom and well-being (Spence 2006, 2009; Gewirth 1978).[5] Insofar as the communication of information constitutes a type of informational action, information as a process and product of communication must not be disseminated in ways that violate peoples' fundamental rights to freedom and well-being (*generic rights*), individually or collectively, or undermine their capacity for self-fulfillment (Gewirth 1998).

In addition, information must as far as possible be disseminated in ways that secure and promote peoples' generic rights and capacity for self-fulfillment (*positive rights*) when those rights cannot be secured or promoted by the individuals themselves and can be so secured and promoted at no comparable cost to their disseminators. The concept of *self-fulfillment* that I am using here is the neostoic equivalent of the stoic concept of *eudaimonia* that I ascribe to Alan Gewirth (Spence 2006, ch. 10; 2021). Due to constrains of space, and because it is beyond the scope and focus of this chapter, I will not attempt to provide a detailed justification for Alan Gewirth's argument for the principle of generic consistency (PGC) on which his derivation of rights is based.[6]

Applying the PGC to information, we can now make the further argument that information generally, both analog and digital, must not be disseminated in ways that violate informational agents' rights to freedom (FR) and well-being (WB), individually or collectively (*negative rights*). Moreover, information must as far as possible be disseminated in ways that secure and promote the informational agents' rights to FR and WB (positive rights). This places significant and important responsibility on the disseminators of information and in particular the media, especially journalists, both offline and online, as well as social media.

In conclusion, the dual obligation information theory (DOIT) demonstrates the dual-normative structure of *informational action*, to which all informational agents are committed by universal necessity, including the media (the legacy media of the Fourth Estate, the digital media of the Fifth Estate [Elliott and Spence 2018] and the Big Tech network media of the Sixth Estate [Spence 2020] such as Facebook and Google). Information generally can be epistemologically and ethically evaluated *internally* by reference to its inherent normative structure. Insofar as the ethical values to which the inherent normative structure of information gives rise requires that the informational agents' rights to FR and

WB should be respected, secured, and promoted, those values are also mandated by the principle of generic consistency (PGC), and thus information can also be *externally* evaluated by reference to the PGC. *Expressive information* can also be evaluated either internally, externally, or both in this way. For example, *identity theft* on the Internet is morally wrong both because it is untruthful (internal evaluation) and because it can cause harm (external evaluation).

# The Right to Privacy and Its Abuse by the Big Tech Companies

Having examined the natural rights that all informational agents have in virtue of the inherent normative structure of information, we are now in a position to examine those fundamental rights of freedom and well-being in terms of the notion of privacy and how that privacy is systemically violated by the Big Tech companies, such as Facebook and Google, through their opaque and unaccountable persuasive algorithms.

As Mittelstadt et al. (2016, 10) correctly observe, "algorithms are also driving a transformation of notions of privacy. . . . A right to identity derived from informational privacy interests suggests that opaque or secretive profiling is problematic." In the important and timely new book *Privacy Is Power*, Carissa Véliz (2020) also correctly argues that,

> Surveillance threatens freedom, equality, democracy, autonomy, creativity, and intimacy. We have been lied to time and again, and our data is being stolen to be used against us. No more. Having too little privacy is at odds with having well-functioning societies. Surveillance capitalism needs to go. It will take some time and effort, but we can and will reclaim privacy. (5)
>
> Aristotle argued that part of being virtuous is all about having emotions that are appropriate to the circumstances. When your right to privacy is violated, it is appropriate to feel moral indignation. It is not appropriate to feel indifference or resignation. . . . Privacy is a right for good reasons. Defend it. (201)

Véliz is of course right in her insightful analysis. Clearly, as per our aforementioned analysis of the universal rights to freedom and well-being agents have with regard to the dissemination of digital information, the control of one's informational privacy is a central part of what it is to be a fully autonomous agent capable of exercising *internal control* over one's judgments and choices made on the basis of one's own volition.[7] The idea that third parties can access one's informational privacy, especially without one's informed consent, and not uncommonly without their knowledge, is a fundamental violation of those rights. For our judgments, choices, volition as free autonomous agents should always be within our control as they have a direct impact on our well-being and eudaimonia. To allow third parties to share control over our informational privacy would amount to surrendering control over ourselves, and hence to our freedom, dignity, and integrity, consequently allowing others to determine what our well-being ought to be according to their interests, not ours.

As Mittelstadt et al. (2016) observe,

> Identity is increasingly influenced by knowledge produced through analytics that makes sense of growing streams of behavioural data. The "identifiable individual" is not necessarily a part of these processes. . . . Profiling seeks to assemble individuals into meaningful groups, for which identity is irrelevant (Floridi, 2012; Hildebrandt, 2011; Leese, 2014). Van Wel and Royakkerss (2004: 133) argue that external identity constructions by algorithms is a type of *de-individualisation* or a "tendency of judging and treating people on the basis of group characteristics instead of on their own individual characteristics and merit." . . . The individual's informational identity (Floridi, 2011) is breached by meaning generated by algorithms that link the subject to others within a dataset (Vries, 2010). . . . A lack of recourse mechanisms for data subjects to question the validity of algorithmic decisions further exacerbates the challenges of *controlling identity and data about oneself* (Schermer, 2011). (emphasis added).

Needless to say, the above astute observations and comments made by Mittelstadt et al. raise some very important and crucial normative issues concerning autonomy, self-sovereignty, identity, privacy, freedom, and especially control, which, as previously emphasized, is the overarching normative issue with regard to the external control exercised by the Big Tech companies over us; as well as the internal control we as individuals ought to have over our own autonomy, freedom, dignity, and integrity, as both agents and importantly as persons owed unconditional respect and an absolute right to our dignity (Spence 2021, ch. 7).

As clearly indicated in the above-quoted passage, our individual identity is under threat by the digitalization and datafication of our identity through opaque, incomprehensible, and unaccountable algorithms that construct our digital identities without our knowledge or consent, based on statistical data gathered at group level that has very little, if anything, in common with our natural individual identities. And yet our group-level identities are the ones that are used as the basis for making decisions that affect our natural identities, which can result, through impersonal profiling, in unjust outcomes for our individual natural selves.

In a paradoxical turn, our digital identity is and can be set in normative opposition and seemingly in conflict with our natural identity, when through profiling someone may be deemed guilty of a crime presumed to have been committed, or likely to be committed, on the basis of the profile of their *digital group-level identity*, which their natural identity is unaware of having committed.

Yet another insidious and potentially crucial existential problem, not just for data subjects but humanity generally, is the split of our identity into two separate identities: a *group digital-identity* controlled externally by algorithms, and our *natural individual identity* controlled internally by us as individuals, but whose autonomy, however, is also precariously under the intended systemic control of the persuasive technologies of the Big Tech companies, such as Facebook and Google. Hence, the abuse of our privacy by the Big Tech companies takes place at two levels: one is the systemic harvesting of the data of our natural individual identity, which is then used to engineer our *group digital-identity* and disseminated to third parties for profit, most often without our knowledge and consent, which as we shall examine below in the Cambridge Analytica case, undermined the democratic system and its associated institutions in the 2016 US presidential elections and the Brexit Referendum in the United Kingdom.

For those of us acquainted with *Star Trek*, this issue of opposing and conflicting identities, our *digital group-identity* vs. our *natural individual-identity*, should remind us of the collective digital identity of the Borg: an alien species that conquers other planets and "assimilates" their citizens within its digital collective hive, without the consent or willingness of the victims, who consequently lose their own personal and individual identities. When the Borg meet resistance from potential victims, their warning is that "resistance is futile." In the *Star Trek* series *Voyager*, "Seven of Nine," a young human woman assimilated by the Borg when still a child, is rescued by the human crew of *Voyager* and restored to her original individual identity, but not before many difficult changes and adaptations that she has to face in learning how to become an individual human person again, with her own thoughts, judgments, choices, volition, and importantly, privacy. One could say, at least metaphorically, that "Seven of Nine's" case is not only one of *identity-theft* but also one of *identity-amnesia* one suffers when one is assimilated into a collective identity hive, through the digitalization and dehumanization of their natural personal identity, which denies them their own natural individual identity, privacy, and autonomy.

This raises a paradox. The autonomy of our natural individual identity (NII) is systemically and methodically usurped by the Big Tech companies through their persuasive technologies, by their autonomous algorithms, which are used through profiling to create our digital group identity (DGI), which is then applied to further undermine our digital individual identity and consequently our autonomy and privacy, which can result in unfair and unjust outcomes resulting from statistical group-level profiling. For the Big Tech companies, it is a case of having their cake (their algorithms) and eating it too (our data). As Shoshana Zuboff (2019) astutely points out, in the surveillance capitalism era, *we are the product*. A very valuable data product, a commodity that the Big Tech companies sell to third parties to make themselves extremely wealthy, very powerful, and very unaccountable.

# The Cambridge Analytica Case

One of the biggest and most controversial cases involving a breach of data subjects' privacy was the Cambridge Analytica case,[8] which exposed the sale of millions of users' data to third-party information brokers without the users' knowledge or consent. As a result of that exposure Facebook was fined $5 billion USD as part of a settlement with the Federal Trade Commission (*USA Today* 2019) and 500,000 GBP by the UK Information Commissioner's Office. What is of interest about this case and other similar cases involving both Facebook and Google as well as other tech companies is the role the Fourth and Fifth Estates played in exposing the unethical and illegal practices of those companies. It's a case of the convergent media of the Fourth and Fifth Estates keeping a check on the Sixth Estate that comprises these new tech media companies (Spence 2021, ch. 6).

A key question of this case and other similar cases involving the collection and distribution of users' data to unknown third parties to be used for unknown purposes, was whether Facebook had obtained *informed consent* from its 87 million users whose data they collected and passed on to Cambridge Analytica. It transpires that only 270,000 Facebook users gave their consent by installing an app that allowed Facebook to collect information from their Facebook profiles and those of their friends' profiles, which they then provided to the makers of the app, who in turn passed it on to Cambridge Analytica. But apart from the 270,000 Facebook users who had installed the app and thus could be presumed to have given their consent, though not necessarily for the purpose for which it was used, most of the remaining 87 million Facebook users whose information was harvested for use by Cambridge Analytica were unaware their data had been collected in this way and that it would be used to form voter targeting for Trump's presidential election campaign (Tufekci and Zeynep 2018). So, most of those Facebook users not only did not give consent for the harvesting of their information by Facebook, but moreover did not provide consent for the purpose of its use, that is, to target voters in the Trump presidential election. Because of those reasons Facebook was found guilty of a breach of users' privacy and fined by the Federal Trade Commission, as well as by the UK Information Commissioner's Office.

## THE NORMATIVE VIOLATIONS BY FACEBOOK IN THE CAMBRIDGE ANALYTICA CASE

Having determined the key facts of the Cambridge Analytica case, let us examine the specific normative issues of this case by application of the DOIT principle we examined earlier.

Facebook's part in allowing the harvesting of its user's information for use by Cambridge Analytica was an epistemic and ethical violation of their *right to informed consent*, their *right to privacy*, and crucially, by implication, their *right to autonomy*, as they were offered no knowledge that their information was collected and sent to a third party, and furthermore this was done without their knowledge of the purpose for which their information was to be used. In doing so, Facebook violated the fundamental communication principles of trust, reliability, and truthfulness, as well as its users' rights to freedom and well-being, which supports their fundamental right to autonomy and privacy as informational communicative agents (Spence 2020, 2021a). In sum, Facebook's actions (in this case at least), by omission and by commission, were unethical.

# The Shared Moral Responsibility of Citizens

If we know or suspect that our information is harvested by Facebook to build virtual profiles of us that are then sold to advertisers and/or other third parties such as information brokers or political actors without our informed consent, as in the case of Cambridge Analytica, are we ourselves as users, in some way and to some degree, ethically responsible for the unethical ways in which our information is applied by Facebook? For example, the Cambridge Analytica case involved institutional political corruption that undermined the democratic system (Spence 2021a), specifically by undermining public trust and in turn damaging the democratic system itself.[9]

In answering that question let us first examine in what different ways, directly or indirectly, fully or partially, our own ethical responsibility or lack of it, as users, might be explained.

Given our retrospective knowledge of the Cambridge Analytica case and the ensuing fallout from the loss of public trust in democratic political institutions and the resulting damage to those institutions, do we as Facebook's users have an ethical responsibility to exercise more vigilance and take more care in ensuring the privacy, security, and the overall integrity of our shared information, which in turn should reciprocally be respected and protected by Facebook? Moreover, are we collectively responsible as users for ensuring that our shared information is not abused and undermined by being used for unethical and illegitimate purposes by

Facebook and by the third parties to which it sells our information, as illustrated by the Cambridge Analytica case? For as we saw in that case, Facebook's actions have the tendency of undermining the normative integrity of users' information, and moreover, the social, financial, and political institutions that together comprise our democratic system. The answers to the above questions is clearly yes. Facebook's users do have those ethical responsibilities by virtue of being bound by the normative requirements of DOIT. That is, they are bound by principles of transparency, truthfulness, reliability, trustworthiness, and respect for the informational rights of all communicators as equal members of the infosphere. A consequence of living in the infosphere is that the normative responsibilities and commitments of informational agents as demonstrated by DOIT are not less but more. And given the global nature of the infosphere and the World Wide Web, these responsibilities and commitments are also global and universal.

Another consequence is that the corruption of information and its communication processes and the resulting corruption of democratic political institutions, as illustrated by the Cambridge Analytica case, is a global concern, one that should also be shared by Facebook's users worldwide, as *global citizens of the infosphere.* Just as climate change affects everyone globally, so does the misuse and abuse of information and its communication, as well as the corrupting effects it has on the infosphere, including of the democratic political institutions it also tends to corrupt. We are, therefore, jointly, collectively, and normatively responsible for the well-being and integrity of the infosphere just as we are of our shared ecosystem (Spence 2021, ch. 4).[10]

Given that Facebook users are also bound, by the normative requirements of DOIT, are they also in any way collectively responsible, at least partly, for any of Facebook's normative transgressions? Here is an argument that at first blush appears to lend support to an affirmative answer to this question.

Insofar as Facebook's users have or ought to have some knowledge concerning

1. Facebook's part in the Cambridge Analytica case and similar other cases; and
2. knowledge of the generic conflict of interest at the heart of Facebook's surveillance business model conducive to such normative misconduct, as demonstrated by the application of the DOIT model above; and
3. that as users of Facebook there is a reasonable presumption that they are expected as institutional role occupants of Facebook for which they provide and share informational content, to have such knowledge; then
4. it is reasonable to conclude that the users of Facebook bear some partial joint and collective normative responsibility pertaining to them as institutional role occupants, for any present and/or future unethical practices that Facebook engages in, through the misuse and abuse of their information.

Being a distributed normative responsibility shared jointly and collectively by Facebook's users, such normative responsibility would be minimal for each of the 2.2 billion Facebook users.

Of course, this would also depend on how much knowledge the users of Facebook have concerning Facebook's operations and financial media activities, especially when often those activities are opaque and shrouded under a cloak of invisibility and concealment. However, despite that limitation or because of it, in the age of information, ignorance of how one's information is being used and for what purposes by tech companies such as Facebook and Google is no bliss and no longer morally excusable. This also entails a normative education of using and communicating information so as to ensure or at least minimize the unethical and corrupt uses and applications of our shared and collective information on Facebook and generally in the infosphere.

# Conclusion

This chapter has demonstrated that the problem of the collection and harvesting of users' information via opaque algorithms that is then sold for profit to third parties, often without the users' knowledge and informed consent, is a *generic, systemic, normative problem* not limited to Facebook. A similar systemic problem is evident in Google's operations, insofar as it, through its *search* function and its communication and curation practices that involve the collection, profiling, and harvesting of users' information via its apps (such as Gmail, for example), which like Facebook it sells for a profit, as well as through its YouTube practices that have been partly shown to be responsible for the spread of misinformation, fake news, and deep fakes. This is also a conflict of interest between its business model, which favors Google's financial interests, and the normative informational rights of it users. Google's systemic problem, just as in the case of Facebook, violates the fundamental rights that users have to their autonomy and privacy, which is particularly harmful to the whole of society as it undermines the collective common good and well-being of society and its underlying democratic system and aligned institutions.

# References

Beyleveld, Deryck. *The Dialectical Necessity of Morality: An Analysis and Defense of Alan Gewirth's Argument to the Principle of Generic Consistency.* Chicago: Chicago University Press, 1991.

Dretske, Fred. *Knowledge and the Flow of Information*. Stanford, CA: CSLI Publications, 1999.

Elliott, Deni, and H. Edward Spence. *Ethics for a Digital Era*. Oxford: Wiley-Blackwell, ch. 5, 2018.

Floridi, Luciano. "The Fight for Digital Sovereignty: What It Is and Why It Matters, Especially for the EU." *Philosophy & Technology* 33 (2020): 369–78.

Floridi, Luciano. "Is Semantic Information Meaningful Data?" *Philosophy and Phenomenological Research* 70, no. 2 (2005): 351–70.

Gewirth, Alan. *Self-Fulfillment*. Princeton, NJ: Princeton University Press, 1998.

Gewirth, Alan. *Reason and Morality*. Chicago: University of Chicago Press, 1978.

Kokolakis, Spyros. "Privacy Attitudes and Privacy Behaviour: A Review of Current Research on the Privacy Paradox Phenomenon." *Computers & Security* 64 (2017): 122–34.

Mittelstadt, Brent. D., Patrick Allo Patrick, Mariarosaria Taddeo, Sandra Wachter, and Luciano Floridi. "The Ethics of Algorithms: Mapping the Debate." *Big Data and Society* (July–December 2016): 1–21.

Spence, Edward H. *Stoic Philosophy and the Control Problem of AI Technology: Caught in the Web*, ch. 6. Lanham, MD: Rowman & Littlefield, 2021.

Spence, Edward H. *Media Corruption in the Age of Information*. Switzerland: Springer, 2021a.

Spence, Edward H. "The Sixth Estate; Tech Media Corruption in the Age of Information." *Journal of Information, Communication and Ethics in Society* 18, no. 4 (2020): 553–73.

Spence, Edward. "Information, Knowledge and Wisdom: Groundwork for the Normative Evaluation of Digital Information and Its Relation to the Good Life." *Ethics and Information Technology* 13, no. 3 (2011): 261–75.

Spence, Edward. "A Universal Model for the Normative Evaluation of Internet Information." *Ethics and Information Technology* 11, no. 4 (2009): 243–53.

Spence, Edward. *Ethics Within Reason: A Neo-Gewirthian Approach*. Lanham, MD: Lexington Books/Rowman & Littlefield, 2006.

Tufekci, Zeynep. "Facebook's Surveillance Machine." *New York Times*, March 19, 2018.

Véliz, Carissa. *Privacy Is Power: Why and How You Should Take Back Control of Your Data*. London: Bantam Press, 2020.

Zuboff, Shoshana. *The Age of Surveillance Capitalism: The Fight for a Human Future at the New Frontier of Power*. London: Profile Books, 2019.

PART THREE

# CHALLENGES

# Section 1

# AI and Its Applications

# CHAPTER 13

# AI in Health Care

## ETHICAL ISSUES

*Rita Manning*

## Abstract

Discussions of AI in health care run the range from hype to panic, opportunity to risk. The explosion of data in electronic health records (EHR), for example, is seen both as a gold mine of data riches and a sink pit of meaningless clerical tasks. There are growing fields in health care awash in reports that tout the next best thing and/or the impending takeover of human professionals by "black box" algorithms, algorithms that even the developers might not understand. This hype is often distracting, especially in robotic surgery, which basically has little to no real current use of AI. Other fields, like imaging, are maturing, while yet others have great potential. This chapter will provide a brief description of what AI is and how it works in health care. Then it will look at the formidable ethical issues that are raised by the use of AI.

### KEYWORDS

AI, artificial general intelligence (AGI), narrow AI, algorithms, principlism, explicability, replacing doctors, privacy, bias, trust, cost of AI

## Introduction

Discussions of AI in health care run the range from hype to panic, opportunity to risk. The explosion of data in electronic health records (EHR), for example, is seen both as a gold mine of data riches and a sink pit of meaningless clerical tasks. There are growing fields in health care awash in reports that tout the next best thing and/or the impending takeover of human professionals by "black box" algorithms, algorithms that even the developers might not understand. This hype is often distracting, especially in robotic surgery, which basically has little to no real current use of AI.[1] Other fields, like imaging, are maturing, while yet others have great potential.[2] In this chapter, I will take you on a journey into AI and medicine. First, I provide a brief description of what AI is and how it works in health care. Next, I will look at the formidable ethical issues that are raised by the use of AI.

# AI: What It Is and How It Works

Artificial intelligence can be divided into two kinds: artificial general intelligence (AGI) and narrow AI. AGI is what many people think of when they hear "artificial intelligence." Like *Star Trek*'s Data, AGI shares with humans "the ability to reason; to process visual, auditory, and other input; and to use it to adapt to their environments in a wide variety of settings. These systems are as knowledgeable and communicative as humans about a wide range of human events and topics."[3] However, like Data, AGI is complete fiction. We do not now have any devices like Data, and there is no reason to think we will, even in the far future.

The reason that we do not expect to see AGI in our computing systems in the near future is because AI as we know it is very narrow. It does not have general knowledge of the world, it cannot experience the world, and it doesn't have what we call "common sense."[4] There is good reason for thinking that AGI is not likely to be part of health care, or any other applications, for a very long time because human intelligence is enormously complex. Take Immanuel Kant's discussion of how humans interpret the world.[5] Kant describes the necessity of using central concepts to be able to organize one's experience of the world, among them the concepts of causality and of object permanence across time and space.[6]

Without these concepts, humans are not only unable to know but also they are unable to experience the world at all.[7] The current AI models

> lack ways of representing causal relationships (such as between diseases and their symptoms), and are likely to face challenges in acquiring abstract ideas like "sibling" or "identical to." They have no obvious ways of performing logical inferences, and they are also still a long way from integrating abstract knowledge, such as information about what objects are, what they are for, and how they are typically used.[8]

Narrow AI, on the other hand, is very real and has already been adopted in medical applications across a wide range of specialties. Narrow AI is a system that can do one narrowly defined task, and can often do it really well. Narrow AI depends, among other things, on algorithms, sets of instructions designed to perform a specific task like multiplying numbers. These algorithms must be trained by importing a huge amount of data and then refining them by testing their output. The data is often imported by humans but much of the training is done by the machines themselves. Often even the data scientists who are creating these systems don't understand some of the algorithms.

# Benefits of AI in Health Care

The use of this narrow AI in health care has demonstrated some real benefits. First, AI excels at well-defined tasks and hence does well in applications that are well-defined. We see this in imaging examples. The input is a digital image and the output is a binary classification: whether a lesion is benign or malignant,[9] or whether the image indicates diabetic retinopathy.[10] At the same time, since all the current AI medical applications are narrow AI, they only excel at well-defined tasks and thus cannot do the kind of synthesis that only human practitioners can do.

Second, AI can support health care systems that are under-resourced. For example, a diabetic retinopathy AI application was studied in Thailand, which has a shortage of ophthalmologists, and this application allowed recommendations to be made without consultation with an ophthalmologist.[11] Third, AI can be used to analyze very large volumes of data. Examples include a breast cancer study that used AI to sort patient responses to chemotherapy[12] and a big data analysis that provided data for improvements in computer-assisted orthopedic surgery.[13] While there are benefits of AI in medical applications, there are also formidable ethical issues raised by the use of AI.

# AI Ethics in Health Care

In order to imagine an ethical response to these problems, we begin with a brief sketch of bioethics and AI ethics. Principle-based and utilitarian models are combined in a widely adopted model of bioethics called principlism.[14] The principles are not ranked in terms of priority and instead are grouped under four general categories: (1) respect for autonomy (liberty; the absence of controlling influences) and agency (self-initiated intentional action); (2) nonmaleficence (do no harm); (3) beneficence (act for another's benefit); and (4) justice. Respect for autonomy reflects the influence of principle-based models. Nonmaleficence and beneficence address utilitarian concerns. Areas of justice in bioethics include rules for allocating health care and protection and aid for vulnerable and disadvantaged parties in local or global health care systems.

## AI ETHICS

In the field of artificial intelligence, principlism is the core ethical model with an additional principle: explicability. AI that is both beneficent and nonmaleficent is avoiding harm and doing good. AI promoting and not constraining human autonomy means "striking a balance between the decision-making power we retain for ourselves and that which we delegate to artificial agents."[15] For AI to be just, the people and organizations who develop and use it should be held accountable when it does harm. The explicability principle involves intelligibility and accountability. This means that both the developers and the users have to understand how AI works.

## ETHICAL PROBLEMS IN AI AND HEALTH CARE

The ethical issues we face with AI applications in health care include the way AI may be replacing doctors; how patients' privacy is at risk; the possibility that bias is built into the algorithms; whether this technology will be provided fairly to all patients; whether medicine should trust AI applications when the algorithms cannot be explained by the developers; whether patients can and should trust their practitioners when they are diagnosed and treated using AI; how putting AI into the larger context of health care creates and addresses its ethical problems; and finally, whether the tremendous effort in human labor and the vast sources of data used to train the algorithms that are the engines of AI are worth it.

# Does AI Replace Doctors?

The success of AI in imaging has been so profound that many radiologists have raised concerns about whether AI will replace MD radiologists. "Machines can be trained to be much less distracted by normal variants and image artifacts, and will be able to access vast amounts of data from other exams quickly and effortlessly. These abilities cannot be replicated by armies of human physicians and thus represent a disruptive change in practice."[16] The study on diabetic retinopathy showed that an AI application can decrease reliance on ophthalmologists.

To the general concern that doctors will be replaced by AI, defenders of doctors have argued that narrow AI, the only kind of AI that is currently used in medicine applications, can only perform relatively simple tasks, while the work of a physician includes many very complex tasks. Consider radiology, for example:

> Although the interpretation of images plays a central role in the radiologist's workflow, the work also goes beyond image interpretation, including consultations with other physicians about diagnosis and treatment, performance of image guided minimally invasive procedures, selection of the most appropriate imaging method, integration of image findings with data from the electronic health record (EHR), discussion of findings with the referring physician and patient, quality control, and education. . . . AI will not carry out those tasks in the short term.[17]

In addition to the complexity of medical care, human doctors have skills, virtues, and temperaments that algorithms lack: "you'll never see 'machine' doctors, because . . . empathy, common sense and instinct play a critical role in medical decision-making."[18] When AI applications involve algorithms that are not transparent, doctors have an even greater role to play.

> [A] black-box model can lead physicians to good decisions but only if they keep human intelligence in the loop, bringing in the societal, clinical, and personal context . . . the unique human brain and clinical training can generate new ideas, see new applications and uses of artificial intelligence and machine learning, and connect these technologies to the humanities and the social sciences in ways that current computers do not.[19]

# Privacy

Privacy is another serious ethical issue that AI raises and all of the current AI ethics models include privacy as a value to be protected.[20] The Health Insurance Portability and Accountability Act (HIPAA)[21] forbids the use of patient medical information without authorization. The American Medical Association Code of Medical Ethics describes privacy as encompassing a number of aspects, including "personal space (physical privacy), personal data (informational privacy), personal choices including cultural and religious affiliations (decisional privacy), and personal relationships with family members and other intimates (associational privacy)."[22]

Informational privacy is an obvious concern for AI applications in medicine because a patient's data, whether anonymized or not, is fodder for these applications. Either it is used as part of the huge dataset that is required to train algorithms, or it is part of the data that the algorithm is analyzing. De-identification (anonymizing datasets before sharing them) has been the main tool used to share personal data while still protecting privacy. Unfortunately, a recent study used a statistical method that showed that 99.98% of Americans would be correctly reidentified in any dataset using fifteen demographic attributes, even when their data was de-identified.[23]

# Bias

Another ethical concern is bias. The Centre for European Policy Studies (CEPS) distinguishes two different kinds of bias in AI. The first is design bias, which refers to assumptions made in "designing the model and its applicability to the overarching research question."[24] One example of design bias is the dermatology application that sorts images of skin lesions into benign and cancerous.[25] Unfortunately the dataset used by this application was composed predominantly of fair skin samples. This is a reason for distrusting the accuracy of this system to categorize skin lesions of individuals with darker skin colors.[26]

Another study looked at an algorithm that sorted patients on the basis of what additional resources they needed to manage their health care.[27] The designers assumed that how much health care patients used was a good metric to decide if they needed additional resources. Using this metric resulted in Black patients being underrepresented in the group of patients needing additional resources. The study pointed out that a more plausible explanation was overlooked, viz. that Black patients used less health care because they were, as a group, poorer and had worse access to health care than the patients, largely White, who used more health care.

Another issue is societal bias "reflected and exacerbated by algorithms."[28] This kind of bias is a function of the information that is included in the data. Since the decisions about how and whether to include information in a dataset are made by humans, this kind of bias is partly a function of the lack of diversity of data scientists.

Another kind of bias is contextual bias.[29] This is not a function of the kind of information included (or excluded) in the data, but the way one dataset is used in a different context. For example, W. Nicholson Price notes that most medical datasets are composed of data collected at high-resource medical institutions, largely academic medical hospitals. Algorithms are trained on huge amounts of data. If the data comes from an academic medical hospital, it may not provide an appropriate decision for doctors working in a low-resource hospital. An example Price offers is gallbladder cancer, which can only be treated safely by a cancer surgeon who is very experienced in this kind of surgery.[30]

An algorithm developed in a high-resource institution would have included data about this surgery performed by such a surgeon and might then recommend surgery when certain diagnostic parameters are met. However, this recommendation offered in a low-resource institution would likely be carried out by a general surgeon with little experience with gallbladder cancer, resulting in a recommendation that the surgery be performed by a surgeon inexperienced in this procedure.

One response to the AI bias problem would be to stop relying on any algorithm that assumes bias and engineers it in its applications. The problem here is that there are many narrow but powerful AI applications that do assume and engineer bias. While we must guard against bias, we also want to make sure that everyone has access to these powerful tools. A prominent European policy research institute combines both of these values in stating one of its fundamental values: "Justice, equity, and solidarity, which entails that AI-enabled systems contribute to global justice and equal access; and accordingly prevent or, where appropriate, timely detect and/or report discriminatory biases in data sets used to train and run AI systems."[31]

In addition to making sure that patients have equitable access to the AI applications that improve health, broad access to data is a way to minimize bias: "Increasing access to high-quality data could help developers address bias concerns by ensuring data are representative, transparent, and equitable." [32]

# Trust

The next concern about AI in medicine is trust. One of the concerns here is epistemological: How can a doctor know that an AI application's output is accurate when the algorithms that generate the output are unknown? This is called the black box problem.[33] The second concern is related to the first: How can a patient trust her doctor when her doctor's diagnosis or treatment advice is based on information that the doctor cannot fully explain to the patient?

One solution to the second problem is to reassure patients that doctors are relying on technology in which they have faith. This requires a solution to the first problem: doctors must be justified in having this faith. The solution to the second problem also requires that the AI applications will not be ultimately in charge of the medical procedures and treatments: "AI commonly handles tasks that are essential, but limited enough in their scope so as to leave the primary responsibility of patient management with a human doctor."[34] This goes beyond merely reassuring the patient that the doctor is in charge—the doctor, and not an algorithm, *must* be in charge. [35] Limiting the role of AI in medicine to supporting and not supplanting the doctor is a policy commitment.

One solution offered to the epistemological problem is that AI is more transparent than the human mind and since we are content to rely on human minds, we should rely on AI algorithms. "Human intelligence can't explain the complex, underlying basis for how we arrived at a particular conclusion . . . compared with human intelligence, A.I. is actually the more transparent of intelligences." [36]

I do not find this argument compelling. We do not rely on judgments by humans just because they were made by human minds, but because they are supported by evidence and reasoning that is transparent. We don't need a full understanding of how human minds work, but we need the evidence and transparent reasoning. This is missing in many AI applications.

A more plausible argument for trusting AI decisions is "that opaque decisions are more common in medicine than critics realize . . . when our knowledge of causal systems is incomplete and precarious . . . the ability to explain how results are produced can be less important than the ability to produce such results and empirically verify their accuracy." [37] How might this work? Consider the skin lesion application. [38] After the AI application categorized 129,450 images of pathologically confirmed benign and cancerous skin lesions, these categorizations were confirmed by board-certified dermatologists. So, while we don't know how the application did the categorizing, we do know that it was accurate.

To provide a degree of comfort to the doctors using these tools, we could "open the black box by presenting to the radiologist the annotated cases (ACs) proximal to the current case (CC), making decision rationale and uncertainty more explicit." [39] This is a policy decision: while developers needn't share their algorithms, they must show the images that they used to train the algorithms.

# Cost of AI in Health Care

The next concern about AI in medicine is its cost, including the cost of gathering the data required to train algorithms and the information needed for the effectiveness of AI in medicine, the environmental cost, and the human cost to both health care professionals and patients.

Pathology is a field that has been skeptical of AI because of its cost:

> An anatomic pathology workflow that includes digital pathology
> will not reduce or remove the need to produce and ultimately store

glass slides of pathology specimens. Instead of any reductions, digital pathology will require additional workflows, personnel, equipment, and importantly storage of data (it is estimated that digital pathology images are at least 10 times larger files than radiology images), all on top of an already financially and operationally stressed health care system.[40]

In addition to the cost of gathering data, there is also an environmental cost of using computing to train the algorithms with huge amounts of data:

> Training large AI models consumes a lot of computer processing power, and hence a lot of electricity . . . a 2019 paper . . . on the carbon emissions and financial costs of large language models . . . found that their energy consumption and carbon footprint have been exploding since 2017, as models have been fed more and more data . . . the sheer resources required to build and sustain such large AI models means they tend to benefit wealthy organizations, while climate change hits marginalized communities hardest.[41]

Finally, there is a human cost to consider. Human labor ranges from the highly educated physician or computer scientist to the large numbers of humans gathering and labeling the data needed to train and upgrade the algorithms used in medicine. Some of this work, often done by Amazon Mechanical Turk (MTurk), for example, does not require any particular education.[42] This work is tedious and underpaid but highly sought by researchers because it is an "efficient, reliable, cost-effective tool."[43] The problem with using Amazon Mechanical Turk is not just that the work is often mind-numbing, but that it pays less than minimum wage because the workers are not considered contractors covered by the Fair Labor Act. One study of 2,676 workers performing 3.8 million tasks on MTurk found that "workers earned a median hourly wage of only ~$2/h, and only 4% earned more than $7.25/h."[44]

These workers have "become crucial for the development of machine-learning applications. MTurk workers are frequently used to build and label . . . training datasets, yet their role in machine learning is often overlooked. . . . We eagerly admire the visage of the autonomous 'intelligent machine,' while ignoring, or even actively concealing, the human labor that makes it possible."[45]

One cost to patients is how much time doctors spend on their iPatients, the electronic shadow of the physical patient. Another cost is the way the need for data pressures patients into providing data not always in the interest of the patient, and the pressure on health care institutions to request, store, and categorize it. Doctors might be unburdened by the onerous task of scribing all the details of their patient interactions, but at the same time they are expected to develop new skills and knowledge in fields far from health care. Some medical professionals will work as data annotators, completing "time-consuming and monotonous" tasks.[46] Many doctors will be expected to work with AI tools, and this will require additional costly education:

> AI and other computational methods must be integrated into all of our training programs. Future generations of pathologists must be comfortable and facile using digital images and other data in combination with computer algorithms in their daily practice; optimistically, it will take 5 to 10 years to build such a workforce, and that is only if the process begins today.[47]

As we dwell on the benefits of AI in medicine, we must consider its cost to the environment; to health care practitioners and patients; and to the humans gathering, categorizing, and labeling huge amounts of data to build algorithms. I do not assume that these costs are never worth it, but we should ask how and when they are worth it.

# AI and Context

The final concern I will address is whether the fascination with AI distracts us from the larger context in which it is developed and utilized. One study looks at the way the collection of data on sexual orientation and gender identity (SOGI) may be perceived by patients as culturally insensitive.[48] Another describes how the obsession with AI can be distracting, as "gurus of data assume once something is identified and known, it is solved. . . . But in health care the goal is often changing an ingrained habit such as eating processed foods, smoking, not exercising, or skipping daily medications."[49]

The other context to look at is the way AI in medicine might change the interaction between patients and their doctors. These concerns range from the appropriateness of treating psychiatric patients with natural language enabled chatbots[50] to patients with total access to their EHR and AI tools who decide they don't need doctors to diagnose or treat them.[51] In response to this concern, AI in medicine will only be effective and ethical when health care practitioners take responsibility for the ethical implications of AI in medicine, including reading AI medical papers critically.[52]

# Conclusion

In this chapter, I surveyed some of the ethical issues presented by AI in health care. This includes the way AI may be replacing doctors; how patients' privacy is at risk; the possibility that bias is built into the algorithms; the worry that this technology will not be provided fairly to all groups of patients; whether medicine should trust AI applications when the algorithms cannot be explained by the developers; whether patients can and should trust their practitioners when they are diagnosed and treated using AI; and whether the tremendous effort in human labor and the vast sources of data used to train the algorithms that are the engines of AI are worth it.

Health care professionals will need a deep understanding of AI to navigate a professional world surrounded by narrow AI tools making their professional lives both more complex and hopefully richer. Patients stand to benefit from this understanding. Policy makers must be ready to provide the structure in which these tools will operate both effectively and ethically. I hope that I have provided a useful beginning as we all navigate this rapidly changing health care environment.

# CHAPTER 14

# The Ethics of Self-Driving Cars

*Jens Kipper*

## Abstract

The goal of this chapter is to provide an overview of morally relevant questions that are raised by self-driving cars. First, the likely effects, both positive and negative, of the use of self-driving cars are examined. Second, the question of how self-driving cars should be programmed to deal with certain critical kinds of situations is discussed. This includes moral dilemmas, exemplified by the much-discussed "trolley cases," but also more mundane situations (e.g., road users trying to exploit the compliance of self-driving cars). Finally, some avenues for future research on the ethics of self-driving cars are identified.

KEYWORDS

self-driving cars, artificial intelligence safety, informational privacy, cybersecurity, trolley cases

## Introduction

This chapter discusses moral issues raised by the use of self-driving cars. The term "self-driving" is here meant to apply to vehicles that can safely operate on public roads without any monitoring or interference by a human—this corresponds to level 4 or 5 on the SAE International's scale of driving automation (SAE International 2018). Self-driving cars have already traveled tens of millions of miles on public roads. At present, they still struggle to deal with some conditions human drivers can face. For instance, current self-driving cars have difficulty driving in harsh weather; in unusual lighting conditions; and in dense, chaotic traffic. It is thus difficult to give a precise estimate for when self-driving cars will become widely available for private and commercial use. Nevertheless, it is very likely that this time will come. And since the use of self-driving cars raises some difficult ethical issues, it is important to address these ahead of time.

The most basic moral question to ask about self-driving cars is whether they should be used at all. The next section of this chapter thus considers the pros and cons of self-driving cars. "On the Interaction between Self-Driving Cars and Other Road Users" then discusses how self-driving cars should react in certain ethically relevant situations, and how their interaction with other road users should be regulated. Here, a focus of the discussion has been on so-called trolley cases. These are situations in which an agent must choose between different options, each of which involves harm being inflicted on someone. As we will see, it is also important to consider how self-driving cars should react in more ordinary, non-dilemmatic situations. The conclusion to this chapter provides a brief summary of the main results, and points toward future work that needs to be done to meet the ethical challenges raised by self-driving cars.

# Pros and Cons of Self-Driving Cars

More than 90% of road accidents are caused by human errors. Unlike human drivers, self-driving cars do not speed or violate other traffic rules; they do not get distracted, tired, or intoxicated; they do not panic in difficult circumstances; and they potentially have much shorter reaction times than human drivers. The introduction of self-driving cars thus has the potential to reduce the number of road accidents significantly. Since more than a million people are killed in road accidents worldwide every year, this means that a huge number of lives could thus be saved. Self-driving cars have many other potential advantages. A significant amount of traffic jams are caused by accidents. Reducing the number of accidents could thus also reduce traffic congestion. Due to their superior reaction time and their ability to communicate with each other, self-driving cars could require much shorter safety margins, which would further increase the efficiency of traffic flow and thus, potentially, reduce congestion.

This reduction in traffic congestion, combined with the fact that self-driving cars are generally able to drive in a more energy-efficient way than humans, could also result in a decrease in emissions. Time spent on commutes could be spent much more productively, or just more pleasantly, if people no longer had to operate their car. The widespread availability of self-driving cars would also increase the mobility of young, elderly, and disabled people, and it would make car-sharing models more attractive. The latter would mean that fewer cars have to be produced and that space used for parking could instead be used for housing, among other things. A further potential positive side effect of the widespread availability of self-driving cars would be that, since space for additional housing would be freed and commutes would become easier, more productive, and less unpleasant, housing in big cities could become more affordable.

For some of the expected changes just mentioned, their net effect is difficult to predict. For instance, it is unclear whether the use of self-driving cars will lead to a reduction in traffic congestion overall. If commutes become less burdensome, people might be willing to commute more, which would be a counterweight to the increased efficiency of traffic flow. In addition, the increased mobility of young, elderly, and disabled people would mean that more people would travel in cars.[1] Still, if time spent on the road can be used more sensibly than today, traffic can flow more efficiently, and traditionally disadvantaged groups can gain mobility, then these are certainly very welcome changes. In light of this, it would seem more reasonable to conceive of new policies to keep traffic in check, rather than to restrict the use of self-driving cars.

However, self-driving cars raise potential problems. One of them concerns software vulnerabilities. In a worst-case scenario, an external party could take control over a moving vehicle by hacking its software—or even the software of many vehicles simultaneously, depending on their level of connectivity. It therefore seems clear that cybersecurity questions should be taken very seriously (McCarthy 2017; Luetge 2017, 554). Ideally, the design of self-driving cars should make it impossible for an external party to gain control of them. This issue is complicated by the fact that law enforcement officials might want to be able to gain such external control and thus push for loopholes.

It is likely that self-driving cars will produce massive amounts of data, recording the vehicle's location and speed, crash data, etc. These data could be used, for example, for mass surveillance and various commercial purposes. Self-driving cars thus raise concerns about privacy (Glancy 2012; Luetge 2017, 555). Here, too, policies would still need to be developed that prevent abuse (e.g., by granting passengers ownership of their data).

It is difficult to give an overall ethical assessment of the introduction of self-driving cars, since some relevant empirical contingencies are still undetermined at this point. However, if they indeed turn out to be much safer than human drivers and if their software is sufficiently secure, then it seems that their advantages far outweigh their potential disadvantages. This naturally leads to the question whether it is human driving that should, eventually, be outlawed (Gogoll and Müller 2020). Once there is a better alternative, the safety risk posed by human drivers may well be deemed unacceptable.

Nevertheless, it will probably take many years before this question becomes relevant, for the following reason: Suppose that self-driving cars were available that are significantly safer than humans in all conditions. It is not to be expected that one could convert all ordinary cars that are in use at this point into self-driving cars. It would also seem logistically unfeasible, and excessively wasteful, to decommission all those cars immediately and replace them with self-driving cars. This means that it is likely that for many years, self-driving cars will operate alongside cars driven by humans. Some of the ethical questions that arise from this interaction between human and artificial drivers are discussed below.

# On the Interaction between Self-Driving Cars and Other Road Users

## TROLLEY CASES AND ETHICS SETTINGS

We just saw that if certain conditions are met, then it is ethically permissible, if not even mandatory, to use self-driving cars. The question that arises then is how such cars should be programmed to deal with certain situations. In most circumstances, it is clear what a self-driving car should do. It should get its passengers to their desired destination as quickly and efficiently as possible, in accordance with the traffic laws and while minimizing the risk of accidents. However, some cases are less clear-cut. As many have pointed out, even if we (somewhat unrealistically) assume that the software and hardware of self-driving cars work flawlessly, it is inevitable that they will occasionally crash. For instance, self-driving cars will encounter wildlife, pedestrians, cyclists, and—at least for the foreseeable future—other cars driven by humans. If a self-driving car is moving at a relatively high velocity, then irrespective of its reaction time, purely physical reasons dictate that it will take a certain time to come to a halt. Thus, if such a car faces an unexpected obstacle, a crash might be unavoidable. In many situations of this type, too, it is relatively straightforward to tell how the car should react.

For instance, all things being equal, a crash at a lower velocity is preferable to a crash at a higher velocity, crashing into a pile of cardboard boxes is preferable to crashing into a concrete wall, running over a soccer ball is preferable to running over a cat, etc. But there are other possible cases that raise deep moral problems. For example, suppose that a car is traveling at high velocity, when a truck driving in the opposite direction suddenly steers into the car's lane. There is not enough time to brake, and a collision with the truck would likely be fatal for the car's passenger. The only alternative is to swerve right. But that would mean that our car crashes into a motorcyclist, who would also likely be killed. Which option should the self-driving car choose in these circumstances? And what if there are two or more passengers in the car, or two people on the motorbike, or if swerving right would steer the car into a group of children?

Cases like these are commonly compared to so-called trolley cases, which have been extensively discussed in ethical theorizing. In Philippa Foot's original case (1978), the driver of a "runaway tram" has to choose between a) letting the tram kill five innocent people, and b) turning the tram such that it runs into and kills one innocent person. Since the publication of Foot's article, countless variations of this case have been devised. In many of these cases, it is difficult to decide what the right course of action is.

It has been argued that the situations self-driving cars might face are importantly different from the standard trolley cases. For instance, Sven Nyholm and Jilles Smids (2016, 1286–1287), Noah Goodall (2014), and Johannes Himmelreich (2018, 677) have noted that real-life circumstances always involve uncertainty—unlike the trolley cases, in which agents are assumed to know the consequences of each of their options. But irrespectively of how comparable the kinds of trolley cases discussed in the philosophical literature are to real-life circumstances, it seems hard to deny that a self-driving car might find itself in a situation that involves a moral dilemma. For instance, a self-driving car might judge that action A (steering straight or left, braking) will result in a collision with a truck at high velocity with a very high probability, whereas action B (steering right, braking) will result in a collision with a pedestrian at high velocity, with an equally high probability. Hence, it appears that self-driving cars will occasionally have to make difficult moral decisions.

It is important to note that the question of how a self-driving car should react in a certain situation differs from the question of how a human who is in the same kind of situation should act. A self-driving car is not a moral agent. Hence, the relevant moral decisions in the case of self-driving cars are made long before the dilemmatic situation occurs, namely, at the time the car is programmed (Nyholm and Smids 2016, 1280). This affects the question of how such situations should be dealt with. For instance, many people think that if one has to choose between killing an old and sick person and killing a young and healthy person, the former option is preferable.[2] Even if this verdict is correct, it might well be problematic, both from an ethical and from a legal perspective, to build self-driving cars that prefer running over old people to running over young people. Therefore, the crucial question is not what the right thing to do is in "trolley-style" cases, but how self-driving cars should be programmed to react in such cases (i.e., what kinds of "ethics settings" self-driving cars should have).

To settle this question, it is important to consider the expected consequences of implementing specific ethics settings. For example, if self-driving cars were programmed to value the lives of some groups of people higher than those of others—as in the above example—then this would likely be perceived as unjust by those disadvantaged and lead to anxiety, frustration, and tensions between different groups. For this reason alone, it would seem advisable to implement ethics settings that don't discriminate between different groups of people.

A related question that has been raised is whether a self-driving car should give preferential treatment to its passengers in situations in which an accident is unavoidable. For instance, such a car might rank a collision with a group of pedestrians higher than a collision with a concrete wall, even if the former option is expected to lead to greater overall harm. The rationale for this suggestion is this: we saw above that the introduction of self-driving cars can save many lives. But people might be reluctant to use self-driving cars that are disposed to "sacrifice" their passengers to prevent greater harm. Hence, implementing ethics settings that always put a car's passengers first could lead to a higher acceptance of self-driving cars and as a result save lives (Coca-Vila 2018, 63).

This line of reasoning is supported by surveys suggesting that people would prefer using self-driving cars that put the passengers' lives first (e.g., Bonnefon et al. 2016). However, the same surveys also suggest that people generally prefer self-driving cars to be programmed to minimize harm. People might be opposed to the introduction of self-driving cars that are disposed to run over pedestrians to save a passenger's life. It is a difficult question whether, to what extent, and how the ethics settings of self-driving cars might affect public acceptance. Serious empirical research would have to be done to settle it. Arguably, the default option should be to not give preferential treatment to passengers in cases of unavoidable accidents, since that would be at odds with the principle of minimizing harm.

## PERSONALIZED VS. MANDATORY ETHICS SETTINGS

It has been argued that the users of self-driving cars should be allowed to choose their car's ethics settings (e.g., Sandberg and Bradshaw 2013). Such "personalized ethics settings" might increase the public acceptance of self-driving cars. This suggestion is motivated by the idea that self-driving cars should be understood as proxies of their users (i.e., as making decisions on their behalf), reflecting their values or preferences (Millar 2014). Patrick Lin (2014) rejects the introduction of personalized ethics settings, since he fears that it would allow users to choose settings that discriminate against people based on, for example, their gender. But this example only illustrates that a self-driving car's settings should not be freely customizable by its user. A more reasonable approach would be to equip self-driving cars with a range of legally and ethically permissible settings. The choice of such settings could still reflect its user's values, but within reason.

Personalized ethics settings might raise questions connected to liability and responsibility for accidents. Many people have argued that owners and users of self-driving cars shouldn't be liable for potential damages, provided that they haven't tampered with the car's settings and that they have utilized it in accordance with its intended use. But what if some harm is caused by settings that were specified by the user? Arguably, users should still not be liable in cases like this, assuming that they made their choice among a set of options that have been deemed legally and morally acceptable. One might nevertheless argue that users would be morally responsible for harm that results from their choice of ethics settings. But this consequence could very well be embraced by proponents of personalized ethics settings who believe that a self-driving car should serve as a proxy of its user.

Jan Gogoll and Julian Müller (2017) raise another objection against personalized ethics settings that is based on game-theoretic considerations. Consider a society in which people can choose between selfish settings (i.e., settings that favor a car's passengers), and utilitarian settings (i.e., settings designed to minimize global harm). According to Gogoll and Müller, an individual user has nothing to gain from choosing utilitarian settings. Choosing those settings would only increase their likelihood of being harmed in an accident, and it would put them at a disadvantage compared to others who choose selfish settings. Hence, in such a society, the choice of selfish ethics settings maximizes any given individual's expected utility, irrespective of what other users choose.

The game-theoretic equilibrium of such a society is one in which everyone uses selfish ethics settings. This is a problem, because in such a society, everyone is worse off than they would be if everyone used utilitarian settings. The following considerations should serve to motivate this claim: By definition, utilitarian settings minimize global harm. Any settings that deviate from this—for instance, by giving preferential treatment to passengers—are thus expected to lead to more harm than utilitarian settings. Assuming that everyone is equally likely to be a passenger or a non-passenger in the relevant kind of accident, this means that the universal adoption of selfish settings makes everyone worse off than if utilitarian settings were universally adopted. Gogoll and Müller thus argue that personalized ethics settings would lead to a prisoner's dilemma (i.e., to a situation in which individually rational [and expected] behavior would lead to a suboptimal outcome for everyone). For this reason, they suggest that there should be mandatory utilitarian ethics settings, since these would yield the optimal outcome for everyone.

Is Gogoll and Müller's reasoning sound? It is unclear whether literally everyone would be worse off in a society in which everyone uses selfish settings, compared to one in which everyone uses utilitarian ones. Depending on the circumstances, some people might well benefit from such a situation. Nevertheless, it is difficult to deny that the universal adoption of selfish ethics settings (as opposed to utilitarian ones) would increase the expected number of casualties in road accidents. In this respect, society as a whole would thus be worse off. The crucial question is therefore whether Gogoll and Müller are correct in assuming that people would prefer selfish ethics settings to altruistic ones, if given the choice. In many other contexts, people do not consistently act selfishly: they help their neighbors and friends or even strangers, donate to charity, etc. Some of this behavior is genuinely altruistic. The issue of how common genuinely altruistic behavior is and to what extent people might display it in their choice of ethics settings is extremely complex and cannot be settled here.

Another relevant question is whether there is some other benefit to be gained by choosing unselfish ethics settings. Notice that since trolley-style dilemmas are extremely rare, users who choose such settings increase their risk only by a minuscule amount. It would therefore take relatively little to offset this cost and thus make the choice of unselfish ethics settings rational. Often, seemingly altruistic behavior in fact benefits an agent. For instance, helping a neighbor, friend, or stranger, or donating to charity can increase a person's social standing. Could something similar apply to the case of ethics settings—could it, for example, increase a person's social standing to use unselfish ethics settings in their self-driving car? It is not obvious that it would, since one's choice of ethics settings need not be visible to others. But there might be ways to make it easy for users to share which settings they choose, and thus to nudge them into choosing utilitarian (or other unselfish) settings.

To sum up: the introduction of personalized ethics settings for self-driving cars would give users more freedom and would enable us to construe a person's car, to a certain extent, as their proxy. Conceivably, such settings could increase people's willingness to use self-driving cars. The most obvious downside of such personalized settings is that they might enable users to choose settings that lead to more harm than necessary. Gogoll and Müller even argue that individual users would have good prudential reasons to choose such nonoptimal settings, meaning that the introduction of personalized ethics settings would create a prisoner's dilemma. As we saw, whether this assessment is correct depends on the details of how personalized ethics settings are introduced. Furthermore, to decide whether the introduction of personalized ethics settings is desirable, one would need to determine whether their costs are outweighed by the increased freedom they bring, and to what extent users even want this kind of freedom.

## BEYOND TROLLEY CASES

The discussion up to this point has focused on how self-driving cars should react to rather dramatic circumstances in which an accident is unavoidable, and in which each choice of action will cause harm. Since it is very plausible that such situations can occur, ethical issues relating to them do need to be addressed. However, as was mentioned above, trolley-style situations are extremely rare. Some philosophers have therefore argued that more attention should be paid to issues regarding how cars should be programmed to react in more mundane situations. Usually, much less is at stake in such situations. But since (by definition) they are much more common, the overall consequences of how cars are programmed to react in mundane situations might well be more important. Some of the relevant issues that have been mentioned in this context are how self-driving cars should deal with the inevitable tradeoff between mobility and safety (Himmelreich 2018, 680), and how self-driving cars should coordinate with each other and with other road users (Borenstein et al. 2019).

Another kind of problem that needs to be addressed concerns the possibility of other road users exploiting self-driving cars (Borenstein et al. 2019, 389). For example, pedestrians might cross the street into self-driving car traffic, trusting that these cars have superior reaction times, are never distracted, and are programmed to prevent harm. Similarly, self-driving cars will probably be programmed to drive very cautiously, if only for reasons of liability. Other road users could exploit this fact by, for example, being less inclined to yield to them. In each case, this would only create a minor nuisance. But if this kind of behavior became common, it might seriously impede traffic flow. Some of the features that make self-driving cars superior to human drivers—their reliability, their predictability, their caution, etc.—thus also make them vulnerable to exploitation. So, what could be done to prevent this kind of exploitation?

One option is to change the behavior of self-driving cars (e.g., by making them more aggressive and less predictable). But it seems clear that this would have to be done within narrow limits, since such measures could otherwise increase the risk of accidents to an unacceptable degree. Another natural option is to penalize exploitative behavior. To be able to pursue violations effectively, self-driving cars' cameras could be used to identify perpetrators. The downside of this option is that it might be accompanied by mass surveillance and a large amount of bureaucratic effort, for the purpose of penalizing what are in fact mostly minor traffic violations. Better solutions to prevent exploitation of self-driving cars are not immediately apparent. Ideally, incentives should be created to discourage exploitative behavior in a minimally intrusive way. More work will need to be done here.

# Conclusion

Self-driving cars will likely transform traffic. This transformation has the potential to bring great benefits, such as a significant reduction of accidents, traffic congestion and air pollution; an increase in productivity; and more affordable housing. If self-driving cars are as safe and efficient as they are promised to be, then their benefits most likely outweigh their drawbacks. Nevertheless, their introduction also raises a number of ethical challenges. Many of these challenges relate to questions of how self-driving cars should react in certain critical situations. Here it is important to keep in mind that the relevant moral decisions are not made by the car itself, but rather by those who determine its programming or its settings. This means that first and foremost, the expected overall effects of different settings need to be considered. These effects will need to be studied in greater detail. For instance, how would it affect the public acceptance of self-driving cars if they were programmed to primarily protect their passengers in cases in which an accident is unavoidable? And to what extent would users choose such "selfish" settings if they themselves were given the choice?

As we saw, it will also be important to think about the behavior of self-driving cars and their interaction with other road users in less dramatic situations. Here, one issue that will have to be addressed is how behavior by other road users that exploits the (otherwise desirable) predictability of self-driving cars can be discouraged.

# References

Awad, Edmond, Sohan Dsouza, Richard Kim, Jonathan Schulz, Joseph Henrich, Azim Shariff, Jean-François Bonnefon, and Iyad Rahwan. "The Moral Machine Experiment." *Nature* 563 (October 2018): 59–64.

Bonnefon, Jean-François, Azim Shariff, and Iyad Rahwan. "The Social Dilemma of Autonomous Vehicles." *Science* 352, no. 6293 (June 2016): 1573–76.

Borenstein, Jason, Joseph R. Herkert, and Keith W. Miller. "Self-Driving Cars and Engineering Ethics: The Need for a Systems-Level Analysis." *Science and Engineering Ethics* 25 (2019): 383–98.

Coca-Vila, Ivó. "Self-Driving Cars in Dilemmatic Situations: An Approach Based on the Theory of Justification in Criminal Law." *Criminal Law and Philosophy* 12 (2018): 59–82.

Foot, Philippa. "The Problem of Abortion and the Doctrine of Double Effect." In *Virtues and Vices: And Other Essays in Moral Philosophy,* 19–32. Berkeley: University of California Press, 1978.

Glancy, Dorothy. "Privacy in Autonomous Vehicles." *Santa Clara Law Review* 52, no. 4 (2012): 1171–239.

Gogoll, Jan, and Julian F. Müller. "Autonomous Cars: In Favor of a Mandatory Ethics Setting." *Science and Engineering Ethics* 23 (2017): 681–700.

———. "Should Manual Driving Be (Eventually) Outlawed?" *Science and Engineering Ethics* 26 (2020): 1549–67.

Goodall, Noah J. "Machine Ethics and Automated Vehicles." In *Road Vehicle Automation*, ed. Gereon Meyer and Sven Beiker, 93–102. New York: Springer, 2014.

Himmelreich, Johannes. "Never Mind the Trolley." *Ethical Theory and Moral Practice* 21 (2018): 669–84.

Larson, William, and Weihua Zhao. "Self-Driving Cars and the City: Effects on Sprawl, Energy Consumption, and Housing Affordability." *Regional Science and Urban Economics* 81 (2020): 103484.

Lin, Patrick. "Here's a Terrible Idea: Robot Cars with Adjustable Ethics Settings." *Wired*, August 18, 2014. https://www.wired.com/2014/08/heres-a-terrible-idea-robot-cars-with-adjustable-ethics-settings/.

Luetge, Christoph. "The German Ethics Code for Automated and Connected Driving." *Philosophy and Technology* 30 (2017): 547–58.

McCarthy, Tom. "Self-Driving Cars Must Have Technology to Prevent Use in Terror, Lawmakers Say." *The Guardian*, September 6, 2017. https://www.theguardian.com/technology/2017/sep/06/self-driving-cars-terrorism-cybersecurity-technology.

Millar, Jason. "Proxy Prudence: Rethinking Models of Responsibility for Semi-Autonomous Robots." *Proceedings of We Robot*, Coral Gables, FL, 2014, The University of Miami School of Law.

Nyholm, Sven, and Jilles Smids. "The Ethics of Accident-Algorithms for Self-Driving Cars: An Applied Trolley Problem?" *Ethical Theory and Moral Practice* 19 (2016): 1275–89.

SAE International. "SAE International Releases Updated Visual Chart for Its 'Levels of Driving Automation' Standard for Self-Driving Vehicles." 2018. https://www.sae.org/news/press-room/2018/12/sae-international-releases-updated-visual-chart-for-its-%E2%80%9Clevels-of-driving-automation%E2%80%9D-standard-for-self-driving-vehicles.

Sandberg, Anders, and Heather Bradshaw-Martin. "What Do Cars Think of Trolley Problems: Ethics for Autonomous Cars." In *Beyond AI: Artificial Golem Intelligence*, ed. J. Romportl et al. Conference Proceedings, University of Western Bohemia, 2013. https://www.beyondai.zcu.cz/files/BAI2013_proceedings.

# CHAPTER 15

# Moral Dilemmas of Self-Driving Cars

*Sven Nyholm*

## Abstract

This chapter provides an overview of some of the most important ethical issues related to autonomous vehicles, also known as self-driving cars. The chapter begins with a discussion of ethical issues related to different levels and kinds of autonomation in cars. It next considers issues having to do with safety precautions, and after that turns to issues related to risks created by self-driving cars. The chapter then discusses the trolley problem, empirical approaches to the ethics of self-driving cars, traditional moral theories, and, lastly, questions related to moral responsibility for harm caused by self-driving cars.

KEYWORDS

self-driving cars, safety, risks, the trolley problem, moral dilemmas, responsibility gaps

## Introduction

This chapter provides an overview of some important ethical issues related to autonomous vehicles, also known as self-driving cars. Notably, automation in vehicles comes in different degrees and kinds (Nyholm & Smids, 2020). Cars can be partially or fully automated. It is common practice to distinguish among five different levels of automation, where level zero means no automation and level five means full automation. In cars with some automation (level one to four cars), drivers are expected to sometimes take over some of the driving tasks. But they are also able to hand over some or perhaps all of the tasks to the car itself, at least in some traffic situations. For the purposes of this chapter, the expression "self-driving car" will refer to any type of vehicle that is either fully automated or could operate in an autonomous mode in at least some traffic situations. Fully autonomous level-five cars may not become available for a very long time. But cars that can operate in autonomous mode in some traffic situations already exist and are on the market.

There are ethical questions related to the differences in levels and types of automation in cars. For example, is it to expect too much of human drivers to require them to sometimes take over the operation of the vehicle, if the artificial intelligence in the car suddenly requests that control be handed back to them? In particular, is it reasonable to expect people to be sufficiently alert at all times, so that they can easily take over if necessary (Hevelke & Nida-Rümelin, 2015)? Some authors argue that it is not reasonable to expect this. So, we should either have fully autonomous self-driving cars or manually driven cars, according to these authors (Sparrow & Howard, 2017).

To this, one might potentially respond that cars should never ask or expect human drivers to take back control, but that it should always be a human choice when one wants to drive and when one wants to hand over control to the artificial intelligence in the car. Such questions about handing control over to, and taking control back from, cars are intriguing. In what follows, however, the focus will not be on that topic. The questions below will all be about those times that the vehicle is operating in autonomous mode, whether or not it is possible to hand control back to the human occupant(s) riding in the car.

This is a fairly new topic. Moral philosophers started investigating ethical issues related to self-driving cars around 2014. Back then, the discussion exclusively involved hypothetical thought experiments. What if there was a crash involving a self-driving car, and somebody was injured? Who should then be held responsible? What if the artificial intelligence in the car had to react to a potential crash? What should the self-driving car do? Legal scholars had started thinking about issues involving crashes with self-driving cars a little earlier (e.g., Marchant & Lindor, 2012; Peterson, 2012) But those early articles in legal theory were also mostly about hypothetical scenarios.

In 2015, what had previously been thought experiments started happening in real life (Nyholm & Smids, 2020). That year, there were around twenty small accidents involving experimental self-driving cars. No human beings were seriously harmed, and there were only some minor scratches on some of the cars. What mostly happened was that people in regular cars rear-ended experimental self-driving cars. This typically happened because those self-driving cars were not behaving as the human drivers in the regular cars expected them to.

For example, the self-driving cars accelerated more slowly than most human-driven cars do.

After those early accidents, human drivers were usually blamed. In 2016, however, for the first time, a self-driving car clearly caused an accident (Nyholm, 2018a). On Valentine's Day of that year, an experimental self-driving car from Google crashed into a bus. Google had to admit that their car had caused the crash. Later in the same year, something more tragic happened. The first person died while riding in a self-driving car. A Florida man was killed in an accident when his Tesla Model S crashed into a truck while operating in the "autopilot" mode. In 2018, in turn, the first pedestrian was hit and killed by a self-driving car. The artificial intelligence in an experimental car operated by Uber failed to recognize a human being crossing the road in time. The victim was Elaine Herzberg. She was first classified as a sign, then as a bike, and then reclassified as a human being. But by then it was too late. The car hit Herzberg, and she died on the way to the hospital.

In recent years, there has been an absolute explosion of philosophical articles about the ethics of self-driving cars. This chapter will not try to summarize everything that has been discussed in academic philosophy related to self-driving cars. The focus will instead be on some of the key issues that have received the most attention.

# The Ethics of Safety and Experiments with Self-Driving Cars

One important reason why many people are excited about the prospect of self-driving cars relates to traffic safety. Eventually, self-driving cars are hoped to become much safer than regular cars (Gurney 2016). So far, though, this has not been proven in practice. This already raises interesting ethical questions.

To improve the safety of self-driving cars in a wide range of real-life traffic scenarios, engineers need to experiment with self-driving cars in actual traffic. This involves imposing risks on people who live in the communities where experimental self-driving cars are being tested. A key question here is how great the risks are that we can justifiably impose on people in this experimental stage to make sure that we later save many lives because very safe self-driving cars have by then been developed. Recall that Elaine Herzberg was killed by an experimental self-driving car. A grim question arises: Should such deaths be tolerated now because of the greater number of lives that might later be saved if the tech industry is permitted to experiment with self-driving cars on public roads?

Robert Sparrow and Mark Howard (2017) present an interesting claim about the ethics of risk and safety in the development of self-driving cars.

They argue that so long as self-driving cars have not been proven to be safer than regular cars, it should be illegal to sell self-driving cars. However, once self-driving cars have been proven to be safer than regular cars, regular cars should be forbidden. That argument seems to implicitly rest on the following general moral principle: if a safer alternative is introduced into some risky domain of life, it is immoral to use older, less safe alternatives. Only the safest alternative should be permitted in a dangerous domain like traffic. Is this right?

What if people who drive older, otherwise less safe cars are willing to use special safety precautions (Nyholm, 2018b; Nyholm & Smids, 2020)? For example, the requirements for getting a driver's license could be made much more stringent. Moreover, manually driven cars could perhaps be equipped with alcohol locks and speed-limiting technologies, which would make it impossible to drive while drunk or to do any dangerous speeding. Could such added safety precautions perhaps offset the greater risks otherwise involved with manually driven cars? Whatever we think about these issues, the following seems to hold true: when or if self-driving cars become safer than regular cars, this will put pressure on those who still wish to drive regular cars to justify why they should still be permitted to do so.

# Ethics Programming and the Trolley Problem

As noted above, self-driving cars hold the promise of eventually becoming much safer than regular cars. Yet they cannot be 100% safe. Even the safest self-driving cars will sometimes crash. Anything that is heavy and moving fast, and that could malfunction, like any technology can, will sometimes cause accidents. So, we need to think about accident scenarios involving self-driving cars (Goodall, 2014).

It is sometimes suggested that humans should always take over control in crash scenarios or that cars should simply brake in risky scenarios. However, these responses are problematic. Average human reaction times are slow. It won't always be possible for people to react in time. Moreover, in some situations, it is not possible to simply apply the brakes. And no option open to the car may be safe for everyone involved. So, it seems that automated cars need to be programmed for how to respond to accident scenarios. Coming up with such programming requires thinking about potential choices that impose serious risks on different people. The issue of what self-driving cars should do in situations in which crashes are unavoidable is an inherently ethical issue. Therefore, some philosophers talk about the need to equip self-driving cars with "ethics settings." For example, should the car always try to protect the people riding in the car?

Or should self-driving cars simply try to minimize overall harm when crashes are unavoidable (Goodall, 2014; Nyholm, 2018a)?[1]

Imagine the following scenario. A self-driving car with five passengers suddenly detects a large obstacle on the road. Unless the car turns, the five passengers are likely to die. The only way to turn is onto a sidewalk. But a pedestrian is walking there. So, the only way the car can save the five is if it sacrifices the one. What should the self-driving car be programmed to do in such a situation? Now consider an alternative scenario: in this case, there is only one person in the automated car. Again, some large obstacle falls onto the road. And again, the car can only save the passenger if it turns onto the sidewalk. This time, however, there are five pedestrians on the sidewalk. What should the car do now? Should it sacrifice the one for the sake of the five?

These examples are designed to sound similar to the so-called trolley problem (Kamm, 2015; Nyholm & Smids, 2016). The trolley problem is a well-known philosophical thought experiment in which an out-of-control trolley is about to hit five people on some train tracks. You are standing next to a switch. If you pull the switch, the trolley will be redirected to a side track, where there is only one person. So, to save the five, one person would have to be sacrificed. In another variation, the only way to save the five on the tracks is to push a large and heavy person off a bridge down onto the train tracks in front of the trolley. The large person's hefty weight will then set off the automatic breaks of the trolley before it hits the five. This would kill the one but save the five. What should be done in these cases? The challenge of explaining and justifying differences in people's intuitions about such cases is what is usually referred to by the phrase "the trolley problem" (Kamm, 2015).

Many articles—both in the mass media and academic literature—have likened the ethics of self-driving cars to the trolley problem. However, we should be careful not to draw too close of an analogy between the philosophy of the trolley problem and the real-world ethics of crashes involving self-driving cars (Hevelke & Nida-Rümelin, 2015; Nyholm & Smids, 2016). There are at least three reasons why.

Firstly, in academic discussions of the trolley problem, we are asked to concentrate only on a small set of stylized situational considerations. In the real-world ethics of automated driving, in contrast, we should take as many considerations as possible into account. Secondly, in philosophical trolley-problem discussions, we are typically asked to completely set aside questions about legal and moral responsibility. In the real-world ethics of automated driving, we cannot simply set aside questions about responsibility. Thirdly, in trolley-problem discussions, we assume that we know with certainty what the outcomes of different possible actions would be. In the real-world ethics of automated driving, in contrast, we are dealing with risks and uncertainty.

For these reasons, the literature on the so-called trolley problem may be less helpful than many people might think when it comes to the ethics of automated driving. That is not to say that the literature about the trolley problem and the comparison between trolley problem-inspired cases and the ethics of self-driving cars is altogether irrelevant. If nothing else, it can be useful to compare the ethics of crashing self-driving cars with the trolley problem because identifying key differences between the two can be a good way of clarifying what matters most in the real-world ethics of self-driving cars.

# Empirical Ethics

There has been some fascinating work about self-driving cars within the field of empirical ethics. Empirical ethics is an attempt to incorporate empirical investigation of ordinary people's intuitive attitudes and judgments into academic ethical analysis. For example, we can systematically study people's attitudes and moral intuitions by letting them make judgments about many different real or simulated scenarios involving crashing self-driving cars. We can then discern patterns in their judgments and intuitions. And we can try to incorporate our findings into ethical arguments.

Several psychologists and behavioral economists have been surveying ordinary people's intuitive opinions about how automated cars should handle crash scenarios. One interesting finding comes from interdisciplinary researchers at MIT (Bonnefon et al., 2016). The finding is that when people are asked about what kinds of accident algorithms they would like others to have, many people say that they want others to have cars programmed to minimize overall harm. However, when asked what kind of accident settings they would like to have in their own self-driving cars, people's responses typically change. They do not want to be required to use or buy cars that are "altruistic" by being programmed to minimize overall harm. Instead, they prefer cars that would be programmed to try to always save the people in the car, even if this does not minimize overall harm.

On the "moral machine" website also created by researchers at MIT, one can explore numerous different dilemmas and cases and make intuitive judgments about them.[2] For example, if a car would hit and kill three senior citizens if it turns left, or hit and kill three children and two cats if it turns right, what should the car do? Or what if a car with five passengers in it can either go straight and crash into a wall, or turn and crash into a pedestrian who is jaywalking when there is a red light? What should the car then do? Those are the kinds of dilemmas people are asked to have intuitions about.

Millions of people around the world have participated in this experiment. The researchers have analyzed widely shared attitudes about these moral dilemmas involving self-driving cars (Awad et al., 2018). An interesting finding is that depending on where people live in the world, they have slightly different attitudes about whose safety should be prioritized in these imagined crash scenarios. In some parts of the world, participants were more likely to favor saving children at risk than saving older people at risk. In other parts of the world, it was the other way around. Moreover, in some parts of the world, someone breaking the traffic rules (e.g., crossing the street at a red light) was seen as weakening their right to not be hit by a self-driving car. In other parts of the world, that factor did not play any significant role in people's intuitions. There were several other fascinating cultural differences in people's attitudes around the world in these surveys.

Is this survey-based empirical methodology a good basis for ethical theorizing about crash scenarios? These findings are certainly very interesting. But there are some reasons for skepticism (Nyholm, 2018a). Here are three.

First, people do not yet have much real-world experience with traffic involving self-driving cars. It is likely that people's attitudes will change once they acquire more experience of what it is like to have lots of self-driving cars in society. This gives us reason to not put too much weight on people's current attitudes. Second, people's spontaneous gut reactions to hypothetical cases do not necessarily tell us what arguments and reasons they would present to defend their intuitive judgments. In ethical reasoning we evaluate arguments, and not only intuitive responses without any arguments or reasons to back them up. Third, people seem to have inconsistent attitudes. As was noted above, most people want others to have harm-minimizing cars. But they themselves want to have cars programmed to save them. Cars that minimize overall harm will sometimes save the car owner. But sometimes cars programmed to minimize overall harm will have to sacrifice the people in the car.

Again, people's attitudes and intuitions are certainly important and interesting to consider when we think about the ethics of automated driving and accident scenarios. But it is not clear that we can easily move from premises about people's intuitive attitudes to any solid conclusions about how best to argue about self-driving cars and accident scenarios.

# Traditional Ethical Theories

We can next briefly explore the option of using traditional ethical theories from moral philosophy when thinking about how self-driving cars should behave. Specifically, let us consider utilitarianism, Kantian ethics, and virtue ethics. Utilitarianism is the theory that we should always promote the overall good, by promoting everyone's well-being. Kantian ethics says that we should adopt a set of basic principles we would be willing to have as universal laws, so that we treat everyone with equal respect. Virtue ethics tells us that we should live our lives in ways that help us to exercise various virtues and excellences. We can use these theories to explore the question of how self-driving cars should handle accident scenarios as well as how they should behave more generally (Gurney, 2016).

Importantly, these ethical theories were originally developed to be about what humans should do, not about what technologies equipped with artificial intelligence should do. So, it is not obvious that we can simply carry over the moral principles that are supposed to guide human choices to the ethics of how self-driving cars should behave. It might be unclear what principles of translation should be used when we export traditional theories about human–human interaction into the new domain of human–machine interaction. This is a new form of ethics, where different rules and principles might potentially be taken to apply.

Let us nevertheless consider how these theories might be used in this context. Some philosophers will say that we need to make a choice here. We can only use one moral theory. But it is also possible to suggest that in thinking about the ethics of how cars should behave around human beings, we could make use of all three moral theories. There is clearly something to learn from each traditional moral theory.

The lesson from utilitarianism (or consequentialism more generally) might be that however cars are programmed to handle crash scenarios or behave more generally, we should think about this issue with an eye to the greater good of society. We should reason carefully about what promotes overall well-being and other important human values.

The lesson from Kantian ethics could be that whatever rules we decide on regarding the behavior of self-driving cars, these rules should be "universal laws" that are respectful of everyone. For the sake of fairness and equal treatment, people's cars should behave and handle crash scenarios according to a shared set of rules, applying equally to everyone.

Consider lastly virtue ethics. Currently, there are important virtues that many people tend to exhibit in traffic. For example, people tend to conduct themselves in fairly responsible ways. Of course, there are many exceptions. But most people feel responsible and mostly also act responsibly when they use very risky technologies like cars. The philosopher Mark Coeckelbergh (2016) has argued that people's tendencies to feel a sense of responsibility when they use cars is influenced by the design and technology of the car. This is relevant from a virtue-ethical perspective. After all, behaving responsibly is an important virtue. So, it can be argued that self-driving cars should be designed to make people who use such cars still feel responsible for what happens when they are riding in these cars. This is an important virtue.

In general, then, we could use the traditional ethical theories of utilitarianism, Kantian ethics, and virtue ethics to argue for the following general moral principle regarding how self-driving cars should behave in society: self-driving cars should be made to behave in a way that promotes everyone's well-being, according to principles that apply equally to all and that are respectful toward all, and that help to promote human virtue. That is a very general moral principle, and there may be lots of disagreement about what this would mean in practice. But it provides general guidelines for ethical thinking about the behavior of self-driving cars that seems highly plausible.

# Moral Responsibility

In the introduction above, it was mentioned that the ethics of self-driving cars has gone from using hypothetical thought experiments to being about real-world events. When this development was mentioned above, there was also a brief mention of the issue of who should be held responsible when there are accidents involving self-driving cars. This has been a key issue in the real-world ethics of automated driving. In this last section, let us therefore briefly consider some issues related to responsibility and self-driving cars.

Starting with the real-world cases mentioned earlier, Google has usually denied responsibility whenever their experimental self-driving cars have been involved in crashes. However, as was mentioned above, there was one case—the case on Valentine's Day of 2016—in which Google admitted that a crash had been caused by their car. The Google car had crashed into a bus. Google admitted "partial responsibility." They also promised to update the software of their car, so that it would become better at predicting the behavior of buses (Nyholm, 2018b).

In contrast, when a man died in a Tesla Model S car operating in "autopilot" mode later that same year, Tesla denied all responsibility. They published a blog post expressing sympathy with the family of the deceased. But the company noted that it was part of their user agreement that users of their "autopilot" function must take responsibility for whatever problems might arise. At the same time, however, Tesla also said that they would update their hardware, so that their cars would be better able to detect dangerous obstacles.

To some people, Google's abovementioned response made more sense than Tesla's. Google assumed partial responsibility. So, it made sense that they would also say that they were going to update their software. This contrasts in an interesting way with Tesla's response. Tesla admitted that it would be a good idea to update their hardware. Was that not an admission of responsibility for the crash? If Tesla was not to blame for the crash, then what need was there to update the technology in their car?

Some commentators find it unfair to blame human users of self-driving cars for accidents that their cars cause (Hevelke & Nida-Rümelin, 2015). Users of self-driving cars who are lucky because their cars do not crash may not do anything differently than users of self-driving cars who are unlucky because their cars do cause accidents.

Why not always simply blame the companies who create the self-driving cars? Some scholars who discuss this issue have worried that this might make car companies less motivated to create these cars (Marchant & Lindor 2012; Hevelke & Nida-Rümelin 2015). That would be a bad development, it has been suggested, since self-driving cars are thought to potentially have many benefits, particularly related to traffic safety.

Another reason that is sometimes suggested for why car designers should not be responsible for crashes involving self-driving cars is that they will not be able to reliably predict what these cars will do once they are on the road. Once the cars are out in traffic and operating autonomously, the people who built the cars will no longer directly control what the cars are doing. After all, they are self-driving cars. They are supposed to be operating autonomously. And no human might be able to fully predict what the artificial intelligence in the car will decide is the best course of action in certain traffic situations (Hevelke & Nida-Rümelin, 2015).

Some philosophers who discuss issues like these worry that self-driving cars might give rise to "responsibility gaps" (Nyholm, 2018b). This would mean that there is nobody who can be sensibly blamed when self-driving cars crash and people are harmed, even though it might seem as if somebody should be held responsible.

Do these worries about possible responsibility gaps make sense? Perhaps some traditional ways of thinking about responsibility for crashes involving human-driven cars cannot be directly carried over to the new case of crashes involving self-driving cars. However, there are ways in which one can under-stand moral and legal responsibility that can be brought to bear on the issue of responsibility for crashes involving self-driving cars. For example, we can think in terms of what roles and rights people have. This can ground responsibilities. There are also other possible arguments. Among other things, one can think about who benefits most from the presence of self-driving cars on the road. If a car company rents out self-driving cars, and that company makes a lot of money, then it might only be fair that they should be held responsible for any accidents that may occur involving their lucrative self-driving cars.

Moreover, even if people may lack direct control over how self-driving cars behave on the road, they will still have indirect control over the behavior of self-driving cars. Self-driving cars will be updated and maintained. And updates and maintenance will be based on people's opinions about how self-driving cars should function (Nyholm, 2018b). This will help to make anybody in charge of updating and maintaining these cars at least partly responsible for how the cars behave on the road. This will give people at least indirect control over what self-driving cars do. That might be enough to make them responsible for the behavior of the cars.

# References

Awad, E., Dsouza, S., Kim, R., Shulz, J., Henrich, J., Shariff, A., Bonnefon, J-F., & Rahwan, I. (2018). The moral machine experiment. *Nature*, *563*, 59–64.

Bonnefon, J-F., Sharrif, A., & Rahwan, I. (2016). The social dilemma of autonomous vehicles. *Science*, *352*(6293), 1573–1576.

Coeckelberg, M. (2016). Responsibility and the moral phenomenology of using self-driving cars. *Applied Artificial Intelligence*, *30*(8), 748–757. https://www.tandfonline.com/doi/full/10.1080/08839514.2016.1229759.

Goodall, N. J. (2014). Ethical decision making during automated vehicle crashes. *Transportation Research Record: Journal of the Transportation Research Board*, *2424*(1), 58–65.

Gurney, J. (2016). Crashing into the unknown: An examination of crash-optimization algorithms through the two lanes of ethics and law. *Albany Law Review*, *79*(1), 183–267.

Hevelke, A., & Nida-Rümelin, J. (2015). Responsibility for crashes of autonomous vehicles: An ethical analysis. *Science and Engineering Ethics*, *21*(3), 619–630.

Kamm, F. (2015). *The trolley problem mysteries*. Oxford University Press.

Marchant, G., & Lindor, R. (2012). The coming collision between autonomous cars and the liability system. *Santa Clara Legal Review*, *52*(4), 1321–1340.

Nyholm, S. (2018a). The ethics of crashes with self-driving cars, a roadmap I. *Philosophy Compass*, *13*(7): e12507. https://onlinelibrary.wiley.com/doi/full/10.1111/phc3.12507.

Nyholm, S. (2018b). The ethics of crashes with self-driving cars, a roadmap II. *Philosophy Compass*, *13*(7): e12506. https://onlinelibrary.wiley.com/doi/full/10.1111/phc3.12506.

Nyholm, S., & Smids, J. (2020). Automated cars meet human drivers: Responsible human-robot coordination and the ethics of mixed traffic. *Ethics and Information Technology*, *22*(4): 335–344.

Nyholm, S., & Smids, J. (2016). The ethics of accident-algorithms for self-driving cars: An applied trolley problem? *Ethical Theory and Moral Practice*, *19*(5), 1275–1289.

Peterson, R. W. (2012). New technology—old law: Autonomous vehicles and California's insurance framework. *Santa Clara Law Review*, *52*: 101–153.

Sparrow, R., & Howard, M. (2017). When human beings are like drunk robots: Driverless vehicles, ethics, and the future of transport. *Transportation Research Part C*, *80*, 206–215.

Section 2

# Cybersecurity

# CHAPTER 16

# AI and Criminal Justice

## INDIVIDUAL AUTONOMY, JOINT RIGHTS, AND COLLECTIVE RESPONSIBILITY

*Seumas Miller*

## Abstract

In this chapter ethical issues that arise in relation to predictive policing, DNA databases, and facial recognition technology are discussed. Moral problems that arise include the potential for the use of AI in law enforcement to violate individual privacy and autonomy rights and, in the case of universal or bulk DNA databases, joint moral rights to genomic data. On the other hand, it is argued that these rights can be overridden under certain circumstances, notably in cases in which there is a collective moral responsibility and, therefore (on the view advanced here), an individual moral responsibility to assist law enforcement in relation to serious crimes.

### KEYWORDS

predictive policing, DNA databases, facial recognition technology, joint rights, collective responsibility

## Introduction

Artificial intelligence is impacting criminal justice systems in the United States, United Kingdom, and other liberal democracies, but even more so in some authoritarian states, such as China. As is the case with other powerful technologies, such as nuclear technology, AI is a dual-use technology; it can be used to provide great benefits but also to do great harm.[1] In this chapter we discuss

207

ethical issues that arise from the establishment of bulk databases, and the use of machine-learning techniques, for law enforcement purposes. The specific areas discussed are predictive policing, DNA databases, and facial recognition technology.

# Predictive Policing

Predictive policing (PP) uses crime mapping data and analysis, social network analysis, bulk databases, and machine learning. Police services have long used crime mapping data and analysis to target crime hotspots, whether on the basis of past crimes in particular locations or because these locations have features that statistically correlate with specific crime types (e.g., they are tourist sites with good escape routes for thieves). Police have also targeted known offenders on the basis, for instance, of a modus operandi (M.O.) used in a spate of crimes, an M.O. preferred by the targeted offender in question. In both these kinds of cases police are, in effect, predicting that crime will take place at a particular location (and distributing their resources accordingly) or that a particular known offender is continuing to commit crimes of a certain type (and acting to prevent the offender from doing so).

PP is used in many jurisdictions in large cities in the United States, such as New York, Chicago, and Los Angeles. PP is controversial. There is a concern that citizens might be arrested for crimes they have not committed and, indeed, have no intention of committing. Part of the moral concern here is based on an epistemic concern; the reliability of the evidence used in predictive policing is questionable, especially when it is used in relation to relatively low-volume crimes, such as murder or terrorism. Arguably, there are no features of a person that would justify the reliable prediction that he or she will commit an act of murder or terrorism. Naturally, multiple past murders or terrorism offenses might provide good evidence that the offender in question would continue to commit such offenses if released. However, this judgment does not seem to require PP and, in any case, even these sorts of prediction are not necessarily reliable. After all, a past offender can choose not to reoffend.

Thus, predictive policing has significant limitations. For some serious crimes, such as murder and terrorism, the databases are small—too small to afford an opportunity to use machine-learning techniques to generate useable profiles of murderers or terrorists (respectively), as opposed to indicators that might guide investigators on an ad hoc basis.

What of high-volume crimes? Certainly, these crime categories (e.g., house burglaries in particular locations) offer more favorable opportunities for PP. However, even high-volume crime categories provide obstacles for PP.

Predictions of future crime using machine learning techniques are based on *the past* (i.e., reported crimes, arrests, prosecutions, lists of offenders, etc.). Thus, if law enforcement agencies rely on machine learning then (other things being equal) offenders and offense types that have escaped detection in the past (e.g., child sexual abuse) are less likely than those that have not (e.g., grievous bodily harm) to be targeted by police.

Naturally, other things might not be equal, and police might choose to target offenders and offense types that are now known to have gone undetected in the past, as has recently happened in the case of child sexual abuse. However, if in doing so police are seeking to predict future crimes by these offenders or these offense types using machine-learning techniques then problems will arise. Problems will arise as a result of the inadequacy of the past datasets (i.e., non-existent, incomplete, and unreliable information about the past offenders and offenses in question).

For the same reason, by relying on past data to predict future crime, communities that have been overpoliced in the past are likely to continue to be overpoliced relative to other communities. This is especially the case if predictive policing techniques utilize socioeconomic indicators that statistically correlate with crime indicators, as is the case with poor Black neighbourhoods in the United States.

Related to this last point, one of the more controversial predictive policing techniques is profiling, and profiling can take the form of morally problematic racial profiling. A famous case of profiling in the United States is that of Sokolow, who was searched by customs officials at an airport and found to possess drugs. He was searched because he fit the profile of a drug courier, and this was taken to constitute reasonable grounds for suspicion. Sokolow argued in court that fitting a profile did not constitute reasonable grounds for suspicion. However, he lost the case because it was held that whereas fitting a profile did not of itself constitute reasonable suspicion the evidence that constituted the profile in his particular case did.[2]

However, there are dangers in the practice of profiling and, of interest to us here, profiling that utilizes machine-learning techniques. Specifically, there is the risk of discriminatory algorithms (e.g., an algorithm that relied on a past dataset that comprised an unjustifiably disproportionate number of "stop-and-frisk" searches of Black citizens). Profiling practices that rely on machine-learning techniques that utilize such datasets can end up generating morally unjustified, racially biased profiles of offenders and, thereby, entrench existing racist attitudes among police officers and others.

There is also the general problem of the effectiveness of PP in criminal justice contexts in which offenders can themselves predict the results of PP processes and thereby thwart them. If, for example, criminals become aware of the profiles used by police, they can adjust their M.O.s so as to escape detection.

Thus far we have focused on predictive policing as it is currently practiced (at least for the most part) in liberal democracies, such as the United States, the United Kingdom, and Australia. However, predictive policing is constantly evolving and in doing so is utilizing new technologies. Fingerprint recognition and DNA identification have a long history of successful use in the criminal justice system to investigate serious crime. However, new biometric identification technologies, such as facial recognition, gait analysis, and voice recognition are rapidly evolving. Moreover, there have been important developments in existing technologies, notably DNA identification, and the expansion, digitization, and interlinking of existing databases with new ones (see "DNA Databases" below).

Recently, biometric databases have been established by governments and the private sector; for example, automated facial recognition is now a key part of passports and border security in many countries. Automated facial recognition is a powerful technology with the potential to identify a face in a large crowd, through integration with closed-circuit television (CCTV) systems, enabling real-time surveillance, identification, and tracking of individuals through public places by police (see "Facial Recognition Technology" below). Further notable applications of facial recognition include the analysis of images taken from the Internet, particularly social media, such as images from Facebook, Twitter, LinkedIn, and Google. The significance of this capability is highlighted by the rapid expansion in the number of images uploaded to the Internet. For example, Facebook alone holds several hundred billion photographs in its database, and uses automated facial recognition software to identify or "tag" users in photographs.

The use of these technologies raises a number of pressing ethical concerns. The capacity to integrate databases of biometric and nonbiometric (e.g., smartphone and email metadata and financial, medical, and tax records) information adds to these concerns. For instance, biometric facial image templates can be used in conjunction with digital images sourced from CCTV, phone GPS data, and Internet history to provide an increasingly complete picture of an individual's movements and lifestyle. As is often noted, privacy and confidentiality in relation to personal data consists in large part in the right to control the access to, and use of, that data. As such, it is a component of individual autonomy, a cornerstone of liberal democracy.

# DNA Databases

As just mentioned, the collection of biometric data, notably DNA and facial image data, is rapidly expanding. In this section our focus is on DNA data, and in the following section on facial image data.

Universal forensic DNA databases include the DNA profiles of all persons in a jurisdiction. To date there are no such databases, other than perhaps in the Xinjiang province in China. However, the technique described as forensic gene-alogy[3] has the potential to enable the creation of what Smith (2018)[4] refers to as *quasi-universal forensic DNA databases*. These databases already exist in several jurisdictions, including not only China but also the United Kingdom and the United States.

National databases of the DNA profiles of convicted offenders and sus-pects have been created in many countries. For example, in the United States the National DNA Index System contains approximately 13 million convicted offender profiles (from a total population of 328 million);[5] the United King-dom's National DNA Database contains about 6 million offender profiles (from a total population of 66 million);[6] and China has established the world's largest DNA database, believed to include approximately 140 million profiles (from a total population of 1.4 billion).[7]

However, forensic genealogy utilizes DNA profiles to identify suspects who are not included in law enforcement's DNA databases. It does so by relying on the genetic relatedness of an offender (whose DNA is found at a crime scene) to a relative who provided his or her DNA to an organization for genetic health or ancestry testing. The best-known example of forensic genealogy is the "Golden State Killer" case in California. The offender was identified because a distant relative had been genetically tested to determine their ancestry. The investiga-tors found a partial match between the DNA of the killer derived from crime scenes and the DNA of the distant relative in the ancestry database. They then used standard investigative methods, firstly to construct a list of suspects from the family tree (derived from birth registry records) and secondly to narrow the list of suspects down to the offender.

Using this technique of forensic genealogy and available law enforcement DNA databases together with access to health and ancestry databases, it is esti-mated by Smith (2018)[8] that if 5% of the total population in a jurisdiction were included in a DNA database, then if an offender leaves their DNA at a crime scene, the offender can be identified via their relatives whose DNA is in an exist-ing database, even if the offender's DNA is not in a database. Accordingly, the need for universal DNA databases is obviated. It is necessary only to have quasi-universal forensic databases, given the availability of the technique of forensic genealogy and law enforcement access to health and ancestry databases.

The genome of a person is not only constitutive of that person's individual-specific (biological) identity; that same genome is *in part* constitutive of the individual-specific (biological) identity of the person's relatives (to a decreasing extent depending on the degree of relatedness, for example, a sibling is more related than a second cousin). Evidently, therefore, genomic data involves joint rights. But what are joint rights?[9] Roughly speaking, two or more agents have a joint moral right to some good, including potentially some data or knowledge, if they each have an individual moral right to the good, if no one else has a moral right to it, and if the individual right of each is dependent on the individual rights of the others. Thus, the right of moral agent A to some good, G (jointly held with moral agent, B), brings with it an essential reference to the right of B to G (jointly held with A), and does so via the good, G. Moreover, being a joint right, neither A nor B can unilaterally extinguish it.

As stated above, the genome of a person is not only constitutive of that person's individual-specific (biological) identity; that same genome is *in part* constitutive of the individual-specific (biological) identity of the person's relatives. Accordingly, there is a species of joint right to control genomic data in play here, and not merely an exclusively individual right. The right to control one's genome data needs to be regarded, we suggest, as a (qualified)[10] joint right (i.e., a right jointly held with the individual's relatives). If these rights are, as we are suggesting, joint rights, then it follows that an individual may not have an exclusive individual right to provide his or her genomic data to consumer genetic testing providers, or to law enforcement. Of course, when it comes to serious crimes, the consent of an individual to access his or her genome data is not necessarily required (e.g., if the individual is a past offender and hence his or her genomic data in the form of a DNA profile is held in a law enforcement database).[11]

However, in cases in which identifying the person who has committed a crime relies on the genomic data of relatives known to be innocent and the relatives in question have a joint right to the data in question, then it may be that *all* of *these* relatives need to have consented to the collection of the genomic data in question.[12] For in voluntarily providing one's DNA to law enforcement a person is, in effect, providing law enforcement with the partially overlapping DNA data of the person's relatives. But presumably a person does not have a moral right to decide to provide law enforcement with another person's DNA data.

Accordingly, it seems that a person, A, does not have a moral right to *unilaterally* provide law enforcement with his or her own data (i.e., A's DNA data, given that in doing so A is providing to law enforcement the partially overlapping DNA data of A's relatives, B, C, D, etc.). Rather, A, B, C, D, etc., have an (admittedly qualified) joint moral right to the DNA data in question and, therefore, the right (being a joint right) has to be exercised jointly (i.e., perhaps all, or most, have to agree).

Naturally, as is the case with individual moral rights, joint moral rights can be overridden. For instance, A's individual right to know whether he is vulnerable to a hereditary disease might justify his providing his genomic data to health authorities and doing so without the consent of any of his relatives. In relation to our concerns here, the joint moral right of a group of persons to refuse to provide law enforcement with the DNA data in a murder investigation, for instance, is presumably overridden by their collective moral responsibility to assist the police.

Here collective moral responsibility is to be understood as joint moral responsibility. Central to joint responsibility and therefore collective responsibility is the responsibility arising from joint actions. A joint action can be understood as follows: two or more individuals perform a joint action if each of them intentionally performs his or her individual action but does so with the (true) belief that in so doing each will do their part and they will jointly realize an end that each of them has and that each has interdependently with the others (i.e., a collective end).[13] In this view of collective responsibility as joint responsibility, collective responsibility is ascribed to individuals;[14] moreover, if the joint action in question is morally significant (e.g., by virtue of the collective end being a collective good or a collective harm), then the individuals are collectively *morally* responsible for it.

Evidently, citizens have a collective moral responsibility to assist law enforcement in relation to serious crime and, in particular, to provide their DNA data, if required. Indeed, this moral responsibility may need to be enforced since in relation to serious crimes it evidently overrides privacy/autonomy rights. However, the collective moral responsibility in question applies in specific cases on a piecemeal basis; it is not a collective moral responsibility to provide their DNA data in a manner that contributes to a universal or quasi-universal DNA database. Moreover, it is not a collective moral responsibility to provide their DNA data on a permanent basis. Rather, they have a joint moral right that the data be destroyed upon the conclusion of the specific criminal investigation and associated trial.

# Facial Recognition Technology[15]

As we saw in the case of DNA, one's face (as opposed to one's facial expressions, for example, whether one is smiling or not) is a more or less unalterable feature of a human being and constitutive (in part) of their identity. However, unlike DNA a human being's face is expressive of their inner mental self (e.g., their emotions as opposed to their physical self), and somewhat under their control. As such, a human being's face is constitutive (in part) of their identity in a different and, in some respects, more profound sense than is their DNA.

Moreover, a person's face, while it is more or less unalterable, does undergo gradual change over time, notably as part of the aging process. In this respect, it mirrors one's changing personal identity (e.g., the adult is the same person as the child he or she was but also importantly different). Given that one's facial image is an image of a constitutive feature of one's identity (i.e., one's face), and given the tight connection between identity and autonomy (of which more below), evidently, control of one's facial image is importantly connected to individual autonomy; specifically, a person has a moral right to control images of his or her face (e.g., digital photos). However, unlike DNA profiles, facial images are easily and surreptitiously obtainable and, as a result of the widespread use of social media, ubiquitous. Accordingly, control of one's facial image is increasingly difficult and to that extent individual autonomy is potentially compromised.

Biometric facial recognition technology involves (1) the automated extraction of facial images from passport photos, drivers' licences, social media sites (e.g., Facebook), and elsewhere; (2) the digitization of these facial images; (3) the conversion of these facial images into a contour map of the spatial and geometric distribution of the facial features on these images; (4) the storage of these facial features (thus extracted and converted); (5) the comparison using algorithms of newly acquired facial images (thus extracted and converted) with those already stored in databases to identify individuals. Biometric facial recognition systems can be integrated with the closed-circuit television systems that already exist in public spaces to search for, identify, and thereby track people in real time[16].

The expanding use of this technology in law enforcement, border protection, and national security contexts raises a number of pressing ethical concerns for liberal democracies[17] in relation to, in particular, individual privacy and autonomy and democratic accountability. Moreover, the fact that this technology is already in widespread use in authoritarian states, such as China in the context of its social credit system, raises the specter of its widespread use in liberal democracies.

We also note that it is not simply a matter of the use of this technology by law enforcement agencies. Criminal organizations, firms, and private individuals now have access to this technology, but also to a very large database of facial images (and associated publicly available information). The latter database has been created by the private firm Clearview. Clearview created a database of literally billions of facial images by scraping them off social media sites and related sources. Moreover, these facial images have links to websites from which the facial images were scraped, thus providing information about the identity of the persons whose facial images are in the database.

Further, Clearview's software enables its buyer to compare a facial image the buyer might possess (e.g., as a result of taking a digital image of a stranger in a public space), with images in Clearview's huge database and thereby (via the publicly available information associated with these facial images), identify the stranger in question (e.g. who they are, what they do, and so on). Accordingly, criminal organizations could use facial recognition technology (and Clearview's database and app, in particular) to thwart law enforcement, (e.g., by identifying an undercover operative whose facial image might be on a police college gradu-ation photo),[18] and to engage in crimes such as stalking (e.g., by using a facial image to gain more information about a person being stalked) and identity theft (e.g., using a facial image in conjunction with other personal data with a view to defrauding potential victims).

Biometric facial recognition is obviously implicated in privacy concerns. Indeed, in privacy concerns it is related to both information and observation. Here it is important to note that the moral right to privacy is closely related to the more fundamental moral value of autonomy. Roughly speaking, the notion of privacy delimits an informational and observational "space" (i.e., the private sphere). However, the right to autonomy consists of a right to decide what to think and do and, of relevance here, the right to control the private sphere and, therefore, to decide *who to exclude and who not to exclude* from it.[19] So, the right to privacy consists of the right to exclude organizations and other individuals (the right to autonomy) both from personal information and facial images, and from observation and monitoring (the private sphere).

Naturally, the right to privacy, including one's control of facial images, is not absolute; it can be overridden. Moreover, its precise boundaries are unclear; a person does not have a right not to be observed in a public space but, argu-ably, has a right not to be photographed in a public space (let alone have an image of their face widely circulated on the Internet), albeit this right not to be photographed and have one's image circulated can be overridden under certain circumstances. For instance, this right might be overridden if the public space in question is under surveillance by CCTV in order to detect and deter crime, and if the resulting images are only made available to police—and then only for the purpose of identifying persons who have committed a crime in that area.

What of persons who are present in the public space in question and recorded on CCTV, but who have committed a serious crime, such as terror-ism, elsewhere, or at least are suspected of having committed a serious crime elsewhere and are, therefore, on a watch list? Presumably, it is morally accept-able to utilize CCTV footage to identify these persons as well. If so, then it seems morally acceptable to utilize biometric facial recognition technology to match images of persons recorded on CCTV with those of persons on a watch list of those who have committed, for instance, terrorist actions, or are suspected of having done.

In addition to the rights of a *single* individual, it is important to consider the implications of the infringement, indeed violation, of the privacy and autonomy rights of the whole citizenry by the state (and/or other powerful institutional actors, such as corporations). Such large-scale violations can lead to a power imbalance between the state and the citizenry and, thereby, undermine liberal democracy itself.[20] The surveillance system imposed on the Uighurs in China, incorporating biometric facial recognition technology, graphically illustrates the risks attached to large-scale violations of privacy and related autonomy rights.

# Conclusion

In this chapter we have discussed ethical issues that arise in relation to predictive policing, DNA databases, and facial recognition technology. In doing so we have seen that a number of moral problems arise, notably the potential for the use of AI in law enforcement to violate individual privacy and autonomy rights and, in the case of universal or bulk DNA databases, joint moral rights to genomic data.

On the other hand, we have also seen that these rights can be overridden under certain circumstances, notably in cases in which there is a collective moral responsibility and, therefore (on the view advanced here), an individual moral responsibility, to assist law enforcement in relation to serious crimes.

# CHAPTER 17

# Ethical Dimensions of Facial Recognition and Video Analytics in Surveillance

*Rosalie Waelen and Philip Brey*

## Abstract

This chapter identifies and analyzes ethical issues in video surveillance, with a focus on applications that involve video analytics and facial recognition technology. The first part of the analysis focuses on ethical issues in video analytics, which are techniques that automatically analyze preexisting or gathered video data. Ethical issues are discussed in relation to processes of identification, classification, detection, and tracking of persons. Next, facial recognition technology is discussed, particularly its use in surveillance, and its ethical challenges are investigated. Finally, we focus on three advanced video analytics techniques: facial analysis, behavior analysis, and emotion analysis, which raise additional serious ethical issues.

**KEYWORDS**

surveillance, ethics, facial recognition, video analytics, behavior analytics, emotion analytics

## Introduction

Some of the most controversial applications of digital technologies are found in surveillance. When worries are voiced about negative implications of digital technologies for privacy and individual rights, applications for surveillance are often mentioned among given examples. Digital technologies have vastly extended the powers of organizations—both governments and private corporations—to engage in surveillance. In this chapter, we will focus on visual surveillance of physical places, undertaken by means of cameras (i.e., camera surveillance), and we will focus on two major digital technologies that have come to be used in camera surveillance in recent years: video analytics and facial recognition technologies. We will carry out an ethical analysis of these technologies and their use in surveillance.

Surveillance is the monitoring of the behavior of individuals and groups through observation and data collection. It is usually associated with government agencies, especially law enforcement, but surveillance is also undertaken by private corporations, health agencies, and criminal organizations, among others. The purpose of surveillance is normally to serve the goals and interests of the surveilling entity, which can be varied. For government agencies, these interests can be to prevent or investigate criminal activity and terrorism; to monitor processes so as to enhance safety and security; to better manage social processes so as to ensure their quality, efficiency, and compliance with law and policy; to protect national security; and to maintain social control and social order in a general sense. For corporations, these interests are to protect property; guarantee the integrity and security of organizational processes; enhance the security and safety of employees and customers; enhance the performance of employees; and analyze and influence customers.

Surveillance practices are as old as civilization, but they have taken new forms in contemporary society, due to the emergence of new surveillance technologies that drastically extend the abilities of organizations to engage in surveillance. Electronic and digital technologies, in particular, have greatly enhanced the possibilities for observing individuals and groups, and their traits, behaviors, and movements; for analyzing information thus gathered; and for exercising real-time influence and control. The emergence of the Internet as a mass medium has enabled large-scale computer and network surveillance, in which the online behavior of individuals is monitored.

The digitalization of the telephone network has enabled large-scale wiretapping and telephone surveillance. In public and private spaces, closed-circuit television (CCTV) systems and satellites have made possible new forms of visual surveillance. And wireless tracking technologies have made it possible to track the location and movement of individuals through devices like mobile phones and radio frequency identification (RFID) tags.

In this chapter, we will investigate how video analytics and facial recognition enable new forms of surveillance, and analyze the ethical issues that arise as a result. In the next section, we start with a review of ethical issues in the use of CCTV, with particular attention to recent developments in video analytics that allow for the intelligent analysis of video images. In the section titled "Facial

Recognition Technology," we turn to facial recognition technologies and their use in surveillance. In the section titled "Facial, Behavioral, and Emotional Analytics," we focus on video surveillance applications that involve facial analysis, behavior analytics, and emotional analytics. The chapter ends with a "Conclusion" section.

# Video Surveillance and Video Analytics

Video surveillance using closed-circuit television (CCTV) has been in use since at least the 1970s. Cameras in buildings and public spaces are used for monitoring and are connected to an observation room in which one or more operators observe the video feed and monitor the places and people in them. Cameras were increasingly equipped with supporting features, like panning, tilting, zooming in and out, sound, and infrared capabilities. However, a genuine expansion of the abilities of CCTV cameras has come with the advent of video analytics in the 2000s and the introduction of deep learning to this field in 2011 (Adjabi et al., 2020).

"Video analytics" is an umbrella term referring to a variety of techniques used to automatically analyze preexisting or gathered video data and retrieve information from that data. This technology has also been referred to as "video content analysis," "video processing," and "smart cameras." The general aim of video analytics is to extract meaningful and relevant information. Whatever information is meaningful and relevant depends on the given context in which video analytics is used. For example, when video analytics is implemented in a store it would be relevant to the store's owner to recognize on video footage when a customer slips something into his or her pocket, or perhaps whether there is a large line for the checkout.

Dependent on the types of information one wants to retrieve from visual data, different techniques can be used. This is then a second important truth about video analytics: it is not a single technique or software system. It is made up of a variety of techniques, the constellation of which differs depending on the purpose for which video analytics is implemented. It typically involves some form of big data analytics for analyzing large amounts of visual information, and machine learning and artificial intelligence techniques, including computer vision algorithms, to segment, categorize, and analyze visual input data.

Video analytics models, and the techniques used to constitute them, can raise ethical concerns regardless of their application. First of all, a model can contain algorithmic biases caused by insufficiently inclusive training datasets, low-quality input data, or prejudices of the developer. Such biases in turn cause low-quality output ("garbage in, garbage out," as they say), which potentially leads to the unjust or discriminatory treatment of certain groups or individuals (see the next section). Secondly, big data analytics and machine learning can be employed to predict, describe, prescribe, or diagnose. The nature of these outcomes is ethically relevant, for example, because prescriptions are inherently normative and because predictions are necessarily uncertain and potentially self-fulfilling (King, 2019).

Another ethical concern related to the technical level of video analytics has to do with transparency and explainability. Machine learning and in particular deep learning, on which computer vision models are usually based, are complex techniques, which is why it is difficult for the average individual, and sometimes even for developers themselves, to understand how a model came to deliver a given outcome. This complexity makes algorithmic decision-making processes opaque, which is an ethical concern because transparency and explainability of decision-making processes make it easier to ascribe responsibility and account-ability, foster trust, and strengthen the epistemic agency and autonomy of those subjected to the decisions made.

Video analytics is carried out through different "tasks," "functionalities," or "modules," which carry out different types of analysis. It depends on the purpose or context of a video analytics application which tasks are implemented and which of the above discussed techniques are utilized. Typical tasks include the following:

- *Segmentation*: The detection and delineation of pixels that appear to belong together within a larger frame.
- *Localization*: The locating of objects and persons within a larger frame.
- *Classification*: The application of categories to localized objects or persons (e.g., "bicycle," "man," "yellow," "seated").
- *Detection*: The combination of localization and classification in which types of objects or attributes are localized in a picture or video
- *Tracking*: Following an object or person in motion through consecutive video frames.
- *Identification*: Recognition of a specific token in a class of objects (rather than a type), by matching an object or person in an image with an image of a specific object or person in a database. *Facial recognition* is a special type of identification.
- *Facial analysis*: This is a task different from facial recognition and involves analysis of facial features and expressions to reveal information about a person, for example, gender, age, or ethnicity, as well as potentially controversial features like sexual orientation, IQ, and character traits.

- *Behavioral analysis*: Analysis of the activity of individuals, crowds, animals, and vehicles, for example, by analyzing walking patterns, facial expressions, and direction of gaze in persons.
- *Emotion recognition*: The recognition and interpretation of emotions and inner mental states of persons based on facial analysis and/or analysis of voice, speech, and behavior.

Segmentation, localization, classification, detection, and tracking are rather basic tasks that video analytics systems are generally able to perform to a greater or lesser degree. Identification, facial analysis, behavior analysis, and emotion analysis are not always part of a video analytics model and allow for more sophisticated, interpretative analysis of persons and their behaviors. As a result, the latter group of tasks raises the most ethical concerns (which we will address in the following two sections). Moreover, the latter group of video analytics tasks are particularly relevant to surveillance, because they can be specifically used to analyze images of human beings and their behaviors (including objects carried or used and vehicles driven or used).

However, the more basic video analytics tasks are not without problems either. Each of these tasks' accuracy affects the overall outcome of a model. If, for example, localization is done poorly, it affects later steps and the overall quality of a model's outcome, which makes a model less trustworthy and more likely to cause discriminatory treatment.

Identification of persons raises privacy issues, since it makes known (aspects of) the identity of a person, which is not immediately apparent from the mere visual image of a person. Identification is therefore intrusive in a way that mere registration of persons through video surveillance is not. Similarly, tracking of persons can be morally objectionable because it follows people over larger distances, and can be argued to violate their "locational privacy": privacy with respect to their location. Especially when combined with identification, so that the identity of the person is known, tracking raises issues of privacy.

Classification can be morally objectionable when stereotyping or discriminatory labels are used. Moreover, when classification is used to profile individuals, this can have a normalizing or generalizing effect on their behavior and identity formation. By categorizing people, by giving them a label and treating them on the basis of it, surveillance should become more individualized. But at the same time, such classification also denies a person's individuality. By treating someone like other people that fit in the same category (e.g., "male," "elderly," "disabled," "White," "sports fan," and so on), they are nudged to shape themselves after others like them. This effect can be referred to as "algorithmic normalization" and is above all a threat to autonomy.

Tasks such as tracking, detection, and identification raise concerns of function creep (Brey, 2004) and over-enforcement (Adams & Ferryman, 2013; Stanley, 2019). The automation of these tasks makes it possible to recognize and follow large amounts of people, in real-time, and to link their actions to past activities. Even if video analytics systems are not used for surveillance purposes today, their use might change in the future. Brey (2004) refers to the risk that a technology gains new functions or purposes as "function creep."

If function creep occurs in the context of video analytics for video surveillance, this will lead to over-enforcement. If it becomes the norm that video analytics is used not just to monitor suspects but to identify and track all individuals in public spaces, this would imply excessive monitoring. Such excessive monitoring, or over-enforcement, would disproportionally threaten individual liberties like privacy, freedom, and autonomy as well as democratic or societal values. As Adams & Ferryman point out, "tracking can be used in oppressive policing in both oppressive and democratic states" (2013, p. 12).

Finally, the rising use of video analytics for video surveillance strengthens preexisting ethical challenges in surveillance. Typically associated with CCTV surveillance and other types of monitoring are implications for privacy, data governance, and informed consent. It is sometimes suggested that video analytics for surveillance is less privacy-invasive than traditional CCTV surveillance, because the automatic analysis of videos makes it superfluous for human operators to monitor video footage, and thus makes the practice of humans watching other humans disappear. However, even though no other human might actually watch a person that is being filmed, video analytics makes it possible to retrieve and aggregate much more information about a person than was the case in traditional surveillance. Smart surveillance also makes it easier to shift information about a person from one context to another. Because of these new dimensions of surveillance, surveillance by means of video analytics actually augments privacy concerns (Nissenbaum, 1998).

Informed consent is challenged by new forms of video surveillance, because it becomes increasingly difficult for an individual to understand what information is gathered when they are subject to surveillance and for what purposes. Although it is already often impossible to consent to video surveillance in public spaces in the first place, the complexity of video analytics technology makes *informed* consent unfeasible. Moreover, video analytics technologies such as facial recognition systems are often built on images scraped online without the knowledge or consent of those who shared the photo or are displayed in it (Van Noorden, 2020).

# Facial Recognition Technology

A video analytics task that is particularly valuable for surveillance is facial recognition. Facial recognition technology is used to identify human faces presented in digital images or video frames by comparing them against a database of faces. The software reads the geometry of the presented face and compares it with geometric features of faces in the database. If there is a match, then there is facial recognition. The faces in the database may be part of a record with further personal information about the identified person that can be used for further identification and analysis.

Facial recognition technology has two main applications: authentication and monitoring. Authentication is the process of determining whether someone is who they declare to be. Authentication is typically used for access to spaces, devices, or services, and whenever there is a need for authorities to establish the identity of a person who is on their premises. Authentication is usually a scripted process in which an individual has to move in front of a camera and follow instructions, after which a photograph is taken and a search is undertaken to match their identity. Upon successful authentication, the individual is given access to the space, device, or service that they are attempting to access, or the relevant authorities take relevant follow-up actions.

Authentication may involve governmental organizations, which have used it, among other purposes, to verify identity in immigration, voting, and applications for driver licenses. It may involve private companies, as when a company restricts access to its buildings with facial recognition technology or uses the technology to authorize financial transactions by customers, and it may involve private applications, for example, for unlocking one's smartphone and for starting the engine of one's car.

Monitoring is different from authentication in that there is no explicit attempt by an individual to claim an identity and the privileges that belong to it. Monitoring is a process that involves the scanning of groups of people, whereas authentication is defined over single individuals. Monitoring usually involves human identification at a distance, with cameras that survey crowds of people rather than persons posing in front of a camera, and with the possibility of people not being aware that they are being monitored by means of facial recognition technology.

Monitoring may be undertaken for at least four reasons. First, monitoring may be done to deny access to individuals who have been identified to present a security or safety risk or who are otherwise denied benefits available to others. This is an opt-out solution, for situations where everyone should have access to a space, device, or service, except for selected individuals, whereas authentication is usually used as an opt-in solution, in which only selected individuals gain access. Companies may, for example, decide to ban certain customers from their stores because of past theft, fraud, or disturbances, with identification at a distance using a database of images of banned individuals.

A second application of monitoring is for the location and apprehension of wanted individuals, usually by law enforcement authorities. In such applications, law enforcement uses video surveillance with facial recognition to find matches against a database of wanted criminals, suspected terrorists, or missing children, and uses positive IDs to apprehend the individual who is a match. A third application is that of flagging individuals. When there is a match, people that are flagged by the system become the subject of extra attention and possible follow-up actions. Video surveillance may be used to track the individual, analysis may take place of his or her behavior or interactions, and actions may be taken when specific circumstances or risks materialize. Such flagging may, for example, be applied to suspected criminals who are tracked by police, or by VIPs who require extra security.

Fourth and finally, monitoring may be used for mass surveillance, as in the Chinese social credit system, in which camera surveillance and facial recognition technology are used to observe and analyze the actions of Chinese citizens and use the result of analysis to update citizen scores that represent their trustworthiness.

Facial recognition at a distance is less reliable than recognition through a proximate camera, because images have lower resolution, lighting conditions are less ideal, and people do not pose for the camera. For this reason, distant cameras are rarely used for authentication, which requires a high degree of reliability. In the future, however, this could change as the technology improves. But for now we will assume that authentication involves proximate cameras and monitoring involves recognition at a distance. Authentication involves posing, awareness of the individual that he or she is being subjected to facial recognition, and more reliable matches than monitoring. Monitoring involves the identification and tracking of often unsuspecting individuals in crowds who engage in natural behavior, and lower reliability (more false positives and negatives).

Authentication processes that make use of facial recognition do not in and of themselves involve surveillance, as they are not directly used to monitor behavior of individuals and groups through observation and data collection. However, it is possible that authentication information is used as data points by organizations in surveillance practices, as they tie a particular individual to a time and location. Also, when people start using an authentication service that involves facial recognition, it is conceivable that the biometric image of their face that is created will be used in a database for future surveillance. Such potential function creep is why authentication makes data protection and privacy, as well as protection against oppressive regimes, pressing topics.

Whereas authentication does not directly involve surveillance, monitoring does. It does so at least in a limited sense, in that data is gathered on individuals; at a minimum, their identity is established, and they are tied to a certain place and time. But monitoring using facial recognition usually involves additional observation and data-gathering practices, such as the observation and analysis of behaviors and location tracking, making facial recognition part of a broader surveillance practice.

Because of the introduction of facial recognition in surveillance practices, surveillance no longer entails the monitoring of anonymous individuals and groups. By identifying people in video footage, surveillance becomes more personal and privacy-sensitive. Before, even with CCTV cameras present, individuals could expect some level of privacy in public spaces. Unless they caused a scene or had security or law enforcement after them, individuals could still expect to move around in public spaces anonymously. With the emergence of facial recognition, privacy and anonymity in public diminish significantly.

If the use of facial recognition in surveillance becomes the norm, people can be recognized everywhere they go, whether they are persons of interest or not. Information about people's behavior and whereabouts can also be aggregated and used later on in different contexts. Anonymity not only protects people's right to privacy, it is also valuable because it promotes freedom and autonomy. With anonymity "people will feel freer to associate with whomever they want, read and watch what they choose, and express their opinions as they see fit" (Doyle & Veranas, 2014, p. 210). Anonymity in public can, for example, help a young man who is exploring his sexuality hide a visit to a LGBTQ bar from his family and friends. Anonymity also safeguards those fleeing oppressive regimes or those who, for good reasons, had to take on a new identity.

In addition, facial recognition poses unique difficulties to informational privacy, because people's faces are directly accessible to everyone people meet and everywhere they go. Because of this, one has no choice but to "share" facial data. Having to hide one's face in public to protect one's privacy is an unrealistic and undesirable option, as it would conflict with other liberties.

Aside from its privacy implications, facial recognition technology has also received a lot of critical attention because it can lead to discriminatory or unjust treatment. As mentioned in the previous section, insufficiently diverse training data or prejudices of developers can cause facial recognition systems to be biased, and errors in any of the tasks on which identification builds can lead to inaccurate outcomes. Both bias and error are problematic because they can lead to false conclusions and, as a result, unwarranted treatment of people.

Bias and error are particularly problematic in the case of facial recognition, because their effects on a system's outcome could directly affect how individuals are treated. Bias in facial recognition is more problematic than mere error, because it does not just randomly produce false positives or negatives, it systematically misrecognizes certain demographics. It is then certain societal groups that disproportionately have to deal with malfunctioning facial recognition systems and the discriminatory treatment resulting from them.

Finally, facial recognition technology gives new meaning to one's face. The face is no longer just a part of one's body, it becomes a means with which we can acquire access to services, devices, buildings or events, or a tool for governments to exercise control. The face is then no longer just "ours," it simultaneously belongs to those who own a certain database or facial recognition system. Such a functional reduction of body parts may be perceived as dehumanizing. Furthermore, the fact that one's face exists and has meaning outside of oneself can alienate one from this very personal part of their body (Brey, 2004).

# Facial, Behavioral, and Emotional Analytics

In the narrow sense, "facial recognition" refers solely to the identification of individuals on the basis of their face. However, the term is often used to refer to a much wider range of applications, namely to the analysis of an individual's characteristics based on their facial features. We will refer to this broader type of facial recognition as "facial analysis." Facial analysis is a more interpretive task and less developed than facial recognition is. It can be used not only to identify characteristics such as a person's gender, age, or race, it also makes it possible to analyze a person's behavior and emotions.

Behavior analysis is the analysis of the activity of individuals or groups. Although we focus here on the analysis of human behavior, it can be applied to analyze nonhuman animals too. People's behavior can be analyzed based on their facial features, but also on the basis of their walking patterns, direction of gaze, driving styles, and more. Behavior analysis technology is of immense value to surveillance practices, because it makes it possible to automatically detect misconduct in real time.

Moreover, the technology is expected to enable the prediction and prevention of misconduct, by recognizing patterns that lead up to unwanted actions and allowing law enforcement or security staff to respond to a situation before any damage has been done. At first sight, such "predictive policing" might appear to be a hyperefficient, promising form of surveillance, but it raises complicated questions regarding responsibility, as we tend to agree that people cannot be held responsible for crimes they did not actually commit.

Emotional recognition takes place when someone's emotion or sentiment in a given moment is derived from their facial expressions. Alternatively, emotions can also be recognized from speech or the tone of one's voice. Most existing emotional recognition systems are based on research done in the 1970s by psychologist Paul Ekman. Ekman distinguished six emotions—happiness, anger, sadness, fear, disgust, and surprise—which, he found, all people express in the same way. The underlying assumption of emotional recognition systems is therefore that it is possible to infer from someone's facial expressions what their emotional state is, and that a specific person's facial expressions can be understood on the basis of data of others' facial expressions.

Emotional recognition can be implemented as a surveillance tool, for example, in schools to check students' engagement, or by the entertainment industry to keep track of viewers' responses to their content. It can also serve state surveillance initiatives, such as the example of the Chinese social credit system, by helping governments judge whether citizens show "appropriate" sentiments in certain situations.

All three types of interpretative video analytics tasks (facial analysis, behavior analysis, and emotional recognition) have faced critique regarding their scientific grounds, or rather, lack thereof. Facial analysis systems have not only been developed to recognize traits like gender, age, or race, there are also more dubious experiments with systems aimed at inferring, for example, someone's sexual preference or criminality likelihood (Van Noorden, 2020). These attempts resemble the long-debunked pseudosciences phrenology and physiognomy. Behavior analysis, and in particular its application for predictive policing, raises the question: To what extent, if at all, can behavior tell us something about a person's inner states or intentions?

While behavior analytics technologies assume that there is at least some relation between a person's behavior and their thoughts and intentions, there is no consensus about this matter among psychologists and philosophers. Similarly, not all psychologists agree that emotions are natural kinds, that they are by nature expressed in a certain way. In fact, there is still uncertainty about what emotions are at all, which means that emotional recognition technology might be built on false assumptions.

Like the aforementioned uses of video analytics for surveillance, facial analysis, behavior analysis, and emotional recognition raise ethical issues with regard to human dignity, privacy, and over-enforcement. Human dignity, first of all, is threatened by the emergence of these tasks, because it is people's subjective identity, personality traits, and feelings, among other things, that are turned into data. The most intimate and vulnerable aspects of our selves are now increasingly accessible to others and potentially commodified. These tools might even allow the surveilling entity to understand a person better than they do themselves.

Also detrimental to one's dignity is misrecognition by facial analysis, behavior analysis, emotional recognition, and even facial recognition systems, especially when misrecognition occurs routinely. Misrecognition entails that the identity, emotions, intentions, personality traits, gender, race, and so on ascribed to a person by facial analysis systems are inaccurate. When a system fails to recognize a Black person as a person or mistakes a woman for a man, this is not only problematic because it can lead to misplaced or discriminatory treatment. Misrecognition is also an ethical concern because it can be experienced as humiliating.

Furthermore, facial analysis systems pose a threat to a very particular type of privacy. The analysis of one's characteristics, behavior, and emotions not only reveals very personal, intimate information, it deals with what is going on inside our heads. By attempting to know our inner states, often without our knowledge or consent, these technologies violate what is sometimes called "mental privacy." Our thoughts, feelings, beliefs, and intentions form perhaps the most intimate and private types of information about us. By trying to obtain and analyze this information, facial analysis systems can take away a person's mental privacy and sense of dignity, as well as make the person vulnerable to the power of the surveillant.

With concerns about facial analysis's implications for mental privacy comes the aforementioned risk of over-enforcement, that is, of excessive exercises of power over individuals through the use of facial, behavioral, and emotional analytics for surveillance. Face, behavior, and sentiment analytics systems are useful tools to realize a kind of "thought police," which in turn threatens individual liberties and democratic societal values.

Surveillance can cause people to self-censor their behavior and refrain from exercising their liberties or rights—a phenomena often referred to as "chilling effects." The use of facial recognition and facial analysis systems that aim to read people's inner states can keep people from exercising their freedom of assembly, freedom of association, or freedom of expression. Knowing they are constantly watched over in public places may make people more attentive to what they say and how they act, meaning they not only act differently than they otherwise would have but also refrain from acting in a certain way or expressing certain opinions. Furthermore, knowing one's face might be identified in a crowd, either in real-time or in hindsight, can keep one from participating in demonstrations.

Such a chilling effect threatens the freedom of association and assembly and, moreover, being discouraged to protest against governments or policies has implications for the functioning of democracy. Given its far-reaching effects on people's liberties, legal experts suggest that the use of facial recognition and analysis in public places, or at least where citizens might come together to share their views or protest, violates the proportionality principle (European Union Agency for Fundamental Rights, 2019). When the technology has chilling effects, the benefits that come with the use of video analytics systems for surveillance would not be in proportion to the harms.

# Conclusion

In this chapter, we undertook an ethical analysis of camera surveillance of physical places that use video analytics and facial recognition technology. After introducing the topic of surveillance, we focused on video surveillance and the use of video analytics technologies in it. We claimed that identification raises privacy issues because it reveals the identity of persons who are watched, and tracking raises privacy issues because it reveals their location, which is particularly invasive if tracking is combined with identification. We also argued that classifications of persons can be biased and discriminatory, and can rob people of their individuality and lead to "algorithmic normalization," which threatens autonomy.

We also argued that video analytics processes can result in function creep, in which the technology is used for new, previously unauthorized purposes and over-enforcement. We also argued that video analytics makes more information available for analysis than traditional video surveillance and makes it easier to reuse data in new contexts, thus imposing additional threats to privacy, and that the complexity and opacity of video analytics technology makes informed consent more difficult to accomplish.

We then turned to facial recognition technology, especially its use in video surveillance. We argued that because this use of the technology involves the monitoring of faces in crowds from a distance, facial recognition has moderate to low reliability. This lower reliability could lead to more false positives and false negatives, imposing a burden especially on people who are falsely recognized as having a particular identity (e.g., that of a wanted criminal). More generally, facial recognition technology discloses key aspects of the identity of persons, and surveillance that uses it is therefore much more privacy-invasive than surveillance without it.

Facial recognition systems also often contain biases, due to insufficiently diverse training data or prejudices of developers, which can lead to stereotyping and discrimination. Facial recognition technology also commodifies faces, in that faces are no longer just expressions of one's identity, but also means by which we can enter buildings or access data, as well as a means through which people are controlled.

Finally, we discussed facial analysis (of which facial recognition is a subset), behavior analysis, and emotion analysis as tasks that can be carried out by smart video surveillance systems. We claimed that the analytics methods used for such analysis are rarely based on sound science, but can lead to far-ranging conclusions about people's behaviors, traits, and mental states that can have serious consequences for them depending on the use that is made of these analyses. We also argued that these practices come with serious risks to privacy, risks of error and misrecognition, and risks of over-enforcement. There is also a potential threat to human dignity, as these technologies turn people's subjective identity, personality traits, and feelings into data, and a special threat to mental privacy, which involves a violation of the privacy of our inner thoughts and feelings.

It should be clear by now that video analytics and facial recognition technology constitute very powerful technologies that raise extremely serious ethical issues when used for surveillance. These technologies, if they are used at all for surveillance, should be used with utmost caution and awareness of ethical limitations. This is increasingly being recognized by both governments and private industry, especially in reference to facial recognition technology. In 2020, major companies like Microsoft, IBM, and Amazon stopped development of facial recognition products, or placed a moratorium on their sale to law enforcement.

In 2021, the European Union started preparing legislation to severely restrict the use of facial recognition technology for surveillance, with very limited exceptions for public safety, such as the localization of missing children and the prevention of imminent terrorist threats. The public and policy debate on these technologies has, however, only begun, and it is to be hoped that wise decisions will be made regarding their future development, use, and regulation that take into account their ethical dimensions.

# References

Adams, A. A., & Ferryman, J. M. (2013). The future of video analytics for surveillance and its ethical implications. *Security Journal, 28*(3), 272–289. https://doi.org/10.1057/sj.2012.48.

Adjabi, I., Ouahabi, A., Benzaoui, A., & Taleb-Ahmed, A. (2020). Past, present, and future of face recognition: A review. *Electronics, 9*(1188), 1–52. doi:10.3390/electronics9081188.

Brey, P. (2004). Ethical aspects of facial recognition systems in public places. *Information, Communication & Ethics in Society, 2*, 97–109.

Doyle, T., & Veranas, J. (2014). Public anonymity and the connected world. *Ethics and Information Technology, 16*(3), 207–218. https://doi.org/10.1007/s10676-014-9346-5.

European Union Agency for Fundamental Rights. (2019, November 27). *Facial recognition technology: Fundamental rights considerations in the context of law enforcement.* FRA Focus. https://fra.europa.eu/sites/default/files/fra_uploads/fra-2019-facial-recognition-technology-focus-paper-1_en.pdf.

King, O. (2019). Ethics of big data analytics and learning techniques. In SIENNA *D1.4 report on ethical tensions and social impacts.* De Montfort University. https://doi.org/10.21253/DMU.8397134.v3.

Nissenbaum, H. (1997). Toward an approach to privacy in public. *Ethics & Behavior, 7*(3), 207–209.

Stanley, J. (2019). *The dawn of robot surveillance: AI, video analytics, and privacy*. American Civil Liberties Union. https://www.aclu.org/sites/default/files/field_document/061119-robot_surveillance.pdf.

Van Noorden, R. (2020). The ethical questions that haunt facial recognition research. *Nature, 587*, 354–359.

# CHAPTER 18

# Cybersecurity in Health Care[1]

*Karsten Weber and Nadine Kleine*

## Abstract

Ethical questions have always been crucial in health care; the rapid dissemination of information and communications technology (ICT) makes some of those questions even more pressing and also raises new ones. One of these new questions relates to cybersecurity ethics in health care. To more closely examine this issue, this chapter introduces Beauchamp and Childress's four principles of biomedical ethics, as well as additional ethical values and technical aims of relevance for health care. Based on this, two case studies—implantable medical devices and electronic health cards—are presented, which illustrate potential conflicts between ethical values and technical aims, as well as between different ethical values themselves. It becomes apparent that these conflicts cannot be eliminated in general but must be reconsidered on a case-by-case basis. An ethical debate on cybersecurity regarding the design and implementation of new digital technologies in health care is essential.

### KEYWORDS

autonomy, beneficence, electronic health card, digital implants, justice, nonmaleficence, principlism

# 1. Introduction: The Value of Health

In the preface of his book *The Value of Life* (1985, xv), bioethicist John Harris writes, with a dash of sarcasm, that

> [n]ot very long ago medical ethics consisted of two supremely important commandments. They were: do not advertise; and avoid sexual relations with your patients. At about the same time as doctors were doing their best to obey these commandments, moral philosophers were more concerned with the meaning of words than with the meaning of life. Now, not just doctors but all health care professionals are interested in ethical questions as they relate to medical practice.

The questions Harris addresses in his book are of fundamental character: the value of life, the beginning and end of life, euthanasia, and the like. Most astonishingly, health is not mentioned at all in the table of contents, although the whole book is dedicated to providing arguments that protecting the life and health of their patients is the most important responsibility of physicians and other health care professionals, since health is seen as the most important prerequisite of a good life.

In Western culture, at least since the time of ancient Greece, there has been a great deal of thought given to the value of health for a good and successful life. Even after more than 2,500 years, the Hippocratic Oath still has an important significance for medical action; the value of health, not only throughout Western intellectual history, is a recurring theme. It is probably no exaggeration that health, despite all the problems inherent in a precise definition of this term, enjoys high priority worldwide. Given this importance, it should be no surprise that in order to protect health, the World Health Organization (WHO) has formulated access to it as a central human right.

If health is actually an important, if not the most important, value to human beings, then a health care system being able to provide effective and efficient help in case of medical problems is also most valuable—from an individual as well as a societal point of view. That immediately raises the question of who must be obliged to provide for the necessary resources to maintain an effective health care system (e.g., Daniels 1985; Harris 1988). Although we do not discuss the benefits and burdens or moral justifications of different ways to maintain and finance an effective and efficient health care system, justice and fairness will be an important issue in what follows. The provision and maintenance of cyber-security in health care can be very resource-intensive; this raises the question of who has to pay for these resources.

Health care systems most obviously need substantial resources—according to the WHO in 2018, $8.3 trillion USD worldwide was spent on health care. This amounts to 10% of the 2018 global GDP (2020, 2). At the same time, in many countries providing these resources is becoming more and more difficult because political or economic factors, as present in most countries with aging populations, make it difficult to finance their respective health care systems. Therefore, as Nancy Lorenzi (2005, 2) puts it, "Almost every major economy in the world experiences the effects of the high cost of health care, and many, if not most, national and regional governments are in some stage of health care reform." Although this was being said more than a decade ago it is still valid—and it is to be expected that it will still be valid in the years to come.[2]

Attempts to reform existing health care systems most often include the development and implementation of information and communication technology (ICT) in order to support the provision of effective and efficient health care services. In other words, ICT shall be employed to reduce or at least stabilize the costs of health. One of the main purposes of ICT systems in health care is the administration of information about patients and treatments that "is a vital but complex component in the modern health care system. At a minimum, health care providers need to know a patient's identity and demographic characteristics, recent and distant medical history, current medications, allergies and sensitivities, chronic conditions, contact information, and legal preferences" (McClanahan 2007, 69). However, McClanahan also stresses that "[t]he increased use of electronic medical records has created a substantial tension between two desirable values: the increased quality and utility of patient medical records and the protection of the privacy of the information they contain."

At the same time, "Improvements in the health status of communities depend on effective public health and health care infrastructures. These infrastructures are increasingly electronic and tied to the Internet. Incorporating emerging technologies into the service of the community has become a required task for every public health leader" (Ross 2003, v). In other words, stakeholders such as patients, health care professionals, health care providers, and insurance companies are confronted with competing or even contradictory aims such as increasing efficiency, reducing costs, improving quality, and keeping information secure and confidential (Fried 1987). Employing new technologies in health care therefore creates new value conflicts or at least makes old conflicts and problems more visible or increases their urgency.

Simultaneously, other moral values also shall be protected and supported, either as fundamental moral values in Western democratic societies and/or as moral values, which are constitutive for the relationship between patients on the one side and health care professionals on the other. Conflicting or even contradictory aims and values raise moral concerns, since it has to be decided which aim and which value should be prioritized. To illustrate this, studying the conflict between beneficence and autonomy—both are important moral values within and outside the medical sphere—can be beneficial: when ICT is deployed in the health sector, it should be aimed at ensuring that patients themselves determine when which information is revealed to whom. Password protection and encryption are common measures to achieve this aim. However, in emergencies, when patients are no longer able to make this decision, there is now a risk that important medical information will no longer be accessible.

Moreover, it might be very helpful to share medically relevant patient information widely among health care professionals to improve the quality and efficiency of treatment. The goal of protecting patients' privacy and autonomy, however, may be at odds with this aim. In addition, in scholarly debates it is often mentioned that to provide cybersecurity it might be necessary to compromise privacy. This can occur, for example, when nonpersonal health information on the Internet is only accessible if potential users of this information have to disclose their identity. It is argued that the respective platforms are better protected against attacks because the identity of the attackers could be determined. The problem here, however, is that anonymous searching, for example, for information on diseases that are socially stigmatized, would then no longer be possible.

Such conflicting aims raise particular concern because it is obvious that both the protection of patients' privacy, as well as the security of information systems and patient data, must be important objectives in health care. Without privacy, trust among patients and health care professionals necessary for medical treatment is jeopardized (Beauchamp and Childress 2009, 288) and without the certainty that patient data will not be tampered with or stolen, treatment itself is at risk.

Approaching cybersecurity in health, in the second section we first discuss the relevant moral principles, values, and technical aims relevant for the health domain. To illustrate the complexity of these issues, in the third section we present case studies from health practice. We furthermore explain in detail the conflicts that have emerged, which are examples of the broad spectrum of existing conflicts and trade-offs in health care. Finally, we outline the relationship between moral values and cybersecurity in health care. In the fourth section, we draw a brief conclusion.

# 2. Principles, Moral Values, and Technical Aims

## 2.1. PRINCIPLISM AS A STARTING POINT OF ETHICAL ANALYSIS

Those involved in scholarly and professional debates concerning biomedical ethics will be familiar with autonomy, beneficence, and justice: together with nonmaleficence, these values—or more accurately "principles"—can be seen as core moral aims, as particularly emphasized in Beauchamp and Childress's considerations on the foundations of biomedical ethics. Their book *Principles of Biomedical Ethics* (Beauchamp and Childress 2009), first published in 1977, is a groundbreaking text. The core features of their approach, based on "principlism," involves four moral principles, namely autonomy, nonmaleficence, beneficence, and justice, which are pertinent to a particular moral situation; furthermore, they use their specification, balancing, and (deductive) application to create a bridge between the moral situation and the relevant principles.

It must be stressed that principlism is far from an indisputable tenet in biomedical ethics; its weaknesses include neglect of emotional and personal factors that are inherent in specific decision situations, oversimplification of the moral issues, and excessive claims of universality (e.g., Clouser and Gert 1990; Hine 2011; McGrath 1998; Sorell 2011). Nevertheless, principlism remains highly influential for scholarly thinking about ethical issues arising (not only) in the health domain (e.g., Reijers et al. 2018). Hence, we use principlism as the starting point of our ethical analysis concerning cybersecurity in health.

As already mentioned, Beauchamp and Childress's four principles of biomedical ethics are *respect for autonomy, nonmaleficence, beneficence*, and *justice,* the definitions of which can be briefly summarized as follows (Loi et al. 2019):

- *Respect for autonomy* as a negative obligation means avoiding interference in other people's freely made decisions. Understanding respect for autonomy as a positive obligation means informing people comprehensibly and thoroughly about all aspects of a decision, for example, about its consequences. Respect for autonomy also may "affect rights and obligations of liberty, privacy, confidentiality, truthfulness, and informed consent" (Beauchamp and Childress 2009, 104).
- The principle of *nonmaleficence* is derived from the classic quote "above all, do no harm," which is often ascribed to the Hippocratic Oath. As Beauchamp and Childress (2009, 149) state, "the Hippocratic oath clearly expresses an obligation of nonmaleficence and an obligation of beneficence." At the heart

of this principle is the imperative not to harm or ill-treat anyone, especially patients.

- *Beneficence* must be distinguished from nonmaleficence. According to Beauchamp and Childress (2009, 197), "Morality requires not only that we treat persons autonomously and refrain from harming them, but also that we contribute to their welfare." Consequently, care must always be taken to ensure that actions that are intended to be benevolent do indeed provide a benefit; the advantages and disadvantages, opportunities and risks, as well as the costs and benefits of those actions must therefore be weighed.

- *Justice* as a principle is even more difficult to grasp than the other three principles, since the different existing theories of justice produce very different results. For the purposes of our considerations, justice is to be translated as a guarantee of fair opportunities and the prevention of unfair discrimination, for instance based on gender or ethnicity. Justice also means that scarce resources should not be wasted; in addition, these resources often have to be provided by others, for example, by the insured (McCarthy 1987), so that economic use is required.

As Beauchamp (1995, 182) emphasizes, "The choice of these four types of moral principle as the framework for moral decision making in health care derives in part from professional roles and traditions." Hence, it should be considered that it might have repercussions on the principles as a framework for moral decision-making in health care if professional roles and traditions change over time. It is most obvious that new technologies contribute to such changes.

## 2.2. TECHNICAL AIMS MAPPING TO ETHICAL PRINCIPLES

Despite justified criticism, we chose to use principlism as a starting point of our ethical analysis because its four moral principles can be mapped to the important aims of the employment of ICT in health care, which are *efficiency and quality of services, privacy of information and confidentiality of communication, usability of services,* and *safety* (this idea was first developed by Christen et al. 2018; see also Fig. 1). The definitions of these four aims can be summarized as follows:

- *Efficiency and Quality of Services:* One of the main purposes of ICT systems in health care is the administration of information to increase the *efficiency* of the health care system and to reduce its costs. Improvements in health care in *qualitative* terms refer, for instance, to new services that provide treatment or processes with better health-related outcomes. Big data, the collection and sharing of as much health-related data as possible, might be used to establish

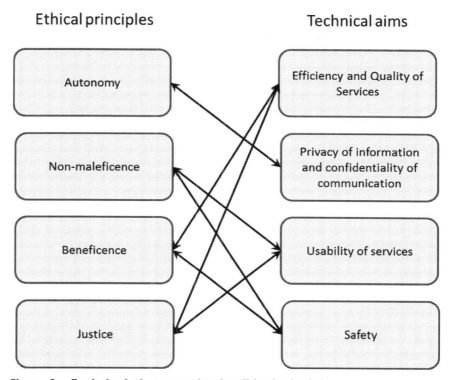

## Ethical principles

- Autonomy
- Non-maleficence
- Beneficence
- Justice

## Technical aims

- Efficiency and Quality of Services
- Privacy of information and confidentiality of communication
- Usability of services
- Safety

**Figure 1.   Technical aims mapping to ethical principles**

new insights regarding diseases and possible treatments (e.g., Vayena et al. 2016). In this regard, *quality and efficiency of services* map to the *principle of beneficence. Efficiency of services* map also to the *principle of justice* insofar as services contribute to the economic use of resources, in this way diminishing the risk of unfair allocations.

- *Privacy of Information and Confidentiality of Communication:* Using ICT to process patient data creates a moral challenge in terms of quality on the one hand and *privacy* and *confidentiality* on the other hand—yet both are important aims in health care. In particular, privacy is often seen as a prerequisite of patients' autonomy and therefore *privacy* maps to the *principle of autonomy.* Privacy and confidentiality are also foundations of trust among patients and health care professionals.

- *Usability of Services: Usability* can be defined as "the degree of effectiveness, efficiency, and satisfaction with which users of a system can realize their intended task" (Roman et al. 2017, 70). With regard to health, users can be patients, medical staff, and/or administrators, who have different degrees of

ICT competences, depending on personal attitudes and sociodemographic variables (Kaplan and Litewka 2008). *Usability of services* map to the *principle of nonmaleficence* since poor usability can hurt people (e.g., Magrabi et al. 2012; Viitanen et al. 2011). Thus, usability, quality, and efficiency are interrelated since reduced usability may compromise quality and efficiency. *Usability of services* additionally maps to the *principle of justice* in that usability for all kinds of users increases the accessibility of services.

• *Safety:* *Safety* can be defined as the reduction of health-threatening risks. Safety, quality, efficiency, and usability are interrelated, but they do not align, because safety measures might reduce the efficiency and usability of services and therefore quality. *Safety* maps to the *principle of nonmaleficence*, as well as to the *principle of beneficence*.

The four technical objectives mentioned above are composed of various sub-goals. For instance, accessibility, availability, responsibility, and transparency can be considered part of safety. Another example is universal design as "design-for-all, barrier-free design, transgenerational design, design-for-the-broader-average, or design-for-the-nonaverage" (Sandhu 2000, 80) that can be understood as part of usability. A detailed ethical analysis of case studies requires a very thorough examination of what subgoals make up the abovementioned technical aims in each case—this can be understood as a "specification" in the sense that Beauchamp and Childress understand it in relation to their ethical principles. This kind of specification is important not only for the technical requirements, but—as will become apparent—also for the identification of moral values that could be affected by technical aims.

## 2.3. OTHER MORAL VALUES

The findings of an extensive structured literature search (Christen et al. 2017; Yaghmaei et al. 2017, 9–17) show that, besides the four principles, additional moral values are affected by cybersecurity in health care. These values may often have a connection to Beauchamp and Childress's principles, but they go beyond them to different extents. The most relevant ones with regard to cybersecurity in health care are *freedom and consent*, *privacy and trust*, *dignity and solidarity*, and *fairness and equality*.

• *Privacy and Trust:* Privacy plays a crucial role, not least because of the use of constantly growing amounts of data (big data). Privacy of patients shall be guaranteed, with particular regard to the sensitive nature of health-related data. Risks such as uncontrolled access by third parties, disclosure of data, and the like are to be eliminated. Patients must be able to trust new health technologies, professionals, and the health care system in general. In other words, they must be certain to be protected from harm, which is connected to the *principle of nonmaleficence.*

- *Freedom and Consent:* Freedom includes both the unrestricted choice of (non) use of new technologies, as well as the unhindered choice of how and for which purposes new technologies are being used. To achieve this, patient consent must be recognized as an important factor in health care. This refers, in contrast to presumed consent, to informed consent. The idea of informed consent and the general freedom of use and freedom of choice emphasizes the *principle of autonomy.*

- *Fairness and Equality:* An important value in terms of health is fairness in treatment. This includes access for all patients to all types of treatment, regardless of, for instance, their ethnicity and social background. This is closely linked to the principle of justice, but emphasizes the protection against subtle unfair treatments (e.g., special consideration for people with a lack of skills, knowledge, or abilities); patients with limited health and technical literacy should be treated equally compared to those who know how to operate health technology. Everybody must be protected from unfair treatment, discrimination, and stigmatization; vulnerable groups shall not be excluded. Fairness and equality are closely linked to the *principle of justice.*

- *Dignity and Solidarity:* Human dignity is a major democratic value. Dignity must always be maintained, regardless of technical innovations, necessary moral compromises, and limited resources. While dignity in its abstract form is difficult to grasp and primarily addresses the individual, solidarity describes a societal value in a more concrete way: the interpersonal commitment of individuals and groups who share both responsibilities and benefits as a community (e.g., in a health insurance system and public welfare). Both dignity and solidarity, especially in relation to health and cybersecurity, are tied to the *principle of beneficence.*

These ethical principles and additional values are often both interlinked and in conflict with each other. In addition, there is the different use of terms: privacy, for example, appears as part of an ethical principle, a technical aim, and a moral value. Privacy as a technical aim refers to data protection whereas Beauchamp and Childress consider privacy as a specification of the principle of autonomy. This ambiguity again demonstrates the importance of a detailed analysis of moral principles and values on the one hand and technical aims on the other.

# 3. Case Studies

## 3.1. CARDIAC PACEMAKERS AND OTHER IMPLANTABLE MEDICAL DEVICES

### 3.1.1. Brief Description of the Case

Implantable medical devices (IMDs) are employed with the intention of improving the quality of a patient's life. Implants such as cardiac pacemakers, insulin pumps, biosensors, and cochlear implants offer therapeutic, monitoring, and even life-saving benefits: medical treatment can be made more precise, efficient, customized, and flexible (Burleson and Carrara 2014, 1; Ransford et al. 2014, 157–67). An increasing number of IMDs are wirelessly networked and can be connected to other devices to, for example, monitor functionality, set parameters, exchange data, or install software updates.

However, for some years, there have been reports about the dangers of implantable medical devices. In addition to the risk of unintentional loss of function due to defects, the connectivity of IMDs leaves them open to malicious attacks. Examples of such possible attacks include the following:

- unauthorized access to sensitive data, and their manipulation or further misuse, such as identity theft;
- spread of malware and viruses to interconnected devices and system networks;
- manipulations of the devices to, for instance, modify the automatic insulin output or the impulse rate of a cardiac pacemaker; and
- switching off devices, which can endanger the health or, in the worst case, even the life of the person carrying the device (Baranchuk et al. 2018, 1285; Coventry and Branley 2018, 48; Mohan 2014, 372; Ransford et al. 2014, 158–61).

Although there have been no real incidents known to date, for years, hackers, security experts, and scientists have been illustrating the vulnerabilities of IMDs: Jerome Radcliffe presented a talk at the Black Hat conference in 2011 at which he explained how he was able to get access to implanted insulin pumps through reverse engineering (Radcliffe 2011); Barnaby Jack showed his successful hack in order to control pacemakers (Burns et al. 2016, 70); and Pycroft et al. (2016) discussed the actual possibilities of "brainjacking" neurological implants. In 2017, the FDA published a safety communications issue in which it announced that almost half a million cardiac pacemakers must get a software update "to reduce the risk of patient harm due to potential exploitation of cybersecurity vulnerabilities" (FDA 2017).

In one of the most recent cases, Billy Rios and Jonathan Butts explained in the abstract of their 2018 Black Hat presentation that they "provide detailed technical findings on remote exploitation of a pacemaker system, pacemaker infrastructure, and a neurostimulator system. Exploitation of these vulnerabilities allow for the disruption of therapy, as well as the ability to execute shocks to a patient" (Rios and Butts 2018). Already some years ago, this issue received special public attention when the media widely reported that the wireless function of then US Vice President Dick Cheney's pacemaker was deactivated due to security risks (e.g., Vijayan 2014).

Although dangers posed by attacks on IMDs should not be underestimated, their occurrence is, due to the complexity of such attacks, not yet too realistic. First, depending on the type of data transmission, a short distance may be required, not least because of the already difficult energy provision of IMDs. Second, the motivation to potentially risk the lives of implant users needs to be a given; if it was a matter of financial gain through access to personal data, other cyberattacks would serve a better purpose. Experts expect a greater risk of malware and viruses affecting medical networks including connected implants (Baranchuk et al. 2018, 1287; Burleson and Carrara 2014, 2–5; Coventry and Branley 2018, 49–51).

Different factors contribute to the lack of security. In addition to the risks posed by interconnectivity, there are other technical difficulties: digital implants are supposed to have a long lifecycle to minimize invasive treatment. Therefore, and due to the required small size and light weight of medical devices, battery capacity and storage space are very limited, which often results in weak or missing encryption; in outdated, weak, or even no virus protection; and/or in the lack of regular software updates. The latter, in particular, creates the risk of endangering patients' health and/or life caused by malfunctions or breakdowns of a device due to the problem of outdated and insecure software used with IMDs (Burleson and Carrara 2014, 1, 4; Fu and Blum 2013, 36; Mohan 2014, 372; Ransford et al. 2014, 162, 166–69).

The development of effective regulations to improve the security of IMDs has proven to be difficult as well: several administrative bodies (e.g., the FDA, see Woods 2017) have been working on such regulations and on certification systems for years without successfully covering all eventualities. Due to the complex combination of various technical factors and different actors, the definition of responsibilities and requirements regarding IMDs seems to be quite difficult and often comes with a substantial time delay with regard to technical improvements (Burns et al. 2016, 70; Cerminara and Uzdavines 2017, 311; Coventry and Branley 2018, 48).

### 3.1.2. Conflicting Ethical Values

The following analysis of possible moral conflicts demonstrates that there are not just management problems that contribute to these conflicts but that competing moral values or different value hierarchies of stakeholders increase the insecurity of IMDs. Furthermore, as already pointed out, moral values can also conflict with technical requirements.

IMDs serve the primary aim of increasing the physical safety of patients. Wireless IMDs are designed to enable the continuous monitoring of vital parameters and faster communication with health care professionals both routinely and in emergency cases. While this faster access aims to enable health care professionals to use medical data more quickly, efficiently, and flexibly to perform successful treatment, lack of transparency about who and under what circumstances people can access what information does not ensure patient consent and control (Mohan 2014, 372). In addition, a key problem is that patients do not have direct access to information stored in IMDs, particularly in the case of so-called closed-loop devices, although these data could inform them about their own body and health status (Alexander 2018; Ransford et al. 2014, 165–67).

If patients think that they might have little or no control over their own health-related data, that could, in the long run, contribute to a loss of confidence in health technology, as well as in health care professionals. Because IMDs can be attacked and personal data stolen, patients may perceive danger for themselves and their data and thus for privacy and trust. Furthermore, there is the risk that implant users will be discriminated against as a consequence of unauthorized access to sensitive data and their uncontrollable use and disclosure to third parties (Burleson and Carrara 2014, 1; Coventry and Branley 2018, 48; Ransford et al. 2014, 158).

Another possible negative effect on patients' trust is the lack of a clear attribution of (moral) responsibility to the various stakeholders involved (e.g., manufacturers and designers, health care professionals and insurance companies, legislators and regulators), who pursue different interests and are not always primarily focused on the patients' well-being (Alexander 2018; Baranchuk et al. 2018, 1285; Burns et al. 2016, 72).

If patients were to decide who exactly has access to their IMDs or if the access would be at least (through technical or regulatory measures) more protected, however, other problems (in addition to the ones mentioned above) would arise:

> Requiring users to authenticate to a device before altering its functionality is a boon for security, but it introduces risks in case of an emergency. A medical professional may need to reprogram or disable a device to effectively treat a patient. . . . [E]ncryption or other strong

> authentication mechanisms could make such emergency measures
> impossible if the patient is unconscious or the facility does not pos-
> sess a programming device with a required shared secret. (Ransford
> et al. 2014, 170)

In this case, the effective use and safety of the IMD would be in jeopardy. The conflict between usability and security does not only occur with the use by health care professionals. In the case of an open-loop system in which patients have access to the information stored in the device, their literacy level must be recognized to ensure that patients with little technical knowledge and understanding of security do not suffer disadvantages. The degree of dependency and the level of risk must also be considered (Alexander 2018; Ransford et al. 2014, 164).

## 3.2. ELECTRONIC HEALTH CARDS (EHC) IN GERMANY AND ELSEWHERE

### 3.2.1. Brief Description of the Case

Conflicts with regard to cybersecurity are often related to privacy and data protection (e.g., Fernández-Alemán et al. 2013). However, there are other types of conflicts. For instance, reaching a high level of cybersecurity might be very expensive. In a health care system financed on a solidarity basis, as it exists, for instance, in many European states, such costs would be passed on to all insured persons and thus potentially make the health care system more expensive for all. In health care systems in which every person insures her own risk, as in the United States, for example, it could be the case that only those who are willing and able to pay for expensive security would be able to enjoy the benefits of appropriately secured technology. This might raise concerns regarding social justice. As mentioned above, cybersecurity can also conflict with usability and accessibility. Despite these potential difficulties, there are high hopes for the use of ICT in health care, in particular regarding electronic health records and electronic health cards. This is demonstrated with reference to the German eHealth Card (eHC):

> As part of the German health-care reform, the current health insur-
> ance card is being upgraded to an electronic health card. On it, data
> on patient investigations, drug regulations, vaccinations and emer-
> gency data are stored. The aim is among other things to improve
> medical care and the prevention of drug incompatibilities and dupli-
> cation of investigations. (Jürjens and Rumm 2008)

The development of an eHC in Germany was already discussed for the first time in 2004. Technical development then began in 2006, but in 2009 the project was halted (Tuffs 2010) because it was feared that the costs and benefits were no longer in reasonable proportion to each other. There was also a great deal of resistance, particularly on the side of physicians. Now, in 2022, the nationwide introduction of the German eHC has yet to begin (Stafford 2015).

In particular, German physicians are quite skeptical with regard to the eHC, since it is feared that its deployment will result in high costs and increase the workload of physicians and health care personnel: "The cost-benefit factor plays an important role in the implementation process, because—in the opinion of many physicians—the financial effort for acquiring and maintaining the system does not sufficiently outweigh the resulting benefit" (Wirtz et al. 2012, 659). As Ernstmann et al. (2009, 185) write, "the ratings of perceived usefulness are rather low, i.e. physicians are not aware of useful aspects of the new technology or do not judge the established aspects as useful in their practice."

It is difficult to make accurate statements about whether this dissatisfaction has improved, as there is little practical experience with the eHC to date. A large-scale study (Schöffski et al. 2018) shows that many practitioners are still skeptical about the benefits. Although it is emphasized that the validity of insurance status can be determined more reliably by the eHC—which is an important (cyber) security aspect—the administrative effort has not decreased. Since the functional capabilities of the eHC have also been very limited to date, it is still not possible to prove any medical benefit. Some scholars (Deutsch et al. 2010; Klöcker 2014) assume that these attitudes result from the perception of different aims on the part of the stakeholders; this would strengthen the assumption that technical, medical, and ethical values or principles often compete or conflict with each other, especially in the health care sector. Although not discussed in detail here, it should be added that economic considerations play a dominant role in this particular case, which may also compete with other goals and values.

This rather skeptical attitude changes if it is assumed that the functional scope of the eHC is supplemented by the storage of a so-called emergency dataset, which, for example, would make it considerably easier for emergency physicians to provide first aid more accurately (Born et al. 2017). Since the medical benefit for physicians and, of course, for patients is most obvious, other considerations such as privacy, data protection, and the like seem to be pushed into the background.

At the same time, at least to some stakeholders, benefits such as increased security are less obvious: "The efficiency of the system is considered as critical by the physicians, particularly in terms of data security and potential misuse of data. The primary concern of the physicians is the unauthorized access of a third party to stored data." In addition, "Regarding the introduction of the eHC to date, most physicians have criticized the very opaque communication and poor instruction on the subject" (Wirtz et al. 2012, 651). Or, to put it in other words (Ernstmann et al. 2009, 181): "Primary care physicians rate their involvement in the process of the development of the technology and their own IT expertise concerning the technological innovation as rather low."

The German eHC is based on a decentralized ICT infrastructure; its security features are strongly dependent on online network connections between end-user terminals and servers. Only if such connections are available can all security features be fully used—two-factor authentication with PIN and eHC, for example, only works if there is an online connection between the terminal and the server. Without being online, end-user terminals can still be used, but with reduced security. In such cases, the application of the eHC comes with a potential conflict of (cyber)security on the one hand and usability on the other (Jürjens and Rumm 2008). Since the provision of mobile Internet has improved since 2008, this problem may have been mitigated. The example shows, however, that cybersecurity builds on infrastructures that are not always and universally available—this might raise questions of social justice.

### 3.2.2. Conflicting Ethical Values

In addition to the obvious conflicts of moral values that could arise from the high infrastructural costs of the introduction of the eHC, this brief description already illustrates that there are other areas of conflict that should be examined in more detail.

Beyond the issue of unfairly distributed economic burdens, which raise moral concern with regard to social justice, the deployment of the German eHC, as well as similar ICT infrastructures in other countries, might be accompanied by another issue concerning discrimination. Due to security considerations (e.g., the need to protect medical data against misuse and unauthorized access), most of these infrastructures employ encryption and password protection of sensitive data. Laur (2014) mentions that "While some people have already difficulty remembering a PIN (especially elderly and disabled people), having many more passwords that are intended to protect them could put them at risk of disclosure, loss or stealing."

Although Laur refers to electronic health records in general, the problem also applies to the German eHC in particular: The eHC not only consists of a database but its core components are a PIN and a credit-card-size chip card for two-factor authentication. Patient data (apart from the emergency dataset) can only be accessed if the chip card and PIN are used simultaneously. For elderly and/or handicapped people, for instance the visually impaired, using the eHC could be difficult. It is very likely that the persons concerned will create their own workarounds, for example, by writing PINs on the eHC or by disclosing them to health care personnel, which will certainly reduce the level of data protection, privacy, and security of those persons.

In such cases, a personal relationship of trust, which was originally intended to be replaced by technology, regains importance. From an ethical perspective, this does not necessarily have to be evaluated negatively, but it demonstrates that security measures can have ambivalent consequences and might raise concerns with regard to equality. Furthermore, it must be considered that in the large study of Schöffski et al. (2018), usability was not really examined. This raises questions regarding the consideration of stakeholder groups such as handicapped or elderly people and their needs.

## 3.3. CYBERSECURITY AND ETHICS IN HEALTH: A TENTATIVE SUMMING-UP

It must be stressed that there is a long history behind the collection, storage, and use of patient data. During that time, moral rules or moral orders developed to manage this data conscientiously and according to the interests of all stakeholders, but these rules related to data storage in paper files. The introduction of new technologies for storing and processing patient data, such as the electronic patient record or the eHC, will undoubtedly affect traditional moral and legal rules "governing health records, for example, consent and access rules, responsibility for data quality, liability for negligence, mistakes and accidents" (Garrety et al. 2014, 72); they will certainly be called into question by the new possibilities. In the future, we will have to prove whether these changes should be called "disruption of moral orders" (Garrety et al. 2014). Nevertheless, digital technologies and their possibilities force us to pay more attention to how moral rights and obligations change with the use of technology.

The case studies described above should already demonstrate that in terms of cybersecurity, the design and application of new technologies in health care affect numerous principles, goals, and moral values that are in competitive, conflicting, or exclusive relationships. Without striving for completeness, the conflicts among technical aims and moral values and/or among different moral values should be briefly mentioned again: security vs. usability, safety and usability vs. privacy and trust, efficiency and quality of service vs. freedom and consent, and security vs. beneficence.

It is likely that in many cases, conflicts can be mitigated or even completely resolved by skillful technical design or by adapting organizational processes. However, it is equally likely that in some cases no such solutions are available. Beauchamp and Childress have often been criticized for not providing a clear hierarchy of principles; this, as often denounced, leaves the prioritization of principles to the discretion of the decision-makers. However, it could indeed be that in many conflicts this is all that can be achieved. It is therefore one of the most important tasks of the value-based design of technology to make considerations that lead to a decision transparent.

This makes it possible for decisions to be reconstructed, questioned, and, if necessary, revised later on. In addition, there is often a demand that as many stakeholders as possible be involved in the value-based design of technology so that their expectations, demands, and fears can be considered (Hennen 2012). However, it should be kept in mind that the participatory design of technology itself raises moral concerns that cannot always be answered adequately (Saretzki 2012).

# 4. Conclusion

Verbeek (2006, 362) writes that "Like a theater play or a movie . . . technologies possess a 'script' in the sense that they prescribe the actions of the actors involved. Technologies are able to evoke certain kinds of behaviour. . . . Technological artefacts can influence human behaviour, and this influence can be understood in terms of scripts." Verbeek (2006, 361) thus stresses that it is necessary to explore technology's normative aspects because "When technologies coshape human actions, they give material answers to the ethical question of how to act. This implies that engineers are doing 'ethics by other means': they materialize morality." As a consequence, we must learn that "information systems are intentionally or unintentionally informed by moral values of their makers. Since information technology has become a constitutive technology which shapes human life it is important to be aware of the value ladenness of IT design" (van den Hoven 2007, 67).

The statements above aim to provide an initial insight into how moral values can conflict with each other in the design and use of medical technology, as well as how technical design decisions can come into competition with moral values. It is to be expected that an investigation of further case studies would reveal other and more conflicts not considered here. Following the concepts of "value sensitive design" (VSD; e.g., Friedman 1996; Friedman et al. 2013) and "responsible research and innovation" (RRI; e.g., Burget et al. 2017; Stahl et al. 2014), every research and development project must therefore ensure that a comparable detailed analysis takes place in order to detect and then avoid or at least mitigate such conflicts.

# Acknowledgments

The original version of this text was written as part of a European research project. Therefore, references to Europe are often implicitly made; however, all statements can be generalized beyond Europe. This text could not have been written without the work done as part of the project "Constructing an Alliance for Value-Driven Cybersecurity" (CANVAS, https://canvas-project.eu/). We are deeply indebted to our colleagues with whom we had the privilege of working on this project and whom we would like to thank for their excellent collaboration. CANVAS has received funding from the European Union's Horizon 2020 research and innovation program under grant agreement No. 700540; additionally, it was supported (in part) by the Swiss State Secretariat for Education, Research and Innovation (SERI) under contract number 16.0052-1.

# References

Alexander, Neta. "My Pacemaker Is Tracking Me from Inside My Body." *The Atlantic*, January 27, 2018. https://www.theatlantic.com/technology/archive/2018/01/my-pacemaker-is-tracking-me-from-inside-my-body/551681/.

Baranchuk, Adrian, Marwan M. Refaat, Kristen K. Patton, Mina K. Chung, Kousik Krishnan, Valentina Kutyifa, Gaurav Upadhyay, John D. Fisher, and Dhanunjaya R. Lakkireddy. "Cybersecurity for Cardiac Implantable Electronic Devices." *Journal of the American College of Cardiology* 71, no. 11 (March 2018): 1284–88. https://doi.org/10.1016/j.jacc.2018.01.023.

Beauchamp, Tom L. "Principlism and Its Alleged Competitors." *Kennedy Institute of Ethics Journal* 5, no. 3 (1995): 181–98. https://doi.org/10.1353/ken.0.0111.

Beauchamp, Tom L., and James F. Childress. *Principles of Biomedical Ethics* (6th ed.). New York: Oxford University Press, 2009.

Born, Judith, Jürgen Albert, Andreas Bohn, Norbert Butz, Karlheinz Fuchs, Stefan Loos, Johannes Schenkel, and Christian Juhra. "Der Notfalldatensatz für die elektronische Gesundheitskarte: Die Sicht von Notfallmedizinern und Rettungsdienstpersonal." *Notfall + Rettungsmedizin* 20, no. 1 (February 2017): 32–37. https://doi.org/10.1007/s10049-016-0197-y.

Burget, Mirjam, Emanuele Bardone, and Margus Pedaste. "Definitions and Conceptual Dimensions of Responsible Research and Innovation: A Literature Review." *Science and Engineering Ethics* 23, no. 1 (February 2017): 1–19. https://doi.org/10.1007/s11948-016-9782-1.

Burns, A. J., M. Eric Johnson, and Peter Honeyman. "A Brief Chronology of Medical Device Security." *Communications of the ACM* 59, no. 10 (September 22, 2016): 66–72. https://doi.org/10.1145/2890488.

Burleson, Wayne, and Sandro Carrara. "Introduction." In *Security and Privacy for Implantable Medical Devices*, edited by Wayne Burleson and Sandro Carrara, 1–11. New York: Springer, 2014. https://doi.org/10.1007/978-1-4614-1674-6_1.

Cerminara, Kathy L., and Marylin Uzdavines. "Introduction to Regulating Innovation in Healthcare: Protecting the Public or Stifling Progress?" *Nova Law Review* 31, no. 3 (2017): 305–12.

Christen, Markus, Bert Gordijn, Karsten Weber, Ibo van de Poel, and Emad Yaghmaei. "A Review of Value-Conflicts in Cybersecurity." *The ORBIT Journal* 1, no. 1 (2017): 1–19. https://doi.org/10.29297/orbit.v1i1.28.

Christen, Markus, Michele Loi, Nadine Kleine, and Karsten Weber. "Cybersecurity in Health—Disentangling Value Tensions." In Ethicomp 2018, SWPS University of Social Sciences and Humanities, Sopot, Poland, September 24–26, 2018.

Clouser, K. Danner, and Bernard Gert. "A Critique of Principlism." *Journal of Medicine and Philosophy* 15, no. 2 (April 1, 1990): 219–36. https://doi.org/10.1093/jmp/15.2.219.

Coventry, Lynne, and Dawn Branley. "Cybersecurity in Healthcare: A Narrative Review of Trends, Threats and Ways Forward." *Maturitas* 113 (July 2018): 48–52. https://doi.org/10.1016/j.maturitas.2018.04.008.

Daniels, Norman. *Just Health Care.* Cambridge: Cambridge University Press, 1985.

Deutsch, Eva, Georg Duftschmid, and Wolfgang Dorda. "Critical Areas of National Electronic Health Record Programs—Is Our Focus Correct?" *International Journal of Medical Informatics* 79, no. 3 (March 2010): 211–22. https://doi.org/10.1016/j.ijmedinf.2009.12.002.

FDA. Firmware Update to Address Cybersecurity Vulnerabilities Identified in Abbott's (Formerly St. Jude Medical's) Implantable Cardiac Pacemakers: FDA Safety Communication (2017). https://www.fda.gov/MedicalDevices/Safety/AlertsandNotices/ucm573669.htm.

Fernández-Alemán, José Luis, Inmaculada Carrión Señor, Pedro Ángel Oliver Lozoya, and Ambrosio Toval. "Security and Privacy in Electronic Health Records: A Systematic Literature Review." *Journal of Biomedical Informatics* 46, no. 3 (June 2013): 541–62. https://doi.org/10.1016/j.jbi.2012.12.003.

Fried, Charles. "The Primacy of the Physician as Trusted Personal Advisor and Not as Social Agent." In *Bioethics: Readings & Cases*, edited by Baruch A. Brody and Hugo Tristram Engelhardt Jr., 221–25. Englewood Cliffs, NJ: Prentice-Hall, 1987.

Friedman, Batya. "Value-Sensitive Design." *Interactions* 3, no. 6 (December 1996): 16–23. https://doi.org/10.1145/242485.242493.

Friedman, Batya, Peter H. Kahn, Alan Borning, and Alina Huldtgren. "Value Sensitive Design and Information Systems." In *Early Engagement and New Technologies: Opening Up the Laboratory*, edited by Neelke Doorn, Daan Schuurbiers, Ibo van de Poel, and Michael E. Gorman, 55–95. Philosophy of Engineering and Technology. Dordrecht, Netherlands: Springer, 2013. https://doi.org/10.1007/978-94-007-7844-3_4.

Fu, Kevin, and James Blum. "Controlling for Cybersecurity Risks of Medical Device Software." *Communications of the ACM* 56, no. 10 (October 2013): 35–37. https://doi.org/10.1145/2508701.

Garrety, Karin, Ian McLoughlin, Rob Wilson, Gregor Zelle, and Mike Martin. "National Electronic Health Records and the Digital Disruption of Moral Orders." *Social Science & Medicine* 101 (January 2014): 70–77. https://doi.org/10.1016/j .socscimed.2013.11.029.

Harris, John. *The Value of Life*. London/New York: Routledge, 1985.

Harris, John. "More and Better Justice." In *Philosophy and Medical Welfare*, edited by J. M. Bell and Susan Mendus, 75–96. Cambridge: Cambridge University Press, 1988.

Hennen, Leonhard. "Why Do We Still Need Participatory Technology Assessment?" *Poiesis & Praxis* 9, no. 1–2 (November 2012): 27–41. https://doi.org/10.1007/ s10202-012-0122-5.

Hine, Kristen. "What Is the Outcome of Applying Principlism?" *Theoretical Medicine and Bioethics* 32, no. 6 (December 2011): 375–88. https://doi.org/10.1007/ s11017-011-9185-x.

Jürjens, J., and R. Rumm. "Model-Based Security Analysis of the German Health Card Architecture." *Methods of Information in Medicine* 47, no. 5 (2008): 409–16. https:// doi.org/10.3414/ME9122.

Kaplan, Bonnie, and Sergio Litewka. "Ethical Challenges of Telemedicine and Telehealth." *Cambridge Quarterly of Healthcare Ethics* 17, no. 4 (October 2008): 401–16. https://doi.org/10.1017/S0963180108080535.

Klöcker, Philipp. "Understanding Stakeholder Behavior in Nationwide Electronic Health Infrastructure Implementation." In *47th Hawaii International Conference on System Sciences*, 2857–66. Waikoloa, HI: IEEE, 2014. https://doi.org/10.1109/ HICSS.2014.357.

Laur, Audrey. "Fear of E-Health Records Implementation?" *Medico-Legal Journal* 83, no. 1 (March 2015): 34–39. https://doi.org/10.1177/0025817214540396.

Loi, Michele, Markus Christen, Nadine Kleine, and Karsten Weber. "Cybersecurity in Health—Disentangling Value Tensions." *Journal of Information, Communication and Ethics in Society* 17, no. 2 (May 13, 2019): 229–45. https://doi.org/10.1108/ JICES-12-2018-0095.

Lorenzi, Nancy M. "Introduction." In *Transforming Health Care through Information* (2nd ed.), edited by Laura Einbinder, Nancy M. Lorenzi, Joan S. Ash, Cynthia S. Gadd, and Jonathan Einbinder, 2–6. New York: Springer, 2005.

Magrabi, Farah, Mei-Sing Ong, William Runciman, and Enrico Coiera. "Using FDA Reports to Inform a Classification for Health Information Technology Safety Problems." *Journal of the American Medical Informatics Association* 19, no. 1 (January 2012): 45–53. https://doi.org/10.1136/amiajnl-2011-000369.

McCarthy, Carol. "The Money We Spend and Its Sources." In *Bioethics: Readings & Cases*, edited by Baruch A. Brody and Hugo Tristram Engelhardt Jr., 206–13. Englewood Cliffs, NJ: Prentice-Hall, 1987.

McClanahan, Kitty. "Balancing Good Intentions: Protecting the Privacy of Electronic Health Information." *Bulletin of Science, Technology & Society* 28, no. 1 (February 2008): 69–79. https://doi.org/10.1177/0270467607311485.

McGrath, Pam. "Autonomy, Discourse, and Power: A Postmodern Reflection on Principlism and Bioethics." *The Journal of Medicine and Philosophy* 23, no. 5 (August 1998): 516–32. https://doi.org/10.1076/jmep.23.5.516.2568.

Mohan, Apurva. "Cyber Security for Personal Medical Devices Internet of Things." In 2014 IEEE International Conference on Distributed Computing in Sensor Systems, 372–74. Marina Del Rey, CA: IEEE, 2014. https://doi.org/10.1109/DCOSS.2014.49.

Pycroft, Laurie, Sandra G. Boccard, Sarah L. F. Owen, John F. Stein, James J. Fitzgerald, Alexander L. Green, and Tipu Z. Aziz. "Brainjacking: Implant Security Issues in Invasive Neuromodulation." World Neurosurgery 92 (August 2016): 454–62. https://doi.org/10.1016/j.wneu.2016.05.010.

Radcliffe, Jerome. "Hacking Medical Devices for Fun and Insulin: Breaking the Human SCADA System. White Paper." In Black Hat Conference, 2011. https://infocondb.org/con/black-hat/black-hat-usa-2011/hacking-medical-devices-for-fun-and-insulin-breaking-the-human-scada-system.

Ransford, Benjamin, Shane S. Clark, Denis Foo Kune, Kevin Fu, and Wayne P. Burleson. "Design Challenges for Secure Implantable Medical Devices." In Security and Privacy for Implantable Medical Devices, edited by Wayne Burleson and Sandro Carrara, 157–73. New York: Springer, 2014. https://doi.org/10.1007/978-1-4614-1674-6_7.

Reijers, Wessel, David Wright, Philip Brey, Karsten Weber, Rowena Rodrigues, Declan O'Sullivan, and Bert Gordijn. "Methods for Practising Ethics in Research and Innovation: A Literature Review, Critical Analysis and Recommendations." Science and Engineering Ethics 24, no. 5 (October 2018): 1437–81. https://doi.org/10.1007/s11948-017-9961-8.

Rios, Billy, and Jonathan Butts. "Understanding and Exploiting Implanted Medical Devices." In Black Hat Conference, 2018. https://www.blackhat.com/us-18/briefings.html#understanding-and-exploiting-implanted-medical-devices.

Roman, Lisette C., Jessica S. Ancker, Stephen B. Johnson, and Yalini Senathirajah. "Navigation in the Electronic Health Record: A Review of the Safety and Usability Literature." Journal of Biomedical Informatics 67 (March 2017): 69–79. https://doi.org/10.1016/j.jbi.2017.01.005.

Ross, David A. "Foreword." In Public Health Informatics and Information Systems, edited by Patrick W. O'Carroll, William A. Yasnoff, M. Elizabeth Ward, Laura H. Ripp, and Ernest L. Martin, vvi. New York: Springer, 2003.

Sandhu, Jim S. "Citizenship and Universal Design." Ageing International 25, no. 4 (December 2000): 80–89. https://doi.org/10.1007/s12126-000-1013-y.

Saretzki, Thomas. "Legitimation Problems of Participatory Processes in Technology Assessment and Technology Policy." Poiesis & Praxis 9, no. 1–2 (November 2012): 7–26. https://doi.org/10.1007/s10202-012-0123-4.

Schöffski, Oliver, Thomas Adelhardt, Stefan Brunner, and Markus Maryschok. "VSDM Ergebnisphase: LG 15: Evaluationsgutachten (inklusive LG 14: Statistische Auswertungen)," 2018. https://www.evaluation-egk.de/wordpress/wp-content/uploads/2018/03/ORS1-WEV-VSDM_LG15_Evaluationsgutachten_inkl.-LG14_v1.0_final.pdf.

Sorell, Tom. "The Limits of Principlism and Recourse to Theory: The Example of Telecare." Ethical Theory and Moral Practice 14, no. 4 (August 2011): 369–82. https://doi.org/10.1007/s10677-011-9292-9.

Stafford, Ned. "Germany Is Set to Introduce E-Health Cards by 2018." *BMJ* 350, no. 1 (June 1, 2015): h2991–h2991. https://doi.org/10.1136/bmj.h2991.

Stahl, Bernd Carsten, Grace Eden, Marina Jirotka, and Mark Coeckelbergh. "From Computer Ethics to Responsible Research and Innovation in ICT." *Information & Management* 51, no. 6 (September 2014): 810–18. https://doi.org/10.1016/j.im.2014.01.001.

van den Hoven, Jeroen. "ICT and Value Sensitive Design." In *The Information Society: Innovation, Legitimacy, Ethics and Democracy*. In Honor of Professor Jacques Berleur S. J., edited by Philippe Goujon, Sylvian Lavelle, Penny Duquenoy, Kai Kimppa, and Véronique Laurent, 67–72. IFIP International Federation for Information Processing. Boston: Springer, 2007. https://doi.org/10.1007/978-0-387-72381-5_8.

Tuffs, Annette. "Germany Puts Universal Health E-Card on Hold." *BMJ* 340, no. 2 (January 12, 2010): c171. https://doi.org/10.1136/bmj.c171.

Vayena, Effy, Urs Gasser, Alexandra Wood, David O'Brien, and Micha Altman. "Elements of a New Ethical Framework for Big Data Research." *Washington and Lee Law Review Online* 72, no. 3 (2016): 420–41.

Verbeek, Peter-Paul. "Materializing Morality: Design Ethics and Technological Mediation." *Science, Technology, & Human Values* 31, no. 3 (May 2006): 361–80. https://doi.org/10.1177/0162243905285847.

Viitanen, Johanna, Hannele Hyppönen, Tinja Lääveri, Jukka Vänskä, Jarmo Reponen, and Ilkka Winblad. "National Questionnaire Study on Clinical ICT Systems Proofs: Physicians Suffer from Poor Usability." *International Journal of Medical Informatics* 80, no. 10 (October 2011): 708–25. https://doi.org/10.1016/j.ijmedinf.2011.06.010.

Vijayan, Jai. "DHS Investigates Dozens of Medical Device Cybersecurity Flaws." InformationWeek, October 23, 2014. http://www.informationweek.com/healthcare/security-and-privacy/dhs-investigates-dozens-ofmedical-device-cybersecurity-flaws-/d/d-id/1316882.

World Health Organization. "Global Spending on Health 2020: Weathering the Storm." Geneva, 2020.

Wirtz, Bernd W., Linda Mory, and Sebastian Ullrich. "eHealth in the Public Sector: An Empirical Analysis of the Acceptance of Germany's Electronic Health Card." *Public Administration* 90, no. 3 (September 2012): 642–63. https://doi.org/10.1111/j.1467-9299.2011.02004.x.

Woods, Michael. "Cardiac Defibrillators Need to Have a Bulletproof Vest: The National Security Risk Posed by the Lack of Cybersecurity in Implantable Medical Devices." *Nova Law Review* 41, no. 3 (2017): 419–47.

Yaghmaei, Emad, Ibo van de Poel, Markus Christen, Bert Gordijn, Nadine Kleine, Michele Loi, Gwenyth Morgan, and Karsten Weber. "Canvas White Paper 1—Cybersecurity and Ethics." *SSRN Electronic Journal*, 2017. https://doi.org/10.2139/ssrn.3091909.

# Technology and War

# CHAPTER 19

# The Ethics of Drone Killings and Assassinations

*Wanda Teays*

## Abstract

The attacks on the World Trade Center on 9/11 gave rise to concerted efforts to punish the enemy. The use of drones became increasingly attractive because of their efficiency and the fact that drone operators were thousands of miles away from the battlefield, protected from harm. However, the extent of the collateral damage to noncombatants raises a number of questions regarding the morality of the drone strikes. The degree of secrecy and lack of accountability also merits our attention, as I will discuss in this essay. Furthermore, the preference of killing suspected terrorists over capturing and detaining them has led to the proliferation of drones on a global scale. However, the lack of due process and inability of suspects to face charges warrants our concern. There needs to be public scrutiny of the policies and operations behind targeted killing and assassination by means of drone strike.

### KEYWORDS

drone warfare, collateral damage, moral injury, proportionality, legality, targeted killing, assassination

## Introduction

> Sometimes you hit innocent people, and I hate that, but we're at war . . . —Sen. Lindsey Graham

> War by remote control turns out to be intimate and dis-
> turbing. —Mark Bowden

After 9/11 the United States vowed to hold responsible those who planned and carried out the devastating attacks on the World Trade Center. With the pressure on, no expense was spared to find and punish the enemy. The result was a "war on terror," with tens of thousands of insurgents and potential or suspected terrorists held in detention centers and CIA "black sites" around the world. It has been a messy, drawn-out business with no end in sight—or way to discern exactly who are the terrorists and when such a war would end.

Meanwhile as the conflict dragged on, the mounting deaths and injuries to troops on the battlefield fueled a quest for alternatives. Unmanned aerial vehicles controlled by an operator on the ground—drones—filled the void by providing a way to take out combatants with little, if any, risk. Or so it seemed.

In time that gave rise to a drone-over-detention mentality. Constitutional law professor Noah Feldman observed that detaining terror suspects exposed the Bush administration to harsh criticism, especially with the increasing accusations of detainee abuse. In contrast, "dead terrorists tell no tales—and have no lawyers shouting about their human rights," he pointed out. The lesson of Guantánamo Bay, Feldman says, was that "extrajudicially killing alleged terrorists, while just as legally dubious, is superior to detaining them" (as noted by Benjamin 2012, 133–34). Consequently, the United States turned to unmanned armed vehicles—drones—as the more efficient solution.

And so it was that the vocabulary of war expanded to allow new terms and euphemisms to make the human costs more agreeable. Instead of "assassination," death-by-drone became "targeted killing," denoting the intentional and premeditated use of lethal force against specific suspected terrorists (Krebs 2017, 5). Jeremy Scahill (2015) puts it succinctly:

> Drones are a tool, not a policy. The policy is assassination. While every president since Gerald Ford has upheld an executive order banning assassinations by U.S. personnel, Congress has avoided legislating the issue or even defining the word "assassination." This has allowed proponents of the drone wars to rebrand assassinations with more palatable characterizations, such as the term du jour, "targeted killings."

This is not the random murder of opponents or the acts of soldiers in combat; rather the victims are selected—targeted—for a planned drone attack. The record of those being targeted is called a "kill list," euphemistically expressed as "removed from the battlefield" (Shane 2015).

The kill list itself is a subset of what has been called "the disposition matrix." Ian Cobain of *The Guardian* (2013) explains: "The disposition matrix is a complex grid of suspected terrorists to be traced then targeted in drone strikes or captured and interrogated." Such euphemisms and bureaucratic doublespeak help neutralize the actions and deaden the resistance. Language shapes the dialogue.

# Characterizing Targeted Killings

Is targeted killing an "assassination"? Under international law, assassinations are not permitted outside of an armed conflict. This is because "they violate international human rights law, as well as an array of domestic laws," states political scientist Michael J. Boyle. He clarifies: "They are permitted only during the context of armed conflict and under exceptional circumstances, where overwhelming necessity to prevent further loss of life dictates that they should be conducted" (Boyle 2015, 119). These are significant restrictions. The question is whether they are recognized and honored.

Proponents of drone strikes seek to avoid the negative connotation of the term "assassination," as well as the restrictions around legality and accountability. "Targeted killing" is the linguistic preference, although it has its own baggage. Former President Jimmy Carter expressed his discomfort with the White House having kill lists, asserting that the United States can no longer speak with moral authority on human rights (Carroll 2012). Its global standing has been tarnished.

Whether we call it a "targeted killing" or an "assassination," the net effect is the death of another person—a person who cannot challenge the grounds for or the severity of their punishment. Moreover, not only those targeted may lose their lives in drone strikes. Women, children, and any number of noncombatants have become "collateral damage," as we will see later. The scope of carnage far exceeds the numbers on the kill lists.

What is striking about civilian casualties, asserts Cholpon Orozobekova (2015), is that the CIA carries out secondary attacks to kill rescuers who come to help the injured after the drone attack. Amnesty International decries follow-up rescuer attacks, saying, "deliberately attacking civilians rescuing the wounded or the wounded themselves is a war crime" (Orozobekova 2015).

Finding a way to assess the policy of drone strikes requires acts of war to be put in perspective. This includes weighing the extent of the harm. "Drone strikes are a far cry from the atomic vaporizing of whole cities, but the horror of war doesn't seem to diminish when it is reduced in scale," argues journalist Mark Bowden (2013). "If anything," he says, "the act of willfully pinpointing a human being and summarily executing him from afar distills war to a single ghastly act." In turn, this calls us to examine the lawfulness of that act.

# The Legality of Drone Strikes

Outside of the context of armed conflict, the use of drones for targeted killing is almost never likely to be legal, human rights advocate Phillip Alston maintains. This is echoed by international law professor Mary Ellen O'Connell, who says, "Outside of a combat zone or a battlefield, the use of military force is not lawful" (Bowden 2013). And drones can certainly be a use of military force—potentially twenty-four hours a day, seven days a week.

Determining the legality of targeted killing operations is not on the front burner, even though critics voice their concerns. Instead, at issue is what makes a successful targeted killing *permissible* given its irreversibility. This suggests that a broader inquiry may be desirable. We need to know "Who constitutes a legitimate target? Are there any restrictions in terms of the timing or location of the targeted killing operation?" (Krebs 2017, 6–7, 29). And are there other considerations we should take into account?

Once the drone attack succeeds, the suspect is no longer a threat, unless there is residual post-mortem influence that they may have. In any case, there may be the "collateral damage" of injuries to civilians or noncombatants that may fuel anti-American sentiment. An ironic reaction is that drone strikes then become terrorist recruiting tools as the hatred percolates.

## KEY QUESTIONS

Key questions include: Who has been killed? Why were they targeted? Were there civilian casualties? Were procedures in place to ensure compliance with international law? (Heyns and Knuckey 2013, 112). A related concern is whether or not suspected terrorists should have the right to surrender and defend themselves in court, states legal scholar Shima D. Keene (2015). This leads us to ask: What about due process—is that on the table?

Unlike detention regimes, underscores law professor Shiri Krebs (2017), drone strikes are designed to kill, not capture. This decision rests mainly on available intelligence information concerning the threat. "It is not the 'heat of the battle' or immediate eyesight evidence that drive the killing operation," contends Krebs. Rather, it is a rational and calculated decision-making process based on secret information—information that the targeted individual is not able to challenge (2017, 29). The irrevocability of this reality should not be underestimated. With targeted killing there are simply no procedures for facing charges or pursuing channels to defend oneself.

However superior drone attacks may seem to the detention alternative, there are these pressing issues. Critics such as Christof Heyns, the United Nations

Special Rapporteur on Extrajudicial Killings, wonders if the use of armed drones constitutes war crimes. That decision is complicated by the fact that there is no central legislative body or controlling authority for international law (Carroll 2012). As a result, this limits what can be done to analyze the policies and assess legitimate options.

## PRACTICALITIES

Counterinsurgency expert David Kilcullen says his objection to the US strategy isn't moral or legal. His objection is practical, in the sense that "the strikes are creating more enemies than they eliminate." Another problem, Kilcullen says, is that "using robots from the air looks both cowardly and weak" (McManus 2009).

Addressing these concerns should take center stage. Drones are now a major factor in fighting battles and destroying enemies; they are thought to be crucial to the war on terror. Furthermore, both perpetrators and victims are on a global scale. Christof Heyns and Sarah Knuckey look at the proliferation of drones, and here's what they see:

> A small number of states with the necessary capabilities—particularly the United States—clearly find targeted killing attractive today. As unmanned aerial technologies become more widely available, many other states may feel the same pull towards the advantages of drone attacks in the future. Some 76 countries now have unmanned aerial systems . . . and reports suggest that an increasing number of countries are developing their own armed drones (2013, 103).

Such predictions are sobering. The view is that drones offer unique advantages for greater surveillance and targeting, "and appear to be facilitating the expanding practice, policy, and legal frontiers of targeted killings" (Heyns and Knuckey 2013, 103). The bottom line is that enemies can be killed without endangering the lives of those operating the technology—a win-win situation.

Proponents of drone attacks contrast the use of air strikes, which result in more collateral damage and endanger American troops. Some go even further to argue that the United States is both legally entitled and morally obligated to use drones on the grounds of safety and accuracy, Keene points out (2015, 17). This assumes that "efficiency" is a sufficient moral rationale. The perceived advantages cast a shadow on the various disadvantages, which tend to be minimized or dismissed altogether.

# The Parameters of Targeted Killing

Targeted killing requires a very narrow focus so only the targets are to be affected and destroyed. Since that is not necessarily the case, we need to broaden the scope to include collateral damage and long-term considerations when we are examining accountability.

For an armed attack to be deemed a legitimate killing, the individual victim must be a legitimate target in the eyes of the law and pose a "direct and imminent threat" (Keene 2015, 16). Assuming that bar has been met, the balance is thought to favor drone killings over using troops to fight terrorism. Not only does this save American lives, but it lessens future threats by eliminating enemy combatants and creating chaos in terrorist groups.

That said, it is not always the case that the target is a direct or imminent threat. Or even a threat at all. Other individuals may be injured or killed in the attack and, since the operation is irreversible, mistakes can carry grave consequences. Attorney John Yoo offers this perspective:

> "I would think if you are a civil libertarian, you ought to be much more upset about the drone than Guantánamo and interrogations," [John Yoo] told [Mark Bowden] when [he] interviewed him recently. "Because I think the ultimate deprivation of liberty would be the government taking away someone's life. But with drone killings, you do not see anything, not as a member of the public. You read reports perhaps of people who are killed by drones, but it happens 3,000 miles away and there are no pictures, there are no remains, there is no debris that anyone in the United States ever sees. *It's kind of antiseptic. So it is like a video game*; it's like Call of Duty." (Bowden 2013, emphasis mine)

According to defense analyst Bradley J. Strawser, drone warfare is the preferable option. "It's all upside. There's no downside. Both ethically and normatively, there's a tremendous value. You're not risking the pilot. The pilot is safe. And all the empirical evidence shows that drones tend to be more accurate. . . . Why not do this?" (Carroll 2012).

Opponents would respond to Strawser that there *is* a downside. While states may engage in self-defense against "imminent" attacks, not all of the thousands who are targeted by drone strikes would meet this requirement. Here's why: "The premeditated nature of targeted killings means that, in many cases, claims of imminence ring hollow. The long periods of time of the names of those on 'kill lists,' for example, undermines claims of such an imminent threat" (Heyns and Knuckey 2013, 108).

Furthermore, argues Michael J. Boyle, "This assertion of a right of anticipatory self-defense—which allows for an unrestricted geographic scope of military action, even in the absence of evidence of an immediate threat—has not been widely accepted by the international community" (2015, 111). Indeed, we might ask if "anticipatory" self-defense is really "self-defense," in light of the fact that it is an action based on what *might* happen—not what has happened. That distinction bears consideration.

# The Proliferation of Drones

The use of drones is widespread, with a growing number of nations turning to targeted killings. According to one 2020 estimate, thirty-nine countries currently possess armed drones while dozens of states and non-state actors have unarmed drones (Barno and Bensahel 2020).

In addition, the relative ease of drone warfare raises important issues. "One of the chief ethical dangers arising from drones is moral hazard," affirms Boyle (2015, 121). "Where the fact that drone technology is low-cost and increasingly accessible to a number of states," he continues, "means that targeted killings becomes easier and therefore more frequent." As a result, drone attacks have become increasingly more attractive, with the range of targets expanding.

Consider a recent high-profile case in which the victim was another country's official—Iranian General Qasem Soleimani. Soleimani's death in January 2020 by a US Reaper drone was the first time the United States had used a drone to kill another country's senior military commander on foreign soil. At that point, "The U.S. administration has shown itself willing to use the precision capability of drones to carry out assassinations" (Warrell 2020). Here's where calling it an "assassination" as opposed to a "targeted killing" gets tricky.

"Should news media reports about the killing use that term?" asks Mary Ellen O'Connell, an expert on the laws of war. "The [Associated Press] Style book defines assassination as 'the murder of a politically important or prominent individual by surprise attack.'" As a result, "the targeted killing of a high Iranian state and military official by a surprise attack was clearly an assassination," concludes O'Connell (Daniszewski 2020).

Quite the contrary, insisted the Pentagon. The killing of Soleimani was *not* an assassination. Instead, it should be seen as an act of self-defense, given that Soleimani was actively developing plans to attack American diplomats and service members in Iraq and throughout the region. The argument is that Soleimani got what he deserved. US Secretary of State Mike Pompeo and President Trump characterized the killing as *punishment* of Soleimani for the past blood on his hands (Daniszewski 2020)—an assessment that's quite different from a self-defense argument.

# The Dilemma of Self-Defense

The assertion that the assassination *was* self-defense has not been met with uniform agreement. O'Connell contends that there was never a full-fledged and direct attack on the United States by Iran. Therefore, the act cannot be considered self-defense.

An attack in self-defense should be "necessary and proportionate," which is not obviously the case here. A more appropriate assessment is that Soleimani's death was an assassination. However, this raises its own set of issues, as O'Connell notes. "Assassination is prohibited both in peacetime law as well as on the battlefield. We have really moved to a nearly lawless state," she says (Daniszewski 2020).

Chris Cole, the director of Drone Wars, is in agreement. "It is surely unarguable now that drones have enabled and normalized a culture of targeted killing which is eroding international law norms and making the world a more dangerous place," he asserts. In his view, the killing of Soleimani could usher in a violent new era in drone warfare (Sabbagh 2020).

If we want to punish other countries we are not (or not yet) at war with, we are not justified in assassinating their leaders via drone. What will such actions unleash? The consequences could be horrific and ratchet up conflicts by escalating retaliatory action.

And what happens when the line between *punishment* and *self-defense* is blurred? Punishment is a response to perceived wrongdoing—an assessment that looks to *past* behavior and seeks retribution by means of a penalty or compensation. Self-defense is a response to present actions—an assessment that looks to *future* behavior and seeks protection from harm or injury. One is focused on what was done, the other on what could be done.

Let's not forget that international law considers state-initiated targeted killings to be acts of self-defense *only if* the threat is imminent (i.e., overwhelming and immediate). In the case of Soleimani, the United States claimed that he was plotting further terror attacks against its citizens in the Middle East (Sabbagh 2020). But it did not release or otherwise make public the supportive evidence.

Instead, Trump said that any legal justification about the death of Soleimani "doesn't really matter" because the Iranian commander was a "terrorist" and had a "horrible past" (Sabbagh 2020). President Trump implied that no further justification was required for killing the general.

# Making the Kill List

Drone attacks are not just aimed at suspected terrorists or military leaders who can be considered participants in "direct hostilities." Being thought a threat is sufficient to make the kill list.

An example is Junaid Hussain, twenty-one, a convicted computer hacker and ISIS recruiter from Birmingham, England. Hussain went to Syria in 2013 and ended up "a high-value target" subsequently killed in a drone strike (BBC 2015). We might wonder if those misdeeds qualified for an assassination. In any case, the irreversibility of the drone strike closed out alternatives like facing criminal charges. And so it was that the finality of the drone attack precluded nonlethal options.

# The Appeal of Drones

FBI Director Christopher A. Wray points out various advantages of drones, such as "Drones are relatively easy to acquire, relatively easy to operate, and quite difficult to disrupt and monitor" (Drehle 2017). The result creates a significant security threat. As David Von Drehle (2017) of *The Washington Post* puts it,

> [f]or the price of a flat-screen TV, a would-be terrorist can go online and purchase a commercial model heavy enough to deliver a small package. You don't need to be a Hollywood screenwriter to imagine what might come next: A nearly silent, low-altitude little helicopter bearing a small bomb or supply of toxic material hums over metal detectors and barriers and bodyguards to strike a public gathering or senior official or hallowed landmark. [For example] in 2015, a hobbyist's drone landed on the White House lawn.

That's not all. In addition to hobbyists' drones being able to land on the White House lawn, they can bring down a plane, says Bernard Hudson, former CIA director of counterterrorism. More troubling, he observes, is that "militarized drones, are heavier . . . and can carry several pounds of explosives at speeds up to 100 miles per hour with a range of 400 miles." They can be programmed to enter active airspace and "wreak havoc without human guidance" (Hudson 2018). This brings to mind Skynet from the movie *Terminator*—when the machines became self-aware and turned on their human creators. By the time it was clear what had been unleashed, it was too late.

Hudson (2018) looks at the appeal of drone warfare and the potential for things to go badly. He warns, "Not only can preprogrammed drones swoop in from almost any direction, they can be used by anyone with the means to buy them." Therefore, the widespread proliferation of drones is to be expected and preventing drone attacks will be increasingly more complicated. This definitely ups the stakes in the war on terror, as the possible scenarios are chilling. One disturbing prediction is that

> [s]ooner or later—and probably sooner—senior U.S. civilian and military leaders will become vulnerable to the same types of decapitation strikes that the United States has inflicted on others. Enemies will almost certainly attempt to target and kill U.S. officials during any future major war, and such attacks will likely become a part of future irregular conflicts as well. [And] committed adversaries of the United States may still find that the advantages outweigh the cost savings. (Barno and Bensahel 2020)

# Unsettling Prospects

Current targeted killing practices risk weakening the rule of law, disrupting restraints on the use of force and setting dangerous precedents, maintain Heyns and Knuckey (2013, 112). They ask, "Should there be an international legal order that permits governments around the world to operate 'secret' and unaccountable programs to eliminate their enemies . . . with few binding limits and no meaningful international scrutiny?" (2013, 114).

Their answer is unequivocal. "This cannot and should not be accepted. The international community should act to uphold and restore the integrity of the international rule of law, and the protections guaranteed by human rights and international humanitarian law" (2013, 114).

And let's not forget the bigger picture or the available options. Historian Waitman Wade Beorn (2019) points out that "Proportionality requires that soldiers weigh the destructive potential of the weapons they use against the potential for harm to noncombatants. For example, if a sniper can be eliminated by another sniper, there is no justification for leveling the building with a bombing raid." Weighing the options should not be lost sight of; consequently, proportionality and restraint should have a role to play in the decision-making.

## DRONE VICTIMS

The deployment of drones over population centers in places like Pakistan and Yemen has been met with protests and has elicited fear and anger. *Reuters* journalist David Rohde (2012) described the effect of hearing drones whirring above him for hours on end. He characterized them as a "potent, unnerving symbol of unchecked American power." In the face of such power, drones create a sense of helplessness for those under their flight paths.

At the other end of the spectrum, American citizens have been insulated from the human toll as well as the political and the moral consequences of drone strikes. For the most part, the victims have remained faceless, and the damage caused by drone attacks has remained unseen, observes Jane Mayer (2009) for the *New Yorker*.

The result is a form of dehumanized killing. US Army Chaplain Keith Shurtleff laments this situation. "As war becomes safer and easier, as soldiers are removed from the horrors of war and see the enemy not as humans but as blips on a screen," he remarks, "there is very real danger of losing the deterrent that such horrors provide" (Bachmann 2013, 26).

We in the public don't see any images of those being targeted or learn why they pose an imminent threat. Nor do we hear about the non-terrorists, including children, killed by mistake or thought to be acceptable collateral damage for destroying the target. The images and details remain secret—they are not shared with the public or generally reviewed by elected officials. This lack of transparency is not a minor problem. Decisions made in secret are not easily subject to review.

## THE LACK OF ACCOUNTABILITY

The escalation of drone attacks has occurred with little discussion and, because of the program's secrecy, with no public system of accountability. What are the channels for analyzing policies or questioning particular drone strikes?

Given the lack of transparency, the exact number of casualties can only be approximated. According to the monitoring group Airwars, the first seven months of the Trump administration resulted in coalition air strikes killing between 2,800 and 4,500 civilians (Feldstein 2017). If accurate this estimate is unacceptably large.

Simply put, drone killings are gruesome. Jane Mayer (2009) tells of Pakistan's then-Interior Minister Abdul Rehman Malik watching the video of a drone attack on suspected terrorist Baitullah Mehsud. Malik said the Predator's targeters could see Mehsud's entire body, not just the top of his head. "It was a perfect picture," Malik stated. He reflected that

> "We used to see James Bond movies where he talked into his shoe or his watch. We thought it was a fairy tale. But this was fact!" . . . [T]he C.I.A. remotely launched two Hellfire missiles from the Predator. . . . After the dust cloud dissipated, all that remained of Mehsud was

a detached torso. Eleven others died: his wife, his father-in-law, his mother-in-law, a lieutenant, and seven bodyguards.

Look at the numbers: eleven people besides the intended victim were killed by the drone strike. Was that a mistake or were they considered expendable? Where do we draw the line? We should keep in mind that death by drone is not restricted to the specific target. All too often others end up on the "killed list."

As pointed out by political activist Medea Benjamin, targeted killing in an armed conflict is legal if and only if the target is a "combatant," "a fighter," or, in the case of a civilian, someone who "directly participates in hostilities." It is not someone who simply planned operations in the past. Nor is it someone who provides financial support, advocacy, or other noncombat aid (Benjamin 2011, 129). That distinction has not been given the weight it deserves. Islamic studies professor Kristina Benson asserts that "the decisive criterion for individual membership in an organized armed group is whether a person assumes a continuous function for the group involving his or her direct participation in hostilities" (2014, 122).

# Weighing Consequences

Jennifer Gibson (2019) of the Extrajudicial Killings Project examines the consequences of targeted drone killings. "For more than a decade now, the U.S. and its European allies have pioneered the use of drones to target and kill suspected terrorists far from the traditional battlefield," she says. "Many people's first and only engagement with the West is when a missile lands on their doorstep." That does not seem like the sort of global standing we should aspire to.

Former CIA lawyer Vicki Divoll contends that, "People are a lot more comfortable with a Predator strike that kills many people than with a throat-slitting that kills one." But, she explains, "mechanized killing is still killing"—a view echoed by human-rights lawyer Hina Shamsi. For Shamsi, the Predator program is "targeted international killings by the state" (Mayer 2009).

The international human rights law governing the use of lethal force outside of armed conflict permits the use of lethal force only in very narrow circumstances; specifically, only where it is "strictly unavoidable" to defend against an "imminent threat of death" (Foa, 2020).

We should also be aware that some countries have used drones to assassinate their own citizens, reports security analysts Peter Bergen and Melissa Salyk-Virk (2018). As with the detention and abusive treatment of American citizen Jose Padilla, Americans are not spared from being targeted by a drone strike. According to the ACLU, American citizen Anwar al-Awlaki is the first American citizen since the Civil War to be hunted and killed without trial by his own government (Shane 2015). This indicates that "the government has unreviewable authority to carry out the targeted killing of any American, anywhere, whom the president deems to be a threat to the nation," asserts Medea Benjamin (2012, 131). The reality of a country assassinating its own citizens is most troubling.

The ACLU and the Center for Constitutional Rights have taken legal action, as we saw in 2012 when they sued the CIA over the deaths of three US citizens killed with drones. Focusing on due process, they argue that these killings were undertaken without due process, in circumstances where lethal force was not a last resort to address a specific, concrete, and imminent threat, and where the government failed to take required measures to protect bystanders. This rises, they infer, to a violation of the most elementary constitutional right afforded to all US citizens—the deprivation of life without due process of law (Amnesty International 2012).

# Drawing Distinctions

A key distinction regarding drone victims centers on combatants vs. noncombatants. "The [Law of Armed Conflict] entitles noncombatants (both uninvolved civilians and fighters who have surrendered) to a wide range of rights, including housing conditions, medical care and humane treatment." Most importantly, it prevents them from being intentionally targeted or killed in cold blood (Beorn 2019).

Both counterinsurgency strategist David Kilcullen and security analyst Andrew Exum question decision-making in drone warfare. They draw attention to drone strikes that are way out of proportion to the situation and offer the following analogy by means of illustration:

Imagine that burglars move into a neighborhood. If the police were to start blowing up people's houses from the air, would this convince homeowners to rise up against the burglars? Wouldn't it be more likely to turn the whole population against the police? And if their neighbors wanted to turn the burglars in, how would they do that, exactly? Yet this is the same basic logic underlying the drone war (Keene 2015).

Attempts to lessen the number of civilian casualties are not without controversy. This can be seen with the development of new weapons such as the modified Hellfire missile called the R9X. Proponents consider the R9X missile a "game-changer" that can spare more civilian lives than traditional Hellfire missiles. The R9X—the "Flying Ginsu"—is reportedly armed with a "halo of six long blades" that can pierce buildings and car roofs before shredding its target. It can kill a passenger in the front seat of a moving vehicle while sparing the driver.

"But the new technology can only be as good as the intelligence and the rules that guide it," notes Letta Tayler (2019) of Human Rights Watch.

Tayler says drones are the US weapon of choice for targeted killings. One advantage is that "They can loiter for extensive periods to better distinguish military targets from civilians without risk to human operators, who often are based thousands of miles away" (Tayler 2019). Secrecy is a big part of the problem, however. The government doesn't even acknowledge most attacks, much less release details of their aftermath (Bowden 2013).

# Drone Operators

Conducting a drone attack may seem like playing a video game. There is little emotional investment or physical risk on the part of the operator, who is far from the point of contact. But however advantageous, there is one big downside. The drone pilot "sees the carnage close-up, in real time the blood and severed body parts, the arrival of emergency responders, the anguish of friends and family. Often he's been watching the people he kills for a long time before pulling the trigger" (Bowden 2013).

With such a voyeuristic proximity, operators are sometimes unnerved. Rather than thinking that he's like a video gamer, detached from the reality of his actions, Bowden posits, "If anything, they are far more attached." This opens the door to self-doubts and moral injury.

# Moral Injury

Not all wounds involve physical suffering; some come from ethical breaches. We see this when an individual experiences a conflict with their moral principles and beliefs—as when they cross a moral boundary and throw their values to the wind. Moral injury is the traumatic psychological, mental, social, or even spiritual suffering that results. Holes in one's moral fabric may have long-lasting effects.

Moreover, reparations may be difficult if not impossible to achieve. Consequently, the result may be overwhelming feelings of guilt or shame. As whistleblower Joseph Darby said of the horrors he witnessed at Abu Ghraib, "it catches up to you later, when you get home. Like, I slept fine while I was there, but now I have nightmares" (Norris 2006).

One manifestation this can take is post-traumatic stress. Drone operators who suffer PTSD may sink into depression or lethargy, and seeds of self-hate take root. There are two sides to this coin.

On one hand are those who find drone killing intensely disturbing and are overcome with guilt feelings. The moral injury they suffer may scar them for years. According to Peter W. Singer, international relations scholar, some Predator operators suffer from combat stress that equals, or exceeds, that of pilots on the battlefield. So "virtual killing, for all its sterile trappings, is a discomfiting form of warfare" (Mayer 2009).

On the other hand, some drone pilots are *not* repulsed by what they see or do. "In the words of one drone pilot: 'It's like a video game. It can get a little bloodthirsty. But it's . . . cool'" (Keene 2015, 22). Trivializing the deaths and destruction helps steady any qualms and provides enough detachment to allow drone strikes to continue.

One way this is done is by controlling the narrative. The terminology shows how. For example, people running for cover in a drone strike have been labeled "squirters." Commentator Joe Chapa (2017) says, "squirters" are so named because, "like a pinprick in a water balloon, through the infrared camera overhead the target they look as though they're squirting out of the target building during a raid or kinetic strike."

Minimizing death by drone may make it easier to sleep at night. For awhile at least. But dreams may turn to nightmares as the moral injury begins to fester. In time, drone pilots pay a price for killing at a distance.

Telford Taylor, an American prosecutor at the Nuremberg Trials, emphasizes the role of distinctions. He argues that "unless troops are trained and required to draw the distinction between military and nonmilitary killings, and to retain such respect for the value of life that unnecessary death and destruction will continue to repel them, they may lose the sense of that distinction for the rest of their lives" (Beorn 2019). The long-term effects should not go unnoticed, nor should the personal impact of the distinctions they draw and the decisions they make.

The loss of that distinction is not inconsequential. Nor is it without ethical impact on the drone operator. Military historian Col. Peter Mansoor states that "The laws of warfare are designed not only to protect civilians, but also to minimize the risk of moral injury to troops." And he asserts, "you want to minimize the damage to our values as much as possible, so you don't go over the edge" (Beorn 2019).

# Conclusion

Peter Singer questions whether drone warfare can be considered "war." He contends that a president who sends someone's son or daughter into battle should have to justify it publicly. But, if no one has children in danger, Singer questions whether drone warfare can be considered warfare at all (Babbage 2010). A "war" with no risks has certain advantages but raises a number of ethical questions.

By sparing drone pilots from danger and sacrifice, says Brian Burridge, ex-Air Chief Marshal, the result may be "a virtueless war." This requires neither courage nor heroism (Mayer 2009). Former Army ranger and security analyst Andrew Exum would concur: "There's something about pilotless drones that doesn't strike me as an honorable way of warfare" (as noted by Jane Mayer 2009).

In his view, "There's something important about putting your own sons and daughters at risk when you choose to wage war as a nation." No risk, no honor. For Exum, "We risk losing that flesh-and-blood investment if we go too far down this road" (Mayer 2009). We also risk the deterrent factor of personal risk-taking.

The question is whether the lack of risk, with or without heroism or courage, makes a convincing case for drone warfare. For many the answer is yes. We need only consider how many service men and women have been killed, lost their limbs, or suffered traumatic brain injuries to want to prevent such costs brought by the war on terrorism. The human toll is heartbreaking. But are drone attacks the solution?

Others are not so quick to jump on the drone bandwagon. Political philosopher Michael Walzer questions the wisdom of an intelligence agency like the CIA wielding such lethal power in secret. In his view, "There should be a limited, finite group of people who are targets, and that list should be publicly defensible and available. Instead, it's not being publicly defended. People are being killed, and we generally require some public justification when we go about killing people" (Mayer 2009). Such disclosure and public debates have been absent and do not appear to be forthcoming.

Although there is evidence to suggest that lethal targeting may be effective in terms of disrupting the enemy in the short term, the medium- and long-term impact of the attacks tend not to be fully appreciated (Keene 2015, 27). This needs to change.

Should there be an international protocol permitting governments to operate programs aimed at eliminating their enemies wherever they are and with no meaningful scrutiny? I would think not. There are serious concerns about the frequency of drone strikes, the use of kill lists, and the number of civilian deaths involved.

More clarity is needed to effectively assess drone warfare—and targeted killing in particular. UN Special Rapporteur on Human Rights and Counterterrorism Ben Emmerson has called for more transparency and accountability (Bachmann 2013, 26). The lack of public disclosure amounts to a form of secrecy. This is unacceptable when so much hinges on what has been done with targeted killing and the policies underlying drone warfare.

An undeniable fact is that drone technology removes the pilot from the actual battlefield. For him there is no "battlefield." In place of the closeness and intimacy of war drones have created a distance between the operator and the target, observes law professor Sasha-Dominik Bachmann. This creates a moral distance. Consequently, he asserts, drone killings have eliminated the "humanity of combat"—and, we may add, the humanity of the individual targets (2013, 26).

If drone strikes are going to continue as a feature of the war on terror, we need to proceed with our eyes wide open and restrictions firmly in place.

# References

American Civil Liberties Union. "ACLU and CCR File Lawsuit Challenging Targeted Killing of Three U.S. Citizens." July 18, 2012. https://www.aclu.org/blog/speakeasy/aclu-and-ccr-file-lawsuit-challenging-targeted-killing-three-us-citizens.

Amnesty International. "Is It Legal for the U.S. to Kill a 16-Year-Old U.S. Citizen with a Drone?" 2012. https://www.amnestyusa.org/is-it-legal-for-the-u-s-to-kill-a-16-year-old-u-s-citizen-with-a-drone/.

Babbage. "Robots at War: Drones and Democracy." *The Economist*, October 1, 2010. www.economist.com/blogs/babbage/2010/10/robots_war.

Bachmann, Sascha-Dominik. "Targeted Killings: Contemporary Challenges, Risks and Opportunities." *Journal of Conflict & Security Law* 18, no. 2 (Summer 2013): 259–88. https://academic.oup.com/jcsl/article/18/2/259/821647.

Barno, David, and Nora Bensahel. "The Drone Beats of War: The U.S. Vulnerability to Targeted Killings." *War on the Rocks*. Special Series, Strategic Outpost, January 21, 2020. https://warontherocks.com/2020/01/the-drone-beats-of-war-the-u-s-vulnerability-to-targeted-killings/.

Benjamin, Medea. *Drone Warfare*. New York: OR Books, 2012.

Benson, Kristina. "Kill 'em and Sort It Out Later: Signature Drone Strikes and International Humanitarian Law." *Global Business & Development Law Journal* 27, no. 1 (January 17, 2014). https://scholarlycommons.pacific.edu/cgi/viewcontent.cgi?article=1001&context=globe.

Beorn, Waitman Wade. "Here's What a Split-Second Combat Decision Looks Like. I Didn't Need to Murder." *Washington Post*, December 2, 2019. https://www.washingtonpost.com/outlook/2019/12/02/heres-what-split-second-combat-decision-looks-like-i-didnt-need-murder/.

Bergen, Peter, and Melissa Salyk-Virk. "Attack of the Assassin Drones." CNN, August 7, 2018. https://www.cnn.com/2018/08/07/opinions/attack-of-the-assassin-drones-bergen-salyk-virk/index.html.

Bowden, Mark. "The Killing Machines." *The Atlantic*, September 2013. www
.theatlantic.com/magazine/print/2013/09/the-killing-machines-how-to-think
-aboutdrones/309434/.

Boyle, Michael J. "The Legal and Ethical Implications of Drone Warfare." *The International Journal of Human Rights* 19, no. 2 (2015): 105–26. https://www.tandfonline
.com/doi/pdf/10.1080/13642987.2014.991210.

British Broadcasting Corporation (BBC). "UK Jihadist Junaid Hussain Killed in Syria
Drone Strike, Says US." August 27, 2015. https://www.bbc.com/news/uk-34078900.

Carroll, Rory. "The Philosopher Making the Moral Case for US Drones." *The Guardian*, August 2, 2012. https://www.theguardian.com/world/2012/aug/02/philosopher
-moral-case-drones.

Chapa, Joe. "Drone Ethics and the Civil-Military Gap." *War on the Rocks*, June 28, 2017.
https://warontherocks.com/2017/06/drone-ethics-and-the-civil-military-gap/.

Cobain, Ian. "Obama's Secret Kill List—The Disposition Matrix." *The Guardian*,
July 4, 2013. https://www.theguardian.com/world/2013/jul/14/obama-secret-kill-list
-disposition-matrix.

Daniszewski, John. "Was the Drone Attack on Iranian General an Assassination?" *Associated Press*, January 3, 2020. https://apnews.com/1f914021bc802931059746a5ce8a
192e.

Feldstein, Steven. "Under Trump, US Airstrikes Are Killing More Civilians." *Salon*,
October 20, 2017. https://www.salon.com/2017/10/20/under-trump-presidency-us
-airstrikes-kill-more-civilians_partner-2/.

Foa, Maya. "Trump's Secret Assassinations Programme." *Reprieve*, 2020. https://reprieve
.org.uk/update/game-changer-trumps-new-attacks-on-human-rights/.

Gibson, Jennifer. "We're Quickly Moving Toward a World Where Drone Executions
Are the Norm." *Los Angeles Times*, November 13, 2019. https://www.latimes.com/
opinion/story/2019-11-13/drone-killings-war-syria-turkey.

Heyns, Christof H., and Sarah Knuckey. "The Long-Term International Law Implications of Targeted Killing Practices." *Harvard International Law Journal* 54 (January
2013). https://repository.up.ac.za/handle/2263/39613?show=full.

Hudson, Bernard. "Drone Attacks Are Essentially Terrorism by Joystick." *The
Washington Post*, August 5, 2018. https://www.washingtonpost.com/opinions/drone
-attacks-are-essentially-terrorism-by-joystick/2018/08/05/f93ec18a-98d5-11e8-843b
-36e177f3081c_story.html.

Keene, Shima D. *Lethal and Legal? The Ethics of Drone Strikes*. Carlisle Battacks, PA:
Strategic Studies Institute and US Army War College Press, 2015.

Kilcullen, David, and Andrew McDonald Exum. "Death from Above, Outrage Down
Below." *New York Times*, May 17, 2009. https://www.nytimes.com/2009/05/17/
opinion/17exum.html.

Krebs, Shiri. "Rethinking Targeted Killing Policy: Reducing Uncertainty, Protecting
Civilians from the Ravages of Both Terrorism and Counterterrorism." *Florida State
University Law Review* 44 (August 22, 2017). https://papers.ssrn.com/sol3/papers
.cfm?abstract_id=3021458.

Mayer, Jane. "The Predator War." *New Yorker*, October 19, 2009. https://www.new
yorker.com/magazine/2009/10/26/the-predator-war.

McManus, Doyle. "The Cost of Killing by Remote Control." *Los Angeles Times*, May 3, 2009. https://www.latimes.com/archives/la-xpm-2009-may-03-oe-mcmanus3-story.html.

Norman, Sonya B. "What Is Moral Injury." National Center for PTSD, May 15, 2019. https://www.ptsd.va.gov/professional/consult/2019lecture_archive/05152019_lecture_slides.pdf.

Norris, Michele. "Abu Ghraib Whistleblower Speaks Out." *NPR*, August 15, 2006. https://www.npr.org/templates/story/story.php?storyId=5651609.

Orozobekova, Cholpon. "The US Drone Policy under International Law." *Spotlight on Regional Affairs* 34, no. 11–12 (November–December 2015). http://www.irs.org.pk/spotlight/spnd2015.pdf.

Rohde, David. "How Obama's Drone War Is Backfiring." *Reuters*, March 1, 2012. http://blogs.reuters.com/david-rohde/2012/03/01/how-obamas-drone-war-is-backfiring/.

Sabbagh, Dan. "Targeted Killings via Drone Becoming 'Normalised'—Report." *The Guardian*, January 19, 2020. https://www.theguardian.com/politics/2020/jan/19/military-drone-strikes-becoming-normalised-says-report.

Scahill, Jeremy. "The Drone Papers." *The Intercept*, October 15, 2015. https://theintercept.com/drone-papers/.

Shane, Scott. "The Lessons of Anwar al-Awlaki." *New York Times*, August 27, 2015. https://www.nytimes.com/2015/08/30/magazine/the-lessons-of-anwar-al-awlaki.html.

Tayler, Letta. "'Flying Ginsu' Missile Won't Resolve US Targeted Killing Controversy." Human Rights Watch, May 17, 2019. https://www.hrw.org/news/2019/05/17/flying-ginsu-missile-wont-resolve-us-targeted-killing-controversy.

Von Drehle, David. "The Security Threat We've Been Ignoring: Terrorist Drones." *Washington Post*, September 29, 2017. https://www.washingtonpost.com/opinions/the-security-threat-were-ignoring-terrorist-drones/2017/09/29/3fbd1374-a51f-11e7-b14f-f41773cd5a14_story.html.

Warrell, Helen. "From Desert Storm to Soleimani: How US Drone Warfare Has Evolved." *Financial Times*, January 8, 2020. https://www.ft.com/content/6346dd78-322d-11ea-9703-eea0cae3f0de.

# CHAPTER 20

# War and Technology

## SHOULD DATA DECIDE WHO LIVES, WHO DIES?

*Shannon E. French*

# Abstract

This chapter examines ways in which new technology such as artificial intelligence (AI) and machine learning (ML) may have life-or-death consequences in modern combat and may pose other related ethical concerns. This includes the effect of this technology on the movements of troops and equipment, including routing and navigation, on military medical triage, on distinction (identifying possible threats, ruling out noncombatants as targets and flagging other non-targets, clearing areas as safe or hostile, surveillance in advance of troop movement, etc.), and the use of lethal autonomous weapons systems (LAWS). Technology may provide some positive opportunities, but there are grave associated ethical risks.

KEYWORDS

artificial intelligence, machine learning, military, ethics, principle of distinction, triage, moral injury

When the ethical implications of the use of artificial intelligence (AI), machine learning (ML), or other forms of computing-based augmentation of decision-making are discussed in the military context, the conversation more often than not centers on lethal autonomous weapons systems, or LAWS. While this is of course an interesting area—and one I will address in this chapter—there has already been considerable attention paid to it by scholars in military ethics and international law. Since LAWS should not be the only focus of ethical analysis when it comes to the deployment of emerging military technology, in this chapter I will begin by looking at other ways in which new technology—especially technology that deals with rapid data processing—may have life-or-death consequences in modern combat and that raise other related ethical concerns.

In particular, I will examine the effect of such technology on the movements of troops and equipment, including routing and navigation, on military medical triage, and on distinction (identifying possible threats, ruling out noncombatants as targets and flagging other non-targets, clearing areas as safe or hostile, surveillance in advance of troop movement, etc.). Each of these areas has its own positive opportunities technology may provide, along with its own associated ethical risks. Then I will relate these to the looming issue of LAWS.

First, I need to make a broad point about artificial intelligence. The term "artificial intelligence" is inherently misleading, as it suggests that what AI systems do is closely akin to the workings of human intelligence. This is not the case. The state of the art is nowhere near producing artificial general intelligence (AGI) that would resemble how humans think. What actually happens in AI systems now is rapid and complex data processing, usually to seek out and identify patterns. These patterns, however, may not be what we expect. Berenice Boutin of the Asser Institute explains this point well with a simple example comparing human and machine recognition of turtles. A young child can be shown cartoon images of turtles in picture books and still go on to recognize a real turtle in a zoo or in the wild as a turtle. Current data-driven AI systems cannot make the same leap.

Human brains do use pattern recognition to reason in some contexts, but the exact mechanism of how this works is not fully understood and is the subject of debate across many disciplines, from philosophy to cognitive science. AI systems are trained to identify items by being fed examples (coded datasets) of objects or patterns until they can successfully pick out fresh examples of the same category of items. This extension from the original data to new examples depends on factors that can be coded in machine language—importantly, it is not based on anything like a form or kind, to use terms from the philosophy of language and epistemology. Willard Van Orman Quine is one philosopher who endeavored to explain how human inductive reasoning occurs in part due to our capacity and tendency (innate or socialized) to see "natural kinds" in the world and to shape our language to reflect these categories, whether or not they exist in reality (an issue I will certainly not attempt to resolve here). Philosophers and cognitive scientists from various schools of thought debate how classifications occur in people's minds and the exact role of language in cognition, but however this occurs, and however vague or irreducible the details may be, we somehow perceive similarities that allow us to make mental leaps like that from a cartoon turtle to the living animal.[1] We grasp "turtleness."

AI systems do not recognize "turtleness" in the same way humans do. They are trained to detect patterns in data, which is an altogether different way of chopping up the world than is found in ordinary human cognition. It is, in a sense, profoundly alien to us. This is why MIT researchers were able to make Google AI mistake a clear picture of a tabby cat for a bowl of guacamole—or, even more relevantly in the context of military technology, a turtle for a rifle—just by manipulating pixel colors and density in an image or an object.[2]

> The problem is that although neural networks can be taught to be experts at identifying images, having to spoon-feed them millions of examples during training means they don't generalize particularly well. They tend to be really good at identifying whatever you've shown them previously, and fail at anything in between. Switch a few pixels here or there, or add a little noise to what is actually an image of, say, a gray tabby cat, and Google's Tensorflow-powered open-source Inception model will think it's a bowl of guacamole. This is not a hypothetical example: it's something the MIT students, working together as an independent team dubbed LabSix, claim they have achieved.[3]

In other words, these systems are not looking for cats, or rifles, in the way that humans would. It is a mistake to anthropomorphize artificial systems as if they were just superintelligent people, doing what we do, only faster and better. It may be more challenging to guard against the kinds of errors a machine would make, as opposed to the all-too-familiar failings to which people fall prey.

How AI classifications work is a "black box" problem. It can be difficult to gauge how trustworthy a classification system is by looking at it from the outside, as it were, because results that may initially seem to be accurate may be based on qualities that are fundamentally unreliable. Marco Tulio Ribeiro, Sameer Singh, and Carlos Guestrin demonstrated this point quite effectively with an experiment that showed how a bad classifier could pick out pictures of wolves from pictures of huskies most of the time, simply by classifying pictures with snow in the background as wolf pictures and those with grass behind the animal as dog pictures:

> Often artifacts of data collection can induce undesirable correlations that the classifiers pick up during training. These issues can be very difficult to identify just by looking at the raw data and predictions. In an effort to reproduce such a setting, we take the task of distinguishing between photos of Wolves and Eskimo Dogs (huskies). We train a logistic regression classifier on a training set of 20 images, hand selected such that all pictures of wolves had snow in the background, while pictures of huskies did not. As the features for the images, we

use the first max-pooling layer of Google's pre-trained Inception neural network. . . . On a collection of [an] additional 60 images, the classifier predicts "Wolf" if there is snow (or light background at the bottom), and "Husky" otherwise, regardless of animal color, position, pose, etc. We trained this bad classifier intentionally, to evaluate whether subjects are able to detect it.[4]

Even though the subjects of the experiment were "graduate students who have taken at least one graduate machine learning course," far too many of them nonetheless trusted the bad classifier, until the patterns on which it had been trained were fully explained to them. Their faith was misplaced, and more robust than it should have been. As the experimenters sagely observe, "Determining trust in individual predictions is an important problem when the model is used for decision making. When using machine learning for medical diagnosis or terrorism detection, for example, predictions cannot be acted upon on blind faith, as the consequences may be catastrophic."[5]

It takes very careful coding and training of classification algorithms to ensure that they are reasonably reliable, and even the best systems remain vulnerable to "adversarial examples," or images intended to trick the classifier. Currently, the most effective systems are those that are able to analyze fairly static, consistent images, with as few variables as possible to interfere with correct classifications. For example, there appear to be genuine benefits from AI systems reviewing mammogram images to look for breast cancer.[6] Unfortunately for those who support military applications for AI classification systems, armed conflict involves ever-changing conditions that do not lend themselves well to automated analysis, combined with the near certainty of adversarial efforts to intentionally push such systems into false classifications.

Why does this matter? After all, humans can also be fooled and manipulated and make identification errors or pattern recognition mistakes. It matters primarily because people have been exposed to quite a lot of "sales pitches" suggesting that AI can do more than it can (or will be able to do for decades, if ever). It is vital not to fall for hype about the capabilities of AI/ML systems for a number of reasons. For one thing, there is the strong danger of automation bias. Automation bias is the tendency to accept the authority of an automated or computerized system as superior to one's own or another human's authority—to assume that the machine knows best. As Lisa Lindsay and I have noted elsewhere, this can be a gravely pernicious aspect of the use of automated systems by the military:

Artificial intelligence, as a technology that is little understood by the general public and often sold as "better" than human ability, puts us at even higher risk for automation bias. Despite documented failures, people focus on reports that seem to suggest that artificial minds are superior to organic ones, including news of computers beating humans at strategy games like chess and Go. While television advertisements find humor in people following incorrect Google maps directions straight into a lake, the reality of overreliance on automation is much less amusing. In a military context, automation bias can have life or death consequences. Just as infantry check the proper functioning of their weapons, those using A.I. systems in their military roles are obligated to make sure their tools—both automated and not—are working correctly, too.[7]

Elke Schwarz warns that "Set against a background where the instrument is characterized as inherently wise, the technology gives an air of dispassionate professionalism and a sense of moral certainty to the messy business of war."[8] While those most critical of the military tend to focus on instances of human error or, worse, intentional evil, examples also abound of human troops showing restraint, compassion, and kindness, even at great risk to themselves. I am reminded of this case, from the United States's engagement in Somalia in 1992:

> Colonel Michael Campbell, another US Marine, was commanding a tank unit in Somalia when he was ordered to destroy three tanks that the enemy had deployed on the outskirts of an impoverished civilian community. When Colonel Campbell's unit, which included both armour and infantry, came into range, the turrets of the enemy tanks turned towards the approaching American troops. The colonel's subordinates in the US tanks urgently requested permission to fire first, to defend themselves and the infantrymen all around them. However, something made the colonel hesitate. Perhaps it was just instinct, or perhaps there was something slightly wrong about the way the enemy turrets turned to bear upon the Americans that set off alarm bells in the colonel's subconscious. For whatever reason, with both his superiors on the radio and his subordinates all around him shouting for him to order the attack, the colonel refused to fire at the tanks. Just then, the hatches on top of the enemy tanks popped open, and Somali children began to crawl out and run back to their homes. The tanks had been abandoned in the middle of the night, and the children had been playing in them.[9]

Imagine how much additional pressure the colonel might have felt to order fire if there had been an AI-enabled targeting system firmly identifying the tanks as urgent military targets. Whether we should trust machine systems more than human systems to make final decisions on use of lethal force is a topic I will return to later when I discuss LAWS, but for human-in-the-loop military decision-making, the risk of individuals allowing automation bias to cloud their judgment must be given proper weight. There is disquieting research that suggests the possible harms that could follow from the effects of automation bias. MIT's M. L. Cummings summarizes some examples of this in the context of automated route-planning systems:

> computer generated solutions are not always truly optimal and in some cases, not even correct. Known as "brittleness," automation decision support models in complex systems cannot account for all potential conditions or relevant factors which could result in erroneous or misleading suggestions.[10,11] In addition, as problem spaces grow in complexity, it becomes more difficult for the human to not only understand whether or not a computer-generated solution is correct, but how any one variable, a combination of variables, or missing information influence the computer's solution. This inability of the human to understand complex algorithms only exacerbates the tendency towards automation bias. For example, in a study examining commercial pilot interaction with automation in an enroute flight planning tool, pilots, when given a computer-generated plan, exhibited significant automation overreliance causing them to accept flight plans that were significantly sub-optimal. When presented with an automated solution, 40% of pilots reasoned less or none at all when confronted with uncertainty in the problem space and deferred to erroneous automation recommendations, even though they were provided with tools with which to explore the automation space.
>
> The authors of this study suggest that even if automated critiquing alerts are provided to warn against possible constraint violations and/or provide suggestions to avoid constraint violations, human decision makers can be susceptible to automation bias. In a similar experiment looking at levels of automated assistance in a military in-flight replanning task, pilots with [automated] assistance exhibited overreliance in the form of complacency. In this study, an automated decision aid planned a route taking into consideration time to targets, possible threats, and fuel state and subsequently presented pilots with its "optimal" solution, which could always be significantly improved through human intervention. Despite having the ability to change and improve the computer's solutions, subjects tended to accept the computer's solution without question.[12,13]

From his extensive research, Cummings concluded that, "in time critical environments with many external and changing constraints such as air traffic control and military command and control operations, higher levels of automation are not advisable because of the risks and the complexity of both the system and the inability of the automated decision aid to be perfectly reliable," further noting that, "there can be measurable costs to human performance when automation is used, such as loss of situational awareness, complacency, skill degradation, and automation bias."[14]

There are other forms of bias to contend with, as well. Systems that are programmed by humans, even if those systems proceed to "learn" on their own, are vulnerable to the same biases and fallibility of humans. There is an essential truth captured in the phrase, "garbage in, garbage out." A grimly humorous example of this can be seen in the case of an AI "chatbot" named Tay that Microsoft designed to interact with people on Twitter.

The intention was for the chatbot to acquire the ability to mimic human interactions more naturally. The result was that Tay quickly began to send out wildly offensive tweets, expressing all forms of hate, including (but not limited to) racism, misogyny, and anti-Semitism.[15] In a similar case, "after Facebook eliminated human editors who had curated 'trending' news stories . . . the algorithm [that replaced the human editors] immediately promoted fake and vulgar stories on news feeds."[16]

Automated systems are certainly not amoral or divorced from the ethical or character flaws of humans. In *Weapons of Math Destruction*, Cathy O'Neill points out, "these models [of AI and ML] are constructed not just from data, but from the choices we make about which data to pay attention to—and what to leave out. Those choices are not just about logistics, profits, and efficiency. They are fundamentally moral."[17]

Even as such systems are improved, they need to be seen as tools that process information only in very specific ways, not as superhuman or godlike intelligences that are necessarily more accurate or objective than human agents. In other words, we need to understand going into any discussion about the ethical use of AI/ML systems that these systems do not think like us and that they can only work with the information (data) that we give them. With this background perspective in mind, let us review some of the ethical issues and the pros and cons that arise when deploying data-driven systems for nonlethal military use.

First, consider the case of military medical triage. As Sara Gaines has explained,[18] the US military, like most militaries, divides military medical care into three categories: (1) care under fire (CUF); (2) tactical field care (TFC); and (3) tactical evacuation care (TACEVAC). All three of these are collectively known as tactical combat casualty care (TCCC).[19] The idea behind AI-augmented military medical triage would be to have an algorithmic, data-based system to help medics on the ground make time-sensitive triage decisions. Gaines explains the complex context in which this technology could be deployed:

> Moral injury can be defined as a "disruption in an individual's confidence and expectations about one's own or others' motivation or capacity to behave in a just and ethical manner."[20] During TFC, the medics making decisions have their dual loyalties to contend with,

meaning that there are times when one decision may go against the expectations of the other role. In the scenarios mentioned before, a medic who follows orders and does not treat a casualty is acting as a soldier, but there is then the psychological cost of not acting within the role of care provider to the casualty. For combat medics who are expected to follow international laws regarding treatment of casualties, they need to be able to have faith in themselves to make the correct decision. For medics suffering from a moral injury and lacking the ability to trust their own decisions, making the tough in-arena calls which must be made would be extraordinarily difficult. If a medic is not able to make the difficult decisions associated with the role and act quickly, then it is the casualties who must incur greater suffering until treatment begins. Not only are there in-arena consequences to a medic suffering from a moral injury and unable to trust that the decisions being made by them and around them are the just and ethical ones, but suffering a moral injury makes them more susceptible to developing Post-Traumatic Stress.[21,22]

In theory, an AI system might spare human medics some degree of moral injury by taking the most gut-wrenching decisions out of their hands. Would that really happen, though, or would medics still second-guess whether they should have, for example, overridden the system's suggestions? I share Gaines's skepticism both that we are anywhere close to having the technological capability to field an AI triage system and that such a system would reduce moral injury for medics:

> even if the medic believes the AI to be an accurate tool, the possibility of a moral injury still remains. Evidence has developed in research on post-traumatic stress that there is often guilt associated with not being subject to the same harm as those who went through the traumatic event as well.[23] Known as survivor guilt, one important component within the context of a combat medic is that this guilt can develop from a sense of feeling as though a different decision could have or should have been made, even when no other option existed.[24] So even if an AI is capable of making the decision, unless the medic fully agrees with that decision, they are still at risk of their loyalty as a soldier conflicting with their loyalty as a medic to care for the casualties around them.[25]

This raises another ethical concern: What does healthy dissent look like when AI systems are given a role in decision-making, either as an advisor or an authority? Again, extensive research on automation bias proves that, consciously or unconsciously, humans often tend to cede authority to automated systems and assume them to be more objective or fair.

Unfortunately, as Safiya Noble unequivocally demonstrates in *Algorithms of Oppression*, it is just as likely such systems will be as much or more biased than their human counterparts, and will amplify that bias by imbuing it with the imagined infallibility of cold machine logic. As Noble states, "Algorithms are, and will continue to be, contextually relevant and loaded with power."[26] In civilian medicine, we have already seen how systems trained on, for example, nondiverse datasets that do not contain data from different races can have a negative impact on patient outcomes if doctors rely on them alone or invest them with too much authority. Interestingly, a recent study revealed that senior medical professionals were much more likely to trust their own judgment than to take the AI system's advice, whereas less-experienced doctors tended to second-guess themselves and defer to the machine.[27] This has implications for a military setting, where differences in experience and rank may either exacerbate or mitigate automation bias. Do we want human medics to "go with their gut," knowing that their "gut" may be honed from years of experience or subject to irrational impulse? Or do we want them to let the data decide who can still be saved?

One way to frame the issues is to ask where is a threshold to know when it is better to let the data decide who lives and who dies. Is there a perfect percentage point where we should feel morally comfortable saying "go with the machines," because, for instance, the machines make X percentage fewer errors than humans do in similar circumstances? This way of approaching the problem, by comparing error rates, is tempting. Yet it may be fundamentally misguided. It matters ethically *what kinds of errors are made*, not just how many errors there are. For example, an AI triage system that makes fewer overall errors than human medics do but that consistently underestimates the survival potential of a particular gender or race would not be ethical to deploy.

To give an everyday example, a few seasons ago, my child's summer camp offered a supposedly AI-enabled system using facial recognition to pick out camp photos for parents that contained their children. Setting aside other ethical concerns with this, I noticed something interesting about the errors that the system made. In one large group of photos, it picked out six that it flagged as containing my child. Of these, four indeed did contain my child, but one did not contain any children at all (only trees and other objects). Another was of a child that was not only not mine but in no way resembled mine. In other words, these were not only errors, they were errors that no reasonable person could have made. Meanwhile, I found a total of sixty-one photos that contained my child, and was able to accurately discern from subtle cues in some of them that she was unwell, which was soon confirmed by the camp. The point of this unscientific case study is that we must approach claims of lower-than-human error rates for automated systems with some skepticism, and ask the right questions.

Let us turn now to another possible military application for automated systems, to see if the same, or different, ethical issues arise. Initially, the movement of troops and equipment (logistics) and routing and navigation seem like areas that would be less fraught with ethical peril than military medical decision-making. The benefits also seem fairly clear if we consider, for instance, the appeal of just-in-time deliveries of correct needed parts to units, made possible by an advanced automated system capable of machine learning that tracks and learns where supplies will run low when. It is also straightforward to grasp the advantages of routing systems that give a commander real-time options to navigate through unfamiliar terrain, updated with more data than human scouts could ever hold in their minds. There is positive potential here to build and increase capacity and efficiency, but once again, the devil is in the details.

As any cybersecurity expert will tell you, even the most seemingly autonomous system remains susceptible to human error, as well as to malicious human attack. A just-in-time supply chain depends on correct, updated information. Once again, it is garbage in, garbage out. Any automated system can be hacked and undermined or simply fall prey to mistakes or unanticipated elements of chaos introduced by nonhuman factors like the environment or human ones.[28] This is especially true of systems that depend on complex digital platforms to collect and communicate information.

> Even as they grant unprecedented powers, [digital technologies] also make users less secure. Their communicative capabilities enable collaboration and networking, but in so doing they open doors to intrusion. Their concentration of data and manipulative power vastly improves the efficiency and scale of operations, but this concentration in turn exponentially increases the amount that can be stolen or subverted by a successful attack. The complexity of their hardware and software creates great capability, but this complexity spawns vulnerabilities and lowers the visibility of intrusions. Cyber systems' responsiveness to instruction makes them invaluably flexible; but it also permits small changes in a component's design or direction to degrade or subvert system behavior. These systems' empowerment of users to retrieve and manipulate data democratizes capabilities, but this great benefit removes safeguards present in systems that require hierarchies of human approvals. In sum, cyber systems nourish us, but at the same time they weaken and poison us.[29]

Every new piece of technology introduces new potential points of failure. As Jacquelyn Schneider explains, this can be understood as the "capability-vulnerability paradox," and it is not a unique problem for digital or computerized systems:

> In examining analogies within infrastructure development and conflict, a historical pattern of capabilities and vulnerabilities that illustrate the logic of the capability/vulnerability paradox emerges. Take, for example, the combustion engine. Internal combustion engines opened up remarkable opportunities for weapons development—from tanks to aircraft to ships, combustion engines made nations more effective on the battlefield. But it also made them more dependent on oil and therefore vulnerable to disruptions in the oil supply chain.[30]

Some of these concerns are practical, not ethical, and as such are not necessarily grounds to refuse to develop and continuously improve such systems. However, ethics will quickly come into the picture if militaries allow themselves to become over-reliant on such systems without establishing appropriate backups and potential overrides. In the tragic Boeing 737 Max airplane crashes, when the automated systems went wrong, the human pilots found themselves unable to seize back manual control and save the lives of their passengers (or themselves).[31] The automation itself blocked recovery of the aircraft. These are design choices that have ethical consequences.

> The U.S. military has a troubling history of implementing systems without ample time for them to be carefully studied and tested from a safety perspective, let alone from a legal or ethical standpoint. The Bradley fighting vehicle and the osprey are just two well-known examples of flawed systems rushed into use. There are also the tragedies of service personnel who were sent into irradiated areas before the effects of nuclear weapons were understood or the combat troops who were given unreliable, jam-prone M-16s in Vietnam: "from Gettysburg to Hamburger Hill to the streets of Baghdad, the American penchant for arming troops with lousy rifles has been responsible for a staggering number of unnecessary deaths."[32,33]

Safety testing is only part of the picture. Great care must be taken before militaries buy into systems that may not only not have humans in the loop but may actively lock humans out of the loop even, or especially, when things go wrong with the system itself. That is unacceptable. There is a reason why the NASA astronauts of the Mercury program strongly objected to complete automated control of windowless capsules, which famous test pilot Chuck Yeager said reduced them to mere "spam in a can."[34]

Progress has been made in this area, and there are hopeful signs, such as military research funding organizations like DARPA increasing their requirements for ongoing ELSI/LME (ethical, legal, and social issues/legal, moral, and ethical) reviews of developing projects that are not mere check-the-box compliance exercises. Nevertheless, legitimate concerns persist in light of the US military's tendency to characterize every potential technological advancement as an urgent upgrade that must be deployed as quickly as possible to gain an advantage. This "arms race" attitude is not only reckless, it also fails to take into account not only possible harms from improperly vetted systems but the uncomfortable truth of asymmetric conflicts. It is simply not the case that the more technologically advanced side in an asymmetric armed conflict always (or even usually) prevails. Nor is it consistently true, even in peer or near-peer conflicts, that the first side to deploy a particular technological advancement always gains the advantage. Sometimes, the second mouse gets the cheese.

The just war tradition (JWT) immediately becomes relevant when we turn to looking at the use of AI/ML systems to attempt to distinguish between combatants and noncombatants. Here it is especially important to remember the point I reviewed at the start of this chapter concerning how these systems "recognize" things and spot patterns. It is a value-laden question to ask, if you want to train a computerized system to determine if a person is or is not a legitimate target in war, what exactly you should tell it to look for—bearing in mind that you cannot rely on human-like cognition and understanding of kinds. Should you try to train it to look for a weapon? What do weapons look like, to a pattern-analyzing machine? What would reliably distinguish a rifle from other objects? What about cruder weapons? What about inherently inconsistently constructed weapons like improvised explosive devices (IEDs)? Humans find these kinds of identifications challenging, too, especially when under extreme stress. Would a system of pattern recognition do better? As before, we have to ask what kind of error rates we need, and if certain types of errors are more or less ethically tolerable than others. For example, is mistaking a child's toy for a gun worse than mistaking a carton of cigarettes for an IED?

Suppose we decide that looking for weapons seems too problematic. The alternatives might be even worse, since they would most likely involve trying to determine combatant/noncombatant status by an individual's hostile intent (or lack thereof). Exactly how would you train a system to pick out hostile intent? It is notoriously difficult to predict and analyze human behavior and responses, and as Ruha Benjamin points out in *Race after Technology*, these issues are even harder when dealing cross-culturally, with diverse races, genders, ages, and communities, all in high-stress circumstances likely themselves to skew "normal" behavior.[35]

In testifying before Congress about the extensive failures of the Transportation Security Agency (TSA)'s Screening of Passengers by Observation Techniques (SPOT) program, psychologist Phil Rubin noted how the underlying "science" behind using things like machine-detected "micro-expressions" to determine potential hostility was nothing but false "snake oil," with no reliable, verifiable basis: "In our desire to protect our citizens from those who intend to harm us, we must make sure that our own behavior is not unnecessarily shaped by things like fear, urgency, institutional incentives or pressures, financial considerations, career and personal goals, the selling of snake oil, etc., that lead to the adoption of approaches that have not been sufficiently and appropriately scientifically vetted."

What we would want from an ethics perspective would be a system that could assist human troops with discrimination in a way that would nudge more toward erring on the side of assuming someone is a noncombatant—that would focus on helping to prevent wrongful targeting and deaths. There are many reasons to hope for the development of such a system, not the least of which is concern for the well-being of the troops themselves, who, as I have argued extensively elsewhere,[36] can suffer moral injury when targeting mistakes are made or collateral damage assessments are incorrect. Cases of troops intentionally committing war crimes against civilians are thankfully rare, but tragic mistakes, including also the category of "friendly fire" incidents, are more common. Assisting troops with avoiding killing those who do not need to die to achieve the mission would be a goal worth achieving. Sadly, though, systems that predict or suggest possible hostility based on bad data or weak (hard or social) science could do more harm than good, leading to more suffering for all those concerned, including the troops.

Last but not least, we cannot ignore the reality that as soon as new technology is fielded, the people exposed to it will quickly adapt or evolve their tactics in response. This is ethically relevant because it highlights a subspecies of automation bias. If troops are assured that they have been given systems that can identify hostile forces, but those systems are learned and fooled by their enemies after the first or second use, they may be more a burden than a boon. People are creative and resourceful. A new system may yield a temporary advantage, but as soon as it is known, its vulnerabilities will be exploited. Where there are humans, there is chaos, and unpredictability is an advantage that does not require a computer.

Up until this point, we have been dealing with systems that have no executive function, where targeting and distinction decisions can be overridden by humans. Now we enter a different world, where such decisions are entirely synthetic in agency—the realm of lethal autonomous weapons systems (LAWS). The core ethical argument in favor of the use of LAWS depends on the claim that such systems present a possible solution to the problem of uniquely human qualities (including character deficiencies; natural reactions to extreme stress; or other psychological, biological, or moral factors) leading to either tragedies or intentional war crimes. One of the strongest proponents of this view is Ronald Arkin, who provides ethics consultation for engineering research and development projects aimed at creating what others call "killer robots," but which he believes could be better stewards of legal and ethical conduct in war:

> Defending the use of robots and other automated systems in the military, Ron Arkin has essentially argued that humans are too emotionally vulnerable to be trusted to do the right thing in combat conditions. Citing surveys in which military personnel admit to unethical views about the importance (or lack thereof) of obeying the laws of war, Arkin asserts that humans are too often overcome by intense feelings such as rage and fear (or terror) that effectively hijack their brains and can lead even to the perpetration of war crimes. In his book *Governing Lethal Behavior in Autonomous Robots*, Arkin avers that, ". . . it seems unrealistic to expect normal human beings by their very nature to adhere to the Laws of Warfare when confronted with the horror of the battlefield, even when trained."[37] He believes robots can do better.[38]

Arkin's claim that robots would do better is difficult to test or refute so long as he is comparing imperfect humans to theoretical future robots. Many others in military ethics, myself included, are unconvinced by the argument that human troops are doomed always to fall into the trap of crossing ethical lines under the strain of combat. While violations of the letter and spirit of the Law of Armed Conflict (LOAC) do occur, with more regularity than anyone would like, at least within regular, well-disciplined units, they are certainly the exception, not the rule. Careful analysis of the causes and contributing factors of such incidents, as is found in Jessica Wolfendale and Matthew Talbert's *War Crimes: Causes, Excuses, and Blame*,[39] for example, and insights on the causes and effects of dehumanization in war as explored by David Livingstone Smith in *Less than Human* and *On Inhumanity*[40] can provide a roadmap for enhanced training and education of troops and their leadership to reduce or perhaps even prevent these occurrences. Meanwhile, there are strong ethical arguments against shifting the responsibilities of killing in war onto machines.

As Elke Schwarz points out, the use of fully autonomous lethal machines in war would damage or severely restrict the proper attribution of ethical responsibility and accountability by creating a "moral vacuum" in which crucial decision-making cannot be traced back to any moral agent. This is especially true in cases (which are common in armed conflicts) where guidance from existing laws and norms is inconclusive:

> What I wish to highlight here is the moral vacuum that technologies of ethical decision-making create in their quest to "secure" moral risk. A moral vacuum opens when certain parameters of harm are no one's responsibility; when the decision that harm is permissible

has been determined through technological means. This moment is, paradoxically, also the very moment of moral responsibility. In other words, the moral vacuum exists exactly in the moment when neither law nor existing moral guides have adequate reach. It is in this moment where responsibility resides. For example, the moral vacuum opens precisely when a specific signature strike is executed. Here the decision to kill someone has been determined by algorithms that feed into a disposition matrix and determine whether an individual's pattern of life analysis betrays terroristic dispositions. The accuracy of the technologically determined kill decision cannot easily (if at all) be verified. Where, then, resides responsibility?[41]

In *Technology and the Virtues*, Shannon Vallor shares a similar ethical unease with the idea of humans off-loading life-or-death decision-making onto machine systems. She argues further that such a shift of responsibility would have a deleterious effect on human community and the human exercise of essential virtues:

> The oft-promised ability of drone warfare to minimize civilian casualties from airstrikes has yet to be empirically demonstrated by any neutral observer, but if the asymmetry that modern warfare fosters plays *any* role in feeding the warped psychology and recruitment successes of groups like ISIS and Al Qaeda, then the claim that robotic warfare will make innocent civilians overall safer from the horrors of war is plainly dubious. Thus the development of lethal military robots that promise to allow a minority of privileged human beings to detach even further from the physical, psychological, and moral horrors of war endured by the rest of humanity is deeply inconsistent with the technomoral virtue of courage, not to mention justice, empathy, and moral perspective.[42]

The principle of distinction is the central tenet of *jus in bello*. Without that core determination of who is or is not a legitimate target, armed conflicts rapidly descend into the utter horror of indiscriminate slaughter. In "59 Percent Likely Hostile," Daniel Eichler and Ronald Thompson give the example of a system of discrimination similar to those being explored now with funding from organizations such as DARPA: "The application warns [the soldier] that a group of three adult males are one kilometer ahead and closing. It assigns them a 59 percent chance of being hostile based on their location, activity, and appearance. Clicking on this message, three options flicker onto his screen—investigate further, pass track to remotely piloted aircraft, or coordinate kinetic strike."[43]

Eichler and Thompson acknowledge the concern that the psychological effect of automation bias and a lack of statistical understanding may drive the soldier to treat the unknown men as definitely hostile and engage them with deadly force without further reflection or evidence. They go on to argue that the remedy for this is to train future troops in a better understanding of how both statistics and algorithms work, so that they will be less likely to leap to conclusions or misinterpret results. This seems to me to miss a critical point. There is an ethically relevant difference between a system that provides additional information (e.g., "their location, activity, and appearance") from which soldiers make their own determination of the possible hostility of unknown persons and one that actually labels those persons—even with the "hedge" of an assigned percentage—as hostile or not a threat.

Ultimately, the question here is can we reduce the principle of distinction to a numbers game? If (and that is very a big "if") we can collect the right data, can machines be designed to tell soldiers whom to shoot, more reliably than their own senses? Noel Sharkey, an expert on AI and robotics and cofounder of the International Committee for Robot Arms Control, is intensely skeptical of any plan to fully automate lethal targeting:

> A computer can compute any given procedure that can be written down in a programming language. We could, for example, give the robot computer an instruction such as, "If civilian, do not shoot." This would be fine if, and only if, there was some way of giving the computer a clear definition of what a civilian is. We certainly cannot get one from the Laws of War that could provide a machine with the necessary information. The 1944 Geneva Convention requires the use of common sense, while the 1977 Protocol 1 essentially defines a civilian in the negative sense as someone who is not a combatant. . . . And even if there was a clear computational definition of a civilian, we would still need all of the relevant information to be made available from the sensing apparatus. All that is available to robots are sensors such as cameras, infrared sensors, sonars, lasers, temperature sensors and ladars, etc. These may be able to tell us that something is a human, but they could not tell us much else. In the labs there are systems that can tell someone's facial expression or that can recognise faces, but they do not work on real-time moving people. . . . There is also the Principle of Proportionality and again there is no sensing or computational capability that would allow a robot such a determination, and nor is there any known metric to objectively measure needless, superfluous or disproportionate suffering. They require human judgement.[44]

Warfare always drives innovation, and it is only to be expected that people will look for ways to use technology to try to better survive future conflicts. From an ethical perspective, however, the type of survival that matters is more than physical. However well intended, the wrong applications of emerging tools could increase rates of moral injury among troops while also causing additional tangible harm to the most vulnerable populations. The incorporation of new technology into military operations must therefore be handled with great care and deliberation, not in a mad rush to be the first out of the gate. War is not a game of chess or Go, nor is it readily reducible to zeros and ones. As World War II combat veteran J. Glenn Gray poignantly reminds us in *The Warriors: Reflections on Men in Battle*, "For all its inhumanity, war is a profoundly human institution." There may be ways to innovate intelligent systems that truly augment troops, but when it comes to deciding who lives and who dies, we have to keep the human in the loop.[45]

# Films and Documentaries on Technology Ethics

*Wanda Teays*

## Films

*The Matrix Trilogy*
*Eye in the Sky*
*War Games*
*The Social Network*
*Steve Jobs*
*The Colony*
*Iron Man*
*Her*
*The Net*
*Disconnect*
*I, Robot*
*Eternal Sunshine of the Spotless Mind*
*Elysium*
*Total Recall*
*Terminator*
*Prometheus*
*Tron: Legacy*
*Blade Runner*
*Minority Report*
*Avatar*

## Documentaries

*Snowden*
*Citizenfour*
*The Assange Agenda*
*In Google We Trust*
*Elon Musk: The Real Life Iron Man*
*Steve Jobs: The Man in the Machine*
*Thoughtcrime*
*An Eye on You: Citizens under Surveillance*
*Inside Bill's Brain*
*The Great Hack*
*Battle Drone*
*Drone Wars*
*Drone Nation*
*Technology of War*
*Robotics*
*Kill Switch*

# Notes

## Preface

1. James Steele, Pier Francesco Ferrari, and Leonardo Fogassi, "Introduction: From Action to Language: Comparative Perspectives on Primate Tool Use, Gesture, and the Evolution of Human Language," *Philosophical Transactions: Biological Sciences* 367, no. 1585 (2012): 4–9; Mary W. Marzke, "Tool Making, Hand Morphology, and Fossil Hominins," *Philosophical Transactions: Biological Sciences* 368, no. 1630 (2013): 1–8; and Jason E. Lewis and Sonia Harmand, "An Earlier Origin for Stone Tool Making: Implications for Cognitive Evolution and the Transition to Homo," *Philosophical Transactions: Biological Sciences* 371, no. 1698 (2016): 1–8.

## Chapter 1

1. Cited in Andy Warhol, *The Philosophy of Andy Warhol* (New York: Harcourt Brace Jovanovich, 1975). At an art exhibition in Stockholm, Sweden, he is reported to have said: "In the future everyone will be world-famous for fifteen minutes." Since that time, the quotation has morphed into several different formulations.

2. To see the structure of the personal worldview imperative within the context of other worldview approaches, see Michael Boylan, *Natural Human Rights: A Theory* (Cambridge: Cambridge University Press, 2014): ch. 6.

3. Since the affective good will comes from the completeness condition of the personal worldview imperative, the conditions of the imperative also apply to this sort of philosophical love that I have set out. Some detractors think that you cannot order love (as I have done). I give a response to this argument in Michael Boylan, "Duties to Children," in *The Morality and Global Justice Reader*, ed. Michael Boylan (Boulder, CO: Westview, 2011), 385–404.

4. This is particularly true of some feminist ethicists. See Rosemarie Tong, "A Feminist Personal Worldview Imperative" in *Morality and Justice: Reading Boylan's* A Just Society, ed. John-Stewart Gordon (Lanham, MD, and Oxford: Lexington/Rowman & Littlefield, 2009), 29–38.

5. The phrase "sure-loss contract" comes from the notion of betting houses. Say you were betting on the finals of the World Cup: Brazil vs. Germany. If you gave 5–1 positive odds for each team, then your betting house will go out of business. A positive assessment of one team requires a complementary negative assessment of the other: failure to observe this rule results in a sure-loss contract.

6. Other aspects of the good can include commitments to aesthetics and to religion.

7. My take on the various real and anti-real theories is generally set out in my text, *Basic Ethics*, 3rd ed. (New York and Oxfordshire: Routledge, 2020): part II.

# Chapter 2

1. I am following W. D. Ross's text *Aristotle's Prior and Posterior Analytics* (Oxford: Oxford University Press, 1949). My translation is of 89b 23–25: Τὰ ζητούμενά ἐστιν ἴσα τὸν ἀριθμὸν ὅσαπερ ἐπιστάμεθα. ζητοῦμεν δὲ τέττρα, τὸ ὅτι, τὸ διότι, εἰ ἔστ, τί ἐστιν.

2. See particularly my books that explore Aristotle: *Method and Practice in Aristotle's Biology* (Lanham, MD, and London: UPA/Rowman & Littlefield, 1983) and *The Origins of Ancient Greek Science: Blood—A Philosophical Study* (New York and London: Routledge, 2015): ch. 3, and my articles "Mechanism and Teleology in Aristotle's Biology," *Apeiron* 15, no. 2 (1981): 96–102 and "The Place of Nature in Aristotle's Biology" *Apeiron* 19, no. 1 (1985): 126–39.

3. The *Oxford English Dictionary* cites four principal categories for the noun form in English and many others in verbal and adjectival forms. For a brief summary of the noun forms see below:

I. Senses relating to physical or bodily power, strength, or substance: e.g., Semen. Occasionally also: the sexual fluid of a woman. Now *rare*; and the vital functions of the human body as requiring sustenance, esp. nourishment. Frequently in to support (also suffice, sustain) nature. Now *rare*. II. Senses relating to mental or physical impulses and requirements, e.g., The vital functions of the human body as requiring sustenance, esp. nourishment. Frequently in to support (also suffice, sustain) nature. Now *rare*. III. Senses relating to innate character., e.g., The inherent or essential quality or constitution of a thing; the inherent and inseparable combination of properties giving any object, event, quality, emotion, etc., its fundamental character. In later use also more generally: kind, type. IV. Senses relating to the material world, e.g., (a) The creative and regulative power which is conceived of as operating in the material world and as the immediate cause of its phenomena. (b) The phenomena of the physical world collectively; *esp.* plants, animals, and other features and products of the earth itself, as opposed to humans and human creations. (c) In a wider sense: the whole natural world, including human beings; the cosmos. *Obsolete.* (d) (Contrasted with art.) In a person's speech, writing, drawing, etc.: fidelity or close adherence to nature; naturalness; (apparent) lack of artifice. *Obsolete.* (e) in nature: (of goods or products) in a natural condition; un-manufactured. *Obsolete. Rare.*

In various ways, this chapter touches on all of these definitions even though many of the texts considered are not written in English. Please also note that these four senses of nature are not to be confused with the three senses of nature that I put forth.

4. I'm thinking here of those who consider the environment as being a constant medium in which humans or some specific human agent seeks to commit purposive action within his own rational life plan. These agents view nature rather like a swimming pool in which they partake for their own pleasure when they want to for their self-oriented purposes. I believe that these sorts of agents are on the front lines of being deniers of environmental change. For a brief discussion of this, see George Marshall, *Don't Even Think about It: Why Our Brains Are Wired to Ignore Climate Change* (London: Bloomsbury, 2015) and Haydn Washington and John Cook, *Climate Change Denial: Heads in the Sand* (New York and London: Routledge, 2011).

5. Arthur O. Lovejoy, *The Great Chain of Being* (Cambridge, MA: Harvard University Press, revised edition 1976) sets out one model in which humans set themselves as above the natures of plants and animals at a place midway between these primitive entities on Earth and angels. Such an ontology is, necessarily, dualistic with humans as the midpoint.

6. Aristotle sets these three powers out in *Peri psuche* (*De anima*): Plants—414:31; Animals—414b:1–415a:13; Humans—III.3–5. For a brief overview on this see my article in the *Internet Encyclopedia of Philosophy*: https://www.iep.utm.edu/aris-bio/.

7. For more context on this, see Michael Boylan, "Mechanism and Teleology in Aristotle's Biology," *Apeiron* 15, no. 2 (1981): 96–102; *Method and Practice in Aristotle's Biology* (Lanham, MD, and London: UPA/Rowman & Littlefield, 1983); "The Place of Nature in Aristotle's Biology," *Apeiron* 19, no. 1 (1985): 126–39; and *The Origins of Ancient Greek Science: Blood—A Philosophical Study* (New York and London: Routledge, 2015).

8. Michael Boylan, *Natural Human Rights: A Theory* (New York and Cambridge: Cambridge University Press, 2014): chs. 2 and 3.

9. I have identified this sense of nature as one of three principal forms in the ancient world in my book *The Origins of Ancient Greek Science: Blood—A Philosophical Study* (New York and London: Routledge, 2015). I have continued with this characterization in subsequent lectures and essays. The other two forms are nature as materially understood under a realistic epistemology and nature understood materially under an anti-realistic epistemology.

10. The literature on this is huge. Some brief suggestions include Lawrence James, *The Rise and Fall of the British Empire* (New York: St. Martins, 1997); Adam Hochschild, *King Leopold's Ghost: A Story of Greed, Terror, and Heroism in Colonial Africa* (New York: Houghton Mifflin, 1999); Gareth Knapman, *Race and British Colonialism in South East Asia: 1770–1870* (New York and London: Routledge, 2018); Shashi Tharoor, *Inglorious Empire: What the British Did to India* (Royal Oak, MI: Scribe Publishers, 2018); James Lehning, *European Colonialism since 1700* (New York and Cambridge: Cambridge University Press, 2013); and Chinua Achebe, *Things Fall Apart* (New York: Penguin Books, 1994). What is common to these and many other studies is that the age of conquest and massive land theft required a sensibility of superiority over the vanquished. This separation and consequent belief in superiority is analogous to the separation that many feel from Nature.

11. Frank Lloyd Wright, *An Organic Architecture*, ed. Andrew Saint (London: Lund Humphries, 2017, rpt. 1939).

12. For an historical survey of such transitions, see Jennifer Birch, ed. *From Pre-Historic Villages to Cities* (New York and London: Routledge, 2014). To Native Americans this European attitude of natural dominion was seen as being against Nature as "To the Indians it seemed that these Europeans hated everything in nature—the living forests and their birds and beasts, the grassy glades, the water, the soil, and the air itself" (from Dee Brown, *Bury My Heart at Wounded Knee* [New York: Picador, 1970]: 7).

13. Michael Boylan, *A Just Society* (New York and Oxford: Rowman & Littlefield, 2004): 115–16.

14. This constraint is the personal worldview imperative: *"All people must develop a single comprehensive and internally coherent worldview that is good and that we strive to act out in our daily lives."* Michael Boylan, *Natural Human Rights: A Theory* (New York and Cambridge: Cambridge University Press, 2014): 166.

15. For a discussion of this distinction, see Michael Boylan, *Basic Ethics*, 2nd ed. (Upper Saddle River, NJ: Pearson, 2009): 30–32.

16. An advocate of this position is Hilary Putnam, *Ethics without Ontology* (Cambridge, MA: Harvard University Press, 2004).

17. The move to ethical anti-realism is no small matter. Ethical anti-realists believe there are no certain facts about ethics in the world. This means that norms are created by force: *kraterism* (might makes right). For my argument on this, see Boylan (2014): 196–202.

18. "All people must develop a single comprehensive and internally coherent worldview that is good and that we strive to act out in our daily lives," Boylan (2014): ch. 6.

19. It is important to distinguish a nonethical (non-moral) practice from an unethical (immoral) practice. The former does not concern ethics while the latter is judged to be wrong by some theory of ethics.

20. I define a micro community as one in which a participant can, in principle, know all the members of that community. Governance in the micro community is via a committee of the whole. A macro community is rather larger and its governance is via elected representatives. See Boylan (2004): 113–15.

21. Of course, if one is in a position to influence the macro community via the media or public lectures, this would be helpful, too. However, this is a position only open to a few. To impose this duty generally upon all would be utopian.

22. "Kraterism" I hold to be the philosophy that "might makes right." Most philosophers disavow this approach. For a famous discussion on this topic, see Plato's *Republic*, Book One, 338c–354a.

23. Of course, the existence of other species poses other problems. For an example of this sort of analysis, see Thomas White, *In Defense of Dolphins* (Oxford: Blackwell, 2008).

24. Boylan, 2014: 176–77.

25. According to the *Washington Post*, around 47% of the world's population has access to the Internet. See https://www.washingtonpost.com/news/worldviews/wp/2016/11/22/47-percent-of-the-worlds-population-now-use-the-internet-users-study-says/?utm_term=.1de178a04090.

26. For an exposition of this argument, see Michael Boylan, "Worldview and the Value-Duty Link in Environmental Ethics," in *Environmental Ethics*, 2nd ed., ed. Michael Boylan (Malden, MA and Oxford: Wiley-Blackwell, 2014): 95–104.

27. One example of this is the false information about childhood vaccinations. For a discussion of this, see http://www.immunize.org/reports/report038.pdf.

28. See Julie Kirsch's take on this: "When Is Ignorance Morally Objectionable?" in *The Morality and Global Justice Reader*, ed. Michael Boylan (Boulder, CO: Westview, 2011): 51–64.

29. This is widely cited but without a clear single reference; see https://www.huffpost.com/entry/our-own-facts_b_542796.

30. Some may say that I am naïve on this aspect of the education requirement. The regular eco-community worldview imperative can be satisfied by one's daily life and interaction with the local ecosystem and the larger biome. But this *extended* eco-community worldview imperative requires *more*. If, as previously established, roughly half the world has access to the Internet, then there is opportunity. But if one is working twelve to fourteen hours a day just to survive, this may not be a functional reality. Here Kant's "ought implies can" caveat can fit in with otherwise sincere individuals seeking truth. Sadly, this group is often exploited by demigods who have their own personally enriching scenarios to set forth in the place of dispassionate science.

31. Michael Boylan, "Worldview and the Value-Duty Link to Environmental Ethics," in *Environmental Ethics*, 2nd ed., ed. Michael Boylan (Malden, MA and Oxford: Wiley-Blackwell, 2014): 95–108.

32. The type-token distinction is variously represented. My use of the distinction owes its source to Paul Grice, "Utterer's Meaning and Intentions," *Philosophical Review* 78 (1969): 147–77 and Willard Van Quine, *Quiddities: An Intermittently Philosophical Dictionary* (Cambridge, MA: Harvard University Press, 1987).

33. Boylan (2014).

34. For the fine points of this see the argument for "The Moral Status of Basic Goods" in Boylan (2014): 182.

35. The relationship between "toolmaking" and the evolution of rationality is a controversial subject. For a general discussion of some of the key points of this discussion, see Alex H. Taylor and Russell D. Gray, "Is There a Link between the Crafting of Tools and the Evolution of Cognition?" *Wiley Interdisciplinary Reviews: Cognitive Science* 5 (2014): 693–703, doi:10.1002/wcs.1322.

36. For a more complete depiction of this in the context of ancient Greek science see Boylan (2015).

37. Of course, there are some who think that *all* interference in nature is improper. These are people who assert that Nature was created by God and since God is perfect, God's *makings* are perfect, too. Any interference will inevitability lead to a diminished outcome. This point of view was set out in the seventeenth century (a time of great scientific questioning and innovation in Europe): "Heaven if for thee too high / to know what passes there; be lowly wise: / Think only what concerns thee and thy being" from John Milton, "Paradise Lost" in John Milton, *The Poetical Works of John Milton*, vol. 1, ed. Helen Darbishire (Oxford: Oxford University Press, 1952): Bk. 8, ll. 172–74.

38. For two different perspectives on this issue, see Beril Idemen Sözman, "Harm in the Wild: Facing Non-Human Suffering in Nature," *Ethical Theory and Moral Practice: An International Forum* 16, no. 5 (2013): 1075–88 and Martin Drenthen, "New Wilderness Landscapes as Moral Criticisms: A Nietzschen Perspective on Our Contemporary Fascination with Wilderness," *Ethical Perspectives: Journal of the European Ethics Network* 14, no. 4 (2007): 371–403.

39. Two studies show the quandary that pollution caused in nineteenth-century Britain: Stephen Mosley, *The Chimney of the World: A History of Smoke Pollution in Victorian and Edwardian Manchester* (London and New York: Routledge, 2008) and Peter Thorsheim, *Inventing Pollution: Coal, Smoke, and Culture in Britain since 1800* (Athens: Ohio University Press, 2006).

40. The human "makings" over and against Nature without this human interference was obviously a controversial topic in nineteenth-century Britain, cf. Thomas Hardy's novel, *A Laodicean*, in which the daughter of a man who made a fortune as an engineer in the new rail service to the West Country (an act which is seen as *unnatural*) follows onto the daughter, who *herself* is unnatural from this background. For a broader historical treatment, see the classic Eric Hobsbawm, *Industry and Empire: The Birth of the Industrial Revolution* (New York: The New Press, rpt. 1999).

41. I distinguish between two sorts of human communities based upon size; see Boylan (2004): ch. 6.

42. In the *Torah*, *Genesis* 2–3 there is a forbidden tree in the Garden of Eden: it is the Tree of the Knowledge of Good and Evil. Adam and Eve are told to forbear eating of this fruit. Since John Milton's *Paradise Lost*, this prohibition was extended to technology that might verge Nature (*para phusin*): the "new science" of the seventeenth century, *op. cit.* n. 37.

43. A very safe ploy against censorship since Eve was the "fallen woman" who doomed humankind. You could put almost *anything* in her mouth. This is Milton playing it cautious.

44. There were a number of individuals in nineteenth-century Britain advocating some form of evolutionary theory. For examples of these, see W. J. Dempster, *Evolutionary Concepts in the Nineteenth Century: Natural Selection and Patrick Matthew* (Bel Air, CA: The Pentland Press, 1995); and *Evolution and Its Influence*, ed. by the staff of *Humanities in the Modern World* (Minneapolis, MN: University of Minnesota Press, 1954). In the context of controlling Nature as a cultural event in this era, see Martin Fichman, *Controlling Nature: Evolutionary Theory and Victorian Culture* (Amherst, NY: Humanity Books, 2002).

45. This distinction in the Western tradition goes at least as far back as the differing views of Parmenides (the static view) and Heraclitus (the constant change position).

46. How biological evolutionary theory ought to be applied to human social society has been a ongoing experiment still in progress. From Herbert Spencer, *The Synthetic Philosophy* (London: Williams and Norgate, 1915, fifth impression) to sociobiology (e.g., Arthur F. G. Bourke, *Principles of Social Evolution* [Oxford: Oxford University Press, 2011]) it has been controversial just how principles of biological evolution might be properly applied to the structure of human society.

47. Note that "better" and "worse" are not a part of biological evolutionary theory. Rather, it is an unproven assumption based upon the connotation of the word "evolution" as applied more broadly to human society, cf. n. 46.

48. Hesiod discusses devolution as five ages of man: the Golden, Silver, Bronze, Heroic, and Iron Ages in *Works and Days*—Hesiod, *Theogony and Works and Days*, ed. Glenn W. Most (London and Cambridge, MA: Loeb Classical Library, 2006): ll. 109–201; cf. Ovid, *Metamorphosis*, ed. G. P. Gould et al. (London and Cambridge, MA: Loeb Classical Library, 1984): Bk. I, ll. 89–150.

49. An example of this in the United States is the politician Donald Trump, whose mantra was to "make America great again." This is an example of devolutionary thinking.

50. It is essential to add a positive outcome to the mechanism, otherwise one might be inclined to view positively intricate systems that cause death and destruction. In this account "animal and plant life" is asserted to be a per se good so long as the sustainability proviso is added. Any predatory element that kills more than it enriches will be viewed negatively in this regard. This could include a judgment against humans.

51. This argument should be seen in the context of my argument in "The Moral Status of Basic Goods" in *Natural Human Rights: A Theory* (New York and Cambridge: Cambridge University Press, 2014): 182.

52. For examples of what I mean by these three forms of logic, see my *The Process of Argument: An Introduction*, 3rd ed. (New York and London: Routledge, 2020).

53. **The Table of Embeddedness (see Boylan, 2014, 186).**
**BASIC GOODS**
Level One: *Most Deeply Embedded* (that which is absolutely necessary for human action): food, water, sanitation, clothing, shelter, and protection from unwarranted bodily harm (including basic health care)
Level Two: *Deeply Embedded* (that which is necessary for effective basic action within any given society)

- Literacy in the language of the country
- Basic mathematical skills
- Other fundamental skills necessary to be an effective agent in that country (e.g., in the United States, some computer literacy is necessary)
- Some familiarity with the culture and history of the country in which one lives
- The assurance that those you interact with are not lying to promote their own interests
- The assurance that those you interact with will recognize your human dignity (as per above) and not exploit you as a means only
- Basic human rights such as those listed in the US Bill of Rights and the United Nations Universal Declaration of Human Rights

**SECONDARY GOODS**
Level One: *Life Enhancing*, Medium to High-Medium on Embeddedness

- Basic societal respect
- Equal opportunity to compete for the prudential goods of society
- Ability to pursue a life plan according to the personal worldview imperative

- Ability to participate equally as an agent in the shared community worldview imperative

Level Two: *Useful*, Medium to Low-Medium Embeddedness

- Ability to utilize one's real and portable property in the manner one chooses
- Ability to gain from and exploit the consequences of one's labor regardless of starting point
- Ability to pursue goods that are generally owned by most citizens (e.g., in the United States today a telephone, television, and automobile would fit into this class)

Level Three: *Luxurious*, Low Embeddedness

- Ability to pursue goods that are pleasant even though they are far removed from action and from the expectations of most citizens within a given country (e.g., in the United States today a European vacation would fit into this class)
- Ability to exert one's will so that one might extract a disproportionate share of society's resources for one's own use

54. As an *assertion* this premise must be accepted on cognitive intuitionism. It can be made plausible via fictive narrative philosophy using my version of abduction—see my *Fictive Narrative Philosophy: How Fiction Can Act as Philosophy* (New York and London: Routledge, 2019): ch. 5.

55. I am using "projection" here in the sense of Nelson Goodman, *Fact, Fiction, and Forecast*, 4th ed. (Cambridge, MA: Harvard University Press, 1983). It is my contention here that the feature of projection for an *overhypothesis* are met as the hypotheses is empirically supported, unviolated, and unexhausted.

56. Cf. the depiction set out in Boylan (2014): ch. 6.

57. I put these two relations as the parts of metaphysics as I characterize them: ontology (the things that *are*) and cosmology (the priority relation between the things that *are*)—see Michael Boylan, *The Good, the True, and the Beautiful* (London: Bloomsbury, 2009): ch. 5.

58. See Gottfried Wilhelm Freiheer von Leibniz, *Discourse on Metaphysics*, ed. Albert R. Chandler, trans. George Montgomery (Lasalle, IL: Open Court, 1924, rpt. 1902).

59. Please note that "making" (in the sense intended above) is under the control of the "maker." Some apparent "makings" really owe their efficacy to some other system (e.g., biological reproduction does not constitute a "making" in this sense). If male A and female B sexually interact so that child C results, there is a sense of A and B being a contributing part of the causal process in C's coming-to-be, but most of the work involves n/Natural processes that are common to all males and females of that species and others, as per phylogenetic relations affected by systematic, evolutionary proximity.

60. One exposition of the principle of precautionary reason I accept is by Deryck Beyleveld and Shaun D. Pattinson, "Defending Moral Precaution as a Solution to the Problem of Other Minds: A Reply to Holm and Coggon," *Ratio Juris* 23, no. 2 (2010): 258–73.

61. For a more thorough treatment of my views on this topic, see Michael Boylan and Kevin Brown, *Genetic Engineering: Ethics and Science on the New Frontier* (Upper Saddle River, NJ: Prentice Hall, 2002).

# Chapter 3

1. See www.sciencedaily.com/releases/2018/07/180703084127.htm.

2. For a general discussion of status quo bias and an illustration of it in action, see Kahneman (2011, 283–84). Bostom and Ord (2006) have developed a widely used test for status quo bias. For an improved version of Bostrom and Ord's test, see Clarke (2016).

3. A famous expression of loss aversion is encapsulated in the sentiment of the tennis player Jimmy Connors, who declared "I hate to lose more than I love to win."

4. For an extended discussion of the relations between conservatism and cognitive bias, developed using the resources of "prospect theory," see Clarke (2017).

5. For further discussion of conservative political thought, see Scruton (2014).

6. Clarke's work on this chapter was supported by Australian Research Council Discovery Grant DP190101597.

# Chapter 4

1. As a lifelong atheist, I don't mean this literally, but see the Kurzweil remark quoted below for a secular analog of this argument. This poem previously appeared in the Opinion Section of the *New York Daily News* on October 12, 2021.

2. Sean A. Hays, "Transhumanism," *Encyclopedia Britannica*, last modified June 12, 2018, https://www.britannica.com/topic/transhumanism.

3. John Harris, "Intimations of Immortality," *Science* 288, no. 5463 (April 7, 2000): 59.

4. "180 Years Old? Experts Debate Limits of Aging," *CNN*, last modified July 19, 2003, http://www.cnn.com/2003/HEALTH/07/19/aging/index.html.

5. For example, see Craig Hamilton, "Chasing Immortality: The Technology of Eternal Life; An Interview with Ray Kurzweil," *What Is Enlightenment?* (September–November 2005): 58–69; Ramez Naam, *More Than Human: Embracing the Promise of Biological Enhancement* (New York: Broadway, 2005); and Tom Huston, "We Will Be the Lords of Creation: Envisioning Our Immortal Future with Science Fiction Writer Robert J. Sawyer," *What Is Enlightenment?* (September–November 2005): 82–90.

6. John Stuart Mill, "Nature," in *Three Essays on Religion: Nature, the Utility of Religion, and Theism* (London: Longmans, Green, Reader and Dyer, 1874), 3–65. Of course, "Killing, the most criminal act recognized by human laws, nature does once to every being that lives" is an oversimplification, since there are also "unnatural" causes of death, such as murder. But nature kills every living being that is not killed by something else.

7. Wikipedia, "In Memoriam A. H. H.," last modified June 3, 2021, https://en.wiki pedia.org/wiki/In_Memoriam_A.H.H.#Quotations.

8. Mill, "Nature."

9. John Stuart Mill, "On the Subjugation of Women," Making of America, University of Michigan, accessed August 17, 2021, https://quod.lib.umich.edu/m/moajrnl/acw8433.1-01.012/381:9?page=root;size=100;view=text.

10. What is familiar does not inevitably seem natural, though. Consider this passage from George Orwell's *1984*:

He meditated resentfully on the physical texture of life. Had it always been like this? Had food always tasted like this? He looked round the canteen. . . . Always in your stomach and in your skin there was a sort of protest, a feeling that you had been cheated of something that you had a right to. It was true that he had no memories of anything greatly different. . . . Was it not a sign that this was NOT the natural order of things, if one's heart sickened at the discomfort and dirt and scarcity, the interminable winters, the stickiness of one's socks, the lifts that never worked, the cold water, the gritty soap, the cigarettes that came to pieces, the food with its strange evil tastes? (Project Gutenberg Australia, 2008, ch. 5, http://gutenberg.net.au/ebooks01/0100021.txt)

11. Gilbert K. Chesterton, "Orthodoxy: The Suicide of Thought," Page by Page Books, accessed August 17, 2021, https://www.pagebypagebooks.com/Gilbert_K_Chesterton/Orthodoxy/The_Suicide_of_Thought_p1.html.

12. Sherwin B. Nuland, *How We Die: Reflections of Life's Final Chapter* (New York: Vintage, 1995), 58.

13. Nuland, *How We Die*, 267.

14. Nuland, *How We Die*, 87.

15. Thomas Nagel, "Death," University of Colorado Boulder, accessed August 17, 2021, https://rintintin.colorado.edu/~vancecd/phil150/Nagel.pdf.

16. Andrew Stark, *The Limits of Medicine* (Cambridge: Cambridge University Press, 2006), 58–61, 207n9, 222–23n33, and 226–27n82.

17. Stark, *The Limits of Medicine*, 31.

18. The President's Council on Bioethics. *Beyond Therapy: Biotechnology and the Pursuit of Happiness* (New York: ReganBooks, 2003), 290.

19. Council, *Beyond Therapy*, 294.

20. Hamilton, "Interview with Ray Kurzweil," 67.

21. Council, *Beyond Therapy*, 290.

22. Felicia Nimue Ackerman, "Death Is a Punch in the Jaw: Life-Extension and Its Discontents," in *The Oxford Handbook of Bioethics*, ed. Bonnie Steinbock (Oxford: Oxford University Press, 2009), 324–48.

23. C. George Boeree, "Erik Erikson," General Psychology, Shippensburg University, accessed August 17, 2021, http://webspace.ship.edu/cgboer/genpsyerikson.html.

24. Thomas Lynch, "Why Buy More Time?" *New York Times*, March 14, 1999, https://www.nytimes.com/1999/03/14/opinion/why-buy-more-time.html.

25. David Gems, "Is More Life Always Better? The New Biology of Aging and the Meaning of Life," *Hastings Center Report* 33, no. 4 (July–August 2003): 35.

26. Richard W. Momeyer, *Confronting Death* (Bloomington: Indiana University Press, 1988), 19.

27. Even the popular phrase "bored to tears" may not have the import commonly supposed. The common view is that it means "Extremely bored to the point of distraction, frustration, or irritation," from "Bored to Tears," The Free Dictionary, Farlex, accessed August 17, 2021, https://idioms.thefreedictionary.com/bored+to+tears. But when I spent an afternoon with a boring man whose feelings I wanted to avoid hurting, I found out that a physiological reaction is relevant here: swallowing yawns makes one's eyes tear up.

28. Christine Overall, *Aging, Death, and Human Longevity: A Philosophical Inquiry* (Berkeley: University of California Press, 2003), 145.

29. For example, the then fifty-seven-year-old Ezekiel J. Emanuel, in "Why I Hope to Die at 75," *The Atlantic*, October 2014, https://www.theatlantic.com/magazine/archive/2014/10/why-i-hope-to-die-at-75/379329/, denies the value of life after that age and affirms his intention to forgo medical tests or treatments aimed at enabling him to live beyond it, although part of his reason is the decline that he takes to be natural but that transhumanism seeks to avert. Note also Emanuel's passage quoted below that gives another sort of objection to longevity.

30. Daniel Callahan, "On Dying after Your Time," *New York Times*, November 30, 2013, http://www.nytimes.com/2013/12/01/opinion/sunday/on-dying-after-your-time.html.

31. S. Jay Olshansky, Letter to the Editor, *New York Times*, December 1, 2013, https://www.nytimes.com/2013/12/05/opinion/when-life-goes-on-and-on.html.

32. Callahan, "On Dying."

33. Callahan, "On Dying."

34. Emanuel, "Die at 75."

35. I offered a variant of this argument in "Assisted Suicide, Terminal Illness, Severe Disability, and the Double Standard," in *Physician-Assisted Suicide: Expanding the Debate*, ed. Margaret P. Battin, Rosamond Rhodes, and Anita Silvers (New York: Routledge, 1998), 149–61; reprinted in Jennifer A. Parks and Victoria S. Wike, eds., *Bioethics in a Changing World* (Upper Saddle River, NJ: Prentice Hall, 2009).

36. According to Ramez Naam,

the history of medical technology and its prices suggests . . . reasons to believe that enhancement technologies could become cheap enough for most of the world to afford. First, although most enhancement techniques . . . are expensive to develop and test, they're cheap to manufacture, so that after the initial research and development, few further investments must be made. Once initial investments have been recouped, prices can fall. *More Than Human*, 61–62.

In "The Coming Death Shortage," *The Atlantic*, May 2005, https://www.theatlantic.com/magazine/archive/2005/05/the-coming-death-shortage/304105/, Charles C. Mann offers a less optimistic view. This empirical dispute is beyond the scope of my essay.

37. Gems, "More Life," 38.

38. Gems, "More Life," 35.

39. Gems, "More Life," 34.

40. These objections come from my letter about Gems's article, "More about More Life," *Hastings Center Report* 33, no. 6 (November–December 2003): 5.

41. Mann, "The Coming Death Shortage."

42. I made this objection in a letter to the editor about Mann's article. Felicia Nimue Ackerman, Letter to the Editor, *The Atlantic*, October 2005, https://www.theatlantic.com/magazine/archive/2005/10/letters-to-the-editor/304240/.

43. See the discussion in Ben Colburn, "Autonomy and Adaptive Preferences," *Utilitas* 23, no. 1 (March 2011): 52–71, https://doi.org/10.1017/S0953820810000440.

44. A version of this poem appeared in the *Providence Journal*, January 31, 2014, https://www.providencejournal.com/article/20140131/OPINION/301319880?template=ampart.

# Chapter 5

1. Interestingly, both of these comments were way off the mark. There are approximately 3,450,120 fast food and counter workers in the United States. According to the Bureau of Labor Statistics, the median age of these workers is twenty-eight; the median wage is $11.47 an hour. Roughly 87% of these workers lack any health insurance benefits, and many are on some form of public assistance. So, implementing a technology that would replace a substantial portion of this largely unskilled workforce with machines would have a serious impact on the well-being of these workers.

2. Selmer Bringsjord and Naveen Sundar Govindarajulu, "Artificial Intelligence," *The Stanford Encyclopedia of Philosophy*, Summer 2020, ed. Edward N. Zalta, https://plato.stanford.edu/archives/sum2020/entries/artificial-intelligence/.

3. A Turing test is one in which a human being attempts to judge who in a conversation between two other individuals is a machine and who is a human being. If the person doing the evaluation cannot distinguish the machine from the human, then the machine is said to have passed the Turing test.

4. Bringsjord and Govindarajulu, "Artificial Intelligence."

5. Bringsjord and Govindarajulu, "Artificial Intelligence."

6. Jean Hampton, "The Common Faith of Liberalism," *Pacific Philosophical Quarterly* 75 (1994): 186–216.

7. Hampton, "Common Faith of Liberalism," 49.

8. Kashmir Hill, "Wrongfully Accused by an Algorithm," June 24, 2020, updated August 3, 2020, https://www.nytimes.com/2020/06/24/technology/facial-recognition-arrest.html.

9. Patrick Grother, Mei Ngan, and Kayee Hanoaka, NISTIR 8280 Face Recognition Vendor Test (FRVT) Part 3: Demographic Effects, National Institute of Standards and Technology, US Department of Commerce, December 2019, https://doi.org/10.6028/NIST.IR.8280.

10. Kate Crawford, *Atlas of AI: Power, Politics, and the Planetary Costs of Artificial Intelligence*, Kindle ed. (New Haven, CT: Yale University Press, 2021).

11. Crawford, *Atlas of AI*, 42.

12. Crawford, *Atlas of AI*, 31.

13. Christopher Clifton, "Data Mining," *Encyclopedia Britannica*, December 20, 2019, https://www.britannica.com/technology/data-mining.

14. Datasets of voice commands culled from Alexa users, mugshots uploaded to computers and shared by law enforcement authorities (whether or not the person in the mugshot is ultimately convicted), Amazon purchase histories, Facebook, Flickr, Google Images, credit card purchases—all impact one's right to privacy as well as possibly one's right to control who utilizes one's data.

15. Crawford, *Atlas of AI*, 110–11.

16. This threat has been compounded as ANI is increasingly used in the development of autonomous vehicles, which will have to make trolley problem–like decisions, as well as in semiautonomous weapons systems where artificial moral intelligence systems are being deployed. For an examination of the challenges these systems pose, see Wendell Wallach and Colin Allen, *Moral Machines: Teaching Robots Right from Wrong* (Oxford: Oxford University Press, 2009).

17. See, for example, Philip A. E. Brey, "Anticipating Ethical Issues in Emerging IT," *Ethics of Information Technology* 14 (2012): 305–17.

18. At the time of this writing—and I suspect for some time to come—there are no AIs that could be classified as having AGI.

19. For skeptics of consciousness in general (let alone for machines), these are controversial assumptions, but debating the existence of consciousness in general is well beyond the scope of this chapter.

20. Mary Anne Warren, "On the Moral and Legal Status of Abortion," *The Monist* 57 (January 1973): 43–61.

21. Warren, "Moral and Legal Status of Abortion," 56–57.

22. Warren does note that it is possible that (1) and (2) alone might be sufficient for personhood, or (1)–(3). See Warren, "Moral and Legal Status of Abortion," 55.

23. One might argue that an AGI that lacked a humanoid body could not feel pain and would thus not count as a person, but that still leaves open the possibility that it could experience mental pain. For example, simply because someone is under a drug-induced paralysis, it doesn't follow that their lack of pain sensation negates their personhood.

24. Warren, "Moral and Legal Status of Abortion," 56–57.

25. Shelly Kagan, "What Is Wrong with Speciesism?" *Journal of Applied Philosophy* 33, no. 1 (2016): 1–21.

26. Kagan, "What Is Wrong with Speciesism?" 2.

27. Kagan, "What Is Wrong with Speciesism?" 9.

28. Kagan's concerns actually go beyond just persons to what he terms modal persons—those that could have become full persons were it not for some cognitive deficiency. Allowing for these other categories of personhood allows differences in essence of degrees of personhood or degrees of consideration. Since AGI easily fits into the category of person species, these degrees are not relevant here.

29. Kagan, "What Is Wrong with Speciesism?" 8.

30. Lantz Fleming Miller, "Granting Automata Human Rights: Challenge to a Basis of Full-Rights Privilege," *Human Rights Review* 16 (2015): 369–91.

31. Miller, "Granting Automata Human Rights," 379.
32. Miller, "Granting Automata Human Rights," 384.
33. John-Stewart Gordon and Ausrine Pasvenskiene, "Human Rights for Robots? A Literature Review," *AI and Ethics* 1 (2021): 3.
34. Ayelet Sheffey, "Elon Musk Says We Need Universal Basic Income Because 'In the Future, Physical Work Will Be a Choice,'" August 20, 2021, https://www.business insider.com/elon-musk-universal-basic-income-physical-work-choice-2021-8.

# Chapter 6

1. Pierre Teilhard de Chardin, *The Phenomenon of Man* (New York: Harper, 1959).
2. Richard Routley, "Is There a Need for a New, an Environmental, Ethic?" Proceedings of the XVth World Congress of Philosophy, Varna, 1 (1973): 205–10. Reprinted in *Environmental Philosophy: From Animal Rights to Radical Ecology*, ed. M. Zimmerman et al. (Hoboken, NJ: Prentice Hall, 1993), 12–21.
3. See Christa L. Taylor, "Creativity and Mood Disorder: A Systematic Review and Meta-Analysis," *Perspectives on Psychological Science* 12, no. 6 (November 1, 2017): 1040–76.
4. In that essay, James was juxtaposing the bucolic and peaceful setting of Chautauqua, in New York, which was and is an interfaith meeting ground for the well-heeled, with the advantages of a life lived, as he put it, "in extremis."

But in this unspeakable Chautauqua there was no potentiality of death in sight anywhere, and no point of the compass visible from which danger might possibly appear. The ideal was so completely victorious already that no sign of any previous battle remained, the place just resting on its oars. But what our human emotions seem to require is the sight of the struggle going on. The moment the fruits are being merely eaten, things become ignoble. Sweat and effort, human nature strained to its uttermost and on the rack, yet getting through alive, and then turning its back on its success to pursue another more rare and arduous still—this is the sort of thing the presence of which inspires us, and the reality of which it seems to be the function of all the higher forms of literature and fine art to bring home to us and suggest. At Chautauqua there were no racks, even in the place's historical museum, and no sweat, except possibly the gentle moisture on the brow of some lecturer, or on the sides of some player in the ball-field. Such absence of human nature in extremis anywhere seemed, then, a sufficient explanation for Chautauqua's flatness and lack of zest.

See John J. McDermott, ed., *The Writings of William James* (Chicago: University of Chicago Press, 1977): 646–49.
5. Margaret A. Boden, *The Philosophy of Artificial Intelligence* (Oxford: Oxford University Press, 1990).
6. Ray Kurzweil, *The Singularity Is Near* (New York: Penguin, 2005).
7. Nick Bostrom, *Superintelligence: Paths, Dangers, Strategies* (Oxford: Oxford University Press, 2014).
8. Lana and Lilly Wachowski, *The Matrix* (Screenplay), 1999, accessed June 30, 2021, https://imsdb.com/scripts/Matrix,-The.html.

9. See Katherine Heires. "The Rise of Artificial Intelligence," *Risk Management* 62, no. 4 (2015): 38–42.

10. Aparna Vidyasagar and Nicoletta Lanese, "What Is CRISP?" Live Science, Future US Inc., October 20, 2021, https://www.livescience.com/58790-crispr-explained.html.

11. See Laura Parker, "Nearly Every Seabird on Earth Is Eating Plastic," *National Geographic*, September 9, 2015, accessed June 15, 2020, https://www.nationalgeographic.com/news/2015/09/15092-plastic-seabirds-albatross-australia/#close.

12. Hans Jonas, *The Imperative of Responsibility: In Search of an Ethics for the Technological Age* (Chicago: University of Chicago Press, 1984), 1.

13. Rocci Luppicini, *Technoethics and the Evolving Knowledge Society: Ethical Issues in Technological Design, Research, Development, and Innovation* (Hershey, PA: Information Science Reference, 2010), 25.

14. Aldo Leopold, *A Sand Country Almanac and Sketches Here and There* (Oxford: Oxford University Press, 1948).

15. David D. Luxton, Jennifer D. June, and Jonathan M. Fairall, "Social Media and Suicide: A Public Health Perspective," *American Journal of Public Health* 102, Suppl. 2 (2012): S195–S200, https://doi.org/10.2105/AJPH.2011.300608.

# Chapter 7

1. Jeremy Rifkin, *The Empathic Civilization: The Race to Global Consciousness in a World in Crisis* (New York: Jeremy P. Tarcher/Penguin, 2009); Marvin T. Brown, *Climate of Justice: An Ethical Foundation for Environmentalism* (Springer, 2021).

2. W. Barnett Pearce, *Communication and the Human Condition* (Carbondale and Edwardsville: Southern Illinois University Press, 1989).

3. Pearce, *Communication and the Human Condition*, 31

4. Rifkin, *The Empathic Civilization*, 543.

5. Rifkin, *The Empathic Civilization*, 516.

6. Michelle Alexander, *The New Jim Crow: Mass Incarceration in the Age of Colorblindness* (New York: The New Press, 2012).

7. Charles W. Mills, *Black Rights/White Wrongs: The Critique of Racial Liberalism* (New York: Oxford University Press, 2017), 4–5.

8. Kwame Appiah, *Cosmopolitanism: Ethics in a World of Strangers* (New York: W. W. Norton and Company, 2006), xi.

9. David Sarewitz, "Pas de Trois: Science, Technology, and the Marketplace," in *Technology and Science: Building Our Sociotechnical Future*, ed. Deborah G. Johnson and James W. Wetmore (Cambridge, MA: MIT Press, 2009), 289.

10. Rifkin, *The Empathic Civilization*, 169.

11. Rifkin, *The Empathic Civilization*, 41.

12. W. E. B. Du Bois, *The Souls of Black Folk* (New York: Penguin Books, 1936), 5.

13. Pearce, *Communication and the Human Condition*, 31.

14. Ta-Nehisi Coates, *Between the World and Me* (New York: Spiegel & Grau, 2015), 150–51.

# Chapter 8

1. "Distribution of the information technology (IT) industry worldwide from 2019 to 2021, by region," Statista, 2021, accessed August 11, 2021, https://www.statista.com/statistics/507365/worldwide-information-technology-industry-by-region/.

2. Chris A. Mack, "Fifty Years of Moore's Law," *IEEE Transactions on Semiconductor Manufacturing* 24, no. 2 (2011): 202–07.

3. Max W. Thomas, "Eschewing Credit: Heywood, Shakespeare, and Plagiarism before Copyright," *New Literary History* 31, no. 2 (2000): 277–93.

4. Leo Zaibert, and Barry Smith, "Real Estate: Foundations of the Ontology of Property," in *The Ontology and Modelling of Real Estate Transactions* (New York: Routledge, 2017), 35–51.

5. Carol Gould, "Contemporary Legal Conceptions of Property and Their Implications for Democracy," *The Journal of Philosophy* 77, no. 11 (1980): 716–29.

6. Oren Bracha, "The Statute of Anne: An American Mythology," *Houston Law Review* 47 (2010): 877.

7. Pamela O. Long, "Invention, Authorship, Intellectual Property, and the Origin of Patents: Notes toward a Conceptual History," *Technology and Culture* 32, no. 4 (1991): 846–84.

8. David R. Koepsell, *The Ontology of Cyberspace: Philosophy, Law, and the Future of Intellectual Property* (Chicago: Open Court Publishing, 2003).

9. Bernard A. Galler, *Software and Intellectual Property Protection: Copyright and Patent Issues for Computer and Legal Professionals* (Westport, CT: Greenwood Publishing Group, 1995).

10. Susan A. Dunn, "Defining the Scope of Copyright Protection for Computer Software," *Stanford Law Review* 38, no. 2 (January 1986): 497–534.

11. Steven Levy, *Hackers: Heroes of the Computer Revolution* (vol. 14) (Garden City, NY: Anchor Press/Doubleday, 1984).

12. Lance Strate, "The Varieties of Cyberspace: Problems in Definition and Delimitation," *Western Journal of Communication* 63, no. 3 (1999): 382–412.

13. Levy, *Hackers*.

14. Shakeel Siddiqui and Farida Rifai, "The Best Things in Life Are Free; the Non-Economic Paradigm of Sharing in Cyberspace," *ACR European Advances* 9 (2011).

15. Chris DiBona and Sam Ockman, *Open Sources: Voices from the Open Source Revolution* (Sebastopol, CA: O'Reilly Media, 1999).

16. Richard Stallman, *Free Software, Free Society: Selected Essays of Richard M. Stallman*, ed. Joshua Gay (Boston, MA: GNU Press, 2002).

# Chapter 9

1. Disclosure: the author was a member of the Ethics Advisory Board for the NHSX app.

2. See YouTube video at time 1:14:13: https://re.livecasts.eu/webinar-on-contact -tracing-applications/program.

3. Part of the failure was also a failure of trust regarding the ethical issues surrounding the coronavirus apps. See Jessica Morley, Josh Cowls, Mariarosaria Taddeo, and Luciano Floridi, "Ethical Guidelines for COVID-19 Tracing Apps," *Nature* 582 (2020): 29–31.

4. Microsoft Corporate Blogs, "Microsoft to Continue Discussions on Potential TikTok Purchase in the United States," August 2, 2020, https://blogs.microsoft.com/ blog/2020/08/02/microsoft-to-continue-discussions-on-potential-tiktok-purchase-in -the-united-states/.

5. Court of Justice of the European Union, "The Court of Justice Invalidates Decision 2016/1250 on the Adequacy of the Protection Provided by the EU-US Data Protection Shield," Press Release no. 91/20, July 16, 2020, https://curia.europa.eu/jcms/ upload/docs/application/pdf/2020-07/cp200091en.pdf.

6. In the Greek sense of the *kubernetes'*, the pilot's, ability to navigate and steer, as discussed by Plato in the *Republic*.

7. Sarah Berry, "2020 Search Market Share: 5 Hard Truths about Today's Market," Web FX, January 1, 2020, https://www.webfx.com/blog/seo/2019-search-market-share/.

8. "Cicilline Opening Statement At Big Tech Antitrust Hearing," July 29, 2020, https://cicilline.house.gov/press-release/cicilline-opening-statement-big-tech-antitrust -hearing.

9. "Ireland v Commission," Wikipedia, last updated September 7, 2021, https://en .wikipedia.org/wiki/EU_illegal_state_aid_case_against_Apple_in_Ireland.

10. "Enhanced Cooperation," Wikipedia, last updated October 30, 2021, https://en .wikipedia.org/wiki/Enhanced_cooperation.

11. See, for example, the proposal made by Guy Verhofstadt, MEP and former Belgian prime minister (Guy Verhofstadt, *The United States of Europe: Manifesto for a New Europe* [London: Federal Trust for Education and Research, 2006]).

# Chapter 10

1. Kim Kardashian, for example, has 245 million followers and Beyoncé 200 million on Instagram. In addition to the normalizing of fashion face and body plastic surgery, the spread of teeth-whitening presents a far more mundane, but nevertheless widespread and compelling, example of fashion sending us astray. The spread has been so great it has left us all with a reason to get our teeth whitened lest we stand out too much from the crowd, and has hijacked much of dental practice. Dentists are increasingly pushed to direct resources toward teeth-whitening to remain competitive.

2. For some recent mass-media articles, see, for example: Tara Bahrampour, "Teens around the World Are Lonelier Than a Decade Ago: The Reason May Be Smart-phones," *The Washington Post*, July 20, 2021, https://www.washingtonpost.com/local/ social-issues/teens-loneliness-smart-phones/2021/07/20/cde8c866-e84e-11eb-8950 -d73b3e93ff7f_story.html; and Cal Newport, "Email Is Making Us Miserable," *The New*

*Yorker*, February 26, 2021, https://www.newyorker.com/tech/annals-of-technology/e
-mail-is-making-us-miserable. In recent times, "ministers for loneliness" have been
appointed in both the United Kingdom and Japan. See, for example, Julian Ryall,
"Japan: 'Minister of Loneliness' Tackles Mental Health Crisis," April 23, 2021, https://
www.dw.com/en/japan-minister-of-loneliness-tackles-mental-health-crisis/a-57311880.

3. We end *Evil Online* with this caution about our moral fate. Dean Cocking and
Jeroen van den Hoven, *Evil Online* (Oxford: Wiley-Blackwell, 2018). We take the
expression from the case of mass murderer Dylann Storm Roof, who under questioning
at his trial described how his racist hatred had been fueled by online searches. When
asked if anyone else was involved, he replied "Just me, and the Internet." See Edward
Ball, "The Mind of Dylann Roof," *New York Review of Books* 64, no. 5 (March 23,
2017): 12–16.

4. Iris Murdoch describes how we need to "unself" from our self-preoccupations
in order to appreciate value and reality. Elsewhere we develop Murdoch's insight and
apply it to our lives online to ask: How do we "unself" in the age of the selfie? See Dean
Cocking and Jeroen van den Hoven, "Moral Fog and the Appreciation of Value," *Evil
Online, Journal of Practical Ethics* (special issue) (Oxford: Oxford University Press, 2022).

5. For example, in the military case of moral fog during which one cannot tell
civilian from enemy, while one's ability to apply a principle respecting innocents has
been compromised, one's awareness of and respect for the principle need not be. So,
for example, one errs on the side of caution, makes extra intelligence efforts, is deeply
distressed by civilian casualties, and so on.

6. See Jami Cotler and Janelle Rizzo, "Designing Value Sensitive Social Networks
for the Future," *Journal of Computing Sciences in Colleges* 25, no. 6 (June 2010): 40–46,
https://dl.acm.org/doi/10.5555/1791129.1791138.

7. Aristotle argued that the power of instruction and so of being informed cannot be
expected to get us very far at all. See Aristotle, *Nichomachean Ethics*, trans. W. D. Ross
(Oxford: Oxford University Press, 1980): 1179a35–b26.

8. Scientific awareness of the problem dates back to the late nineteenth century. In
1896, Nobel Laureate Svante Arrhenius linked atmospheric $CO_2$ to land temperature
increase. See "Svante Arrhenius," Wikipedia, last updated November 1, 2021, https://en
.wikipedia.org/wiki/Svante_Arrhenius.

9. The quote is from Phillip Adams, @PhillipAdams_1, August, 15, 2021. Adams
was Chair of the committee in 1985.

10. This is known as the so-called privacy paradox; see Susanne Barth and Menno
D. T. de Jong, "The Privacy Paradox: Investigating Discrepancies between Expressed Privacy Concerns and Actual Online Behavior—A Systematic Literature Review," *Telemat-
ics and Informatics* 34, no. 7 (November 2017): 1038–58.

11. For discussion of such blindness, even between friends, see Dean Cocking,
"Friendship Online," in *Oxford Handbook of Digital Ethics*, ed. Carissa Veliz (Oxford:
Oxford University Press, 2021), 1–22.

12. Notably, of course, reason, but also (notably) sympathy and love.

13. See Richard G. Henson, "What Kant Might Have Said: Moral Worth and
the Overdetermination of Dutiful Action," *The Philosophical Review* 88, no. 1 (January,1979): 39–54.

14. See, for example, Viktor E. Frankl's descriptions of finding value within the horrific world of the concentration camps in his *Man's Search for Meaning* (Boston, MA: Beacon Press, 2006). (Originally published 1946.)

15. We take the phrase from the wonderful BBC documentary *The Century of the Self*, which provides many insights about the rise of our self-preoccupation over the past one hundred years (including about Bernays). See *The Century of the Self*, produced by The BBC and RDF Television, 2002.

16. Richard Gunderman, "The Manipulation of the American Mind: Edward Bernays and the Birth of Public Relations," The Conversation, July 9, 2015, https://theconversation.com/the-manipulation-of-the-american-mind-edward-bernays-and-the-birth-of-public-relations-44393. The quote we take from this excellent article is from Bernays's early "ground-breaking" work *Propaganda* (New York: Horace Liveright, 1928). See also his *The Engineering of Consent* (Norman: University of Oklahoma Press, 1955).

17. If people were not "buying" the "torches of freedom," similar ploys were used by the "merchants of doubt" (also brainchildren of Bernays). The merchants of doubt super-critically (we are independent thinkers) pointed out all the methodological and statistical errors in studies (e.g., purportedly showing the carcinogenic properties of tobacco smoking); "You don't want to be a gullible follower of what these studies tell you, do you?" See Naomi Oreskes and Erik M. Conway, *The Merchants of Doubt: How a Handful of Scientists Obscured the Truth from Tobacco Smoke to Climate Change* (New York: Bloomsbury Press, 2010).

18. For extended discussion of the "It's just a tool" defense, see *op. cit.* Cocking and van den Hoven, "Moral Fog and the Appreciation of Value."

19. Alex Zhavoronkov, "Elon Musk's Big NeuraLink Paper: Should We Prepare for the Digital Afterlife?" *Forbes*, June 17, 2021, https://www.forbes.com/sites/alexzhavoronkov/2021/06/17/elon-musks-big-neuralink-paper-should-we-prepare-for-the-digital-afterlife/?sh=3b61949d554d.

20. On the problem of not being able to see others (or oneself), see an excellent interview with actor/director Clint Eastood by Andrew Denton, *Enough Rope*, ABC Television, Australia, November 24, 2008. As well, of course, as our opening quote from a reality TV star suggests, people can "over-identify" with their image or artifice.

21. Casey Newton, "Mark in the Metaverse," The Verge, July 22, 2021, https://www.theverge.com/22588022/mark-zuckerberg-facebook-ceo-metaverse-interview.

22. Robert Stickgold, Antonio Zadra, and AJH Haar, "Advertising in Dreams Is Coming: What Now?" June 7, 2021, https://dxe.pubpub.org/pub/dreamadvertising/release/1.

23. Stickgold et al., "Advertising in Dreams Is Coming."

24. Stickgold et al., "Advertising in Dreams Is Coming."

25. Stickgold et al., "Advertising in Dreams Is Coming."

26. G. E. M. Anscombe, "Modern Moral Philosophy," *Philosophy* 33, no. 124 (January 1958): 1–19.

27. See Elizabeth Schulze, "The Man Who Invented the Web Says It's Now Dysfunctional with 'Perverse' Incentives," *CNBC*, March 12, 2019, https://www.cnbc

.com/2019/03/11/tim-berners-lee-the-web-is-dysfunctional-with-perverse-incentives.html.

28. All summarized in the story of surveillance capitalism, comprehensively described and analyzed by Soshanna Zuboff. See Soshanna Zuboff, *The Age of Surveillance Capitalism: The Fight for a Human Future at the New Frontier of Power* (London: Profile Books, 2019).

29. Philip Kitcher, "Losing Your Way in the Fog: Reflections on Evil Online," *Evil Online, Journal of Practical Ethics* (special issue) (Oxford: Oxford University Press, 2022).

# Chapter 11

1. On the apparent demise of understanding and of our capacities to appreciate value as we live online, see Dean Cocking and Jeroen van den Hoven, "Moral Fog and the Appreciation of Value," *Evil Online, Journal of Practical Ethics* (special issue) (Oxford: Oxford University Press, 2022).

2. Including in many disturbing ways, such as the selling and commodification of violence and gangster life. See, for example, Forrest Stuart, *Ballad of the Bullet: Gangs, Drill Music and the Power of Online Infamy* (Princeton, NJ: Princeton University Press, 2020).

3. See R. Jay Wallace, ed., *Joseph Raz: The Practice of Value (The Berkeley Tanner Lectures)* (Oxford: Oxford University Press, 2003), 15–37.

4. Wallace, *Joseph Raz*, 78–79.

5. Aristotle, *Nichomachean Ethics,* trans. W. D. Ross (Oxford: Oxford University Press, 1980), 1179a44–49.

6. Aristotle, *Nichomachean Ethics*, 1179b23–33.

7. Thanks to Roger Crisp for discussion and clarification on Aristotle's view of the relationship between reason and habit formation in moral education.

8. Aristotle, *Nichomachean Ethics*, 1179b35–46.

9. Aristotle, *Nichomachean Ethics*, 1180a14–28.

10. Immanuel Kant, *The Groundwork of the Metaphysic of Morals*, translated and analyzed by H. J. Paton (New York: HarperCollins, 1964), Ak 4:394.

11. On our "radical evil," see Immanuel Kant, "Religion within the Boundaries of Mere Reason," in *Immanuel Kant: Religion and Rational Authority*, trans. and ed. Allen W. Wood and George di Giovanni (Cambridge: Cambridge University Press, 1996), 39–216.

12. Iris Murdoch, "The Sovereignty of Good over Other Concepts," ed. Robert B. Kruschwitz and Robert C. Roberts, *The Virtues: Contemporary Essays on Moral Character* (Belmont, CA: Wadsworth Publishing Company, 1987), 84–98.

13. J. S. Mill, *On Liberty* (vol. 18), in *The Collected Works of J. S. Mill*, ed. J. M. Robson (Toronto: University of Toronto Press, 1977), 260–67.

14. See, for example, https://en.wikipedia.org/wiki/Star_Wars_Kid (accessed August 14, 2021).

15. See, for example, many of the cases described in Jon Ronson, *So You've Been Publicly Shamed?* (London: Picador, 2015).

16. For discussion of these issues, see Ronson, *ibid.,* and Cocking and van den Hoven, *op. cit.,* "Moral Fog and the Appreciation of Value."

17. There are now also multiple apps designed to protect you from making poor online decisions: "Drunk Mode Keyboard" and "Drunk Dial NO!" allow you to lock features on your phone when your inhibitions are down. You need not use them only to stop yourself from making poor choices while drunk, but also to prevent emotionally or exhaustedly posting on social media. The "No Contact Rule" app allows you to input messages that will pop up when you go to contact someone that you know you shouldn't be contacting. Unlike the drunk lock apps, this type of "reminder to self"–style app might have a better chance of instilling good habits as we *practice* control rather than give control over to the app.

# Chapter 12

1. See Kokolakis, *Computers and Security* (2015, 122): "Do people really care about their privacy? Surveys show that privacy is a primary concern for citizens in the digital age. On the other hand, individuals reveal personal information for relatively small rewards, often just for drawing the attention of peers in an online social network. This inconsistency of privacy attitudes and privacy behaviours is often referred to as the 'privacy paradox.'"

2. The paper Spence (2009), provides the basis for this part of the chapter.

3. These three normative terms, the epistemological, ethical, and eudaimonic, can be jointly understood in this chapter by the collective term *axiological,* as *normatively conferring values.*

4. For a more detailed account of the epistemological and ethical commitments to which information as a process and product of communication gives rise, see Spence (2009).

5. Alan Gewirth's main thesis in *Reason and Morality* (1978) is that every rational agent, by virtue of engaging in action, is logically committed to accept a supreme moral principle, the *principle of generic consistency,* which commits every agent to respect their own and all other agents rights of freedom and well-being. The basis of his thesis is found in his doctrine that action has an inherent normative structure whose necessary features are freedom and well-being, and because of this structure every rational agent, just by virtue of being an agent, is committed to certain necessary prudential and moral constraints.

6. A full and detailed defense of the argument for the PGC against all the major objections raised against it by various philosophers can be found in Spence 2006 (chs. 1–3), Beyleveld (1991), and Gewirth (1978).

7. As Floridi correctly argues, "The ultimate form of control is individual sovereignty, understood as self-ownership, especially [over] one's own body, choices, and data. The fight for digital sovereignty is an epochal struggle" (Floridi 2020).

8. For details of that case see https://en.wikipedia.org/wiki/Cambridge_Analytica.

9. Constrained by space and being beyond the scope of this chapter, for more information on media corruption generally, and specifically how it applies to Facebook in

its role in the Cambridge Analytica case and its similarities to Google, see Spence 2021, 2021a.

10. Carissa Véliz argues also that privacy is a collective normative responsibility of all data subjects (2020, 75–82).

# Chapter 13

1. Some researchers describe surgical robots as "automonous" when they do not even display narrow AI. See, for example, Frederic Picarda, Angela Helen Deakina, Philip E. Riches, Kamal Deepa, and Joseph Baines, "Computer Assisted Orthopaedic Surgery: Past, Present and Future," *Medical Engineering and Physics* 72 (2019): 55–65, https://doi.org/10.1016/j.medengphy.2019.08.005; and Ming Han Lincoln Liow, Pak Lin Chin, and Seng Jin Yeo, "Total Knee Arthroplasty Technique: TSolution One (Robodoc)," in *Robotics in Knee and Hip Arthroplasty*, ed. Jess H. Lonner (New York: Springer, 2019), 195–201, https://doi-org.libaccess.sjlibrary.org/10.1007/978-3-030-16593-2_19.

2. For a discussion of many of the uses of AI in medicine, see Onur Asan, Alparslan Emrah Bayrak, and Avishek Choudhury, "Artificial Intelligence and Human Trust in Healthcare: Focus on Clinicians," *Journal of Medical Internet Research* 22, no. 6 (2020): 1, http://www.jmir.org/2020/6/e15154/; Varun H. Buch, Irfan Ahmed, and Mahiben Maruthappu, "Artificial Intelligence in Medicine: Current Trends and Future Possibilities," *British Journal of General Practice* 68, no. 668 (March 2018): 143–44, https://doi.org/10.3399/bjgp18X695213.

3. Steven Shwartz, *Evil Robots, Killer Computers, and Other Myths* (New York: Fast Company Press, 2021), 4–5.

4. Schwartz, *Evil Robots*, 4–5.

5. The central text here is Immanuel Kant, *A Critique of Pure Reason*, trans. and ed. Paul Guyer and Alan W. Wood (Cambridge: Cambridge University Press, 1998).

6. For a good introduction to Kant's theory of objects, see Yirmiyahu Yovel "Preliminary Observations: Rethinking the Object," in *Kant's Philosophical Revolution: A Short Guide to the Critique of Pure Reason* (Princeton: Princeton University Press, 2018), 1–20.

7. A study that was accepted at a May 2021 conference described teaching object permanence to a computer system by having it play hide-and-seek. They don't plan on using this in a robot because they don't believe it could be done in the real world, not to mention it being possibly dangerous. See Eliza Strickland, "AI Agents Play 'Hide the Toilet Plunger' to Learn Deep Concepts About Life," *IEEE Spectrum*, February 11, 2021, https://spectrum.ieee.org/tech-talk/artificial-intelligence/machine-learning/ai-agent-learns-about-the-world-by-gameplay.

8. Gary Marcus, "Is 'Deep Learning' a Revolution in Artificial Intelligence?" *The New Yorker*, November 25, 2012.

9. Erik R. Ranschaert, André J. Duerinckx, Paul Algra, Elmar Kotter, Hans Kortman, and Sergey Morozov, "Advantages, Challenges, and Risks of Artificial Intelligence for Radiologists," *Artificial Intelligence in Medical Imaging*, eds. Erik R. Ranschaert,

Sergey Morozov, and Paul R. Algra (New York: Springer, 2019), 331. https://doi.org/10.1007/978-3-319-94878-2_20.

10. Emma Beede, Elizabeth Baylor, Fred Hersch et al. (GDH), "Paisan Ruamviboonsuk, Rajavithi Hospital, Bangkok, Thailand, A Human-Centered Evaluation of a Deep Learning System Deployed in Clinics for the Detection of Diabetic Retinopathy," CHI 2020, April 25–30, 2020, Honolulu, HI, USA.

11. Id.

12. Alexander W. Forsyth, Regina Barzilay et al., "Machine Learning Methods to Extract Documentation of Breast Cancer Symptoms from Electronic Health Records," *J Pain Symptom Manag* 55, no. 6 (June 2018): 1492–99.

13. Frederic Picarda, Angela Helen Deakina, Philip E. Riches, Kamal Deepa, Joseph Baines, "Computer Assisted Orthopaedic Surgery: Past, Present and Future," *Medical Engineering and Physics* 72 (2019): 55–65, https://doi.org/10.1016/j.medengphy.2019.08.005.

14. Tom L. Beauchamp and James F. Childress, *Principles of Biomedical Ethics* (Oxford: Oxford University Press, 2012).

15. Floridi (2018), 698.

16. John C. Gore, "Artificial Intelligence in Medical Imaging," *Magnetic Resonance Imaging* 68 (2020): A1–A4, A3.

17. Ranschaert et al., "Advantages, Challenges, and Risks of Artificial Intelligence for Radiologists," (2019), 331.

18. Aziz Nazha, "Does AI Have a Place in Medicine?" Cleveland Clinic Center for Clinical Artificial Intelligence, November 11, 2019, https://blogs.scientificamerican.com/observations/does-ai-have-a-place-in-medicine/?print=true.

19. Abraham Verghese, Nigam H. Shah, and Robert A. Harrington, "What This Computer Needs Is a Physician: Humanism and Artificial Intelligence," *JAMA* 319, no. 1 (January 2, 2018): 19–20, 19.

20. Asilomar principles: https://www.oecd.org/going-digital/ai-intelligent-machines-smart-policies/conference-agenda/ai-intelligent-machines-smart-policies-oheigeartaigh.pdf; Health Insurance Portability and Accountability Act of 1996, Pub. L. No. 104–191, 110 Stat. 1936 (codified as amended in scattered sections of 26, 29, and 42 U.S.C.); https://www.ama-assn.org/delivering-care/ethics/privacy-health-care.

21. Public Law 104–191, Health Insurance Portability and Accountability Act of 1996.

22. American Medical Association. (n.d.). "Code of Medical Ethics Opinion 3.1.1." Privacy in Health Care. https://www.ama-assn.org/delivering-care/ethics/privacy-health-care.

23. Luc Rocher, Julien M. Hendrickx, and Yves-Alexandre de Montjoye, "Estimating the Success of Re-Identifications in Incomplete Datasets Using Generative Models," *Nature Communications* 10 (2019), https://doi.org/10.1038/s41467-019-10933-3.

24. Andrea Renda, "Artificial Intelligence Ethics, Governance and Policy Challenges," Report of a CEPS Task Force Centre for European Policy Studies (CEPS), Brussels, February 2019, 31.

25. Andre Esteva, Brett Kuprel, Roberto A. Novoa, Justin Ko, Susan M. Swetter, Helen M. Blau, and Sebastian Thrun, "Dermatologist-Level Classification of Skin Cancer with Deep Neural Networks," *Nature* 542 (2017): 115–18.

26. Joy Buolamwini and Timnit Gebru, "Gender Shades: Intersectional Accuracy Disparities in Commercial Gender Classification," *Proceedings of Machine Learning Research* 81 (2018): 1–15.

27. Ziad Obermeyer, Brian Powers, Christine Vogeli, and Sendhil Mullainathan, "Dissecting Racial Bias in an Algorithm Used to Manage the Health of Populations," *Science* 366, no. 6464 (2019): 447–53.

28. Renda, "Artificial Intelligence Ethics," 31.

29. W. Nicholson Price II, "Medical AI and Contextual Bias," *Harvard Journal of Law & Technology* 33, no. 1 (Fall 2019): 65–116.

30. Price, "Medical AI," 96.

31. Renda, "Artificial Intelligence Ethics."

32. US Government Accountability Office, *Artificial Intelligence in Health Care: Benefits and Challenges of Technologies to Augment Patient Care*, jointly published with the National Academy of Medicine, November 30, 2020. 33

33. For a discussion of the black box problem, see Daniel Greenfield, "Artificial Intelligence in Medicine: Applications, Implications and Limitations," June 19, 2019, https://sitn.hms.harvard.edu/flash/2019/artificial-intelligence-in-medicine-applications-implications-and-limitations/; and W. Nicholson Price II, "Artificial Intelligence in Health Care: Applications and Legal Issues," *SciTech Lawyer* 14, no. 1 (Fall 2017): 10–13.

34. Varun H. Buch, Irfan Ahmed, and Mahiben Maruthappu, "Artificial Intelligence in Medicine: Current Trends and Future Possibilities," *British Journal of General Practice* 68 (March 2018): 143–44, doi:https://doi.org/10.3399/bjgp18X695213.

35. Buch, Ahmed, and Maruthappu, "Artificial Intelligence in Medicine," 143.

36. Vijay Pande, "Artificial Intelligence's 'Black Box' Is Nothing to Fear," *New York Times*, January 25, 2018, https://www.nytimes.com/2018/01/25/opinion/artificial-intelligence-black-box.html.

37. Alex John London, "Artificial Intelligence and Black-Box Medical Decisions: Accuracy versus Explainability," *The Hastings Center Report* 49, no. 1 (January–February 2019): 15–21.

38. Esteva et al., "Dermatologist-Level Classification of Skin Cancer."

39. Giuseppe Baselli, Marina Codari, and Francesco Sardanelli, "Opening the Black Box of Machine Learning in Radiology: Can the Proximity of Annotated Cases Be a Way?" *European Radiology Experimental* 4, no. 30 (2020), https://doi.org/10.1186/s41747-020-00159-0.

40. Jeffrey Alan Golden, "Deep Learning Algorithms for Detection of Lymph Node Metastases from Breast Cancer Helping Artificial Intelligence Be Seen," *JAMA* 318, no. 22 (December 12, 2017): 2184–86.

41. Emily M. Bender, Angelina McMillan-Major, Timnit Gebru, and Shmargaret Shmitchell, "On the Dangers of Stochastic Parrots: Can Language Models Be Too Big?" *Proceedings of the 2021 ACM Conference on Fairness, Accountability, and Transparency*, March 2021, 610–23, https://doi.org/10.1145/3442188.3445922.

42. For a searing critique of MTurk, see Alana Semuels, "The Internet Is Enabling a New Kind of Poorly Paid Hell," *The Atlantic*, January 23, 2018, https://www.theatlantic.com/business/archive/2018/01/amazon-mechanical-turk/551192/.

43. Karoline Mortensen and Taylor L. Hughes, "Comparing Amazon's Mechanical Turk Platform to Conventional Data Collection Methods in the Health and Medical Research Literature," *Journal of General Internal Medicine* 33, no. 4 (2018): 533–38, doi: 10.1007/s11606-017-4246-0.

44. Kotaro Hara, Abi Adams, Kristy Milland, Saiph Savage, Chris Callison-Burch, and Jeffrey Bigham, "A Data-Driven Analysis of Workers' Earnings on Amazon Mechanical Turk," ACM Conference Human Factors in Computing Systems, 2018, arXiv:1712.05796.

45. Oscar Schwartz, "Untold History of AI: How Amazon's Mechanical Turkers Got Squeezed Inside the Machine," *IEEE Spectrum*, April 22, 2019, https://spectrum.ieee .org/tech-talk/tech-history/dawn-of-electronics/untold-history-of-ai-mechanical-turk -revisited-tktkt.

46. Bertalan Meskó and Marton Görög, "A Short Guide for Medical Professionals in the Era of Artificial Intelligence," *NPJ Digital Medicine* 3, no. 126 (2020): 6, https://doi .org/10.1038/s41746-020-00333-z.

47. Golden, "Deep Learning Algorithms for Detection of Lymph Node Metastases," 2286.

48. Taylor M. Cruz, "Perils of Data-Driven Equity: Safety-Net Care and Big Data's Elusive Grasp on Health Inequality," *Big Data & Society* (January–June 2020): 1–14, doi: 10.1177/2053951720928097.

49. Ezekiel J. Emanuel and Robert M. Wachter, "Artificial Intelligence in Health Care: Will the Value Match the Hype?" *JAMA* 321, no. 23 (June 18, 2019): 2282.

50. A survey of the views of psychiatrists on AI in psychiatry revealed a great skepticism about the ability of AI to treat patients because algorithms are incapable of empathy. C. Bleasc, C. Locher, M. Leon-Carlyle, and M. Doraiswamy, "Artificial Intelligence and the Future of Psychiatry: Qualitative Findings from a Global Physician Survey," *Digital Health* 6 (2020): 5. Psychiatrists are open to the possibility that AI might be useful in diagnosis (8–9). Another study described a "highly accurate algorithm able to identify suicide attempts in patients with mood disorders using clinical and demographic data." Ives Cavalcante Passos, Benson Mwangi, Jair C. Soares et al., "Identifying a Clinical Signature of Suicidality among Patients with Mood Disorders: A Pilot Study Using a Machine Learning Approach," *Journal of Affective Disorders* 193 (March 15, 2016): 109–116.

51. Mark Henderson Arnold, "Teasing Out Artificial Intelligence in Medicine: An Ethical Critique of Artificial Intelligence and Machine Learning in Medicine," *Bioethical Inquiry* 18 (2021): 121–39, https://doi.org/10.1007/s11673-020-10080-1.

52. Meskó and Görög, "A Short Guide for Medical Professionals," 5.

# Chapter 14

1. Cf. Larson and Zhao (2020) for an analysis of the impact of self-driving cars on cities.

2. Awad et al. (2018) present the results of a large survey probing people's attitudes toward such questions.

# Chapter 15

1. At one point, Mercedes said that its self-driving cars would always prioritize saving the people in the car. But this was met with strong criticism. A representative from Mercedes then quickly retracted the stance that Mercedes had previously taken about this, announcing that Mercedes would leave it to others to decide how self-driving cars should handle accident scenarios (Nyholm 2018a).

2. See https://www.moralmachine.net.

# Chapter 16

1. Seumas Miller, *Dual Use Science and Technology, Ethics and Weapons of Mass Destruction* (New York: Springer, 2018).

2. *United States vs Sokolow*, 490 U.S. 1, 109 S. Circuit 1581 (1989), https://caselaw.findlaw.com/us-supreme-court/490/1.html.

3. Nathan Scudder, Dennis McNevin, Sally Kelty, Christine Funk, Simon Walsh, and James Robertson, "Policy and Regulatory Implications of the New Frontier of Forensic Genomics: Direct-to-Consumer Genetic Data and Genealogy Records," *Current Issues in Criminal Justice* 31, no. 2 (2019): 194.

4. Marcus Smith, "Universal Forensic DNA Databases: Balancing the Costs and Benefits," *Alternative Law Journal* 43, no. 2 (July 2018): 131–35.

5. Federal Bureau of Investigation, *CODIS-NDIS Statistics*, accessed February 2, 2021, http://www.fbi.gov/about-us/lab/biometric-analysis/codis/ndis-statistics.

6. Marcus Smith, United Kingdom Home Office, *National DNA Database Statistics*, accessed February 2, 2021, https://www.gov.uk/government/statistics/national-dna-database-statistics.

7. Emile Dirks and James Leibold, "Genomic Surveillance: Inside China's DNA Dragnet," *ASPI Policy Brief* (Report No. 34, 2020).

8. Smith, "Universal Forensic DNA Databases."

9. Seumas Miller, "Collective Rights," *Public Affairs Quarterly* 1, no. 4 (1999): 331–46; also published in chapter 7 of *Social Action: A Teleological Account* (Cambridge: Cambridge University Press, 2001) and chapter 2 of *Moral Foundations of Social Institutions* (Cambridge: Cambridge University Press, 2010).

10. It is a qualified joint right given that the genomic data of any one of the persons is not identical to the genomic data of the other persons (i.e., the sets of genomic data are not overlapping). Moreover, there is a further question with respect to the degree of overlap that would underpin a joint right. Presumably, two persons, A and B, who are very distant relatives and therefore only have marginally overlapping genomic data, might not have a joint right to the data in question; the degree of overlap is very slight

and their familial relationship too tenuous to underpin a *joint* right. Accordingly, the boundaries of joint rights are vague and, as a result, fixing the limits of joint rights is somewhat arbitrary.

11. On the other hand, there is the potential collateral damage to the relatives of criminals, given partially overlapping DNA profiles.

12. This consent issue adds to other problems that exist with direct-to-consumer genetic testing, such as the accuracy of the tests and the fact that the results are not provided in a clinical setting by a health care professional.

13. Seumas Miller, "Joint Action," *Philosophical Papers* 21, no. 3 (1992): 275–99; "Intentions, Ends and Joint Action," *Philosophical Papers* 24, no. 1 (1995): 51–67; chapter 2 of *Social Action*.

14. Seumas Miller, "Collective Responsibility and Omissions," *Business and Professional Ethics* 20, no. 1 (2001): 5–24; "Collective Moral Responsibility: An Individualist Account," *Midwest Studies in Philosophy* 30 (2006): 176–93; chapter 4 of *Moral Foundations of Social Institutions*.

15. An earlier version of some of the material in this section appeared in the open access publication Marcus Smith and Seumas Miller, "The Ethical Application of Biometric Facial Recognition Technology," *AI & Society* (2021), https://doi.org/10.1007/s00146-021-01199-9.

16. Marcus Smith, Monique Mann, and Gregor Urbas, *Biometrics, Crime and Security* (Abingdon, UK: Routledge, 2018).

17. John Kleinig, Seumas Miller, Douglas Salane, Peter Mameli, and Adina Schwartz, *Security and Privacy: Global Standards for Ethical Identity Management in Contemporary Liberal Democratic States* (Canberra, Australia: ANU Press, 2011).

18. Kelly W. Sundberg and Christina M. Witt, "Undercover Operations: Evolution and Modern Challenges," *Journal of the AIPIO* 27, no. 3 (2019): 3–17.

19. Kleinig et al., *Security and Privacy*.

20. Patrick Walsh and Seumas Miller, "Rethinking 'Five Eyes' Security Intelligence Collection Policies and Practice Post Snowden," *Intelligence and National Security* 31, no. 3 (2016): 345–68.

# Chapter 18

1. © Springer Nature Switzerland AG 2019 139 M. Christen et al. (eds.), *The Ethics of Cybersecurity*, The International Library of Ethics, Law and Technology 21, open access, https://link.springer.com/book/10.1007/978-3-030-29053-5#about.

2. This article does not yet take into consideration the changes due to the COVID-19 pandemic. However, it can be assumed that it reflects, if not intensifies, the issues outlined.

# Chapter 20

1. Willard Van Orman Quine, "Natural Kinds," in *Ontological Relativity and Other Essays* (New York: Columbia University Press, 2012), 114–38.

2. Katyanna Quach, "How We Fooled Google's AI into Thinking a 3D-Printed Turtle Was a Gun: MIT Bods Talk to El Reg," *The Register*, November 6, 2017.

3. Quach, "How We Fooled Google's AI."

4. Marco Tulio Ribeiro, Sameer Singh, and Carlos Guestrin, "'Why Should I Trust You?' Explaining the Predictions of Any Classifier," KDD '16: *Proceedings of the 22nd ACM SIGKDD International Conference on Knowledge Discovery and Data Mining*, August 2016, 1135–44.

5. Ribeiro et al., "'Why Should I Trust You?'"

6. Scott Mayer McKinney, Marcin Sieniek, Varun Godbole et al., "International Evaluation of an AI System for Breast Cancer Screening," *Nature* 577 (2020): 89–94.

7. Shannon E. French and Lisa N. Lindsay, "Artificial Intelligence in Military Decision-Making: Avoiding Ethical and Strategic Perils with an Option-Generator Model," in *Emerging Military Technologies: Ethical and Legal Perspectives,* ed. Bernard Koch and Richard Schoonhoven (The Netherlands and Boston: Brill/Martinus Nijhoff Publishers, forthcoming).

8. Elke Schwarz, "Technology and Moral Vacuums in Just War Theorising," *Journal of International Political Theory* 1 (2018): 280–98.

9. Shannon E. French, "An American Military Ethicist's Perspective: Such Waste in Brief Mortality," in *The Price of Peace: Just War in the 21st Century*, ed. Charles Reed and David Ryall (Cambridge: Cambridge University Press, 2007).

10. P. J. Smith, E. McCoy, and C. Layton, "Brittleness in the Design of Cooperative Problem-Solving Systems: The Effects on User Performance," *IEEE Transactions on Systems, Man, and Cybernetics-Part A: Systems and Humans* 27 (1997): 360–71.

11. S. A. Guerlain, P. J. Smith, J. H. Obradovich, S. Rudmann, P. Strohm, J. W. Smith, and J. Svirbely, "Dealing with Brittleness in the Design of Expert Systems for Immunohematology," *Immunohematology* 12 (1996): 101–7.

12. Kip Johnson, Liling Ren, James Kuchar, and Charles Oman, "Interaction of Automation and Time Pressure in a Route Replanning Task," 132–37 (Cambridge, MA: International Conference on Human-Computer Interaction in Aeronautics, 2002).

13. M. L. Cummings, "Automation Bias in Intelligent Time Critical Decision Support Systems," *Decision Making in Aviation* (2017).

14. M. L. Cummings, "Automation Bias."

15. James Vincent, "Twitter Taught Microsoft's AI Chatbot to Be a Racist Asshole in Less Than a Day," *The Verge*, March 24, 2016.

16. Sam Levin, "A Beauty Contest Was Judged by AI and the Robots Didn't Like Dark Skin," *The Guardian*, September 8, 2016.

17. Cathy O'Neill, *Weapons of Math Destruction: How Big Data Increases Inequality and Threatens Democracy* (New York: Crown Publishing Group, 2017), 218.

18. Sara Gaines, "Who Should Choose? Impacts of Artificial Intelligence Use in Tactical Field Care," MA candidate graduate term paper for PHIL417, "War and Morality," Case Western Reserve University, Fall 2018.

19. Stephen D. Giebner, "The Transition to the Committee on Tactical Combat Casualty Care," *Wilderness & Environmental Medicine* 28, no. 2 (2017): S18–S24.

20. Kent Drescher, David W. Foy, Caroline Kelly, Anna Leshner, Kerrie Schutz, and Brett Litz, "An Exploration of the Viability and Usefulness of the Construct of Moral Injury in War Veterans," *Traumatology* 17, no. 1 (2011): 9.

21. Brett T. Litz, Nathan Stein, Eileen Delaney, Leslie Lebowitz, William P. Nash, Caroline Silva, and Shira Maguen, "Moral Injury and Moral Repair in War Veterans: A Preliminary Model and Intervention Strategy," *Clinical Psychology Review* 29, no. 8 (2009): 702.

22. Gaines, "Who Should Choose?"

23. Sadie P. Hutson, Joanne M. Hall, and Frankie L. Pack, "Survivor Guilt," *Advances in Nursing Science* 38, no. 1 (2015): 20–21.

24. Hutson et al., "Survivor Guilt," 27.

25. Gaines, "Who Should Choose?"

26. Safiya Umoja Noble, *Algorithms of Oppression: How Search Engines Reinforce Racism* (New York: New York University Press, 2018), 171.

27. Susanne Gaube, Harini Suresh, Martina Raue, Alexander Merritt et al., "Do As AI Say: Susceptibility in Deployment of Clinical Decision-Aids," *NPJ Digital Medicine* 4, no. 31 (2021).

28. I am reminded here of the character "Crapgame" from the 1970 war movie *Kelly's Heroes*, who is an apt fictional—but not unrealistic—example of a human in the mix capable of adding considerable chaos to any system trying to track military supplies.

29. Richard Danzig, "Surviving on a Diet of Poisoned Fruit: Reducing the National Security Risks of America's Cyber Dependencies," Center for New American Security, July 2014.

30. Jacquelyn Schneider, "Digitally-Enabled Warfare: The Capability-Vulnerability Paradox," Center for a New American Security, 2016.

31. Dominic Gates, "Pilots Struggle Against Boeing 737 Max Control System on Doomed Lion Air Flight," *Seattle Times*, November 27, 2018.

32. Robert H. Scales, "Gun Trouble," *The Atlantic*, January/February 2015.

33. French and Lindsay, "Artificial Intelligence in Military Decision-Making."

34. Jannelle Warren-Findley, "The Collier as Commemoration: The Project Mercury Astronauts and the Collier Trophy," https://history.nasa.gov/SP-4219/Chapter7.html.

35. Ruha Benjamin, *Race after Technology: Abolitionist Tools for the New Jim Code* (Cambridge: Polity Press, 2019).

36. See Shannon E. French, *The Code of the Warrior: Exploring Warrior Values, Past and Present* (2nd ed.) (Lanham, MD: Rowman & Littlefield, 2017).

37. Ron Arkin, *Governing Lethal Behavior in Autonomous Robots* (Boca Raton, FL: Taylor & Francis Group, 2009), 36.

38. French and Lindsay, "Artificial Intelligence in Military Decision-Making."

39. Matthew Talbert and Jessica Wolfendale, *War Crimes: Causes, Excuses, and Blame* (Oxford: Oxford University Press, 2018).

40. David Livingstone Smith, *Less Than Human: Why We Demean, Enslave, and Exterminate Others* (New York: St. Martin's Press, 2012) and *On Inhumanity: Dehumanization and How to Resist It* (Oxford: Oxford University Press, 2020).

41. Elke Schwarz, "Technology and Moral Vacuums."

42. Shannon Vallor, *Technology and the Virtues: A Philosophical Guide to a Future Worth Wanting* (Oxford: Oxford University Press, 2016), 216.

43. Daniel Eichler and Ronald Thompson, "59 Percent Likely Hostile," War on the Rocks, *Texas National Security Review*, January 2020.

44. Noel Sharkey, "Grounds for Discrimination: Autonomous Robot Weapons," RUSI Defense Systems, October 2008.

45. J. Glenn Gray, *The Warriors: Reflections on Men in Battle* (New York: Harper and Row, 1970), 152–53.

# Index

"What's Wrong with Speciesism?"
   (Kagan), 69–70
white supremacy, 92–94
WHO. *See* World Health Organization
Wikipedia, 140
Williams, Robert Julian-Borchak, 64–65
wireless IMDs, 244
Wolfendale, Jessica, 290
women's rights, 54–55
World Health Organization (WHO),
   234–35
World Trade Center attacks, 257
worldview approaches: for community,
   17–18; eco-community worldview
   imperative, 23–24, 301n30; extended

community worldview imperative,
21–23; personal worldview imperative,
7–9, 13; prudential worldview, 6;
psychology of, 18–20; science in,
23–24; utopian worldview, 13
Wray, Christopher A., 265
Wright, Frank Lloyd, 17

Yeager, Chuck, 287
Yemen, 266–67
Yoo, John, 262

Zuboff, Shoshana, 160
Zuckerberg, Mark, 120, 137